**The Informal and Underground Economy
of the South Texas Border**

Number Thirty-six
Jack and Doris Smothers Series in Texas History, Life, and Culture

The Informal and Underground Economy of the South Texas Border

BY CHAD RICHARDSON AND MICHAEL J. PISANI

University of Texas Press ◄◊► *Austin*

Publication of this work was made possible in part by support from the J. E. Smothers, Sr., Memorial Foundation and the National Endowment for the Humanities.

Requests for permission to reproduce material from this work should be sent to:
  Permissions
  University of Texas Press
  P.O. Box 7819
  Austin, TX 78713-7819
  utpress.utexas.edu/index.php/rp-form

Library of Congress Cataloging-in-Publication Data
  Richardson, Chad, 1943–
The informal and underground economy of the South Texas border / by Chad
Richardson and Michael J. Pisani. — 1st ed.
    p.   cm. — (Jack and Doris Smothers series in Texas history, life, and
culture)
  Includes bibliographical references and index.
ISBN 978-0-292-75683-0
  1. Informal sector (Economics)—Texas.   2. Informal sector (Economics)—
Mexican-American Border Region.   3. Labor—Texas.   4. Labor—Mexican-
American Border Region.   5. Crime—Texas.   6. Crime—Mexican-American
Border Region.   7. Texas—Economic conditions.   8. Mexican-American
Border Region—Economic conditions.   I. Pisani, Michael J., 1962–   II. Title.
  HD2346.U52T467   2012
  330—dc23

                                                          2011048580

doi: 10.7560/739277

To the individuals along this great fault line we call the border who shared their lives. They illuminated ours in the process.
CR & MJP

For Jana, William, Carina, & Geoffrey, borderlanders, in one way or another, all.
MJP

Contents

Preface

The people of South Texas are amazing. Like population groups everywhere, they have their mix of saints and scoundrels. We have found, however, a far heavier mix of individuals at the saints' end of the continuum than one might find in many other locations. We admit to a bias in this conclusion, though it is a bias borne of extensive research and some very poignant personal experiences over a period of more than thirty years. Our challenge has always been not only to understand, but to hold back our own biases and let the people of the region tell their own story.

We have devoted a lifetime of academic study to the South Texas border region, which in 2010 comprised over 1.5 million inhabitants. Yet South Texas, both in Texas and within the nation, is often overlooked, disparaged, and regarded as a backwater—even an embarrassment. We believe that, to the contrary, South Texas is a vibrant region full of life and hope. It is essential that academicians, as well as political and economic leaders, understand this people and their borderlands location. Latinos are the overwhelming majority in South Texas and the soon-to-be majority population in Texas and many other regions besides the U.S.-Mexico border. We believe, then, that the tapestry of contemporary life in South Texas is a harbinger in many ways for trends elsewhere in the United States.

This book is the third in a series of monographs (all published by the University of Texas Press) exploring contemporary life in South Texas. The previous two books explored culture and cultural beliefs, class, race relations, ethnicity, immigration, education, health, criminal behavior, and labor issues. In this volume, we explore informal and underground economic activities that are generally overlooked or demonized. As with

our previous efforts, we seek to share informed insights that may benefit students, academics, and policy-makers interested in the borderlands
and Latinos within a unique region of Texas.

The present book, as well as its two preceding companions, is possible because of an innovative approach to teaching and research that officially began in 1982 with the Borderlife Project. Early in his appoint-
ment at the University of Texas-Pan American[1] (then, Pan American
University), the first author, Chad Richardson, engaged locally embedded students to undertake ethnographic field interviews of family,
friends, and members of social networks to document the life experiences of borderlanders in South Texas/Northern Mexico.[2] Thirty years
later, the Borderlife Project Archive now houses over ten thousand in-
depth interviews and ethnographies, and an additional 6,000-plus survey responses. Recently, an outside evaluator estimated the economic
value of the archive at two million dollars.[3] Work is currently underway
at the University of Texas-Pan American (UTPA) to make the context-
rich archive accessible through the internet to outside investigators.

The greatest value of the Borderlife Project, however, is not its monetary significance but its impact in the lives of students, researchers,
and research subjects touched by the Project. From the storyteller to
the student, from the reader to the researcher, the Borderlife Project
provides convergent space. Storyteller and student often reflect on the
importance (and personal reward) of documenting their experiences.
Readers from South Texas and beyond marvel at the intimacy of context bounded by empiricism that the archive provides in the two initial
publications, *Batos, Bolillos, Pochos, and Pelados* and *On the Edge of the Law*.
We hope this third volume accomplishes the same purposes.

The second author, Mike Pisani, has been fortunate enough to have
served in three of the previously mentioned roles, first as a student of
Professor Richardson at UTPA in the 1990s, as a reader of his books,
and then as a researcher employing a version of the Borderlife meth-
odology for a time in Laredo (and utilizing the Borderlife Archive at
UTPA). One of the joys of a teacher using the student-ethnographer approach is the deeper connection between subject matter and student and
the increased learning commitment between student and teacher.

The nexus of ethnography and empiricism and the successful integration of each research design (i.e., qualitative, quantitative) is rare in
the academy. Borderlife researchers have offered these timeless gifts to
students and to the coauthors.

The genesis of the current book can be traced to a meeting of the coauthors at UTPA in May of 2006. While the meeting ostensibly was about sharing current and independent research projects, it quickly moved to one of collaboration. As a comprehensive study of informality or the underground economy in South Texas had yet to be produced, we decided to undertake the research for and the publication of the current volume.

As coauthors, we share the common ground of having lived and worked not only on the border but in Mexico and Central America as well. We also have personal experience working with migrant farm workers in the U.S., teaching at both the community college and university level, and affection for South Texas. These points of commonality have made this joint effort fun, collaborative, and easy-going. We also hope our different academic approaches and disciplines (sociology and international business) enrich this volume.

Acknowledgments

We wish to thank the many thousands of people of the South Texas borderlands who have shared their life stories with us since the initiation of the Borderlife Project at the UTPA in 1982. This book would not have been possible without our students at UTPA and Texas A&M International University. Embedded in the local environment, our students, through ethnographic interviews and semi-structured surveys, artfully collected and shared the experiences and stories of informal and underground participants in the region.

Some of the draft chapters were presented at the Association of Borderlands Studies annual conferences over the past few years, a wonderfully collegial environment in which to share academic papers. We wish to thank all the conference participants who came to the sessions and offered feedback and support. We are indebted to Theresa May, editor-in-chief of the University of Texas Press, who gave us valuable encouragement for the project, from the early stages of writing through the reviewing and editing. Her suggestions were always timely and valuable. We also wish to thank the reviewers of this volume for their critical insights; they challenged us to improve the text and found worth in our effort. Any remaining errors are ours alone.

Chad Richardson's Acknowledgments

I would like to gratefully acknowledge the support of key UTPA administrators (Guang-zhen Wang, Kristin Croyle, Van Reidhead, and Paul Steele), as well as UTPA colleagues (José Pagán, Darrin Rogers, and Dejun Su), and an outstanding department secretary, Jesse Medina.

But special mention needs to be made of some student assistants whose research and collaboration were invaluable, including Carlos Sepulveda, Omar Camarillo, and, especially, Amelia Flores. Amelia deserves special mention, not only for the quality of her work, but also for her heroism in the face of tragedy and obstacles that would have overwhelmed almost anyone.

Mike Pisani's Acknowledgments

For me, the study of the informal economy began while I was a doctoral student at UTPA. Professors José Pagán, John Sargent, Alberto Dávila, and Chad Richardson, all of UTPA at the time of my studies, were instrumental in my training. All have been true mentors. While my dissertation focused on informality in Central America, I was able to quickly adapt my training to the local South Texas environment where I studied (UTPA) and where I taught full-time in Laredo at Texas A&M International University (TAMIU).

At TAMIU, Michael Patrick fostered and encouraged my interest in South Texas and David Yoskowitz became a valued coauthor. Both have moved on to new institutions but remain my good friends. During my time at TAMIU, there were many others who had a positive impact on my research; they include Larry Boyd, Jorge Brusa, Beau Duncan, Baldomero García, Roberto Heredia, Ray Keck, Tony Rodriguez, Jerry Thompson, Carol Waters, and Michael Yoder.

Many at Central Michigan University (CMU) have facilitated my ongoing research of the South Texas borderlands. First in line for thanks include Professors Van Miller and Luis Perez-Batres, departmental colleagues who make up our research cluster. I am very lucky to have these two great colleagues and even better friends to be associated with. In the College of Business I thank the financial support and encouragement of the dean's office, including current dean Chuck Crespy and previous deans Dan Vetter, Mike Fields, and John Schleede. In addition, I thank my current and previous chairs of the Management Department for their financial support, including Mahmood Bahaee, Kevin Love, and Kumar Palaniswami. Special thanks go to Mary Jones, Management Department secretary, who provided invaluable support services cheerfully and expeditiously. More broadly within CMU, I thank the Office of Sponsored Research & Programs, past president Mike Rao, and current provost Gary Shapiro for financial support and encouragement. Additionally, I am indebted to CMU for a semester-long sabbatical in the fall of 2008 that launched the initial writing of this book project.

Lastly, I wish to thank the love of my life, Jana, for allowing me the time and space to complete such a project. She has always been there for me, in more ways than she knows. Our three children—William, Carina, and Geoffrey—have also contributed through many conversations, willing and (mostly) unwilling, but more importantly through living and growing up into wonderful young people right before our eyes.

Introduction

Growing up in the Valley is not the easiest thing to do, especially when you're a pale, blonde-haired white girl. The population is about 90% Hispanic, and the majority of residents are bilingual. My family moved to this unique part of the world in 1989 when I was in fifth grade. It was a tough adjustment, as I did not speak Spanish and had a west Texas accent. It was a difficult transition and a major case of culture shock. I remember a small group of kids in my class who were dropped off at school in Jaguars, Mercedes Benz, and BMWs. They all had the nicest designer clothes and trendy haircuts. When someone asked them their parent's jobs, they could not, for the most part, come up with a job title; they had no idea what their parents did for a living. I thought I was really smart because I knew exactly what my parents did for a living. As I grew up, I began to realize that drugs were a big part of Valley culture. Drug money had bought those big, fancy cars and designer clothes. I wasn't at all smarter than my classmates—they just didn't have a word for what their dads did.

So, for my course project, I decided to interview one of them. I had been to his house before to buy drugs. As I pulled up to his house, he walked to the car and asked "How much?" He is now 25 years old. He dropped out after seventh grade. His family has lived in the same colonia (rural slum) for almost his entire life.

—**Wanda Falding,**[1] **graduate student**

As visitors pause to reel in the sights, sounds, and smells of South Texas, many of the daily activities they sense may originate in the informal and underground economy. The hustle and bustle of a flea market or the serenity under a shade tree often finds vendors and workers operating informally—outside the range of government regulations—selling their wares or labor with little government authority or protection. Closer to the Rio Grande, clandestine movements of people and illegal drugs are common underground activities. In this volume, we will document the informal and underground economy of South Texas with survey data and life stories of those who participate in informal and underground economic activities. In addition, we will relate these micro-level activities to macro-level factors of the larger global economy.

It would be well also to relate current informal and underground activities to the larger historical context. Perhaps no regional historical figure better connects the dots of this volume than Juan Nepomuceno Cortina, the quintessential informal/underground South Texas–Northern Mexico borderlander. Cortina was born in 1824 in Camargo, Tamaulipas, Mexico, across the river from present-day Rio Grande City. Camargo, the first settlement on the Lower Rio Grande, was founded in 1749 by Cortina's great-great grandfather, Blas María de la Garza Falcón. At Cortina's birth, the Rio Grande was not a boundary, but simply a river running through the lower Rio Grande Valley.[2] Even after Texas declared independence in 1836, his homeland on both sides of the river was not part of Texas (though Texans agitated to have it declared so). When President Polk sent American troops into this disputed territory to provoke a war on May 8, 1846, Cortina, a corporal in the Mexican militia and a rancher with lands on both sides of the river, joined with other Mexican residents to unsuccessfully fight off the invaders in the battles of Palo Alto and (the next day) Resaca de la Palma, the first battles of the U.S. war against Mexico. In the three decades that followed, Cortina fought over 30 other battles and skirmishes without being wounded.

One of Cortina's contemporaries, John S. ("Old Rip") Ford, had a love-hate relationship with Cortina. He described Cortina, on the one hand, as possessing high native intellect and behaving toward enemies with a clemency worthy of imitation. On the other hand, he also depicted him as being more willing to fight than to learn to read and write and a "marauding chief . . . a frontier pirate, a notorious champion . . . and the Red Robber of the Rio Grande."[3]

Ford, who repeatedly faced Cortina in battle, described one skirmish where his forces defeated Cortina's small army near Rio Grande City. "Cortina was the last to leave the field," he stated. "He faced his pursuers, emptied his revolver, and tried to halt his panic-stricken men." When Ford ordered his men to fire at Cortina, "one shot struck the cantle of his saddle, one cut out a lock of his hair from his head, a third cut his bridle rein, a fourth passed through his horse's ear, and a fifth struck his belt. He galloped off unhurt."[4]

This battle was one of many in the "Cortina Wars," a series of battles in which Texans largely failed to stop cross-border raids by Cortina and his small army. Many of the raids were against Texas ranches and aimed to steal cattle and horses. James R. Douglas, a Cortina biographer,[5] claimed that Cortina did engage in extensive cattle rustling, but he also maintained that ". . . such behavior was not at all unusual among the populace, both Mexican and American, along the Lower Rio Grande." Douglas continues, "Just as the Texans used the courts to take Mexicans' lands, or violence to subdue them, so did Juan Cortina resort to violence to defend his dignity and rights. Simply put, Juan Cortina behaved more like the wealthy and powerful Anglos of South Texas than most observers have cared to admit."[6]

One incident that illustrates this portrayal and that led to the Cortina Wars occurred when Cortina witnessed the Brownsville town marshal, Robert Shears, viciously pistol whipping an elderly Mexican ranch hand who had worked for Cortina's mother. When Cortina intervened, the marshal insulted him. Cortina shot and wounded the marshal and then lifted the injured Mexican onto his horse and rode out of town to the cheers of Mexican witnesses. Three months later, Cortina led 75 men into Brownsville and killed two men who Cortina accused of having killed Mexicans with impunity. He also killed the jailer who refused to open the jail and then freed the prisoners.[7]

For two months, Brownsville residents lived in fear of another raid by Cortina. Unable to get help from Austin or the U.S. Army, they appealed to Mexican authorities in Matamoros. Thompson[8] relates:

> In response, Matamoros authorities sent a company of fifty militiamen across the river to help defend the town. Brownsville residents watched in awe as Mexican soldiers crossed the Rio Grande to Texas to protect United States citizens from an irregular army of Mexicans being led by a man who considered himself a United States citizen and who had once been a member of the Matamoros militia that now came to protect his enemies. In Austin and Washington it all seemed very confusing.

Soon thereafter, both Mexico and the United States were gripped by major civil wars; in the U.S., between the North and the South, and in Mexico, between the aristocrats who, with the French, supported the Imperialist monarchy of Maximilian, and Mexicans who supported the elected president, Benito Juárez. Both wars soon came to the South Texas–Northern Mexico borderlands. The Confederacy sought to break a Northern blockade by shipping cotton (and importing arms) overland through South Texas and across the Rio Grande to and then out from the Mexican port of Bagdad (near Matamoros). Cortina joined the Union forces, helping them take Brownsville in their (unsuccessful) efforts to end the blockade-busting cotton trade.

Cortina also got heavily involved in the war in Mexico. The French had driven Benito Juárez and his army to the Texas border. Cortina captured and executed the Tamaulipas governor who had pro-Imperialist loyalties. He skillfully played the opposing sides (in both wars) to his advantage, eventually becoming a governor and military commander in northern Mexico. For a brief time, Cortina switched loyalty to the Imperialist cause, though it is unclear whether he did so (as he claimed) as a tactical maneuver to save his army and his artillery to fight again, or because the Imperialist forces seemed to be on the point of winning the war. After six months, he switched support back to Benito Juárez. He recovered arms he had hidden and contributed significantly to the defeat of the French-supported Imperialist army.[9]

At the close of these two wars, Cortina's power began to ebb. After the death of Benito Juárez, he lost the governorship of Tamaulipas, though he continued as mayor of Matamoros. He returned to his practice of stealing Texas cattle, gaining the reputation of having stolen more Texas cattle than any other individual. Texas Rangers retaliated by invading Mexico, burning villages, and indiscriminately hanging Mexican citizens. Eventually, under pressure from the U.S. government, Mexican president Lerdo de Tejada arrested Cortina and imprisoned him in Mexico City.

Never one to give up, Cortina managed to align himself with Tejada's enemy, Porfirio Díaz. With the help of Díaz, Cortina returned to Tamaulipas to battle the Tejada forces. Though he eventually defeated the Tejada army in Reynosa and Camargo, another Díaz general, Miguel Blanco, attacked and defeated the Tejada army in Matamoros. Cortina and Blanco soon became bitter rivals, however. Blanco managed to arrest Cortina and ordered him shot. Cortina's old friend/enemy, Rip Ford, crossed the river to successfully plead for leniency.[10] Porfirio Díaz, under pressure from the Americans to rid the border of a "cattle thief" and to avoid a fight between two of his *caudillos*, had Cortina again arrested and imprisoned in Mexico City. He remained under arrest there for 16 years until his death in 1894.

This brief account of Juan Cortina helps illustrate several points we will return to throughout the book. First, informality and underground economic activities are well entrenched and have a long history on the South Texas border. We will make the point (with supporting evidence) that the South Texas borderlands have one of the highest rates of informality in the United States. This long history dates back to when the border came to South Texas, as described in the Juan Cortina episode. Indeed, the ability of the Confederacy to smuggle cotton through Mexico and on to Europe (as well as smuggling arms and ammunition) had a profound effect not only on South Texas but on the rest of the United States and on Mexico.

Second, informality seems to increase when economic and political institutions are not generally regarded as legitimate.[11] If individuals see state intervention in their lives (taxes, regulation of their property, fees, licenses, inspections, etc.) as illegitimate, they often rebel or turn to informal activities, as did Cortina. In democratic societies, individuals accept governmental intrusion in their lives to the extent that they believe it is fair, evenly applied, and capable of contributing to the general welfare. Juan Cortina experienced invasion of his homeland, oppression of his fellow Mexicans and Mexican Americans by Texas and federal authorities, and state-supported land grabs—actions that produced deep resentment, rebellion, and underground economic activity (e.g., cattle rustling). In the early twentieth century, the Mexican-origin people of the "Nueces Strip" (South Texas) continued to experience brutal repression by Texas Rangers and then disenfranchisement at the voting booth, segregation, and inequality of opportunity in the marketplace.

Third, merchants and residents of the borderlands often benefit by evading, manipulating, or selectively playing the laws of one nation or faction against the other. Border merchants in Cortina's time were able to exploit the laws of several nations to their advantage. One historian of the Civil War and the Valley, James A. Irby, for example, comments,

> For France, the Rio Grande trade was especially perplexing. Although Confederate cotton was indispensable to French looms, munitions had to be kept from Juárez. Therefore France did everything possible to promote the exportation of cotton and prevent the importation of arms unless assured they were for the Confederacy. The United States, meanwhile, made every effort to stop cotton exportation, but in sympathy with Juárez, permitted the passage of munitions to him. In this situation, the speculators again took full advantage of their opportunities.[12]

A fourth point we wish to introduce here is that South Texas–Northern Mexico borderlanders have often had to maintain somewhat divided loyalties. When they are unable to count on their respective national governments for aid or when these national governments make decisions that hurt them, they often turn to each other, using informal arrangements to solve local problems (as did Brownsville residents in asking Matamoros to help against the attack by Cortina). Today, the communities along both sides of the Rio Grande/Bravo border, for example, have united to condemn and oppose the border wall.

Finally, Cortina's story reminds us that there are no easy answers as to the morality of informal and underground activities. From a distance it is easy to label those who, like Cortina, engage in informal or underground activities as "law breakers." The harsh rhetoric against undocumented workers in the United States today is one example of this, as are the strong denunciations of Juan Cortina as "a cattle thief" and "a bandit." Such rhetoric, however, hides the fact that people in power are often able not only to manipulate definitions of morality, but also the laws that allow them to exploit or steal with impunity. Many South Texas ranches, for example, were built in Cortina's day when Anglo ranchers colluded with Anglo[13] politicians to pass property tax laws on unsuspecting Mexican American landowners. They would then foreclose on the land and buy it in auctions open only to themselves. This is the point that historian Douglas (quoted earlier) makes when he says, "Texans used the courts to take Mexicans' lands, or violence to subdue them . . ." He further points out that Juan Cortina's resorting to violence to defend his dignity and rights made him similar to the wealthy and powerful Anglos of South Texas, though history counts his enemies as the heroes and Juan Cortina as a villain.

Today, those who condemn undocumented (informal) Mexican workers and call them "illegal aliens" ignore the fact that there are few *legal* avenues through which poor Mexican workers can fill the insatiable demand for cheap labor in the United States. Similarly, when the poor experience significant health problems, most have no health insurance, and conventional (formal) health care is out of their reach. As a result, many self-medicate, get prescription medicine in Mexico without seeing a doctor, or visit folk practitioners. Informality is one of their few options. While we, the authors, do not wish to condone informal and underground activity, we also do not wish to too quickly condemn it. In many cases, informality is one of the few avenues open to the poor and powerless.

Our Geographical Focus:
The South Texas–Northern Mexico Borderlands

The land that Cortina and his compatriots sought to preserve (and regain) as part of Mexico was called the "Nueces Strip." When Mexico gained its independence from Spain in 1821, the Nueces River was the official boundary between *Tejas* and Tamaulipas (formerly Nuevo Santander). The Strip included the land south of the Nueces River to the Rio Grande, encompassing everything from present-day Laredo and on to the mouth of the Nueces, just south of present-day Corpus Christi. Even maps used by Stephen F. Austin to attract settlers to Texas showed the southern boundary of Texas as the Nueces River. When Santa Ana was defeated, he was captured and forced to sign the Treaty of Velasco, which named the Rio Grande as the southern boundary of Texas. Mexico, however, refused to concede that the Strip was or ever had been part of Texas. The treaty was never ratified or accepted by the Mexican congress.[14]

Today, this region is not only a land bordered by two rivers and the Gulf of Mexico, but a distinct historical and cultural region (see Figure I.1). Daniel D. Arreola calls it the *Tejano* homeland. He states, as the underlying assertion of his book, ". . . Mexican South Texas is a distinctive borderland, unlike any other Mexican American subregion."[15] One of our underlying assertions in this book is that this distinctiveness is closely tied to the high level of participation in the informal and underground economy of South Texas. To understand this distinctiveness and how it is related to informality, we will briefly describe the two major sections of this region: Webb County (which includes Laredo) and the Lower Rio Grande Valley (LRGV).

While most of the Spanish settlements along the Lower Rio Grande River were on the southern bank (Matamoros, Reynosa, Camargo, and Mier), Laredo was mostly on the northern bank when originally settled in 1755. In 1846, Zachary Taylor led U.S. troops into Laredo and declared it part of the United States. When the Treaty of Guadalupe Hidalgo ended the war with Mexico in 1848, the Rio Grande River was finally established as the southern boundary of Texas. Residents of Laredo who did not want to be Americans moved across the river into Mexico and established Nuevo Laredo as a separate (though connected) city. As a result, the cities of Laredo and Nuevo Laredo not only border each other (as do Matamoros and Brownsville), but include many residents who have common family lines.

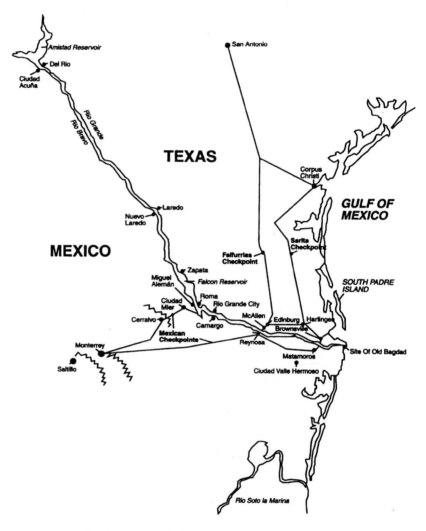

Figure I.I. The South Texas Borderlands

A key distinguishing feature of Laredo is that it has always been predominantly Latino[16], with an entrenched Hispanic elite. Though Anglos arrived after the war with Mexico, they mainly intermarried with Hispanic families. McAllen and Brownsville in the LRGV, in contrast, were established by Anglo elites who marginalized the Mexican residents. As a result, Latinos in LRGV communities struggled for many years, gaining significant political power only in the last 25 years of the twentieth century.

Since its establishment in the 1750s, Laredo has been an important crossroads between San Antonio, Texas, and Monterrey (Mexico's third largest city and an industrial center). With the coming of the cross-border railroad in 1881, Laredo became even more recognized as a gateway for trade between Mexico and the United States. Today, more commercial trade between the United States and Mexico passes through the city of Laredo than by all land routes and through all sea ports in the entire state of California. Indeed, products shipped through the Port of Laredo today account for more than 60% of the entire import and export trade between the U.S. and Mexico.[17]

According to the latest U.S. Census Bureau figures, Hispanics are the largest ethnic group in both Laredo and the LRGV. They comprise 87% of the population of the LRGV and 95% of the Webb County population.[18] In the LRGV, Anglos make up around 10% of the population, while in Webb County their representation in the total population is about 4%. Blacks comprise less than 1% of the population in each of these two border locations.

Both areas have also experienced very rapid population growth. The LRGV and Webb County are home to three of the fastest growing metropolitan statistical areas (MSAs) in the nation: Between 1999 and 2009 the McAllen-Edinburg-Mission MSA showed a 33% growth rate (from 555,875 to 741,152). During this same period, the Laredo MSA grew from 189,014 to 241,438, a 28% growth rate. Not too far behind these two was the Brownsville-Harlingen MSA in Cameron County, which increased at a 20% growth rate (from 330,277 to 396,371) in this same period. The growth rate for Texas as a whole during this ten-year period was 18%.

This rapid population growth has been accompanied by very strong job growth in the border metropolitan areas. The McAllen-Edinburg-Mission MSA, for example, led the state in the percentage growth in nonfarm employment (47.8%) during the period from 1999 to 2009. The Laredo MSA was second with a nonfarm employment growth rate of 33.4%, and the Brownsville-Harlingen MSA was sixth in the state, with a growth rate of 19.6%.[19]

Though such rapid population and job growth is generally associated with rapid economic growth, these border areas continue to be plagued with poor socioeconomic indicators, as they historically have been. For instance, according to census figures, 36% of individuals in the LRGV population and 29% in Webb County lived below the national poverty level in 2008. This compares with 16.3% for the rest of the State of

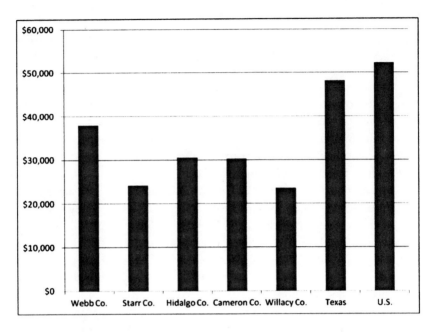

Figure I.2. 2008 median household income (in inflation-adjusted dollars) for five South Texas counties, Texas as a whole, and the U.S.

Texas and 13.2% for the entire United States.[20] Similarly, as one can determine from Figure I.2, the median household income for the LRGV counties in 2008 was around $29,000. It was somewhat better for Webb County ($37,923), though each county in the region was considerably below the median household incomes for Texas and the United States ($48,078 and $52,175, respectively).

These dismal income figures are related to other characteristics of the South Texas border population. In the United States as a whole, 12.5% of the population in 2008 was foreign born. In Texas as a whole, the comparable figure was 15.9%. Along the border, however, 27.9% in Webb County, 31% in Starr County, 28.7% in Hidalgo County, 25.1% in Cameron County, and 13.6% in Willacy County were estimated to be foreign-born, by the 2006-2008 American Community survey.[21] Having a large percentage of the population being foreign born does not, in itself, produce poverty. When a large foreign-born population arrives in the United States with minimal levels of education, however, the results are predictably dismal. Figure I.3 shows the percentage of adults 25 years of age and older in the five border counties who in 2008 had completed high school or a higher level of education. It also provides comparable data for Texas as a whole and the United States.

The effects of low education levels are predictable. The three South Texas MSAs, for example, rank at the very bottom of MSAs in Texas in 2008 hourly wage levels. While the average hourly wage for the whole of Texas in 2008 was $18.90, in the Laredo MSA it was $14.74; in the Brownsville-Harlingen MSA it was $14.08, and, at the very bottom, in the McAllen-Edinburg-Mission MSA the average hourly wage was only $13.85.[22]

As we shall show in the chapters that follow, the demographic character of these border counties is closely associated with informality and underground economic activities. For example, in an examination of Mexicans migrating to the border areas, Dávila and Mora[23] documented an earnings penalty for English-deficient speakers, as well as a tendency for English-deficient Mexican migrants to trend toward "relatively low-skill jobs." The structural unemployment found along the U.S.-Mexican border in South Texas will also be shown to be a contributing factor to the self-employed informality in the region.[24] In addition, areas with many people who live below the poverty line, with large numbers of

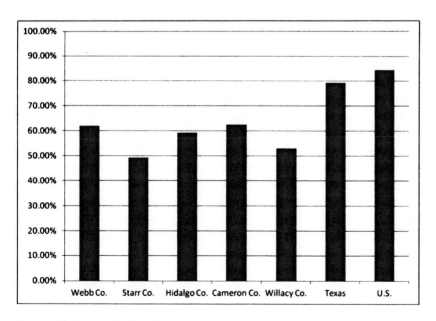

Figure I.3. Percent of adults 25 years of age and older who are high-school graduates in five South Texas counties, in Texas, and in the United States, 2008.

foreign born (living next to the country from which they emigrated), who have seasonal or part-time jobs, and who experience frequent periods of unemployment, are more likely to see high levels of informal activities.

Research Projects and Methodology

Much of the data reported in this and subsequent chapters is from the Borderlife Project, a research endeavor established at the University of Texas–Pan American in Edinburg, Texas, and subsequently incorporated at Texas A&M International, or TAMIU, in Laredo. Since 1982, faculty in this project have trained embedded student interviewers to investigate social situations along the South Texas–Northern Mexico borderlands. To date, the project has completed approximately 6,500 in-depth (ethnographic) interviews and over 5,500 survey interviews from a variety of populations on both sides of the border.[25] Most research topics start out as in-depth (ethnographic) descriptions. The patterns revealed in these anecdotal accounts suggest questions that are built in to in-person survey interviews.

The basic purpose of Borderlife is to help students develop an appreciation for their own culture and place. It is also designed to give voice to the distinct populations of South Texas, many of which receive little notice or, when notice is given, harsh and stereotyped notice.[26] The research generated through this process is more exploratory than explanatory; more hypothesis-suggesting than hypothesis-testing. We offer three major reasons for this. First, the ethnographic research techniques used are much better suited to exploratory and descriptive research than to hypothesis-testing or theoretical research. Second, many of the topics selected in this South Texas environment are still in the exploratory or descriptive stages. Finally, the use of student (embedded) researchers lends itself much more to in-depth ethnographic and exploratory research. Though we do utilize survey research to propose and test select hypotheses, the project emphasizes in-depth understanding of informality in this border environment.

This methodological approach also allows us to paint a broad picture of life on the South Texas border, focusing on many populations and topics, as opposed to a single issue or phenomenon. In the *Batos, Bolillos, Pochos & Pelados* volume (University of Texas Press, 1999), for example, we were able to describe migrant farmworkers, *colonia* residents, undocumented domestic servants, *maquila* workers in Mexico, and Mexican street children. In addition, we looked at racial and ethnic relations among such diverse South Texas groups as Latinos, Mexican immigrants, Anglo newcomers or tourists, and African Americans. In the follow-up volume, *On the Edge of the Law* (coauthored with Rosalva Resendiz and also published by the University of Texas Press, in 2006), we extended the analysis to descriptions of traditional cultural practices, displaced and undocumented workers, drug and immigrant smuggling, cross-border property crimes, the Mexican criminal justice system, and school dropouts. In the current volume, we continue that multidimensional approach, focusing on a fairly diverse set of issues of particular importance to the people of the Rio Grande/Rio Bravo Valley of South Texas and Northeast Mexico.

The vast majority of our data in this volume comes from several recent studies of informal and underground economic activities on the South Texas border. An overview of all the primary data sources is available in Appendix A.[27] The first study includes approximately 600 ethnographic interviews that have been conducted over the past five years by student interviewers on topics related to the informal and underground economy of South Texas and Northern Mexico.[28] Based on the patterns suggested by these ethnographic or in-depth interviews, we designed and conducted our Informal and Underground Survey of 526 adults using a purposive sampling design. Prior to this survey, we conducted a pilot survey of 309 adults. This pilot survey had fewer questions, so data from it will usually not be included. In the cases where the questions were identical, however, we combine the samples, for a total sample size of 835.

The hidden nature of the subject we were researching, along with our use of embedded student researchers, suggests a combination of both ethnographic and survey approaches. In our Informal and Underground Survey, we asked students to include anyone who was doing work "on the side" or being paid "under the table" and who did not report their income. We also asked our interviewers to include at least one individual who did cross-border trade either from or into Mexico (and as either formal or informal work). As a result, 121 respondents (23%) listed their current residence as Mexico, though virtually all of the interviews were conducted in the U.S.

In the chapters that follow, survey data will provide a quantitative portrait of informal and underground activities. As important as this is, we believe that the qualitative (ethnographic) accounts by students provide a richer description of these life situations, as well as insight into the personal causes and effects of informal and underground activities.

We are deeply indebted to the students and to the people who opened their lives to them for the richness of detail that these stories provide. The names of the students whose accounts were used in this book are listed in Appendix B.

The value of these student interviews can best be illustrated by including a few examples related to our opening account of Juan Cortina. Too much time has passed, of course, for students to have interviewed actual participants in these events from the mid-nineteenth century. But the influence of those times carried on into the early twentieth century. Some students were able to capture the shadows that still lingered in the collective mind from people who lived through such events.

One man, for example, remembered how his family had lost land to one of the large South Texas ranches built during that era. "The (Anglo) rancher would buy a few acres of land," he said, "and then fence off more than he originally bought. He would put a couple of armed men on the borders he claimed in case anyone wanted to cause trouble. It was hard to prove them wrong with that kind of system. Every time you would go to the courthouse, the paperwork would be lost or inaccurate. Who could win in a situation like that?"

Two of the subjects interviewed had witnessed brutality committed by the Texas Rangers. One woman said she was on her way to get firewood out in the country around San Manuel, Texas, when she discovered the bodies of two Mexican men who had been hanged. "Most people knew who committed these injustices," she said—"*Los Rinches* (the Texas Rangers). That was the reason we moved to Mission, Texas."

Another Mexican American interviewee, however, reported good relationships between her family and the Rangers. "My sister and I were raised in our grandparents' house," she said. "It was a big house and there was a constant flow of people coming and going. My grandparents spoke English and Spanish and I was raised with both languages. Mexican Americans and Anglos alike came to visit. The Texas Rangers often ate with us."

Hearing such different accounts about relations with the Texas Rangers causes one to wonder how such varying stories could all be true. Part of the explanation might be found in an important sociological principle—that our behavior, as well as our perceptions of the behavior of others, depends more on the cultural and structural situation than most of us care to admit. In this case, a series of events and circumstances took place in Mexico and in South Texas that produced a perfect storm of violence against the Latino residents of the Rio Grande Valley during the decade from 1910 to 1920.[29]

In Mexico, Porfirio Díaz (the same one who imprisoned Juan Cortina) had ruled for over 30 years as a dictator, igniting the Mexican Revolution. Again, the northern border became a focus of violence to remove him, followed by in-fighting among the victorious generals. Thousands of Mexican citizens fled to South Texas, creating hostility and suspicion among Anglo residents of the Valley. The victorious generals included Venustiano Carranza, Pancho Villa, and Emiliano Zapata. When Carranza turned on his former allies, the United States gave him extensive support, igniting a retaliatory raid on Columbus, New Mexico, in 1916 by Pancho Villa. Carranza fomented violence across the border in South Texas to pressure the United States to recognize him as the president of Mexico (with the promise that he would quell the violence). One of his leaders, General Nafarrate, used his forces to instigate cross-border "bandit raids" into South Texas. The *Carrancistas* took advantage of the long-simmering resentment among Hispanic Tejanos for the injustices they had endured since Texas was wrested from Mexico. As a result of this bitterness, and with the backing of Carranza, "El Plan de San Diego" emerged in San Diego, Texas. This document, known to very few South Texas Hispanics, called for a new nation in the lands lost by Mexico in 1836 and 1848 and for the extermination of every Anglo male in Texas.

Meanwhile, Texas had elected James "Pa" Ferguson, arguably the most corrupt governor in Texas history. One of his first actions was to appoint political cronies as leaders of the Texas Rangers, driving out many Rangers who had the respect of South Texas Hispanics. The railroad had also ended the isolation of South Texas, bringing in trainloads of Anglo farmers who, unlike the Anglo ranchers who preceded them, spoke no Spanish, despised Mexicans, and generally relegated Mexican Americans to a status of servitude. With Carranza instigating cross-border raids and wild newspaper accounts of "El Plan de San Diego," South Texas Anglos called on the governor for drastic action to end the "bandit raids."

Ferguson appointed Henry Ransom, a killer who had shot an attorney in cold blood, as captain of a special company of Texas Rangers, many of them vigilantes. He ordered Ransom to ". . . go down there [to the Valley] and clean it up if you have to kill every damned man connected with it."[30] In the ensuing five years, thousands of Hispanic U.S. citizens and Mexicans were rounded up, shot, hanged, or driven across the border into Mexico. Mexicans who were arrested were often shot "trying to escape," and the vigilantes photographed themselves next to piles of bodies of "bandits."

When Carranza received diplomatic recognition from the United States, the raids ended. Virtually nothing was done to the Rangers and others who had perpetrated this campaign of extermination. For years, "*Los Rinches*," (a derogatory term for the Rangers) were seen as the enemy, though few of the pre-Ferguson Rangers actually took part in the brutality. These feelings are illustrated by an interview with an eighty-seven-year-old native of the Valley. "The Rangers caught a man accused of stealing a cow," he said, "and they hung him. People tried to stay clear of the Texas Rangers and not cause any trouble or draw attention to themselves." Another reported that family members were often not even allowed to bury or remove the bodies.

Relations between Anglos and Hispanics in South Texas today are vastly different from those just described. One piece of evidence of this is the reactions to these stories by the students who conducted the interviews. Almost without exception, these student interviewers reported that this was the first time they had ever heard of such events. When they asked the family member they were interviewing why they had never talked about it before, almost uniformly the reply was something like, "We didn't want you to suffer what we did."

Nevertheless, some of the factors that produced such harsh treatment in earlier years still shape events and conditions in South Texas today, often in ways associated with the informal or underground economy. The entire U.S.–Mexico borderland, for example, continues to experience the effects of Mexican and U.S. national policies more harshly than is experienced in interior locations. The drug wars, for example, are fought mainly on the border, with a death toll in Mexico (mainly on the border) reported to be 28,000 in 4 years.[31] Approximately 25% of these deaths have been in the border city of Ciudad Juárez alone.

Similarly, the demand for drugs and cheap labor throughout the United States is met by official actions (often merely posturing that does little to end these trades) mainly at the border. As the federal government builds more fences and puts more "boots on the ground," the power of the cartels increases. Local families with property on the border, however, have land expropriated (often land that has been in their family for generations) to build a wall that many see more as a slap in the face of Mexico than an effective way to deter drugs or illegal immigration. Both the interdiction and the antismuggling efforts have their greatest impact in the border zone.

Likewise, as in the two previous centuries, politicians in Washington, D.C.; Mexico, D.F.; and border state capitals often exploit the borderland for political advantage. Recent examples include Governor Brewer in Arizona and Governor Perry in Texas talking about beheadings and bombings in the border zones of their respective states. In both cases, the violence they reported actually happened across the border, though these politicians chose to portray their own border communities as lawless and violent. In truth, cities on the U.S. side of the border have comparatively low rates of violent crimes.[32] Nevertheless, rhetoric drives policy and trade. The borderland continues to see a buildup in troops and a falling off of tourism resulting from the speech making. In Arizona, the rhetoric culminated in the passage of very strong anti-immigrant legislation that mandated racial profiling. Such policies have their greatest impact in the border zones.

As we shall point out in the following chapters, the U.S.-Mexico border (especially the portion in South Texas) is a magnet for informality and underground activity. Mostly, informality is a means of survival for the very poor. Occasionally, however, it is used by ruthless individuals to exploit the poor and powerless. And, as in past centuries, individuals, good and bad, find in this border location ways to use conflicting laws to their advantage. They also find understandings and arrangements in the local culture and structure that support informality as a way over, under, and around some of the harsh policies imposed on them by outsiders.

CHAPTER 1

Culture, Structure, and the South Texas–Northern Mexico Border Economy

I am a very social person. I do business with different kinds of people. I used to sell clothes at my house in Mexico. I used to buy cars and re-sell them without any titles because they were stolen. I had a bar where I could sell beer to anyone who could afford it. I opened up a bar in Texas, but could only sell beer or alcohol to people over 21. I couldn't sell clothes at my house anymore. They fined me for not having a per-mit. All the businesses there have to be legal, and there is no way you can make money your own way in the United States. That is why I moved back to Mexico. Now I can do business any way I want, so I only go back there once in a while. The United States is OK for people who like being controlled, but not for me.

—Antonio Aguilar,[1] a Mexican citizen who lived for several years in the United States, explains why he returned to Mexico

Introduction

Antonio is a man who has engaged in unregulated and illegal economic activities on both sides of the border. He skirts regulations not only to make money, but also to be free from governmental controls. He is not alone. Many people in the South Texas–Northern Mexico region take part in the informal and/or underground economy. For many, the reasons are economic—the struggle to survive. Others, like Antonio, want freedom from government controls.

The South Texas border offers informal and underground economic opportunities that are quite different from those available in other parts of either the United States or Mexico. What is the nature of this economy, and what factors help explain why informality is so pervasive in the South Texas borderlands? What are the effects of a very robust informal economy in this region of the United States?

The Informal and Underground Economy of the South Texas Border

The *informal economy*,[2] according to economic and sociological conceptualizations, consists of work that is in itself legal but that avoids government regulation, oversight, and/or taxation. While Antonio lived in Texas, his informal work included selling clothes from his home without a permit and selling liquor without a license. Other informal jobs common to South Texas include street vendors, day workers, flea market concessionaires, undocumented workers, people doing extra work "on the side," and even contractors doing unreported "cash only" work.

This is further illustrated in the case of Rosita Alonso, who has personally experienced many of the nuances of the informal and underground economy of the South Texas border.

> My husband never worked; I was the one working. I have three children. Their father does not send them any money because he's in jail for drug trafficking. Now I clean motel rooms during the week, and on weekends I sell plants at the flea market. Sometimes I don't make any money, so I have to go to Reynosa and borrow money. This lady there lends me money, but I have to pay her monthly interest. I get food stamps to feed the children. My *comadre* [female friend] next door is separated also, so we help each other in any way we can.—Rosita Alonso

The complexities of the informal border environment illustrated by Rosita's story include engaging in informal economic activities to survive, having a husband in jail for underground (criminal) drug activity, and needing to use varied, informal support systems (e.g., cross-border informal financing and an informal neighborhood assistance network).

Rosita's informal work includes her unreported sales at the flea market and her work in cleaning motel rooms (for cash) during the week. Informal work activity is not said to be criminal since the work itself is legal, but it is generally undertaken outside the scrutiny and legal bounds of government-mandated regulation and legislation.[3] Thus, a street vendor selling *cascarones* (eggshells filled with confetti, popular around Easter) might be able get a government permit to sell his product, but this is unlikely because the cost of the permit will cut deeply into his low profit margin. The more likely scenario in the border region is for the *cascarones* vendor to both produce and sell his product away from the formal auspices, taxation, and reporting requirements of the government.

The *underground economy*, in contrast, involves economic activities that are not only evasive of governmental oversight but are also criminal in nature. Antonio, in our opening case, was involved in underground economic activities that included selling stolen cars. Drug smuggling is an even more common form of underground economic activity in South Texas. Such activities often provide large profits but with correspondingly high risks associated with government prosecution and/or being preyed upon by other criminals (and such victims are often reluctant to report these crimes).

Many individuals in the South Texas border area utilize the underground and/or the informal economies of the region. Virtually everyone is affected by these economic activities. The economic reasons for involvement vary; some individuals are seeking to eke out a bare subsistence, and some wish to purchase informal or underground services or products. For some, like Antonio (in the opening vignette), the economic reasons involve cultural or personal considerations.

Structural and Cultural Factors Favoring Informal/Underground Activities

In addition to the demographic character of the border population, we propose a number of additional aspects of the South Texas borderlands that contribute to informality. Though many researchers often dichotomize such factors as either economic or noneconomic (or personal vs. contextual), we include a distinction between factors that are cultural and those that are structural. Before proceeding, we need to clarify how we are using these terms and then summarize how they are related to the high rates of participation in the informal and underground economy of South Texas.

We conceptualize "culture" and "structure" as major social forces that affect human behavior. Culture, as we define it, includes the meanings and understandings shared by a society or social group that give common meaning to their way of life and bind them together. For example, the use of a somewhat unique form of "border Spanish," or Tex-

Mex, not only conveys a unique set of shared understandings but is also a binding influence among those who know how to understand and speak it.

Structure, as we identify it, includes patterns of established relationships among the component parts of a society or social group.[4] The structure of the family, for example, would be the established relationships among its different "parts" (father, mother, children, grandparents, etc.). Likewise, the structure of South Texas society is the established relationships among such institutions as religion, government, education, commerce, health care, and criminal justice *on both sides of the border.*

Though these two forces—culture and structure—are often complementary, they also sometimes pull in opposite directions. The structure of the U.S. economy, for example, draws undocumented immigrants northward from Mexico to fill labor demands. This structural (and economic) force is countered by powerful demands among cultural conservatives in the U.S., whose nationalistic calls for "cultural integrity" lead to the building of multibillion-dollar border walls and the placement of federal troops on the border to repel the "alien invaders."

Though culture and structure each exert both positive and negative influences on informality everywhere, our data suggest that their net influence on informality is stronger in South Texas than in other regions of the U.S. We will describe, for example, how cash transactions, which appear to be more common on the South Texas border than in other parts of the U.S., allow market exchanges to go undetected—as long as both parties share the understanding that neither party will report the transaction. Similarly, we will show how the structure of different laws and enforcement mechanisms on both sides of the border facilitate cross-border informality/illegality.

The culture and structure of the family in South Texas may also trump American individualism in ways that facilitate informal and underground activities. Family members who become involved in informal or underground activities (either through choice or perceived necessity), often rely on the embedded social trust strongly associated with powerful family bonds to hide their actions from government agents. Likewise, the cross-national relationships that many Latinos in South Texas have with individuals in Mexico contribute to and facilitate informality and an underground economy.

In the South Texas borderlands, informal and underground activities often produce rather bizarre outcomes. For example, one undocumented informal worker we interviewed, Roberto Ordaz, experienced underground activities in a most unusual manner. He recalls:

> One day while I was almost finished with a roof, a strange thing happened. My truck got stolen. The person who stole it was my boss—the owner of the house I was roofing. The reason for stealing it was that he was trying to get away from the police, because they came with a warrant out for his arrest for drug smuggling. After hearing this from the police officers I was speechless.

Underground and informal activities in South Texas are complicated by the fact that activities outlawed in one country may be legal or winked at across the border. Thus, while selling and possessing firearms in the U.S. is not only legal but is generally considered a constitutional right, the same activity is outlawed and severely punished in Mexico. Similarly, though prostitution is illegal in almost all parts of the U.S., it is regulated in only 18 of Mexico's 32 states. Most cities on the Mexican side of the border permit and regulate prostitution by setting up "zones of tolerance" where prostitutes get monthly government-mandated health checks. In addition, though U.S. laws strictly prohibit and severely punish sex with children, Mexican laws against child prostitution are not well enforced.[5] Likewise, different age requirements, such as is the case for alcohol consumption (18 years old in Mexico and 21 in Texas), may result in activities that are legal on one side of the border but illegal (or even criminal) on the other.

In their comprehensive treatment of underground economies around the world, Bajada and Schneider[6] argue that "crime and other underground economic activities" are simply "a fact of life" which "most societies have attempted to control" with uneven success. We distinguish the term *underground* from *informal* activities and find it useful to highlight the illicit nature of the underground economic activity. The underground economy, then, can be viewed as both a definitional device and a behavioral one to describe illegal economic activities.[7] By definition, the underground economy includes those economic activities that legal authorities have declared illicit, a definition offering operational measurement.

The magnitude and the total economic impact of informal and underground activities are difficult to measure because participants engaged in these activities obviously do not wish to be identified.[8] Still, estimates have been attempted. Schneider and Bajada provide aggregate informal and underground GDP estimates comparing informality in many nations.[9] They estimate that in 2002–2003, the rate of informality in the U.S. was 8.4% of total economic activity. Their corresponding estimate of informality for Mexico for the same period was 33.2%. Further, they estimated the average rate of informality for all 145 countries in their study at 35.2% (an unweighted average). Perhaps because of the low estimate of informality in the United States, one finds relatively few studies of informality or of the underground economy here and elsewhere in the developed world, compared to the Third World.

There is an even smaller (but developing) literature concerning informal and underground activities in areas where First World nations border less developed ones. We see this paucity of studies as an important gap in the literature, both because informality seems more likely in border areas (for reasons soon to be spelled out) and because understanding informality in these areas holds the promise of important insights about informality itself. In Chapter 2, we examine underground economic activities in much greater detail. However, we should point out that much (and probably most) of the underground activity in South Texas is directly related to its geographical location next to the Mexican border.

Though very few empirical calculations have been made for informality in the Texas-Mexico border region, some estimates suggest that at least 20% of the production end of economic activity (by value) in the U.S. border region is undertaken via informal means.[10] For the U.S. as a whole, informal activity of about 10% is the accepted norm.[11] We estimate that along the South Texas border, approximately 30% of economic activity is extralegal, or conducted outside the formal economy, of which 20–25% is *part of the informal economy* and 5–10% is *part of the underground economy*. This relationship is illustrated in Figure 1.1[12] which includes estimated shares for informal, formal, and underground activities.

Informality as a Field of Study

In 1970, Keith Hart introduced the term "informal economy" in his description of large numbers of petty entrepreneurs in Ghana who worked beyond the regulation of government officials. Their behavior, he proposed, was not inherently illegal, but simply occurred outside of state authorization, control, and taxation. He utilized, perhaps for the first

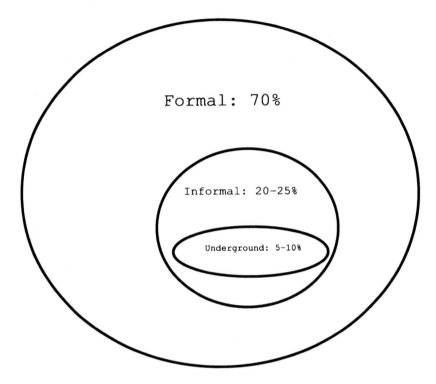

Figure 1.1. Economic activity by value: formal, informal, and underground activity in South Texas

time, the term "informal economy" to describe this large economic sector in Ghana and many other developing countries.[13]

Following his lead, researchers throughout Latin America, Asia, and Africa identified large segments of economic activity in developing countries that came to be classified as part of the informal economy. Some saw it as a natural stage in the economic development of modern capitalist nations. Others argued that the excesses of capitalism were, in fact, the causes of informality and that informality was another means whereby the poor were exploited. Regardless of how researchers interpreted the theoretical importance of the informal economy, they found it to be a major form of livelihood for much of the world's population. Portes and Hoffman, for example, state that it currently accounts for one third to one half of the economically active population of Latin America.[14]

Our model of informal and underground activities (illustrated in

Figure 1.2) takes issue with investigators who see informal and underground activities as unidimensional, with underground activities as simply an extreme form of informality.[15] Utilizing the works of Portes and Cross as a foundation, we posit two separate dimensions—one a continuum of formality-informality and the other a continuum of legal-illegal (or criminal) activities.[16] This dualistic construct yields different economic returns (earnings), as well as vastly different levels of exposure to risk from governmental prosecution, confiscation of assets, or being cheated by clients or associates. Figure 1.2 illustrates these two separate dimensions, and shows four quadrants: 1) Legal/Formal (very low risk); 2) Legal/Informal (low to medium risk); 3) Illegal/Formal (medium to high risk); and 4) Illegal/Informal (very high risk). In addition, following Max Weber, we see each quadrant as an "ideal type" (extreme case).[17]

The first quadrant, Legal/Formal, would include established businesses that conform to all the mandates of government in its roles as regulator, policeman, and tax collector (to use Portes' terminology). An "ideal type" of the first quadrant, to use Weber's heuristic device, would be a legitimate business that always follows *every* single city, county,

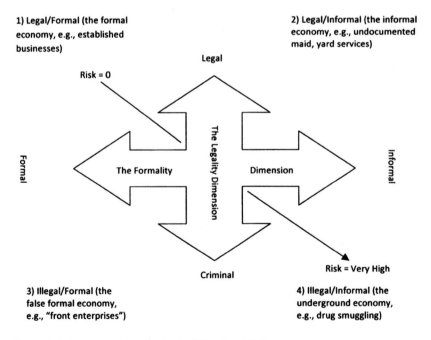

1) Legal/Formal (the formal economy, e.g., established businesses)

2) Legal/Informal (the informal economy, e.g., undocumented maid, yard services)

Legal

Risk = 0

The Legality Dimension

Formal

The Formality Dimension

Informal

Criminal

Risk = Very High

3) Illegal/Formal (the false formal economy, e.g., "front enterprises")

4) Illegal/Informal (the underground economy, e.g., drug smuggling)

Figure 1.2. Labor participation in the (il)legal and (in)formal sectors

state, or national regulation and pays every mandated fee or tax. Although many businesses approach this standard, few realize it completely. Thus, this and the other three quadrants are presented in their "pure" or idealized version and not necessarily as representations of reality. Most enterprises will fall somewhere along the continuum of the two dimensions, between the extremes, or ideal types.

One enterprise, for example, that we would place toward (but not completely in) the Legal/Formal quadrant is a business operated by Anna, a local entrepreneur in the *ropa usada* (used clothing) business in South Texas whom one of our students interviewed in 2009. Her form of border business enterprise was highlighted by Helen Thorpe in a *New York Times Magazine* article in October of 2000.[18] Thorpe reported that Americans gave away as much as 2.5 billion pounds of clothes each year, much of it ending up at huge warehouses in South Texas where people like Anna sort through enormous bales of clothing, prior to its sale into Mexico and beyond. Anna looks mainly for antique linens. She pays about 30 cents a pound for items she selects. She then cleans and sells them through a local antique shop, on eBay, or to individual customers, all at a large markup. She marvels that *ropa usada* warehouses are found almost exclusively on the border and that they provide her with an edge over other antique linen dealers across the nation. On occasion, she sells three to four thousand dollars worth of salvaged items in a month. She offers a discount if people pay cash so that she does not have to report all of her income. She used to sell out of her home to stay under the radar from the sales tax officials. After a while, however, some of her neighbors began to complain about the frequency of her "garage sales," so now her "on-the-side" sales are primarily from inside her home to a select group of customers.

Since Anna pays taxes on most of her income and obeys most regulations in conducting her business, we would classify her business as a legal/formal enterprise. Such overlap illustrates the difficulty of placing individual cases in any one quadrant. Indeed, most of the people we interviewed work in *both* of the top quadrants, having formal jobs with informal enterprises on the side. The product or labor they sell is generally legal, and few of them engage in criminal activities. Thus, most of the people we interviewed fall more into the Legal/Informal quadrant. These individuals undertake normally legal trades, away from the watchful eye of the government (such as undocumented maids or yard-service providers). A street vendor, for example, may be operating without a permit to sell and without documentation to legally work in the

U.S. or may avoid paying taxes while selling legal fruits and vegetables in South Texas. Because the nature of their work is hidden from the purview of governmental authority, the greatest risk is the detection of their otherwise normal business activity. This quadrant will be the main focus of all chapters except Chapter 2.

The third quadrant, Illegal/Formal, reflects the false economy of front enterprises where seemingly legitimate businesses launder money or serve as "fronts" for illegal enterprises. One example from this quadrant is an attorney we interviewed who is paid under the table by people from Mexico and other countries who don't want anyone to know about their illegal activities. This attorney makes around $200,000 a year in his regular business, but would not specify how much he makes under the table from his Mexican clients. Through family members, he also owns other businesses. When asked what laws he is breaking, he replied, "Probably IRS fraud and money laundering. I would have to pay too much in taxes if I claimed everything, and I would also put my clients at risk. I can't do that. My clients give me a lot of business."

The fourth quadrant, Illegal/Informal, describes the world of the high-risk underground economy where illicit activities are combined with illicit goods and services. Typical economic activities include illegal drug smuggling and selling, as well as human trafficking. As Figure 1.2 illustrates, each quadrant carries a different risk associated with the degree of legality/illegality and formality/informality. For the *formal* sector, the legal and authorized risk of participation is essentially nil. As one moves to the second quadrant the risk increases. Participants in the informal economy risk fines, confiscation, deportation, and/or even jail time. However, few public resources are committed to combating the small-time enterprises within the informal economy, as the majority of the enforcement activities concentrate on the more egregious actions of criminals. So the risk is either low, for residents, or medium for undocumented workers who risk being deported. The enforcement emphasis is on the two quadrants involved in the underground economy, particularly the illicit drug trade in South Texas. In the false formal economy (the third quadrant), the potential punishments are harsh, though mainly from arrest and confiscation of assets. The greatest risk is found in the fourth quadrant, Illegal/Informal, where participants not only risk loss of assets and jail time, but substantial danger to life and limb from associates or enemies in the underground economy (as evidenced by a phrase popularized by the media, "a drug deal gone bad"). This risk is illustrated by the case of Luis.

Luis is 30 years old and owns a small construction company that he started two years ago. He only makes about $15,000 a year from it. He earns more, however, from working for smugglers, pressing marijuana into bundles and loading the bundles onto trucks to be transported farther north. He started smuggling small loads on his own but quit when a recent incident taught him how dangerous it is.

> I had a deal with a buyer in Florida. My mistake was to let a friend I partnered with sell that load to a man in Michigan instead. My friend's brother had just gotten out of prison and said someone he knew there would pay a lot more if we would get them the 130 pounds. We had gotten the marijuana from a cartel in Matamoros (Mexico), and we still owed them $22,000. I told the cartel guys that I was suspicious, but they let my friend take the drugs on the promise that he would pay them within two weeks. Well, he and his brother went to Michigan and only got part of the money, with the promise that it would be paid in two or three days. When the money did not arrive, they realized that their buyer had disappeared. When my friend called to tell the cartel what had happened, they told him to just come to Matamoros to get another load from which he could pay off what he owed. Once my friend showed up there, the leader approached him and shook his hand while another man came up behind him and hit him across the head with a gun, splitting his head open. Then they beat him, leaving him bloody and bruised, with four broken ribs. He called me that night to tell me that he was being held hostage. They were going to kill him if we didn't come up with the $22,000 we owed. I picked up my friend's two Jettas, fully loaded with rims and stereo systems and a Chevy short bed truck. My two brothers and I drove the vehicles to Matamoros with the titles and turned them over to them. They claimed we still owed them $7,000, but they let us go, with threats of the same treatment if we didn't pay. We drove my friend to the McAllen hospital. That was the last time I ever tried to get directly involved in transporting marijuana.

This case illustrates the extreme risks involved in activities in the Informal/Illegal quadrant. Smugglers risk not only arrest and prosecution, but even greater dangers from suppliers and those to whom they sell. They find it difficult to appeal to the legal system to uphold a broken agreement, as when the buyer in Michigan failed to pay the full amount. Nor are they likely to appeal to the law to protect them against violence from their suppliers. As a general principle, the further outside the law such transactions are, the greater the risks, not only from the law, but from other underground operators.

Theoretical Observations and Research Questions Related to Informality in South Texas

Alejandro Portes and his colleagues have pointed out the difficulties that governments often encounter in trying to regulate economic activities in developing nations. Portes and Haller, for example, state, "The *basic paradox* of state control is that increased official regulation of economic activity does not necessarily reduce the informal economy, but may expand it by creating opportunities for profitable violation of the rules."[19] This suggests several research questions. First, how might attempts to control the underground or informal economy actually make it larger and more profitable? This is perhaps best seen in the underground drug trade passing through South Texas, but it is also evident in many of the informal economic activities of the area. Several years ago, one Starr County land owner with very little initial capital was reported by neighbors to have made a large profit while other ranchers in the area were experiencing hard times. He reportedly did so by secretly driving cattle purchased in Mexico across the river to his land on the banks of the Rio Grande, fattening them up on his land, and selling them on a cash basis. His profit came not just from buying cheap in Mexico and selling high in the U.S. market, but also from skirting all the very expensive and time-consuming regulations required to import cattle from Mexico.

Portes points out that the profitability of informal or underground opportunities is related to how much control is attempted, how effectively the controls can be enforced, and the power and resourcefulness of individuals to resist or bypass official rules. In the example of the Starr County rancher, the control attempted, i.e., state and federal regulations, was rather large, but the ability of the government to effectively prevent undocumented cattle from coming into the U.S. is no greater (and probably less) than its ability to keep out undocumented immigrants, especially on land adjoining the Rio Grande.[20]

Centeno and Portes argue that informal enterprises seek to avoid the state in its roles as "regulator, policeman, and tax collector."[21] As a result, they argue, the relationship between the informal economy and the state is one of inevitable conflict. The whole point of the state, they argue, is to assert the monopoly of its authority within its territory, while the whole point of informal entrepreneurs is to avoid or to subvert that authority.

Centeno and Portes also point out some paradoxes that result from the opposition between informal entrepreneurs and control by the state. One paradox is that official efforts to obliterate unregulated activities by creating more and more rules often end up expanding the very conditions that give rise to these informal activities. In other words, creating more rules against informality often creates even more opportunities for informal economic activities. Regulations requiring social security and other documents for employment, for example, have spawned a major industry of counterfeiting and selling fake documents.[22]

Another paradox described by Centeno and Portes is that informality and the breaking of government rules and regulations commonly yields some positive benefits for the state, the very institution that tries to prevent these rule breakers from operating. In South Texas, for example, the building of informal *colonia* housing violates many building codes, but the government gains the benefits of greatly reduced homelessness and a reduced need for government-provided low-income housing.

Is the South Texas Border a Special Case of an Informal and/or Underground Economy?

Though the preceding discussion is helpful in understanding informality in developing nations, we need to ask, is informality in the South Texas borderlands a response to somewhat different factors than informality elsewhere in the world? In two previous works, Richardson makes the point that South Texas is unique not only in the context of the U.S. as a whole but even in the narrower context of the U.S.-Mexico border.[23] We propose that the poverty and inequality, the borders, the ethnicity and culture, the cross-border ties, and the large undocumented population of this border area are all factors that contribute to making the informal and underground economy of this area unique.

Inequality and poverty in the borderlands. Though extensive international transportation corridors connect the South Texas–Northern Mexico region to the economic centers of the United States and Mexico, respectively, the region is at the same time isolated from the main centers of power at both the state and national levels in each country. This isolation tends to produce a power disparity—one highlighted in 1998 by the Texas Comptroller of Public Accounts, John Sharp, who characterized the Texas border as the fault line between two tectonic plates, with the power that moves both those plates originating far beyond the border region.[24] This power inequality shows up in multiple ways. It is reflected, perhaps most importantly, in the region's high poverty rate. In 2000, the family poverty rate for the Texas borderlands was 23.2%, compared to 18.4% in the Mississippi Delta (the next poorest region) and only 9.2% for the nation as a whole.[25] It is also reflected in resources available for education. Among Texas border counties, the average revenue available to educate each student in 1998 was $4,341, compared to school districts elsewhere in the state that averaged two or three times that amount.[26] In large measure, this difference was due to a wide disparity in revenue generated by property taxes. In 1998, school districts in the Texas border region had approximately $82,400 worth of property wealth per student, compared to the state average of $137,000 per student.[27]

For the poor living in South Texas or Northern Mexico, the border offers many informal economic opportunities. One South Texas woman who supplements her formal income with informal work describes how use of an informal medical network in Mexico also helps her obtain limited and somewhat risky medical care in Mexico. "Doctors and medicine are just too expensive here," she says, "so I have to take my family to Mexico when we get sick. The people at the pharmacies are really good. You tell them what is wrong and they give you the medicine to fix you. Two birds with one stone, if you ask me."

While such strategies might save money, the obvious risks of getting a medical diagnosis from a pharmacist are compounded by buying prescription drugs in Mexico without a doctor's prescription (technically illegal, but seldom enforced). She must then also transport the medicine into the U.S. for herself or her family (also technically illegal, but seldom enforced). Thus, economic necessity pushes many individuals into medical informality, which includes none of the protections of the usual formal process.

Clearly, poverty and inequality have many connections to informality, so we ask: How much do poverty and inequality promote informality and underground activities? Without doubt, those in poverty often resort to informal means when they believe that formal sources are out of reach. Some are also tempted by the seeming "easy money" to get involved in underground activities, as the following account provided by Mario, a resident of Starr County, illustrates.

The money we make off drugs allows us to afford things we couldn't when growing up. Now we can afford nice things for our children. Guys over here really like trucks like the Wild Child. When those Chevys came out, all the young ones wanted one. Chevy is the truck for these areas. When you go out to the main street you see Chevy upon Chevy *dando la vuelta* (cruising). A few people have sports cars, but they're pretty rare. Another luxury we can now afford is nice homes and furnishings. Many of us have homes that would fit into executive neighborhoods in the bigger cities. We can buy homes like this because there are many ways around government questions. Many of the builders, for example, lie about the cost of building the house. These contractors build a $150,000 home, charge the drug smuggler that much, but then record that the house only cost $90,000. The bank as well as the real estate company are in on it and make their own profit through payoffs or interest on the loan. Even though we don't need a loan, we will get one to cover our tracks.

Borders and Informality. Many writers raise a related question: How do borders facilitate informal and criminal activities? Miller,[28] for example, proposes a direct linkage. "Where a boundary divides a market by restricting the exchange of goods and people," he states, "it can generate illicit cross-border traffic." He further argues that "smuggling and black market networks typically arise when commodities available in one nation are generally desired, but prohibited or heavily taxed in the other. A boundary also sets jurisdictional authority, and consequently may constrain police responses to local crime by limiting essential investigation or by providing refuge in the other nation for lawbreakers."

Culture, ethnicity, and inequality. The ethnic distribution of the South Texas region raises another key research question: To what extent does the culture of Mexico spill over the border into South Texas in ways that might foster or facilitate informality? Unlike some of the other U.S.-Mexico borderlands, where a fence is the border, in the South Rio Grande border area Mexican-origin people make up approximately 90% of the population. About one fourth of the adults in this Hispanic population were born in Mexico, and almost one fifth of workers are undocumented.[29] As a result, the majority of the population is of Mexican ancestry, and the influences of the cultural traditions of Mexico are very strong. As we will demonstrate throughout this book, informality is an omnipresent part of Mexican society. Thus, it would be well to examine how much informality is part of the cultural experience that these immigrants and cross-border traders bring with them.

The structural web of cross-border relationships and informality. Another key question is to what extent does the web of cross-border relationships promote, or at least facilitate, informality by opening up supply and trade opportunities, providing human capital resources (by which to make or sell items informally), and providing assistance to relatives or individuals from Mexico? Martina, for example, is a legal U.S. resident, but maintains ties with Mexico that facilitate informality. "I often call my mother in Mexico," she says, "to place orders with one of her neighbors who frequently comes to the Rio Grande Valley. I have her bring me medications, clothing, and/or accessories, some of which I use for myself and others that I sell to my neighbors who can't cross into Mexico."

Undocumented Immigration and Informality. Related to the preceding factors is the issue of undocumented immigration. To what extent does the presence of large numbers of undocumented, Mexican-origin workers contribute to informality? The work of undocumented immigrants in the U.S. is related in at least three ways to informality; first, these workers are informal because they work without government authorization; second, most of them have to hide their earnings to avoid detection; and third, many produce food or other commodities or services without appropriate licensing or inspection—some midwives and street vendors of tacos are but two examples.

The complexities of the impacts of undocumented immigration to the area are illustrated by the case of Hector Briones, an undocumented young man who initially immigrated to the midwestern U.S. and now continues to work in the South Texas borderlands without legal authorization.

> I was so young when I came to the U.S., and I had never seen a place so clean and full of hope. We were so thankful to the woman who employed my mother as a maid who let my mom bring us here to the U.S. and let us live with her. She even paid for us to cross over. I felt I had to repay her by making something of my life, so I went to work with a friend's papers. He wasn't working so he let me use his papers because the income tax refund would be his at the end of the year. I didn't care. I was going to be working. Little did I know how difficult the work would

be in a chicken processing plant. It smelled bad, we worked long hours, and it was dangerous. I hated working there. So I came back to the Valley and found a job washing dishes. By then, I had a wife and a baby to feed. I lost my papers because the guy who loaned them to me owed child support and they found him and put him in jail. I was just lucky they didn't get me. So I started washing dishes at a restaurant for 9-hour days at $5.15 an hour. It was hard! I still don't earn enough for diapers or food. My wife has college hours from Mexico but she doesn't have papers. If she works and reports an income, we won't get food stamps and Medicaid for the baby. I don't have enough for food as it is, and she would only be making minimum wage anyway. So we are better off the way we are. Just hoping we make it to the next check.

Even if individuals like Hector pay taxes and report their income, they would still be considered informal workers because of their unauthorized work status. If they are apprehended, they may be charged with an immigration violation, as well as with document fraud, a felony. Likewise, many who come with a laser (shopper's) visa may engage in formal work, but the visa does not legally authorize them to do so. Similarly, those who knowingly hire workers with fraudulent documents may be prosecuted, though demonstrating that the employer had knowledge of a worker's undocumented status is difficult to establish. This puts employers in the difficult position of having to judge whether an employee's papers are fraudulent, borrowed, or real. Though the law requires only that papers must *appear* to be legal, an employer may face legal difficulties if the Department of Homeland Security decides to prosecute.

In the South Texas border region, an estimated 20–25% of the adult population is undocumented;[30] activities which otherwise would be considered legal could be classified as informal or even underground activities for such individuals. Even among the 90% of the population of the six-county area—from Laredo to the Lower Rio Grande Valley—who are of Mexican origin, many have parents and/or grandparents with a history of undocumented immigration. In 2005, the McAllen Sector of the Border Patrol recorded 11% of all Border Patrol apprehensions (134,188 out of close to 1.2 million total apprehensions). This was more than any other Border Patrol sector except Tucson and Yuma, Arizona (which are both larger than the McAllen Sector).[31]

Though most undocumented migrants who enter the U.S. through South Texas do not remain in the border area, many do. The Texas Comptroller of Public Accounts in 2006, using data from the Pew Hispanic Center's study of the undocumented population of the United States, projected that if the estimated 1.4 million undocumented immigrants in Texas were deported, it would produce a net decline in the Texas workforce of 6.3%. This same hypothetical deportation, however, would produce a net decline of over 20% of the labor force in the border region from Laredo to Brownsville (and 23% in the area from McAllen to Brownsville).[32] Clearly, such a large, undocumented labor force has a major impact on the informal economy of the area, a phenomenon we will examine in greater detail in Chapter 4.

There are many ways that large numbers of undocumented residents have an impact, directly or indirectly, on the informal and underground economy. The first and most obvious one is an abundant informal labor pool. Many local residents know, for example, which supermarket or flea market (*pulga*) or bus stop to go to if one wants to hire an undocumented maid or gardener. Second, in an environment where the perception is that "everybody does it," one is less likely to see such activities as immoral. Third, large numbers of people living in violation of the law produces a reduced probability of detection. Finally, the presence of many undocumented residents greatly increases the probability that newcomers can more easily "learn the ropes," blend in, and perhaps find a mentor who can teach them not only how to find informal work but also how to minimize the risks of detection and abuse (a form of human capital).

Other Factors Related to a Large, Informal, and Underground Border Economy

In addition to the preceding factors in this border area, there are other border-related factors that contribute to the informality of the area's economy. Besides the numerous undocumented residents, many Mexicans who reside in the area—though on the Mexican side of the border—regularly cross to and from Mexico to engage in trade. To what extent do these cross-border traders contribute to the informal economy of South Texas? Many cross-border traders have jobs or small businesses in Mexico, commuting daily or weekly using a *mica*, a border-crossing card issued by American consulates in Mexico to Mexican border residents (more recently issued as and called the "laser visa").[33] These traders are neither residents of nor official, long-term visitors to the U.S., but they do significantly contribute to the informal and underground economy of the area (as do Mexican drug and immigrant smug-glers who reside in Mexico but cross frequently, often without inspec-tion, into South Texas).

The border is an important factor in informality in other ways. Some residents on both sides of the border are pushed into informality by con-fusion over the laws of the two very different countries. Eduardo Ba-rrera, for example, came from Mexico and started his own business sell-ing patio furniture. He manufactures all of his merchandise in Reynosa and used to bring it into the U.S. in small amounts, pretending to be an American tourist so that he wouldn't have to pay customs duties. One time, as he was bringing furniture into the U.S., a Customs officer rec-ognized him and remembered him bringing similar furniture on other occasions. The officer investigated and discovered that Eduardo owned a small furniture business. He told Eduardo that he could face jail time and a fine and have his vehicle confiscated. Fortunately, the officer saw Eduardo's son asleep in the back seat and decided to give him a severe warning. Eduardo stated, "When the officer told me all the penalties I faced, my heart stopped. Thank God he had sympathy on me. From that point on, I began using the required importation procedures."

Though Eduardo began to comply with formal importation proce-dures, he continues to skirt other U.S. laws. In Mexico, dealing strictly in cash to avoid taxes is a widespread practice, not only among the poor, but among professionals and established business people. When infor-mality becomes "standard business practice," it contributes greatly to a culture of informality that some immigrants bring with them to the U.S. Eduardo hides some of his sales in the U.S. by dealing in cash and not giving a receipt unless customers specifically request one. He stated that most of the sales that he does not report are the deals that he makes with less than reputable individuals. "I immediately know when a *mafioso* (drug dealer) comes into my store," he says, "because he starts choosing things without looking at the price and he always pays cash. *Los mafiosos* really don't want a receipt because the less of a trail they leave to show how they spend money, the better."

Micro-Level and Macro-Level Factors

An additional distinction we need to consider in examining the informal and underground economy of this region is two main aspects of infor-mal or underground economic activities: production/sales versus con-sumption. This distinction suggests that we consider that the informal economy includes not only those producing and selling informally, but also consumers who skirt the law to purchase such goods and services. The *production/sales* aspect of informality ranges from special-event vendors selling *cascarones* (confetti-filled eggshells) during Easter or flowers around *El Día de la Madre* (Mother's Day) to full-time employment endeavors in the service sector—construction, day labor, domestic servants, and so on.

If we consider *consumption* informality, however, participation rates in South Texas would increase dramatically, certainly surpassing 50% and possibly reaching as high as 80–90% of the general population.[34] Consumption informality includes such economic activities as employing a domestic worker or a gardener, paying cash for home repairs that will not be reported, or buying alcohol or prescription medicine in Mexico and then not declaring the purchase when returning to the U.S.

One Customs agent described how otherwise law-abiding people often become participants (as consumers) in informal economic activities. "I often deal with elderly 'Winter Texans' who go into Mexico to shop," he says. "When they come back, I first ask them, 'Are you an American citizen?' Then I ask them what they are bringing back. Just recently, I asked one of them if he was an American citizen. He just laughed and said, 'Yes, of course.' Then I asked him how many bottles of alcohol he had purchased and he said, 'Only one.' When I checked his automobile I found 15 bottles."

Border residents living closer to the economic edge may find that combining informal economic options with more formal activities can expand their options considerably. Many people living barely above the official poverty line, for example, may fail to report all their income in order to maintain even meager welfare benefits. "I'm not a bad mom and I want the best for my kids," said one single mother, "but because I work, I don't qualify for any Medicaid health insurance for my kids. They say I make too much money. How can they say that? I barely make ends meet. Sometimes I just think it's better to quit my job and go on welfare."

The Texas-Mexico border also contributes to informality and underground economic activity in Mexico. This is illustrated by Carlos Calderón, a young boy who seeks out American tourists in Nuevo Progreso (a small, Mexican border town in the Rio Grande/Bravo Valley).

> My family moved from the interior of Mexico to a Mexican border town several years ago. My dad told us it would be better to move to Nuevo Progreso [across from Hidalgo County] because there was more Amer-

ican money there. After living there for several years, though, my dad decided to cross illegally into the United States to get a job as a construction worker in Houston. Later, he called my mom to say that he was going farther north with the company that had hired him, but not to worry because he would be sending money. Well, he left, but he never sent any money back to us. We have not seen him nor heard from him for three years. I think he found another woman prettier than my mom. I stopped going to school, and now I shine shoes to help my mom take care of my two brothers. I only earn enough when it's gringo season [when the seasonal retirees, or "Winter Texans" come back to the Valley].

As Carlos' story illustrates, the economy on both sides of the border is strongly influenced by factors from the opposite side. Many Americans shop in, get medical/dental services in, or buy other goods and services in Mexico, while Mexicans are attracted to the much higher-paying opportunities in the U.S. For many workers, this involves informal means (crossing to work with permits that do not authorize employment) or underground methods (such as fraudulent papers). Carlos' story also illustrates that people who live "on the margins" may have few options available in the formal economy. Such individuals (and especially those in Mexico) may feel that the informal or underground economy is their only alternative.

Structural Bias as a Macro-Level Contributor to Borderlands Informality

Though the region is isolated from political and economic power, it is not isolated from the effects of decisions made in the far-off power centers.[35] Border residents are seldom consulted about national decisions that have their greatest impact in the borderlands. Recent examples include the war on drugs, the North American Free Trade Agreement (NAFTA), the growing militarization of the border, and increasingly stringent and exclusionary border-crossing policies. Such decisions and agreements are generally made elsewhere, with only minor efforts made to consult border residents or to investigate how such policies will affect their lives.

For example, in 2007 former mayor of Brownsville, Eddie Treviño, Jr., stated that the fence being built along the U.S.-Mexico border is like the Great Wall of China and is a thirteenth-century solution to a twenty-first-century problem. He argued that the border fence and the absence of such fences at the Canadian border and in Florida (to keep Canadians and Cubans from entering the U.S.) implies that "Canadians and fleeing Cubans are good neighbors but that Mexicans are not."

The differentials between the wealth and power of the South Texas borderlands and that of Mexico City, Austin, Washington, D.C., and other centers of regional, national, and global power create a form of structural bias.[36] According to Richardson, inequality can produce harmful consequences from cultural and structural sources. Such harm can be either direct and intentional (bigotry and exploitation) or indirect and unintentional (cultural bias and structural bias). In other words, structural bias is a form of unintended harm resulting from imbalanced structural arrangements in which some groups have more power than others. Richardson uses examples such as slow response time to reports of crime in *colonias* (which is unintentional because the colonias are located in the county where the sheriff has fewer deputies to cover a larger area) and how minority individuals in many organizations are the most recently hired and will also be the first fired because of low seniority. Again, the harm is indirect and unintentional and based on inequality in the structural arrangements. A final example of structural bias is when migrant children have greater difficulty in school, not so much because of prejudice, but because their parents' work requires that the families migrate from state to state, making it difficult for these students to stay in the same school for the entire school year. Like the preceding examples, this harm comes not from prejudice or exploitation, but from inequality in the structural relations of the institutions of employment and education.

In each of these examples, the harm is indirect and unintentional— it is caused by bias in the systems of society, producing negative side effects for some groups while providing positive results for others. Though negative side effects can impact any segment of society (just as a medicine can produce negative side effects for the rich and the poor), over time the negative side effects of unequal structural arrangements hurt those with less power and resources almost exclusively. This lopsided result comes about because the wealthy and powerful can use their political and economic power to block or mitigate the side effects that could work against them.

To further illustrate, property taxes are today the major source for funding Texas public schools. This arrangement leaves "property poor" districts, many of which lie along the Texas-Mexico border, with meager budgets with which to compete for good teachers and pay for adequate resources. If a new tax system were to be proposed that had an opposite side effect, one that ended up providing less money for the well-to-do, these affluent parents would use their considerable political power to raise a firestorm of protest, reminding legislators who got them elected and threatening to turn them out in the next election. The proposed change would likely never take effect or would be rapidly changed if they did. When structural arrangements negatively affect those with less power, however, these citizens can muster far fewer political resources to block the changes. Those who do benefit can express regret for the negative effects while claiming the harm to the poor was not intended and that they only acted democratically to protect their interests.

With this background, we propose that much of the informality in the South Texas borderlands today is a result of structural bias, mainly at the macro-level. The South Texas borderland is a region of strategic importance but with little power to influence strategic decisions. Today, immigration is an issue of great national concern and has the potential to deeply impact border areas. Nevertheless, local governments in border areas have little power to make or enforce immigration laws and regulations. These are claimed as exclusively within the federal domain.

The U.S. demand for drugs and the violence in Mexico that results from our "drug wars" is another area where local jurisdictions have far less power than the federal government. With massive increases in the number of Border Patrol, Customs, Immigration and Customs Enforcement (ICE), and Drug Enforcement Administration (DEA) agents being sent into the border areas, arrests may skyrocket. But the resources of the federal prosecution agencies are not increasing correspondingly. So drug cases are turned over to state prosecutors and courts with little federal funding to support the vastly increased caseloads.

Health care is another major national issue, and there are a large number of uninsured in the South Texas borderlands. In the great political debates about the uninsured, however, little attention was given to the effects that the proposed legislation would have on these border residents. For example, the undocumented residents were excluded from being able to purchase health insurance, with far-reaching potential effects on the public health of the region.

Although these and other borderlands issues command considerable national and statewide attention, the discussions surrounding them reveal scant concern about how the policies generated in the centers of power will affect those on the border. And those at the border often turn to informal activities not only because they are shut out of legitimate activities by increasing regulation, but also because increasing regulation, as Portes points out, produces more income-generating opportunities. And local governments, strapped for resources by structurally biased funding mechanisms that divert resources from where they are most needed, are not only unable to meet local needs, but may find it best to not look too carefully when local residents solve some of their own problems through informality.

To give one example, the immigration conundrum could be solved simply by issuing a national identification card that one must present when applying for work and then fining employers who hire anyone that does not have the card. But this universal solution would be threatening to certain economic elites (e.g., large agricultural interests who need cheap field labor, or average citizens who don't want to show a federal identification card). Such groups have systematically rejected such plans as being "disruptive to business." Rather, it is more expedient, politically, to build walls and put more Border Patrol officers on the border to dispatch "illegal aliens" back to their home countries. So while the border enforcement option is more painful for border populations, they are expected to put up with these "side effects" because no one really *meant* to harm them.[37]

One primary avenue by which these populations along the border and in South Texas make do is to turn to informal and underground means, since many of the formal paths that might work better are blocked or mandated away by far-off capitals. So if one cannot afford health insurance, then one crosses the border into Mexico for cheaper (and often more risky) health care (Chapter 7). If there is a shortage of affordable housing, then self-build a home in a *colonia* where developers can fail to put in proper infrastructure and can keep you in debt bondage until you have completely paid for your lot (Chapter 6). If one cannot earn enough playing by the rules (e.g., formal work at less than minimum wage) or might lose familial benefits (i.e., health insurance, food stamps) through formal wage employment, then work on the side and get paid under the table (Chapter 8). For Mexicans suffering from the economic rationalization of NAFTA, particularly those practicing subsistence agriculture or displaced from their communal land holdings, the "make do" alternative is to come to the U.S. illegally to find work under precarious circumstances (Chapter 4).

Informality at the Micro-Level:
Why Do Individuals Engage in Informality?

Though macro-level forces do have a major impact on informality, individuals still must make micro-level decisions. In any rational decision-making model, individuals attempt to compare the benefits of a choice they are considering with its potential costs. This model certainly applies when individuals are considering participation in informal or underground economic activities. While we do not propose that such decisions are completely rational (estimating the potential costs and benefits of some economic enterprises may often be simply "hunches" or guesses), certainly some prior cost-benefit thinking takes place. Will enough customers want the product or service to make it pay? Can one adequately hide the activity and/or the profits to avoid governmental oversight, penalties, and/or taxation?

To illustrate, Roberto and Ana Canales live near a poor neighborhood called "*México Chiquito*" (Little Mexico) in a community near McAllen. Roberto is now self-employed as a diesel mechanic and also has a special-purpose vehicle that cleans supermarket parking lots late at night. He reluctantly reports to the government his income from these two businesses. Before he set up these businesses, he earned money buying merchandise in the U.S. and taking it to Mexico to sell at a profit. Roberto said,

> I would buy all types of American foods from supermarkets, as well as used bikes and appliances and make the trip to Mexico once a week. To prevent problems with the Mexican officials, I would pay Mexican border officials a bribe. This ensured that they would not charge me import fees for taking merchandise into Mexico. I never reported any of the money I made in Mexico to *Hacienda* (the Mexican IRS). My wife, Ana, also keeps her income hidden from the U.S. government. She works part time as a sales person at a bridal store earning roughly $200 a week. She doesn't report it because she can't accept losing money to the government out of the little that she earns every week.

In Roberto and Ana's story, we find participation in the formal and informal sector in the U.S. as well as participation in the informal sector in Mexico. Roberto now dutifully complies with U.S. law for his two small businesses, though his wife avoids reporting her wages earned in the U.S. Earlier, Roberto participated in the Mexican informal sector by reselling in Mexico merchandise purchased in the U.S. He also bribed Mexican officials (a criminal act, but fairly common) to pass the merchandise without inspection at the Mexican border. Why? Like other economic actors, he and Ana are attempting to reduce uncertainty and prevent detection by buying off border officials to avoid fines or import duties and are seeking to maximize benefits by buying where costs are lowest and selling where they can make the greatest profit. But such decisions are not made easily. What are the benefits and the risks of participation in the informal economy, and how do individuals decide whether or not they should move outside the formal economy to engage in informal or underground economic activities?

Why Informality? A Migration Analogy

In the preceding account, Roberto and Ana, like many border people with roots in Mexico, moved in and out of the formal economy, paying duties and taxes when necessary and avoiding them when possible. How do they make the decision to move from formality to informality and even back again? In some respects, these decisions are not unlike the decision of migrants trying to decide whether to leave their homeland for another country. In both cases, individuals must weigh perceived costs of the action against anticipated benefits.

In discussions of migration theory, demographers often employ a "push-pull" model of analysis. What factors push migrants out of their home environment and pull them to the new location? The same push-pull model applies to decisions about whether one should leave the safety of formality to engage in informal (or even underground) economic activities. Again, certain unpleasant aspects of the formal economy may "push" them into informality, just as other factors in the informal economy may be seen as attractive "pull" factors—or at least, as not unattractive.

Often overlooked in both the migration literature and in the literature on factors influencing informality, however, are a second set of forces—those that work to "hold" individuals in their current geographical or economic position and those in the prospective position that might "repel" a move. When making a choice about informality, individuals not only reflect on factors that push them from formality or pull them into informality, but they will also consider factors in the formal economy that hold them there, as well as aspects of the prospective

Location	Formal Economy	Informal (or Underground) Economy
Impact	─────────────▶	
Encourages Informality	──▶ Push (costs of remaining in the formal economy)	Pull ──▶ (benefits of moving to the informal economy)
Discourages Informality	Hold ◀── (benefits of remaining in the formal economy)	Repel ◀── (costs of moving to the informal economy)

Figure 1.3. Factors (push-pull and hold-repel) affecting movement from the formal economy to the informal (or underground) economy

informal/underground situation that would repel their participation.[38] The confluence of all four factors in deciding whether or not to engage in informal or underground activities is shown in Figure 1.3.

Figure 1.3, of course, assumes that individuals start from a position in the formal economy. We recognize not only that the reverse might also be true, but also that individuals can be involved in both sectors and that they may move back and forth between formal and informal economic participation, even across borders (as Roberto and Ana did). Nevertheless, because formal economic activity in the U.S. is legally and statistically considered the norm, we wish to explain deviation from this norm (i.e., moving from formal to informal and/or underground activities).

Push factors might include high regional unemployment; bureaucratic over-regulation; limited upward mobility options; poverty; limited education or language skills; welfare earnings limits; or lack of work authorization. *Pull* factors may include entrepreneurial freedoms; high demand for informal labor; paying lower taxes; skirting governmental regulation; economy of discards; demand for illegal goods and services;

lower start-up costs; greater earnings potential; and social capital networks among informals.

Some of the *hold* factors that can keep economic participants in the formal labor market might include governmental protections against predatory practices or contract violation; consumer protections; access to formal banking services (loans, etc.); family obligations; possessing skills in industries that are highly regulated; stable employment and paycheck; an acceptable quality of life; a positive social safety net; and adequate social capital. Similarly, the things in the informal activity being considered that might *repel* someone from participation there could include a lack of skills and knowledge in navigating in a context of uncertainty; the fear of being apprehended; possible civil or criminal prosecution; a stigma of criminality; a decreased ability to enforce contract obligations; and a fear of social rejection by those who regard informality as immoral.

Antonio, in our opening vignette in this chapter, worked through the dueling forces of push-pull, hold-repel in his decision to return to Mexico. While economic opportunity *pulled* Antonio to open his bar and used clothing businesses in South Texas, he was *pushed* back to Mexico by zealous government regulations and enforcement. Furthermore, the positive and familiar cultural environment of his natal community functioned as a force to *hold* him in Mexico, where his inability to navigate the legal business environment once his informal enterprises were uncovered served as a force to *repel* Antonio from South Texas.

The South Texas border environment, as we have pointed out, presents a unique mix of these four factors—a mix that, on balance, seems much more favorable to informality than the mix that exists in other parts of the U.S. Low education levels here leave many individuals unable to find formal employment in an environment that has a glut of low-skilled workers but a high number of professional jobs being filled by professionals from outside the area. Here also, large numbers of undocumented residents are denied formal employment because their immigration status renders them ineligible for it. In addition, the region has many incentives for informal cross-border trade where one can take advantage of (or skirt) the different laws in either country. In addition, the greater acceptance of informality in Mexico often carries over to the Texas side of this border region. Finally, one also finds extensive social capital networks that enable individuals to acquire skills, contacts, and the economic capital needed to start up informal or underground enterprises. We will discuss these and other factors in this and subsequent chapters.

Economic vs. Noneconomic Factors
(*"It's not just the economy, stupid."*)

As individuals consider informality, weighing costs against benefits, economic considerations are, of course, of fundamental importance. Still, noneconomic concerns are also very important. Individuals not only ask "What will it do to my finances?" but also think about these several questions: "What will it do to my family if I am caught?" "Am I turning my back on my principles?" "What will the people I care about think?" "Who wants me to do it (or not do it), and how important are they to me?" In some cases, economic factors may not even be the primary consideration.

Likewise, the tendency of many Mexicans to avoid governmental taxation and regulation in Mexico may be based on a widespread cultural suspicion that government officials there are prone to abuse the public trust, collect bribes, and assess fees and taxes for their own personal gain. The degree of perceived legitimacy of government (and its ability to tax or to regulate), as Max Weber pointed out, is a shared social definition—one that has a powerful impact on the behavior of individuals. Though we found in our interviews that Mexicans, in general, have more confidence in American public officials (police, etc.) than in Mexican officials, they bring with them a certain general level of distrust of government officials.

The majority of our respondents did not see governmental oversight or taxation as illegitimate. Indeed, most regretted having to work outside the system. Some, however, like Antonio in our opening case for this chapter, feel resentful of governmental controls and taxation. Eduardo Alamía is another individual who makes no excuses for working outside the system. He came to the U.S. from Mexico many years ago and started his own business selling furniture. He was more familiar with the customs in Mexico, where the taxes were not nearly as high as in the U.S. So Eduardo does not report most of his sales. When he files his income tax, he claims far less than he actually earns. "I don't understand the system," he says. "Why must people that bust their ass and make a good wage, only to have to give their money back to the government? That's our hard-working money."

Nelson and De Bruijn are more negative in their portrayal of the feelings that informals have for government.[39] They describe informals as "operators who, by custom and practice, have evolved a negative attitude towards formal government regulations." Our own research suggests that the negative attitude toward formal government regulation in the South Texas borderlands is *not* universal (or even widespread). Many informals simply may not consider themselves *able* to conform, either because they need to hide themselves from the government (e.g., undocumented workers) or because they need to hide income to be able to continue receiving government assistance (e.g., CHIP, Medicaid). Many even prefer the order and predictability of greater formality in the U.S. Their decision to remain hidden from public purview may be purely economic, or it may involve many other considerations, such as tradition, perceptions of governmental honesty, documentation, or other considerations of "what is fair."

Conclusion

Clearly, many individuals in South Texas find that it does pay to engage in underground and informal activities. That point, however, is only part of the story. In the following chapters, we will combine qualitative personal histories from the region collected over several years with quantitative data from our survey sources to point out how the cultural, economic, and sociopolitical aspects of this South Texas and Northern Mexico region operate together to help stimulate informal and underground activities.

Throughout the chapter, we have emphasized several factors related to the unique South Texas border environment that help explain the high levels of economic informality in the region. Our position, however, is that the region, though unique, can teach us much about informality and borders elsewhere in the U.S. and in the world. Individuals the world over turn to informality, we believe, when formal systems do not or cannot meet their needs. Likewise, borders not only create opportunities for informality; they can also make participation in formal systems much more problematic, especially when the population of these areas is very different from their fellow citizens in other parts of their respective nations.

In the chapters that follow, we will take up the multiple facets of informality and propose research-based answers to the questions we have posed about why the informal and underground economy is so robust on the South Texas border. We will also examine some of the major effects of informality on the lives of individuals in this region.

CHAPTER 2

Underground Economic Activities

Well, I like to gamble but I don't like to lose. Unfortunately, while play-ing poker, I lost a lot of money. So I decided I should switch it up a bit. I have friends who raise cocks, sell them, and enter them in cockfights. I figured if I raised my own roosters and trained them really well, [then] the risk of losing money in bets would be lower. Also, I could always sell off the offspring from my winning roosters for good prices.

—Sergio Sánchez

Introduction

Like most entrepreneurs, Sergio engages in his own version of cost-benefit analysis. When he finds himself losing, he looks for ways to cut his losses and increase his prospects of winning. He used informa-tion from a small circle of friends to begin an enterprise that involves not only betting on cockfights, but influencing the outcome by rais-ing, training, and fighting his own birds. And he hopes for additional profit from selling the offspring of his winning roosters. Unmentioned, of course, are the risks he runs by engaging in these illegal or under-ground enterprises.

Sergio is, in numerous ways, representative of many of the South Texas underground "entrepreneurs" we interviewed. Most, for example, do not carefully and systematically gather objective information in or-der to weigh risks against benefits. Many rely on friends and family for information about how to carry out such activities. And most do not become "big-time" operators, though, in general, they do make more money than those engaged in informal enterprises (at least until the risks finally catch up with them).

Using the border to enhance life opportunities and earnings is a theme present throughout this book. The effective arbitrage of the border is not just the domain of multinational corporations; it is also the economic terrain of those able to leverage supply and demand cross-nationally—even if they are one-person, underground concerns.

Many underground activities on the South Texas border are single owner, small-time operations. Many are also part-time. Victor, for example, burns DVDs and CDs at his home in South Texas and sells these items at flea markets in Mexico. Using his status as a legal alien to quickly and easily cross the border, Victor earns nearly $5,000 annually by engaging in the underground activity he learned from a colleague at his formal place of employment

Underground activities are also strongly influenced by the culture of the area. Many of those we interviewed concerning cockfighting, for example, indicated that they were first introduced to the sport by a father, uncle, or grandfather who had taken them to cockfights when they were children. Jorge recalled, "I got involved in this because I feel it is a part of my culture. Since I can remember I have been around the *gallos* (cocks). My uncle had a bunch in his backyard. I remember I would help him feed them when I was a kid. My dad would take me to go see fights along with my cousins all the time. I figured I could make money doing something I like by raising, selling, and fighting the birds." Eduardo recalled his childhood with cockfighting: "I was only six years old when my father took me to the rooster fights. And I loved it because the weekend was the only time me and my father had to bond together."

Who Are the Participants in the South Texas Underground Economy?

Our combined 2006–2009 surveys (described in the introduction and in Appendix A) yielded 157 respondents who engaged in underground economic activities in South Texas.[1] Their economic activities included dealing or transporting drugs; smuggling people across the border ("*coyotes*"); gambling; exotic dancing/prostitution; selling stolen, counterfeit, or pirated merchandise; and dogfighting or cockfighting, which we will describe shortly. The demographic profile of underground and informal economy participants in South Texas may be found in Table 2.1; we include data for informal activities (to be described in Chapter 3) as a point of comparison.

Table 2.1 reveals a substantial difference between individuals involved

Table 2.1. Descriptive statistics for underground and informal economic agents (N = 835)

Variable	Underground (N = 149)[#]	Informal (N = 653)
Gender	N (percent)	N (percent)
Male	113 (75.8%)	334 (50.1%)
Female	36 (24.2%)	332 (49.8%)
	Cross-tab Pearson Chi-Square = 32.445; p = .000***	

	Underground (N = 149)	Informal (N = 653)
Education Level	N (percent)	N (percent)
0–4 Years	6 (4.0%)	83 (12.9%)
5–8 Years	15 (10.1%)	180 (28.0%)
9–11 Years	31 (20.8%)	125 (19.5%)
12 Years	39 (26.2%)	118 (18.4%)
12+ Years	58 (38.9%)	136 (21.2%)
	Cross-tab Pearson Chi-Square = 47.384; p = .000***	

	Underground (N = 149)	Informal (N = 656)
Immigration Status	N (percent)	N (percent)
U.S. Citizen	130 (87.2%)	232 (35.4%)
U.S. Resident	7 (4.7%)	162 (24.7%)
Other Visa (e.g., laser)	3 (2.0%)	113 (17.2%)
Undocumented	9 (6.0%)	149 (22.7%)
	Cross-tab Pearson Chi-Square = 132.506; p = .000***	

	Underground	Informal
Total Generation Score^	N | Mean	N | Mean
	79 | 10.1	447 | 4.8
	ANOVA, F = 102.308; df = 1; p = .000***	

	Underground N | Mean Years | (std. dev.)	Informal N | Mean Years | (std. dev.)
Age	148 | 31.3 | (10.0)	653 | 38.7 | (12.7)
	ANOVA, F = 43.311; p = .000***	

^The higher the Generation Score, the more likely it is that he/she, his or her parents, and his or her grandparents were born in the U.S. The total N for Immigration Status is much larger than that used for Generation Score because the variables needed to calculate Generation Score were included only in the second iteration of the survey instrument administered to a total of 526 individuals.

#As the study of underground and informal activities concerns sensitive information, non-randomized sample designs are required, inhibiting the acquisition of large sample sizes.
Source: Informal and Underground Survey.

in underground economic activities and those involved in the informal economy. Informals had a gender distribution very close to the gender makeup of the general population, while the gender makeup of the sample of underground operators was highly skewed, with more than three times as many males as females. The difference between male and female participation in underground activities may be explained largely by the danger involved and the corresponding perceptions that drug dealing, drug smuggling, cockfighting, and human smuggling are "men's work."

Underground operators in our sample were also more highly educated. While only 14.1% of our sample of underground operatives had an eighth-grade education or less, fully 40.9% of those in the informal economy reported having this low level of education. Similarly, almost two-thirds (65.1%) of our sample of participants engaged in underground activities had completed high school and some college, compared to only 39.6% of those engaged in informal economic activities. The percentage of individuals in the underground economy who have attained these higher levels of education is actually greater than the percentage of the general adult population of South Texas with these levels of education— only 57% of adults in South Texas have completed high school.

Table 2.1 reveals that the mean age of underground operatives in our samples was at least seven years younger than the mean age of those involved in informal activities. With regard to immigration status, underground participants in our survey were almost entirely U.S. citizens (87.2%), with an additional 6.7% in the U.S. legally (e.g., U.S. residents and laser visa holders). Only 6.0% of underground participants were undocumented. And underground participants were far more likely to have parents and grandparents who were born in the U.S. than informal participants (see Generation Score). This comparison reveals clearly that participants in the underground economy are overwhelmingly U.S. citizens, have parents and grandparents who were U.S. citizens, are male, have attained better-than-average levels of education, and are younger in age. We have been unable to determine whether the lower average age of underground participants follows from a need for more energy and vigor in these activities or if younger people are more prone to take risks. We suspect both factors are involved.

Major Underground Economic Activities

Most underground participants do not physically cross the border, though most do leverage the border as a conduit for their economic activity. *Coyotes* and drug smugglers are the primary border crossers, as they actively engage in the smuggling of people and drugs across the border (though many involved in smuggling employ "mules" to do the risky border crossing for them). This and other aspects of the underground economy will become clear as we present a brief overview of each of the major underground "occupations" in the South Texas borderlands.[2]

Drug Dealers

Ismael Cardoza works full-time as a store clerk. He uses this public position to cover and facilitate his drug dealing. Ismael stated, "I can't just depend on the minimum wage I get at the store." Ismael insisted he could make up to $2,000 in a good week selling drugs to provide for his family. Ismael said, "Can't you see my family would die if I didn't do this? Besides it's easy. I have my regulars and they always come back for more." The attraction to the drug trade begins early, especially for those that find school challenging. Another smuggler, Humberto Arriaga, was sixteen and only a freshman in high school when he began to buy and sell marijuana. Humberto noted, "I knew it was wrong, but I was tired of seeing everyone else with all these expensive things, and here I was working at a grocery store for minimum wage. We [he and his family] had just enough money to eat and pay bills." Soon Humberto was making $150 a day packaging marijuana. Eventually Humberto began to transport the drugs north past the checkpoint for $5,000–$8,000 a load. Humberto declared, "I'm now eighteen years old and have all the stuff I ever wanted and more."

Without a doubt the rewards are great in the underground economy, but so are the risks. The stories of being constantly on guard or of getting caught are plentiful. Often, the underground economy destroys families, as we will see. Julio Pecina has come to understand this. He began selling drugs at age fifteen. He quickly dropped out of school and began to support his family, primarily his parents. He currently earns about $2,000 a week in the underground economy, selling marijuana, cocaine, and ecstasy. Now twenty-three, Julio wishes he could start over again because he senses he will be caught soon. Julio said, "I'm constantly worried, and I can't help but look over my shoulder a lot. A lot of people hate me, and they are extremely jealous. They want what I have. But I can tell you, I'd trade this all in. This life isn't as glamorous as you'd think. I would prefer to support my family the right way."

Human Smugglers

The border acts not only as a conduit for drug smugglers, but as a strong enticement to engage in human smuggling as well. Some otherwise legitimate enterprises (like farms and ranches that border Mexico) become involved, spreading involvement in smuggling to more than just a few. Some smugglers traffic in both humans and drugs, and the Mexican drug cartels are more active recently in bundling drug transshipment with human smuggling. Andrés Sevilla is a boss who employs "mules" to help him smuggle both illegal aliens and drugs. Instead of charging the would-be illegal immigrants a fee, his operation requires that they carry—i.e., smuggle—drugs across the border for him.

Javier Cedillo, another smuggler, reported, "I don't get into the small-time selling. That's for the mules to do. My concern is with getting the drugs to this side of the river without being caught. I have a lot of *coyotes* that smuggle people in to the ranches along the border. The ranchers are old friends of the family, and I give them a cut for letting us use their land. The Mexicans coming north will do anything to come, so we tell them we'll bring them for free if they carry the drugs, and many do it." [3]

Gamblers

Mary owns a gambling business that consists of slot machines known as "*las maquinitas.*" This business is illegal but is found in many border cities. Local news channels occasionally report raids and busts that take place. This form of gambling is illegal in the state of Texas except on a very few Indian tribal reservations. Mary sees her business as a good way to sustain herself and her family. She stated, "I will never stop my business until they catch me. Even then I will just move to another location because the money is good and I can't ask for anything better." Her machines are rigged to pay out only 20%, so she keeps 80% for herself. Mary said she could get in trouble not only for gambling but for not reporting her income.

Josué Galindo is another person who conducts illegal gambling operations. He claims that many city officials and even police officers participate in his "pots" for sports gambling. He is fifty-six years old (but looks sixty-five), has almost no education, and was raised in Mexico. He is trying to save money to send his children to college. For many years he did farm and ranch work, but he became ill and resorted to gambling, or selling numbers for football, basketball, and boxing matches. He even sells numbers for local high school football games. "You would be surprised how many people buy pots on a weekly basis," he said. "I make the most money during Super Bowl time. I also have a place on my small ranch where I organize cockfighting every other Sunday. Many prominent, church-going, educated individuals here in Starr County know about it and either come or leave me alone."

Strippers and Prostitutes

Whether it involves exotic dancing, working as a barmaid, or "turning tricks" as a prostitute, the sex trade is vibrant along both sides of the South Texas border. Like other underground activities in South Texas, it also is strongly influenced by the different laws on both sides of the U.S.-Mexico border. Though technically illegal, for example, prostitution in Mexico is either tolerated or facilitated by many local governments and officials, especially along the border. It is often open to public access (i.e., "Boys Town") in very specific locations in Mexican border communities. In South Texas, in contrast, prostitution is illegal.

One set of interviews from "Boys Town" in Reynosa reveals the connection between the sex trade and cross-border sex tourism. A major source of "johns" is American *maquiladora* (assembly plant) managers, tourists, and university students crossing into Mexico for paid sex. Many sex customers are locals from both sides of the border. The Mexican prostitutes are stratified according to "looks" and work locations. The prostitutes, lured into the trade primarily by economic needs, have many additional roles—including mothers and family remittance providers. Some hide their work from family. Others sell themselves for drugs. Most never completed school, and few have dreams of a better tomorrow.

The stories about how people get into the sex trade are all too common—sexual abuse, abandonment, drug addiction, low education, survival. Linda Zavala came to South Texas as a seasoned prostitute at the age of sixteen. She was raped by her teacher in Mexico, had a child at eleven, was abandoned by her family in Mexico because of her "scandal," and was taken in by a twelve-year-old in Mexico who showed Linda how to survive as a prostitute. At sixteen, Linda illegally crossed the border into the U.S. to leave prostitution and earn more through exotic dancing. She said, "I like it here because I do not have to prostitute myself for money any more like before, but I will if I have to. Because this is all I know how to do. I have to support my son and myself."

Monica Cisneros, born to an immigrant prostitute and a drug dealing father, became a prostitute while she was in high school.

> My family and I have earned an income in things like drug dealing and prostitution. My mother, Nadia, is now forty-three years old, and she was a prostitute in Peru since she was thirteen. At the age of seventeen, she came to the U.S. My father, Ramón, was a drug dealer who would pay my mother for sex. They eventually stayed together. I was born here in the United States. My mother is still a prostitute. At the age of sixteen, I dropped out of school to become a full-time prostitute. Now I am 27. My mother taught me how to make money the "easy way," and now I can't get out of it. My family and I risk our lives daily to do this job. There was one time I was with a client and we were in a motel in Hidalgo County. This motel is known to be for prostitutes. With my luck, the police knocked at our door. My client got dressed and opened the door to the cops. He calmed them down and told them he was just visiting town and was trying to get to sleep. I was hiding under the bed. I was afraid of getting jailed. Recently, my father was jailed for selling marijuana, so my mother and I had to increase the number of clients we saw in order to make ends meet. At times, we even had to lower our prices in order for the clients to accept. We get welfare because we do not report the income we make from this job. I can't claim my income since it is illegal and I would be arrested. I go to Mexico at least every 3 months to see the OB/GYN. I am very afraid of getting AIDS.

The seediest side of the sex trade is child prostitution in the Mexican border towns. Little Diego Hidalgo washes car windshields during the day, but some nights he spends with other men when he feels desperate and hungry. "Men come by themselves," Diego said. "When I am working washing windows, they come and ask me if I want some extra money. I already know what they want, so I wait for them in the same corner later that night." Diego is disgusted by this nighttime activity, but he insisted that "they pay good money to do those things. Besides, almost everyone I know has done it before too."

Rolando Contreras sells bracelets on the street in Mexico. He is fourteen years old and without a family. Rolando recalled, "A lot of 'bolillos' [Anglos] offer me good money to sleep with them. I do it to survive—

not because I'm gay. It's embarrassing for me, but I have to make money somehow." Like Diego, Rolando knows others who do the same to survive. "I have other buddies who do the same thing. We don't talk about it, but we know where the money comes from; you don't make twenty dollars in one day selling bracelets."

Theft and Selling Pirated/Counterfeit Goods and Services

Theft from inside a firm is just as big a concern for businesses as is theft from outsiders. Though employee theft is a widespread problem throughout the U.S., employee theft in South Texas has an added dimension of leveraging the border. Two stories from a stocker and a bag boy at a local grocery store illustrate this. One bag boy stole bicycles and tires and re-sold them in smaller towns in Mexico. At the same time, this same bagger conspired with customers to switch goods already purchased, for tip money. Before long, he was fired for stealing. The other, a stocker named Esteban Morelos, was able to steal from his company for two years before getting caught. Esteban recalled his actions, "I would do a lot of stuff at the store for extra money. When I would stock up merchandise in the back, I would leave some boxes on the side for myself. They were usually smaller items like DVD players that I would sell later, mainly to people from Mexico, for about $35 each. The other ways I would make extra money at work was by switching the smaller items that customers had purchased with bigger items and they would give me tips, five dollars or so." Since both workers made less than $12,000 a year in formal income, they felt justified in enhancing their incomes at the expense of their respective firms.

There are some goods which are legal on one side of the border but illegal on the other side—guns and steroids, for example. Roberto Dávalos enjoys keeping in shape, so he often goes to the gym. At the gym, he would overhear people complaining about the cost of nutritional supplements and steroids. For Roberto, a light bulb turned on . . . He could supply other "gym rats" with the supplements and steroids they desired but at a reduced cost by acquiring the same supplies in Mexico. Roberto recalled, "I knew I could get these body building supplies in Mexico. I live near the border, so it is easy for me to cross and get these supplies. I figured I could make a killing because people are so image conscious. I do a lot of research over the Internet on what works best. Women want to be skinny and men want to be muscular." Roberto has been selling steroids and nutritional supplements on the U.S. side of the river for over five years, earning up to $1,000 in a good week. Roberto confided that he must be careful. "I only sell to people I trust," he says. "I have been banned from gyms that found out about my dealings."

The border is also a thriving market for pirated goods and services. José Delgado sells pirated DVDs to earn "a little extra spending money" for his family. Like José, most of our informants who sell pirated DVDs/CDs do not do so full-time, but rather on a part-time basis as a means to earn supplemental income. The income generated is often irregular, as José noted: "Sometimes I get lucky and make two, three sales a day. Other times I won't sell anything for over a week."

Another respondent who pirates media is Ricardo de la Fuente. A waiter in South Texas, he supplements this minimum-wage job with earnings from selling pirated DVDs/CDs. Ricardo is able to use his formal-sector position to enlarge his circle of potential clients and his network in Mexico. Ricardo's brother lives in Mexico and operates as his sales agent for distributing pirated DVDs/CDs across the border. Ricardo is married with three children and saves his underground earnings to pay for unplanned expenses. He said, "My children do not have medical insurance, and in my job or my wife's job, we can't get insurance either. When anyone in the house gets sick, we have to take them to Mexico. The money that I get with the music and the movies that I burn helps me pay those last-minute or medical expenses."

Those who sell pirated services (for example, pirated cable and satellite signals) often do so as an extension of their regular employment. Hector De Leon, for example, has a full-time job as a delivery driver, but he illegally installs satellite programming on the side. Hector estimated that his side job earns him an extra $10,000 per year. Essentially, Hector hooks up friends and friends of friends to digital satellite programming through contraband digital television boxes and cards. Hector uses the border to acquire the presumably stolen digital cards in Mexico.

Dogfighting and Cockfighting

Though in Louisiana and New Mexico cockfighting was legal as recently as 2007, cockfighting and associated gambling are illegal in Texas (and in the U.S. generally). The "sport" of cockfighting may be 4,000 years old and is still common and popular in Mexico. Occasionally, news-popping headlines about cockfighting appear, such as the *Laredo Morning Times* headline that read "80 Fighting Cocks Seized in Houston."[4] According to the Humane Society of the United States, Texas ranks thirty-third

out of the 50 states in strength of penalties for cockfighting (it is a felony punishable with a sentence of 180 days to two years in prison and
a maximum fine of $10,000). Texas currently does not prohibit the pos-
session of birds or implements for fighting or watching cockfighting as a
spectator, but some Texas legislators are aiming to criminalize those activities also.[5]

Carlos Diaz, another individual involved in cockfighting, makes a rea-
sonably good living from this activity. While cockfighting was just a side
pleasure before he injured his back in the oil fields, Carlos then plunged
full time into the underworld of cockfighting. He stated, "What better
way to spend [time] than fighting roosters? It's something I've loved all
my life." Though Carlos received monthly disability checks that managed to keep the family afloat, he said, "I take better care of my family
with the money I bring in dedicating myself to the roosters." With his
earnings from cockfighting (acquired from betting on and raising and
selling cocks), Carlos earned an estimated annual underground income
of $100,000.

For many, the allure of cockfighting—the wagering, the pent-up aggression displayed in the birds, the adrenaline rush of combat, and the
camaraderie—keeps them coming back to the sport. For others, the
cockfights allow them the opportunity to socialize, display their *ma-
chismo*, participate in (and bet on) the rush and thrill of the fight. Heriberto Dominguez closely watches the rooster's trainer and bets according to the trainer with the higher winning percentage. By keeping
tabs on trainers, Heriberto boasts of annual winnings of $47,000 from
his cockfighting wagers. His friend, Gustavo Elizondo, said he spends
all of his work time in the underground sport of cockfighting, earning
$260,000 a year. Gustavo launders this money through the purchase of
legitimate concerns, including several apartment complexes.

A Demographic and Economic Profile of the
Major Underground Activities in South Texas

Table 2.2 provides a demographic breakdown of each of the preceding
categories. It shows, for example, that men in our sample are more likely
to be engaged in the drug trade, gambling, the pirating of goods, and
the fighting of animals (dogfighting and cockfighting). Women in our
sample, on the other hand, participate in the underground economy primarily as prostitutes/strippers, fencers of stolen goods, and, to some ex-

Table 2.2. Respondent demographic profile of underground economic activity

	Underground Economic Activity^					
Variable	Drug Dealer	Coyote	Gambling	Stripper/ Prostitute	Selling Pirated & Stolen Goods	Dog-fighting/ Cock-fighting
Gender (N)						
Male	69	4	14	0	11	11
Female	12	7	1	8	7	0
Mean Age (years)	31.1	41.2	31.0	23.9	29.4	32.6
Immigration Status (N)						
U.S. Citizen	74	10	12	3	10	6
U.S. Resident	2	1	2	1	0	0
Undocumented	3	0	0	4	1	0
Other (laser visa)	1	0	0	0	1	0
Education (N)						
0–4 Years	2	1	0	0	0	2
5–8 Years	7	2	3	1	0	2
9–11 Years	22	3	0	3	1	1
12 Years	17	2	2	2	9	4
12+ Years	34	3	10	1	2	2

Note: Cross-tabulation and test of means results indicate that gender (Chi-square = 57.607, p = .000), age (F = 2.266, p = .021), immigration status (Chi-square = 49.209, p = .006), and education (Chi-square = 56.338, p = .017) are all significantly different between the seven groups of underground occupations. Annual underground earnings (F = 0.984, p = .457) and annual total earnings (F = 1.271, p = .258) were not significantly different between the seven categories.
^As the study of underground and informal activities concerns sensitive information, nonrandomized sample designs are required, inhibiting the acquisition of large sample sizes.
Source: Informal and Underground Survey.

tent, as coyotes. Youth seems to be most important for the eight strippers or prostitutes in our sample, who had an average age of twenty-four years old (compared to a mean age of around thirty years old for most other underground categories). Coyotes were older, with an average age of just over forty. Overwhelmingly, those who participate in underground activities are U.S. citizens and U.S. residents; only prostitutes had a plurality of undocumented participants, suggesting that this occupation is often a form of exploitation.

Table 2.3 provides an occupational earnings overview for participants in the underground economy in South Texas. The table shows how much they make, on average, from each of the underground categories, as well as their average income from formal work (if any), and their combined annual earnings. As Table 2.3 shows, people who work in these underground occupations do quite well on average, earning close to $50,000 annually from their underground endeavors—over $60,000 annually in combined underground and formal earnings. In contrast, we found that the average combined formal and informal earnings for the 589 individuals involved in informal economic activities was $18,785, of which the average annual income from informal activities was only $9,536.

Table 2.3 also indicates that the high end of annual earnings associated with underground activities is the trafficking of drugs that are illegal on both sides of the border, as well as the smuggling of humans. In the middle area, we find participants engaged in dogfighting and cockfighting and prostitution. At the low earnings end of the underground economy are participants who make and sell pirated goods (mostly music CDs and movie DVDs), are involved in gambling, and who acquire and sell stolen or illegally obtained merchandise.

Most of those at the lower end have low earnings because they participate in the underground economy only part-time. Cristina Encina, a single mother of three, finds it difficult to make ends meet with her low-wage, full-time job. With tears in her eyes, she stated, "It's hard to get by, you know. Nobody helps me. The ones that suffer are my children, but I'd do anything to support them." So on her day off each week, Cristina travels to Mexico to buy $300 worth of prescription pills (an amount people are generally allowed to transport "for personal use"). With her brother, Cristina sells the pills throughout South Texas to earn enough to "take care of the rent, bills, insurance, and childcare for the month." Though she is part of a "drug trade," she is at the very low end of it, illegally importing and selling prescription medicine to low-income or undocumented people who cannot themselves obtain such medicines in Mexico.

As in the informal environment, underground participants may engage in more than a single illegal activity. Many simply complement their formal jobs or business with underground activities. Often, these formal activities are a cover for their underground activities. For most but not all of our respondents in this area, underground activities earn them much more than their formal occupation or business. Having a legal immigration status also seems to increase these earnings, whereby those with the legal right to work earn far more ($70,220 annually) or

Table 2.3. Annual underground earnings [or, How much does crime pay?]

Underground Occupation^	Mean Annual Earnings (in U.S.$)		
	Underground Earnings	Formal Earnings	Total Earnings*
Drug Dealer/Grower/Mule	70,596	16,309	82,598
(N)	(80)	(69)	(82)
Coyote	61,736	14,333	73,464
(N)	(11)	(9)	(11)
Gambling	13,961	19,688	31,461
(N)	(18)	(16)	(18)
Stripper/Prostitute	41,138	7,333	48,471
(N)	(9)	(9)	(9)
Selling Pirated/Stolen Goods	9,104	14,757	22,379
(N)	(36)	(33)	(36)
Dogfighting/Cockfighting	48,045	10,833	53,955
(N)	(11)	(6)	(11)
Total (Mean)	$48,154	$17,740	$61,870
(N)	(164)	(142)	(167)

*Total Earnings is not the sum of Underground Earnings and Formal Earnings due to varying sample sizes (e.g., missing data) across the groups.
^As the study of underground and informal activities concerns sensitive information, non-randomized sample designs are required, inhibiting the acquisition of large sample sizes.
Source: Informal and Underground Survey.

about twice as much as those who do not have the legal right to work in the U.S. (who only average $36,614 annually).

A variety of factors help explain the preponderance of U.S. citizens in underground activities. Unlike the undocumented, they do not have to hide their "illegal" status from the host of federal agents in the area. This allows them to operate more openly. In addition, because most U.S. citizens acquire their citizenship through birth in the U.S., they also are more likely to have the economic, human, and social capital (e.g., financing, U.S. street smarts, and trusted contacts) needed to enter and finance underground operations and avoid detection. Most also speak English well and are acculturated into life in the U.S., and thus do not call undue attention to themselves. Essentially, the undocumented face a much greater weight of hold and repel factors, including a greater risk of detection and a greater threat of punishment (such as deportation) rather than just arrest.

The additional ease of crossing the border is another draw for U.S. citizens and U.S. residents. The border facilitates their work and offers ways to reduce risks. Imelda Escobar is a resident alien who works part-time as a home health provider, making just over $10,000 a year from that formal employment. To make extra income, she occasionally engages in prostitution. "I go to Mexico," she said, "and find men and have sex with them. This way I don't have to see them again, I just take their money."

Armando Espinoza, a U.S. citizen, finds the border useful in another way. He was born in the U.S. but was raised in Mexico. He has been involved in the drug trade for many years. "I decided to move back to Mexico because I found out that U.S. federal officers were trying to arrest me. Since then, I haven't returned or even thought about crossing back to the U.S." He said he has no regrets except that when his mother died he was not able to attend her funeral. "Still," he said, "I had her buried here in Mexico."

The Risks of Underground Enterprises: The Other Side of the Equation

In the preceding case, Armando found the risk of being apprehended so great that he moved away from loved ones. John Cross proposes that the risks of underground enterprises are four-fold: 1) *market risks* (the risk of not making a profit because of competition); 2) *transaction risks* (the risk of being cheated by customers, suppliers, or associates); 3) *liability risks* (the risk of being sued or forced to pay damages); 4) *enforcement risks* (the risk of being caught and prosecuted for violating a law or regulation).[6] To those four we would add *personal risks*, or the risk of personal injury or death, damaged family relationships, entanglements that one can break only with great difficulty, and other personal costs such as becoming obsessed with money or feeling compelled to engage in even more extreme criminal activities to protect or further one's business.

Though many assume that underground operators make large amounts of money, the uncertainty of making enough money to even get by is very real.[7] Abelardo Flores is involved in cockfighting. "Making money off my birds every single week is not a certain thing," he said. "Sometimes there have been weeks where I have lost $50–$300 in a single night. Other nights I have made up to $600." He continued, "It's all a matter of luck when it comes down to the actual cockfights." Some participants actually attempt to alter (or fix) their luck through the injection of drugs into the roosters before matches. There's no government agency monitoring the fights, so such practices are not easily monitored. Abelardo's earnings increase when he is able to sell some of his fighting birds. He stated, "Sometimes I will get an occasional customer that will want to buy some of *mi cría* (breed). I treat that as an added bonus to all of my hard work."

In reality, underground entrepreneurs often pay a high price for their seemingly high earnings. In addition to an increased risk of economic loss, they risk their lives, their families, their peace of mind, and even their character (the personal risks mentioned two paragraphs back). This is further illustrated by the case of Carlos Fuentes, a man who was initially very successful in the drug trade but then was betrayed by it. Carlos began his involvement in the trade through the influence of his father-in-law, who had been in the illegal drug business for about 30 years. When asked why he chose drug trafficking, he said, "Simple—the money." Nevertheless, near the end of his career when he was earning nearly $500,000 annually, he found that the money was not as easy as he thought. Carlos has five children and was once married. Early on, his wife worked, but their combined income was not sufficient to support the family. Since Carlos had little education, he saw himself with limited job opportunities. Initially, he managed to build a small, three-bedroom house for his family. He yearned for the other nice things a "regular" family had, so, seeing no legal ways to do so, he inserted himself into drug trafficking. Soon he was able to buy two new cars—a Camaro and Trans Am. "I was moving on up," he says. Everything seemed to be going well. After a few years, he managed to find some mules to cross the Border Patrol checkpoints for him. This reduced his enforcement risks somewhat but may have increased his transaction risks, or the risks of being cheated or betrayed by his mules or associates.

With his increasing success came bigger profits, along with increased personal risks. Carlos sold his first house and bought 10 acres on which he built a huge home. He believed he had accomplished everything he wanted and more. He stated, "The only thing I did wrong was to trust my friends. Never trust your friends because they are the first ones to screw you over." Carlos' friends knew where all the drugs and money were hidden. In the middle of the night, Carlos and his family had guns pointed at them by these "friends." "They stole all my money, the drugs, and all our valuables," he says. "I tried to turn to people who I thought would help me, but everyone I knew had either been aware of or in on the hit, so no one helped."

Carlos was devastated. To get back in the game and make back the money he owed on the drugs seized from his home, he tried to make a drug run north past the checkpoint. "I was busted at the checkpoint with 200 pounds of marijuana," he says. "I went to jail for ten years. When I was released from prison two years ago, I found myself without a family or a home. My wife had sold everything, and, in order to survive, had divorced me and remarried."

Often, underground operators look back with regret on the ferocity, the corruption, and the dangers involved. Hector Gamboa had that experience when he became deeply involved in cockfights. "I could handle the bloodiness of the fights," he said. "It was all the related activities, like the wagering, the drinking, the drugs, and the inhumane treatment of the birds that made me regret my involvement with cockfighting. I also lost my wife and family due to my obsession with cockfighting. I often just got lost in the business and forgot about them. My wife left me because she didn't appreciate what I was doing."

Both Carlos and Hector came to see that involvement in underground activities can become an obsession. This was a pattern frequently repeated in the interview accounts. Individuals deeply involved in the underground economy get caught up in the lifestyle, the "easy money," and the attempt to show off their success. They also find that they must project a tough, even violent, image to protect their assets and their turf. This may involve them in crimes much more serious than drug running. As a result, many find their character changed—they are not the same people. In addition, they may also find relationships, especially with family, destroyed or seriously undermined.

It is hard to resist getting one's family involved. Oftentimes, innocents are used to deflect attention when crossing drugs on the international bridges. Sergio García, an immigration agent, noted, "Many times the load car is driven by families that appear to be headed on vacation. Parents use their children's innocent faces to throw off the Border Patrol."

Families suffer in other ways. Humberto Arriaga (mentioned earlier in this chapter) got caught with drugs in his possession that he intended to sell. He served a few months in jail and received five years probation. For now, he has abandoned drug dealing and has gotten a job as a delivery truck driver earning $8 per hour. Humberto lamented, "My wife and I are struggling a lot financially. We had to move in with her parents and rent out our house so we can save some money. It's hard with two kids and a wife now." Humberto believes his present course is humiliating because he must rely on the good will of his in-laws to make ends meet. The lure of just one more deal is very powerful. Humberto said, "Sometimes I want to go back to selling drugs. I know just one big load will get us back on our feet again."

Finally, one of the greatest risks of getting involved in the underground economy is the risk of exploitation of lower-level operatives by those at higher levels (a form of transaction risk). Indeed, Cross and Johnson propose that the "passing down" of the risk of arrest is one of the hallmarks of the underground economy (which they label "illegal informality").[8] However, the tendency of higher-level operatives to hide behind lower-level associates, exposing them to greater risk of arrest in order to protect themselves, is only part of the exploitation that takes place in the underground economy.

Lupe Garza works in local bars as a barmaid. The bar owners hire her to be flirtatious with customers, encouraging them to buy more drinks. Lupe stressed to her interviewer that most of the money she makes comes from tips. "We work for *fichas* (tokens)," she said. "At the end of the night, if we turn in thirty tokens, we get thirty bucks. There are times that I make about fifty dollars a night. I have learned not to drink all my beer because I will get drunk and then my boss tries to cheat us out of the *fichas*." When asked if she participated in prostitution and drugs, she was hesitant in answering. "When you work in a place like this you get street smarts. You figure out that by engaging in *servicios sexuales* (sexual services) you earn more money. I refuse to waste my hard-earned money in drugs, but I do them when I sleep with men. Smoking *marijuana* makes me not feel so bad. The men that I perform this favor for are the ones that usually buy it for me. I am not proud of how I get the money, but it has helped me raise money to get my legal residency."

Lupe is vulnerable. She is undocumented, doesn't report her tips (thus engaging in informality), and occasionally performs illegal acts—prostitution. She cannot call the police when the bar owner cheats her. She is also at risk from being abused or cheated by customers. Because people in the underground economy work outside the regulatory oversight of the state, they are ill-positioned to call upon the state to protect them from contract violations, physical harm, and other forms of abuse or exploitation.

Children are the most vulnerable in society. For some border children who engage in innocuous street labor such as selling gum, their nightmare deepens when they turn to selling themselves. Alma Gomez was thirteen when she went from selling gum to selling herself. She said, "I was selling on the streets and Margarita (a local bar owner) came up to me and offered to buy me dinner. If I agreed to work with her, I could eat and sleep there." Previously, Alma was spending her nights sleeping on the roof of an old building, so she accepted her new work, thinking she had improved her lot in life. Alma continued, "I never thought I was going to have to go to bed with ugly, fat men, but I did. Margarita pays me well when I work good. But when the men complain, she doesn't pay me at all. That is when I sell gum on the streets during the day. Those men are gross and sometimes I can't stand them to be on top of me. That is when they complain to Margarita."

Though the great risk of exploitation of underground "underlings" is not unique to the South Texas borderlands, the border facilitates exploitation in numerous ways. The very substantial flow of drugs and human cargo through this area is one major factor. Drug cartels have, in recent years, gotten into the human smuggling business because it is very profitable and because they can reduce the risks of drug seizures. They will send a group of undocumenteds across at points where they want to ship drugs, drawing off Border Patrol agents who not only will arrest the illegals but will have to leave the area to take them in for processing.[9] Some undocumented women in the borderlands are enticed by smugglers to take a job to pay off their smuggling fees, only to find themselves held under guard and forced into prostitution.[10]

Strategies Employed by Underground Operatives to Manage Risks

In all economic systems, individual actors seek to find ways to manage risks. This, of course, is a primary function of government regulation in the market. As Cross and Peña point out, those who claim that informal and underground markets are not regulated should understand that they *are* regulated—though informally or illegally. For all actors ". . . risk management involves reducing uncertainty [to] the point that liabilities can be calculated based upon the probability that transaction partners will act in predictable ways assuming common cultural values and norms."[11] When government cannot be called upon to perform this function, informals and underground operators will find informal and illegal means to reduce risks so that they can calculate liabilities.

One way to manage enforcement risks is to pay off or corrupt government officials. This strategy, much more common in Mexico, is also occasionally found on the Texas side of the border, especially when the stakes are very high. Jaime Garza, a drug dealer, insists, "It always helps that I know a lot of people, especially in law enforcement because they always got my back." A tremendous amount of drug money is estimated to traverse the border, so the temptations can be very large. It is not uncommon on the South Texas border to find local officials and some federal officers charged with taking bribes. On Wednesday, October 15, 2008, *The Monitor*, the primary newspaper in the McAllen region, reported that Sheriff Reymundo Guerra of Starr County had been named on three federal counts of conspiracy to distribute narcotics, aiding and abetting drug possession, and using a phone to further drug conspiracy.[12]

According to a recent article in the *Houston Chronicle*,[13] a former Customs and Border Protection inspector in Brownsville received two years in prison for accepting a bribe of $7,500 to allow smugglers to bring illegal immigrants into the country. Also, on July 15, 2008, *Reuters* reported that U.S. Border Patrol agent Reynaldo Zuniga was arrested the previous month lugging a bag of cocaine up from the Rio Grande, one of a growing number of law enforcement officers accused of taking bribes from drug gangs.[14]

Data on federal agents convicted of graft are not generally publicly available, but in 2009 the Center for Investigative Reporting[15] reported data obtained using the Freedom of Information Act. They found that corruption-related investigations of federal immigration and border agents in the Southwest had increased for the third year in a row. They also found that more than eighty investigations were opened in 2008 by the Department of Homeland Security's Inspector General in the four Southwest border states. These investigations were of employees of Customs and Border Protection (CBP), Immigration and Customs Enforcement (ICE), and Citizenship and Immigration Services— the federal agencies that police the border and immigration. In 2008 Homeland Security's Inspector General, whose office takes the lead in investigating criminal corruption cases involving related agencies, had more than 170 open cases, some dating to 2003. That figure does not include cases being investigated by the FBI or the internal affairs offices of CBP or ICE.

For underground operators at the lower end of the earnings scale, one of their greatest risks is being exploited. Often, when a customer, client, associate, or even law enforcement official takes advantage of them, they have little recourse. Several women that occasionally engage in prostitution spoke of their vulnerability. "The light and water bills have to be paid," said Martha Guzman. Even though she can make an honest living, she believes she has to occasionally engage in an illegal and dangerous occupation to earn more income. Another woman, Chita Hernandez, said, "We are used to working for little money, but sometimes people take advantage of us, and we have to just take what they give us."

A third woman who occasionally sells sex for money, Maria Herrera, is not so resigned to being exploited. She became pregnant by a married man and uses blackmail to force him to help pay for their child. "I tell him I will tell his wife about our child," she said, "so he gives me the money."

Another way to reduce risks is to let customers know they will suffer with you. Ernesto Hinojosa, who works two jobs (his wife also works) tries to supplement his income with government assistance and with earnings from selling pirated DVDs.[16] Ernesto said, "My underground activity is to help with the bills around the house, and that extra money also helps to take my family to watch a movie once in a while." Ernesto sells his pirated DVDs at the flea market, even though he is always watchful of the law. Even when law enforcement cracks down on pirated sellers and publicizes busts through spectacular television video, Ernesto does not experience a drop in sales, but he does become even more cognizant of his surroundings. Ernesto boasted, "If I go down, my customers go down with me."

One of the most favored strategies to reduce risks is to try to pick one's clients or associates carefully (an underground form of social capital). Some underground operatives prefer to "keep it in the family," depending on the loyalty they assume characterizes family relationships. Others work only with close friends. Such strategies, however, are often unsuccessful when law enforcement agencies offer plea bargains or other incentives to lower-level operatives. Jaime Ortega became involved in the drug business through his father. When his father died, he tried to rely on close friends.

> A year after my dad was gone, one of my partners was taken to jail and began working with a federal agent. I was very worried. I spent many sleepless nights worrying that at one point or another I was either go-

ing to die or get caught. I thought about finding a decent job that would help me support my family, but there is just no way out of this business. Once you are in, you are in it for good. You may see it as being dumb, but there is great loyalty in this business. Still, it is scary at times because you're never sure who you can really trust. Just two weeks ago a friend of mine was shot to death because of a crooked deal. I did not choose this way of living. It was given to me. There is no other way for me. I have to look after my family.

Juan Hurtado, a high school graduate born and raised in Brownsville, works full-time as a waiter in a local restaurant. Juan supplements his $14,000 per year formal restaurant job with smuggling drugs and people across the border. Juan's neighborhood is rife with other underground participants, perhaps one in every two working people. The neighborhood is closely knit with familial ties to try to insulate against the law uncovering their activities. Despite the precautions, many have gone to jail. Now in his fifth year smuggling people and drugs across the border (as well as packaging drugs for distribution), Juan earns $60,000 annually in the underground economy. The juxtaposition of Juan's formal and underground earnings details in a nutshell the economic decision many in the Lower Rio Grande Valley face. Calculating the opportunity cost and the trade-off with the risks they face can make this a very difficult choice.

When the monetary stakes are high, the means of reducing risks may also become more illegal and more extreme. One man remembers witnessing a torture session. "I really don't remember why this man was being tortured," he said, "but I must admit I was terrified. Two men were beating him up pretty bad. They were choking him, burning him, and also forcing water down his nose. It was the sort of thing you see on T.V. but think it doesn't happen. Well believe me, it does. I wanted to get out of there, but I knew I couldn't. People might say you get used to this sort of thing, but I never did."

Perhaps because most risk-reduction strategies are not very dependable, underground operatives in South Texas and elsewhere may turn to more other-worldly means of protecting themselves, even though such means may seem bizarre and irrational. Some small-time smugglers, for example, admitted to seeking the aid of a *curandera* (folk healer).[17] One such local *curandera* frequently assists people in a serious financial situation where they don't have very much money and have resorted to transporting drugs. She "sweeps" them and their car with herbs and asks what time they will cross the checkpoint so that she can concentrate at her home altar and distract the Border Patrol agents' minds with the help of the spirits.

In recent years, the number of smuggling-related protective cults has dramatically increased.[18] Many smugglers, for example, make promises to Jesús Malverde, a Mexican outlaw who was killed in the early 1900s and who supposedly robbed the rich to give to the poor. Many smugglers make promises to images of him prior to crossing the border with drugs or human cargo. Another folk saint (i.e., a popular saint, not one recognized by the Catholic Church) that in recent years has become quite popular among smugglers is *La Santísima Muerte* (The Very Holy Death). She is portrayed as a skeleton in robes of varied colors (white is for protection, red for love, black to do harm, etc.). In border cities and along the Mexican highways leading to border towns, there are many shrines where drug runners and smugglers pay homage and make promises to her. These icons are given offerings of food, drink, and other items as their faithful plead for special favors. Believers also frequently return to leave money or some other object in fulfillment of promises made. Recently, the police in Nuevo Laredo, Mexico, destroyed more than 30 altars and chapels to *Santa Muerte* along Mexican Federal Highway 85, about thirteen miles south of Nuevo Laredo. The demolition was done as a joint operation of local, state, and federal governments, but no official would admit on the record to taking part in the destruction.[19]

In South Texas border cities, one can see many vehicles with the image of *La Santísima Muerte*. Many local police agencies suspect that such vehicles belong to those involved in smuggling, though they recognize that her following is somewhat wider than just smugglers. Still, many in the drug underworld seem to make promises to her as a way to reduce risks, relying on her protection. Some even carry the cult into prison, carving statues of her to keep in their cells. They also seem to believe that if they are caught or harmed, it is because they failed to keep a promise to her, as she is reputed to be very vindictive.

Some individuals in South Texas operate informal businesses related to such beliefs. One woman, Carolina, makes religious candles to sell in the local "*yerberias*" (folk pharmacies) and directly to individuals. She stated that her best-selling candle is *La Santísima Muerte*. "This candle is used to protect the *narcos* and their families against the evil that surrounds them on a daily basis," she said. "I myself have one constantly lit in my house to ward off any evil spirits from my association with the *narcos.* Every week, I make special deliveries of my candles to families that live in huge houses in La Joya, Rio Grande City, and Roma."

To an outsider, such activities seem highly irrational. Many outsiders would consider such beliefs and rituals ineffective and would regard them as bizarre and counterproductive. In other words, one not only doubts their efficacy but realizes that they could tip off police agencies to the illegal activities of their adherents. So why have the beliefs and practices related to folk drug saints been spreading? From our research, especially using ethnographic accounts, we speculate that their value is that they give believers an enhanced (even if false) sense of protection. Cognitive dissonance theory (from social psychology) suggests that humans become very uncomfortable when they experience dissonance between beliefs and actions. The two major means of relieving the dissonance are to either change the beliefs to match behavior or to change behavior to match the beliefs. Because underground activities like drug running tempt underground operators with a very high rate of return, those who give in to the temptation can relieve the dissonance of knowing they are taking extremely high risks by accepting the belief that some otherworldly force will protect them. We suspect that this is not unlike the practice of many military pilots in wartime who carry "lucky" amulets when they are undertaking extremely high-risk operations—they do so as a way to live with the risk of extreme danger.

Why The Border Underground?

It would be truly unfortunate if our discussion of the underground economy of the South Texas border were to contribute to a stereotype of rampant violence and criminality in this region. Indeed, the rate of violent crime in Texas border cities is relatively low. According to the FBI Uniform Crime Reports, in 2008 Texas cities had the following violent crime rates (per 100,000): McAllen, 165; Brownsville, 203; Laredo, 302; and El Paso, 234, as compared to rates of 553, 425, and 326 for Houston, Dallas, and San Antonio, respectively. The largest of the Texas border cities, El Paso, had the third lowest homicide rate in the United States. Clearly, the border is *not* the violent wasteland portrayed by much of the media.[20]

This, however, is not how much of the U.S. population views the U.S.-Mexico border. They see it as a violent, crime-ridden wasteland. Part of this is due to erroneous stereotypes about the population of the South Texas borderlands, with its heavy population of immigrants. These immigrants, particularly those from Mexico, are seen as more criminal than the general population. Indeed, according to the 2000 General Social Survey of the National Opinion Research Center, 73% of Americans believed that immigration is causally related to higher levels of crime.[21]

Such perceptions are often fed by official sources. California's Proposition 187 (which was eventually ruled unconstitutional by a federal court), for example, asserted in its introductory statement that "the people of California . . . are suffering economic hardship . . . and damage caused by the criminal conduct of illegal aliens in this state".[22] Even President George W. Bush, often seen as a moderate on the issue of undocumented immigrants, stated in his 2006 address on immigration reform, "Illegal immigration . . . brings crime to our communities."[23]

The results of data accumulated over many years show exactly an opposite pattern. Despite their poverty, their having to live in depressed neighborhoods, and their need to live apart from their families, foreign-born men had an incarceration rate in 2000 that was two and one-half times *less* than that of native born (non-Hispanic) white men. Native-born Hispanic men were nearly seven times more likely than foreign-born Hispanic men to be in prison. According to Rumbaut and Ewing, the lower incarceration rate among immigrants was found in every pan-ethnic category, without exception.

The disparity between native-born and foreign-born also shows up very strongly in our analysis of the ethnic and national origins of those involved in the underground (compared to the informal) economy. Table 2.1 examines the differences in immigration status between these two groups (informal and underground) and calculates the Generation Score for each group.[24]

As these results indicate, the underground economy is overwhelmingly dominated by U.S. citizens and individuals whose parents and grandparents were born in the U.S. Less than a third of those who participate in the informal economy are citizens; informals also have a lower Generation Score, indicating that very few participants in the informal economy have parents and/or grandparents born in the U.S. Counter to the image portrayed in the popular media of large numbers of "illegal alien criminals," we found U.S. citizens were more than seven times as likely to be involved in criminal underground activities as all of the other immigration categories combined.

This statistically significant contrast may be explained in part as a function of the opportunity costs associated with detection. The quasidocumented and undocumented mostly avoid detection through more benign informal economic activity because the risk of exposure results in expulsion (deportation) from the U.S. Those without work authorization papers are simply at greater risk and, hence, much more apt to choose informal activities over underground ones. As explained earlier, most U.S. citizens, on the other hand, do not risk deportation if their activities are detected.

There is another important factor, however, that might serve as an even better explanation as to why U.S. citizens of Mexican origin are much more likely to be drawn into underground activity than are Mexican-origin legal and quasilegal residents and the undocumented. When Telles and Ortiz conducted a longitudinal analysis of a 1965 survey of Mexican Americans in Los Angeles and San Antonio, they found that education and other socioeconomic measures rose quickly from the immigrant generation to their children, continued to rise but more slowly for their grandchildren, and then began to decline for those of the fourth or fifth generation.[25] Complementing Telles and Ortiz, Duncan and Trejo's comprehensive study found that educational and wage growth stalls for third generation Mexican American men.[26]

One of the factors they found that might explain the drop for U.S.-born youth was association with a very American institution—street gangs. Telles and Ortiz state: ". . . U.S.-born Mexican Americans were widely familiar with the gang lifestyle, but immigrants were less likely to be."[27] Our ethnographic data also suggest that Mexican Americans drawn into the underground economy may be strongly influenced to engage in criminal activities by the presence and the influence of gangs in Latino border neighborhoods.

Gangs and the Underground Economy

We scouted out an abandoned house to "hit" at midnight. Angel checked the yard for a dog. When he didn't find one, Rudy broke a window and five gang members entered the house. Marcos stayed outside to watch for neighbors or police, and Angel remained on the lookout at the opposite side of the house. Javier, Ricardo, Francisco, and Luis crept inside looking for valuables—they stole jewelry, lamps, cameras, televisions, etc. The next day, we fenced our take with drug dealers who traded us $400 worth of drugs. The drugs lasted about six weeks, even with

> some of our gang members selling their drug share to other students in
> school. After that, if the gang needed more money, we simply "stole" an-
> other house.

South Texas, like most other areas of the United States, has problems
with gangs. Often gangs conduct underground economic activities, such
as burglarizing homes and dealing drugs, as the preceding story illustrates. Unlike gangs in other areas, however, gangs in South Texas are
virtually entirely made up of Latinos. In addition, the South Texas border figures prominently in many of the crimes committed, especially in
relation to drug dealing, auto theft, and other crimes that benefit from
the proximity of the border.

The Latino makeup of gangs here is often revealed by much of the
language used by gang members. For example, one young gang member
who was interviewed stated,

> Well, being in a gang is sort of being in a family. If you see a *vato* (dude)
> getting his ass kicked, you go help him—and the reverse is true. Never
> back down in fights and never be a traitor. The *vatos* in my gang are the
> only people that accept me for what I am. Having too many problems at
> home, at school, and with the authorities, we turn to drugs and alcohol.
> With rival gangs, revenge is our only motive. Nobody f---s with us, and if
> they do, they pay the price. In a gang, your first name is forgotten and is
> replaced by names such as "*El Tío*," "*El Perro*," or "*El Vato Loco*." You wear
> what they wear. You talk Tex-Mex. People hate you—that's fine. They
> cross the line—you and your gang kick their ass.

Not only is the language of gangs apparent in this statement, but
their subculture and prominent values come through clearly as well. A
strong emphasis on being tough (even violent), loyalty to the gang, and
always responding to insults with extreme measures are clearly part of
the life view of gang members.

Sociologist Robert J. Sampson sees this culture as very American,
even though its form among gangs is exaggerated. As he examined immigrant communities, he found that crime rates seemed to be much
lower, even among those residents who were not immigrants.[28] In other
words, in neighborhoods where one would expect a lot of crime, the
presence of an immigrant population seemed to lower the crime rate,
even among nonimmigrant neighbors.

Sampson speculates that the culture of the street (which is most pronounced among nonimmigrants) demands respect and "saving face" and might be behind much of the crime in inner-city areas. These shared expectations lead young male residents of poor inner cities to ". . . react violently to perceived slights, insults, and otherwise petty encounters that make up the rounds of daily life."[29] He proposes that immigrants bring a culture that attributes a different meaning to such events—that every slight does not have to be met with violence or the threat of it. In other words, they bring a culture that is more disposed toward nonviolent response and expression.

Gangs, on the other hand, indoctrinate the children and grandchildren of immigrants to exaggerate the importance of toughness, violence, and protecting one's reputation (and that of the gang). For one local gang we examined, stealing an item worth at least $300 permitted membership. For another, a series of escalating criminal acts beginning in elementary school proves one worthy to join a gang. These acts include breaking downtown storefront windows, stealing, and stripping down a car. In many gangs, however, initiation requires demonstrating toughness—such as by showing one can survive a beating from other gang members, as the following account illustrates.

> I'm twenty-five and I've been a gang member . . . for about ten years. I've been in the heat of trouble. We've kicked ass left and right, just for the hell of it, and we liked it too. I've stolen cars and sold them for parts. I'm one of the main guys now in this outfit. I take part in the initiation processes. Now I can kick the new recruits' asses for a change and see what the hell they're made of. I've wanted to get out of the gang a couple of times when the heat got too hot, but when you're in, you're in for life.

Gangs along the border can be roughly divided into the categories of street gangs and prison gangs. Street gangs are usually localized within particular neighborhoods and have a strong sense of territoriality, or turf. Street gangs often battle each other for control of urban neighborhoods, though some *colonias* have spawned several street gangs. They are also constituted primarily of teens and very young adults. Making money is often secondary to a sense of belonging, gang loyalty, and protecting one another and gang territory.

For these youths, street gangs provide a sense of belonging and security that relates to the underground economy in other ways. Those particularly susceptible to taking part in criminal activities are youths who lack a strong supportive family environment and economic opportunities. For some young women, this may be the entry into prostitution. For example, early in life Norma bounced around foster homes. She made it through high school, but she felt she was all alone until she joined a gang. Her initiation into the gang was to survive not a beating, but being gang raped by the gang leaders. Later in life Norma became a prostitute to survive and continues her connection to the gang membership.

Prison gangs, on the other hand, are more likely to be constituted of young adult men who have served time in prison and who joined a gang for protection while serving time. They are more likely to engage in large-scale underground activities and have a much stronger structure and culture of discipline (deviations and/or snitching, for example, are often punished by extreme sanctions). Some gangs that start out as street gangs may, over time, become prison gangs as their members serve time in prison and operate criminal enterprises from within prison walls.

In recent years, Mexican drug cartels are thought to be establishing relationships with prison gangs on the U.S. side of the border.[30] Mostly, such contacts have been with the more established prison gangs. The street gangs, however, tend to be less organized and less dependable than prison gangs, which can more easily enforce discipline over a much wider area.

Border Trafficking and Gangs

In recent years, there has been an increase in the use of U.S. border gangs by various Mexican drug cartels. The National Criminal Justice Reference Service estimates that the drug cartels are now moving large amounts of illegal drugs and illegal immigrants by means of these gangs.[31] As a result, some of these gangs seem to be moving from vandalism, petty turf fights, and victimizing immigrants and other low-income border residents to trafficking, distribution, extortion, money laundering, and murder. They are apparently also involved in smuggling arms and ammunition into Mexico (for use by the cartels), alien smuggling, protection rackets, and, lately, kidnapping (mainly of wealthy Mexicans who are moving to the U.S. for safety).

Burton and West claim that at least nine well-established prison gangs have connections to Mexican drug cartels.[32] In a February 2010 report of the Attorney General to Congress, the National Drug Intelligence Center proposed that gang members, especially in border states, are increasingly conducting criminal activities across the U.S.-Mexico border. This report further alleges that drug-trafficking organizations are improving the organizational effectiveness of these local gangs, such as by teaching them to use prepaid cell phones and the Internet to communicate, organize, and recruit.[33] According to one recent STRATFOR report, the Gulf Cartel could well be applying the same model by linking up in South Texas with such gangs as Hermanos de Pistoleros Latinos in Houston and the Texas Syndicate and Tango Blast in the Rio Grande Valley.[34] This current trend toward cartelization of gangs and cross-border smuggling on the border may be an ominous one.

Conclusion

The underground economy is an economy that is based on and benefits from government intervention. Cross and Johnson point out that every time the state makes a commodity illegal and imposes high criminal penalties for producing and trading in this commodity, the state prevents competition from legal enterprises, barring them from producing or trading in that commodity.[35] Portes and Haller see a similar benefit of government intervention in what they call the Paradox of State Control.[36] Essentially, absent a change in demand, the more the state seeks to obliterate underground activities such as the smuggling of immigrants and drugs, the more profitable these activities become.

Thus, when the government seeks to curtail an activity, it may increase the profitability of the activity in two ways: First, by restricting supply through interdiction efforts; and, second, by eliminating all formal means of meeting this demand, leaving the field open exclusively to underground operators. Those willing to take the risks are thus doubly benefitted by government efforts to control the underground economy. And this benefit increases on the border, where the disparate laws of the two nations promote an underground economy by opening up enormous economic opportunities while eliminating competition from formal enterprises.

We have argued that the Texas-Mexico borderlands area is unfairly stereotyped as a violent wasteland. The level of violent crime on the South Texas border is far less than this stereotyped image suggests. We have shown that the undocumented and quasidocumented, for the most part, avoid the underground economy in favor of the informal economy (and, where possible, the formal economy). Our results suggest that those with the permanent right to reside in the U.S. (U.S. citizens and U.S. residents) comprise the vast majority of the participants in the underground economy of South Texas. Nevertheless, the increasing violence of the Mexican cartels and their growing ties to border gangs threaten to spill across the border.

It would be wrong, however, to blame this violence mainly on Mexico. We should also fault the distortions caused by our insatiable demand for drugs and cheap labor in the U.S. heartland and our national strategy to interdict these flows by putting more boots on the ground and more fences on the border. We see this as a major manifestation of structural bias. Though the demand for drugs and labor is by far stronger in the interior of the United States, the drug and labor wars are fought primarily on the border. In essence, these far off power centers create conditions in the border region that make the area resemble Mexico—much more than Mexicans living in South Texas make it resemble Mexico.

Mexicans on their own side of the border also suffer from structural bias. Mexican federal troops are sent to the border to solve a problem that is caused mainly by decisions made by power centers in the interior. It is no coincidence that a border city, Ciudad Juárez, which lies across the Rio Grande from El Paso has become the murder capital of Mexico—and ironic that neighboring El Paso has the third lowest homicide rate in the U.S.

This deadly situation thus reflects not only the lure of high profits on the border, but the very high risks. As we have shown throughout this chapter, the level of risk tends to rise with the profitability of each underground enterprise. Unfortunately, those who make the greatest profits are not necessarily those taking the greatest risks. Very wealthy underground operators frequently shift the risks to the weak, to their families, and even to the local border population. As one African proverb suggests, when elephants fight, it is the grass that suffers. That grass being trampled, however, is not just another case of structural bias (in which unequal results are indirect and unintentional). Rather, it is exploitation, where the harm produced is direct, intentional, and very self-serving.

CHAPTER 3

Informal Economic Activities

Several years after her mother died, Amelia Salinas started a small business making tacos around Laredo. She and her husband of ten years had been having severe economic problems. They both had regular jobs in a cafeteria, but the pay was low and their family was growing. Since neither of them had finished high school, they didn't see many options. Amelia said,

> I would pray every night for God to help me find a way to earn more money. After many prayers, the answer came. One night my mom, who had died years earlier, told me in a dream to take advantage of what she had taught me. I didn't really know what she meant, so it was a mystery. But a week later I had the same dream again. This time, though, she mentioned something about selling tacos. My husband and I talked to our families and everybody gave their opinion about the dream. They all decided to lend me the money to start a taco business. Since it was all family, they didn't charge me any interest on the loan. They only asked me to pay them back whenever I had enough money coming in. The business has really taken off because of my secret ingredient—the salsa my mom taught her daughters to make. Today, my business is a success.

Introduction

The taco stand that Amelia and her family run is truly an informal enterprise. They do not pay income taxes and do not charge their customers the mandated state sales taxes. Nor do they have the required sales tax permit. In addition, the food they make and sell is not inspected by the Texas Department of State Health Services, and they do not have a license to sell food. Further, as Amelia's account illustrates, they avoid formal business practices, such as taking out a bank loan. Rather, they chose to ask family members to provide the needed capital. And family members accepted her account of the dream as sufficient reason to advance her an unsecured loan. As a result, no business plan was requested and Amelia and her husband were able to remain "off the books."

In Chapter 1, we indicated that an informal economic enterprise is one that produces a product that is otherwise legal (in Amelia's case, tacos) but that the enterprise's production and sales are unregulated, unreported, and unrecorded. Sociologists and economists generally agree with the distinction made by Feige that informal economic activities are those that evade tax codes, circumvent reporting, and bypass the costs of administrative rules covering labor, property, credit, and benefits.[1]

As a result, these informal enterprises are excluded from the protection of the official rules and the legal systems they evade. If someone refuses to pay or if they are involved in property or labor disputes, these informal operators are largely on their own. Javier Hernandez, another informal vendor, sells hot dogs, *elotes* (corn on the cob), and other Mexican-made snack foods through itinerant snack carts. He and his workers have to face the risks of operating a business informally. Javier, himself once an undocumented immigrant, purposefully seeks out newly arrived undocumented Mexicans to staff his carts. In part, this hiring preference is altruistic, as he seeks to provide opportunities for those who cannot work legally in the U.S. But he also reduces his labor costs through employing illegal immigrants informally. Yet this comes with some risk. As Javier stated, "Whenever one of my guys doesn't return for that day, I know something is wrong and I go out looking for him." Typically what has gone wrong is related to increased border enforcement. Most of the time, Border Patrol officers have taken one of his workers and have left the food cart behind. "I may never see that cart again," he says. "Someone is likely to steal it so they can start their own business with it. I lose a lot of money when my people get picked up because I lose everything. I lose the cart, the products, and the money they made for the day." Because he avoids taxes, permits, and inspections, Javier is not in a position to report these losses or acquire property insurance.

Generally, enterprises with few employees and a moderate volume of trade cannot afford to go without the protections offered by formal systems. If Javier were to have his workers deported and lose his carts more frequently, he would soon be unable to operate. And if he becomes too successful, he would also have great difficulty staying under the radar of officials looking for violators of the codes governing labor, health, property, and business transactions. But since his business is a small mom-and-pop operation, he doesn't attract much attention. Informal operators whose businesses grow too large risk being shut down, but they could also face jail time and could lose their often substantial initial investment as a result of governmental intervention or claims from employees, landlords, or customers.

Such is the case of a convenience store owner in McAllen. The owner started small and was soon able to open a second store. In December 2009, he was arrested and indicted for tax fraud. According to the indictment issued by a grand jury in Austin, he was alleged to have collected more than $100,000 in sales tax in 2008 and a similar amount in 2009. He was charged with collecting but failing to pay sales taxes to the state of Texas over a three- or four-year period. The Texas Comptroller's office in the state capital of Austin was able to bring the charges because a law passed in 2007 requires wholesalers to report tobacco and alcohol sales to stores like these. This gives regulators the means of comparing reported sales tax collections against the amounts that are suggested by the volume of sales anticipated based on the reports submitted by suppliers.[2] Many small-time operators, however, simply avoid using large wholesalers, thus leaving few clues of their informality.

Informality and Social Life

It is tempting to think of the informal economy as an aberration. While it is somewhat abnormal in the U.S. and Western Europe, the *formal* economy is more the aberration throughout history and throughout much of the world. We have become so accustomed to living with a regulated economy that we do not recognize what it has taken to create it. Likewise, formal operators are prone to criticize regulators as "blundering bureaucrats" without realizing the economic benefits government makes possible. As Portes and Haller point out, "In the absence of a stable legal framework and credible enforcement of contracts, long-term productive investment becomes impossible . . . Since there is no outside arbiter of market competition, the rules become uncertain, frustrating systematic capitalist planning and the development of a modern bourgeoisie."[3]

The formal economy, however, comes at a price. Essentially, we suggest, the trade-off is this: You give up some of your freedoms and some of your income and the state will provide you the protection and the muscle needed to enforce contracts and assure good working conditions. In European countries (and to a lesser degree in the U.S.) the agreement provides not only regulation, but also a safety net to protect workers from unemployment, health problems, and unjust labor demands. As a result, the formal controls in those countries are much more extensive.[4]

Even today, many businesses find informality attractive. Employers seeking workers who will not demand formal wages and benefits find informality enticing. By hiring such workers, employers can reduce their wage bills, undercut the prices of formal enterprises, avoid government regulation, and add or fire employees at will. Employers who need workers for special projects, events, or opportunities; those who seek to practice cultural traditions brought from Mexico; and consumers who want special goods or services also find informality attractive. But for many, informality is more a necessity than a preference. Relatively low per capita incomes in South Texas oblige many individuals and families to engage in consumer behavior that stretches out their purchasing power by engaging the informal sector, where the cost of goods and services may be substantially lower than in the formal marketplace.

Getting Started: Leveraging Human and Social Capital for Start-up Capital

Each time an informal operator, whether documented or undocumented, engages the informal economic sector for the first time, his or her story is unique, full of risk, and full of hope. After a falling out with the new owner of a tuxedo rental shop, for example, Ernestina Cantú quit her regular job as a seamstress. Months later, Mrs. Cantú was still out of a job, desperately searching for employment but limited because she couldn't drive. As the new owner of the tuxedo shop where she had previously worked began alienating customers with her dreadful demeanor, a former customer found Mrs. Cantú at home—she lived only a couple of blocks from the tuxedo rental store—and asked her to fix a prom dress. Mrs. Cantú happily assisted with the dress and, more importantly, realized that she could work informally as a seamstress from her home.

Though each story is distinct, a pattern emerges as to how people get their start in the informal market of South Texas. Aspects of the pattern include the use of networks, learning skills on a job and then starting one's own business, serendipity, turning a hobby or labor of love into a job, generating a formal idea, utilizing family support, going door-to-door, crossing the border, and utilizing the fluidity of the border economy.

In our 2006–2009 Informal and Underground Survey designed specifically for this book, we asked, "How did you learn about, or get started doing each of these [informal] activities?" The top three responses were family connections (31.3%), friends and coworkers (29.5%), and self-motivation (11.1%). These answers accounted for more than 70% of the responses. Though less often indicated, word of mouth (3.8%), previous employment (3.5%), training programs (2.3%), and hobby (1.3%) were also mentioned by our survey respondents as key entry points into informality. The remaining responses were a mixture of the above or simply "other."

Social networks, or social capital, are critical in finding informal employment, reducing risk, and eliminating time lost searching for jobs. This is especially true for maids and gardeners. In their study of both gardener and maid markets in Laredo, Pisani and Yoskowitz found that social networks (family, employer recommendations, and word-of-mouth) accounted for 70.5% and 86.8% of all placements for gardeners and maids, respectively.[5] Pisani and Yoskowitz also found that, in the event of job displacement, 64.9% of maids could secure replacement work within seven days through their preestablished social networks.[6]

Without established social networks, finding a job can be difficult and discouraging. Socorro Hinojosa experienced difficulty finding work because she lacked a strong social network. She laments, "I have been living here for almost seven months now, and I have not been able to find a job. I have asked people that I know, gone looking door to door, even tried to use my cousin's papers, and I still can't find a job. I think that's due to the fact that I know no English."

Many informals who lack social capital start by going door to door, soliciting work. Omar Carrizales of Pharr at first sought new clients for his landscaping business by going house to house seeking yard work. Pisani and Yoskowitz found in their study of self-employed gardeners in Laredo that 42% of gardeners reported going door to door in search of their first job.[7] Once these gardeners established a network of many regular customers, only 22% of their new clients were obtained through door-to-door solicitation. The rest of their new clients were obtained through referrals, another use of social capital.[8]

Maids are the quintessential informal actors or informal economic agents in South Texas. Pisani and Yoskowitz establish in their study of maids in Laredo that 64.9% of maids found new employment within a week and only 12.4% were still looking for employment after one month when in search of new employment.[9] Richardson describes the ease with which maids find work when facilitated by social networks 77% of the time.[10] And less than one-third of maids in Laredo were required to show any proof of immigration papers to employers, indicating a wide acceptance of "employment as is" rather than "employment as verifiable to work."[11]

One use of a social network leading into informality represents a betrayal of trust. Some informals secretly steal clients from their employers. One local graphic designer, Rafael Huerta, does informal work on the side, offering clients a cheaper alternative to the fees his boss will charge for work he does at the company. The business he works for caters mostly to small firms that are just starting out. Many of these clients, seeking a cheaper alternative, take him aside and ask if he can do work for them after hours. Other clients come more directly from personal recommendations, some from satisfied customers he has siphoned away from his boss and others as a result of active promotion from his family and friends.[12]

Often, informality begins with an economically desperate situation. Teresa Jimenez, a twenty-seven-year-old mother of two in Hidalgo County, resorted to scavenging for aluminum cans when her husband was incarcerated.[13]

> When my husband went to prison I thought I would go crazy. I had a three-year-old daughter and a newborn son. I wasn't prepared to get a job but I had to find one. I also needed someone to take care of my son. I didn't have money for a day care, and even if I would have I was scared to leave my baby there; he was only a few weeks old. I took a part-time job at night so my mother could take care of my kids. After a few weeks I realized I wasn't making it. I was barely making enough to pay my bills. My mother-in-law told me that I could make a few extra dollars by selling aluminum cans. I was so embarrassed but I knew I had to come up with more money. I started selling cans and then other things like old bikes, or junked metal stuff, whatever I could find. I never thought I would ever have to sell metal. *Yo pensaba que eso era para drogadictos o gente con vicios* [I thought that was for druggies or people that had vices]. Now I know that it can happen to anyone, just like it happened to me.

Most of the informal business enterprises we examined did not start from catastrophic family events, however. A far more common pattern is to start out as an informal employee until one accumulates enough capital (economic, social, and/or human capital) to start a business. Paco Infante came to the U.S. with his family from Mexico. He did not have much money, but he came to Laredo to find a better life. He recalled that this better life "would not happen for his parents" as their lack of education (human capital) severely limited them to such jobs as a janitor or as a maid. When Paco managed to get a GED, he was able to find work in the fast-food industry and over the years managed to save $1,500. "At the age of 31," he said, "I decided I wanted to make some money on my own without having to take orders from everyone that was above me. And I had trouble keeping my job as many more young teenage kids with much more energy and learning ability came into the picture. So I started a fruit business [itinerant and informal] from my car with the money I saved. I have provided for my family, and I hope my kids will have better opportunities than me by finishing high school." Paco quickly came to understand the importance of human capital and intends that his children take advantage of the opportunity to develop it through education.

Once individuals begin participating in informal activities, they may find that they can switch from formal to informal activities and back again, or from one sector of the informal economy to another. This is common for those with the immigration status that allows them to work in the formal sector. The formal sector may provide a safe haven for income, benefits, and future earnings, while the informal sector allows them to augment their income.

One of the key features of informality along the border that is illustrated by the preceding stories is its attraction to those with very little capital—economic, social, or human. The start-up costs are often facilitated by these other forms of capital, but often do not require a large monetary investment. That is, social and human capital often make up for a lack of financial capital. Consider the case of Marco Sanchez, who started a shade-tree automotive repair business. Unlike gardening and maid work, automotive repair generally requires a substantially greater knowledge, as well as one's own tools (similar to self-employed carpenters). Marco is a forty-four-year-old self-taught auto mechanic born in Reynosa, currently a permanent U.S. resident. Mr. Sanchez has "always liked working on cars" and has achieved most of his skills through informal experience in helping his friends fix cars. Mr. Sanchez suggests that there is an abundant demand for his work as a mechanic as "there are always clients with cars that need fixing." Fixing cars generally requires some capital outlay up front, but Mr. Sanchez has been able to purchase the tools he needs with income from his formal job as an oil rig worker. He also rents tools for special jobs, when needed. Mr. Sanchez is able to earn about $7,000 in informal income, some of which also comes from odd jobs in construction.

Types of Informality

Portes, Castells, and Benton make useful distinctions among three types of informality.[14] The first they call *survival informality*. This type is illustrated in most of the cases just presented. Survival informality is what we find among individuals or families who engage in direct subsistence production or the simple and direct sale of goods and services. Even though some may operate a business with several employees, they still just manage to stay above a subsistence level. Often, those engaged in survival informality sell from their home or sell items on the street. Most of the cases we explore in this chapter fall into the category of survival informality.

Another form of informality that is less common on the South Texas border today than in the past is *dependent exploitation*. This form of informality consists primarily of owners and managers making great profits, often at the expense of workers. Enterprises that engage in dependent exploitation reduce labor costs through off-the-books hiring and subcontracting informal workers, who are often undocumented workers. In the Rio Grande Valley, some large produce operations have grown this way, by contracting with labor bosses for undocumented workers, offering piece-rate contracts, encouraging "union busting," and other means of extracting a large profit from the labor of informal workers.

Zulema Iglesias has been a farm laborer all her life. When asked to compare the differences between working in the fields twenty years ago and today she remembers picking cabbage in Mission, Texas, for $1.40 an hour. "Back then," she said, "those wages were the best around. Nobody was ever paid over $1.50." She also stated that today, by law, workers should be earning minimum wage but usually do not because farmers prefer to pay a piece rate.

Portes, Castells, and Benton call the third form of informality *growth informality*. This refers to cooperative efforts organized for accumulating capital, lowering costs, and facilitating greater flexibility among networks of microproducers. Artisan microproducers would be an example of this. We found very few examples of this form of informality in South Texas.[15] So, by far the most common form of informal enterprises that operate in South Texas are forms of survival informality— very small, involving minimal capital investment and only bare survival levels of revenue.

An important aspect of survival informality for informal entrepreneurs is having an equally poor clientele that needs cut-rate goods or services. The South Texas border economy provides such a clientele, which adds to the size of the informal sector.[16] Daniel, who does mechanic work on cars for neighbors, justifies his participation in the informal sector by explaining that he offers a lower price and payment plans for his economically challenged neighbors. He stated, "I know people think that those of us who do things under the table are trying to keep some type of welfare assistance, but that [is] just not always the case. I've been doing mechanic work on most of my neighbors' cars for years now, and I tell you most people come to me because they can't afford to go to some dealer mechanic that will charge them an arm and a leg. Sometimes they pay me by trading an old car or some other form of barter. Sometimes, I hang on to a car for years before they are able to pay for it."

Beto Perez offers a good example of how entrepreneurs move up but often not out of poverty with survival informality. Beto owns a scrap metal business.

> When I started doing this, I was desperate. I would go to people's homes and ask them if they had things they wanted to throw away. It was really embarrassing, but I didn't have much choice. Sometimes I would offer to clean up their lot and throw away all their garbage for free. Of course I knew that anything I could take I could sell. Now almost 20 years later I have my own little business. I still look for cheap metal but now I get a lot more of it; so much that people actually come to my place looking for spare parts. I make good money. Now I even hire people that need a job. I have about four people working for me. They don't have papers, so I give them a place to stay and some work. I don't look for things anymore. They do it for me. All I have to do is sell it. I can't pay them much, and after a while they leave, but when they first come here I give them a job. I used to be ashamed, but not anymore. Sometimes I can even help out my son who is studying to be a doctor. He supports himself, but once in a while I have enough to help him out a bit. I think I set a good example for my kids. I have always worked hard and now they do too.

As Beto's business has grown, his level of risk has also grown. But even though he hires undocumented workers and pays them below minimum wage, he is still at a marginal economic position, only being able to help his son occasionally with his education. Most of the informal enterprise owners we interviewed hover on the edge of subsistence, engaging in informality more out of necessity than choice. A few, however, grow large enough to find ways to move to the formal economy, including developing a sufficiently large capital investment to enable them to operate openly with government regulators or tax agents.

Beto's situation is very common in the South Texas borderlands. Even though some businesses that start in the informal economy may grow, most could not transition to the formal sector. The more common form is for an individual to start from scratch, get enough income to hire a few workers, and then pay them below market wages while the owner also continues living at a subsistence level. And though they pay their workers below-market wages with almost no benefits, they do not exploit their workers, in the neo-Marxist sense, because they earn little real profit.[17]

Measuring the Unmeasurable:
How Large Is the Informal Economy of South Texas?

According to Portes and Haller, attempting to measure the size of the informal economy is "measuring the unmeasurable."[18] Participants in the informal economy deliberately seek to mislead tax-collecting agencies, inspectors, and statisticians. As a result, the informal economy can only be measured indirectly. One method of indirectly determining the size of the informal economy of a given population is the labor-market approach, which is based on the assumption that people in certain labor categories—specifically, the self-employed, the unemployed, and the undocumented—are more prone to hide their income-generating activities than those in other categories. We present data in each of these three areas to support our finding of a robust informal sector in South Texas.

The Self-Employed

Self-employment rates have been found to be positively correlated with participation in the informal economy. In a comprehensive and serious

Table 3.1. 2007 Self-employment data for South Texas, Texas, and the U.S.

Location	Self-Employment* (Total)	Workforce (Total)	Self-Employment Rate (%)
Brownsville-Harlingen MSA	26,676	143,314	18.61
Laredo MSA	18,415	89,644	20.54
McAllen-Edinburg-Mission MSA	59,205	272,708	21.71
LRGV MSAs	104,296	505,666	20.63
Texas	1,819,963	11,514,790	15.81
U.S.	21,708,021	153,124,000	14.18

*Nonemployer statistics (self-employed own account firms)
Source: Bureau of Labor Statistics (www.bls.gov) & Small Business Administration (www.sba.gov).

effort to measure informal sector self-employment using a case study, Tienda and Raijman found that members of 38% of Mexican immigrant households in Chicago worked in the informal economy, often in work considered self-employment.[19] Ivan Light cites this as a reason for exaggerated unemployment rates among these low-end minority workers. They are officially unemployed, but they are working in the informal economy. Those who cite high unemployment among certain ethnic groups tend to overlook these high participation rates in the informal (ethnic) economy.[20] Sanders, Nee, and Sernau stress that we must not only track labor movements across borders, but should also take into account the high rates of participation of immigrant communities in the informal economy.[21] Otherwise we vastly miscalculate the number of economically active people and misunderstand the labor market.

We believe that, as in Chicago, high rates of unemployment in the South Texas borderlands disguise informality. Self-employment rates are considerably higher in South Texas than in the rest of Texas or most elsewhere in the U.S. Utilizing official data from the U.S. Bureau of Labor Statistics, the official federal government agency for collecting employment data, we find that the rates of self-employment in the three metropolitan statistical areas of South Texas (Laredo, McAllen-Edinburg-Mission, and Brownsville-Harlingen) were 30.5% higher in 2007 than the state average and 45.5% higher than the national average (see Table 3.1). Additionally, businesses of the self-employed in the region are generally very small enterprises, and only one in ten has any paid employees.[22] This makes it relatively easy to evade government detection and blend into the local entrepreneurial landscape of the informal economy.

Nearly 90% of Hispanic-owned businesses in the South Texas borderlands region are own-account enterprises, that is, they have no paid employees. The recent work of Alberto Dávila and Marie Mora, economists at the University of Texas–Pan American, adds substantially to our knowledge of Hispanic and immigrant self-employment along the U.S.-Mexico border and its relation to informality. Utilizing data from the 2000 U.S. Census, Mora and Dávila find strong empirical support for estimates of high rates of Mexican immigrant self-employment along the entire border.[23] They also note that Mexican immigrant self-employment is higher than native self-employment in the region or elsewhere in the interior of the U.S. Mora and Dávila argue that along the border Mexican immigrants are positively selected into self-employment, which suggests self-employment is a decision based on choice—that is, the best earnings alternative for this group is self-employment.[24] They contend, however, that self-employment is not nearly as attractive an option for Mexican immigrants who settle within the interior of the U.S. Further analysis shows that Mexican immigrants are 1.9 times more likely to be self-employed within the border region than those Mexican immigrants who settle further into the interior of the U.S., though by locating within the border zone, their earnings are depressed.[25]

Mora and Dávila suggest that the border environment induces self-employment for the newly immigrated.[26] They propose that this "finding could also indicate that Mexican immigrants unable to find paid employment near their homeland prefer to become self-employed rather than leave the region".[27] According to Dávila and Mora, entrepreneurship on the border perhaps allows for a leveraging of the border southward into Mexico, as well as within the border area. Hence, Mexican immigrants with ties to both sides of the border can effectively utilize the border to maximize their benefits—as through self-employment.

Although Mora and Dávila do not estimate the amount of informality among the self-employed immigrants of the border area, self-employment has been found to be closely associated with informality. This is especially true for the undocumented, who are often self-employed so that they do not need to show documents (Social Security card, driver's license, etc.) to be able to work. A study by the Internal Revenue Service, for example, estimated that 47% of workers classified as independent contractors did not report any of their earnings to the IRS. So the high rates of self-employment in the South Texas border region are a strong indirect indicator of a vibrant informal economy in the region.[28]

The Unemployed

Mora and Dávila also argue that the higher the self-employment rate, the higher the unemployment rate.[29] Explaining this connection, they suggest that the possible lack of employment alternatives creates an environment along the border where self-employment becomes a sector of refuge; they state "that many workers in the United States become self-employed instead of (or in addition to) being unemployed, reflecting more of the 'push' phenomenon into business ownership".[30] And Sharif adds the following paradox: Where labor is too abundant (oversupplied) and wages low in developing contexts, even more self-employed labor will be supplied in order to eke out an existence—a situation which persists where human capital accumulation is low.[31]

Unemployment in South Texas historically is more severe than elsewhere in Texas or the U.S.[32] In Table 3.2, we examine the official unemployment rates of the three metropolitan statistical areas (MSAs) in

Table 3.2. Unemployment in South Texas, Texas, and the U.S., 1991–2009

| | Location | | | | |
Year	Brownsville-Harlingen MSA (%)	Laredo MSA (%)	McAllen-Edinburg-Mission MSA (%)	Texas (%)	USA (%)
2005–2009	7.3	6.0	7.9	5.4	5.9
2000–2004	8.4	6.8	9.8	5.7	5.2
1995–1999	12.2	11.4	18.1	5.4	4.9
1990–1994	13.8	10.9	21.5	7.0	6.6
Period Average (1990–2009)	10.5	8.8	14.3	5.9	5.7

Sources: Texas Workforce Commission (www.tracer2.com), U.S. Bureau of Labor Statistics (www.bls.gov).

South Texas, Texas as a whole, and the U.S. over a twenty-year period. This table shows that during all the periods examined, unemployment in the South Texas MSAs was up to three times higher than the national and Texas state averages. Though there has been a generally improving employment situation in recent years (perhaps the early results of NAFTA), stark comparisons stand out. For the entire period, on average, the unemployment rates for the Brownsville-Harlingen, Laredo, and McAllen-Edinburg-Mission MSAs are 1.8, 1.5, and 2.4 times higher than the rates for Texas as a whole, respectively; the South Texas unemployment gap widens slightly more as compared to the national average. High unemployment is a systematic problem in South Texas.

The unemployed often move to the informal economy in order to generate income under the table—some to survive and others to still be able to receive welfare and other benefits.[33] Gutmann and other researchers have estimated that 20% of those officially classified as unemployed are informal workers hiding their income.[34] So we add the unemployed to the self-employed as major contributors to the informal economy of the region.

The Undocumented

The Pew Hispanic Center, a nonpartisan and highly respected authority on Hispanic issues, argues that 55% of all Mexican immigrants in the U.S. are unauthorized (undocumented) for work.[35] From the 2000 U.S. Census, foreign-born population percentages are available by city. Calculating a foreign-born aggregate utilizing the communities in our study area of South Texas reveals that 26.3% of those present in South Texas at the time of the 2000 U.S. Census were foreign-born. The 2008 Census estimate for the six South Texas counties we are focused on (Cameron, Hidalgo, Starr, Webb, Willacy, and Zapata) counts 1,452,977 people in the region. Applying the 26.3% foreign-born and 55% unauthorized benchmarks to the region, we estimate 210,173 unauthorized persons were present in South Texas in 2008. This unauthorized count represents a city the size of Laredo, the largest city in the South Texas borderlands.

While these figures provide a rough estimate, we note that this total probably undercounts the number of undocumented in the region. Based on our experience, we believe the rate of unauthorized persons is higher than the national average suggested by the Pew Center because of the ability of the unauthorized to more easily blend into the local population, as well as to access (travel to) and leverage the border within this region. Hence the estimate of 210,000 is more likely low, and a more accurate number may be double this estimate. Since undocumented workers are almost by definition participants in the informal economy (because they are not authorized to work)[36] and often resort to self-employment, they constitute a large segment of informal workers or informal entrepreneurs and are discussed more fully in Chapter 4.

Combining these three areas—the self-employed, the unemployed, and the undocumented—allows us to more confidently propose that the rates of informality are much higher in South Texas than elsewhere in the country. We support this claim with studies of regions with a comparable labor-force makeup. Based on her surveys for El Paso, Staudt suggests that approximately 30% of the self-employed participate in informal activities.[37] One of the few studies to reliably estimate the size of a regional informal economy in the U.S. was conducted by the Economic Roundtable and examined the informal economy of Los Angeles County. Their mid-range estimate was that 15% of the labor force of Los Angeles was in the informal economy in 2004. They found that the undocumented made up roughly 65% of these informal workers. Unlike South Texas, however, the majority of informal workers in Los Angeles seem to be employed in factories, mills, warehouses, workshops, restaurants, nursing homes, and office buildings—making the informal economy there more of the dependent exploitation type than the survival informality more characteristic of South Texas.

The informal economy of South Texas has other features not common in places that are farther from the border, like Los Angeles. Border locations, particularly those in South Texas, have much higher rates of poverty than most nonborder locations. Poverty plays an important role in facilitating informality. Those living in dire poverty often face choices that affect their very survival. Also, poverty creates incentives to hide income to obtain or retain government services. In addition, South Texas border locations often have fairly large numbers of informal workers who live in Mexico and cross the border regularly for their informal employment. For example, we found a group of Mexico-based sheetrock workers who cross the bridge each morning in Laredo using a laser visa—a local border crossing, or "shopping," card. They are picked up by their supervisor not far from the bridge, are transported to their job drywalling new homes, and are paid in cash. These construction workers resort to the informal sector to earn a living. The desire to earn a living in order to survive also motivates the buyers of discarded clothing in flea markets and used clothing warehouses; they cross the border daily, sorting and purchasing discards in Texas border cities and taking them to Mexico to sell.

In conclusion, we propose that informality in the South Texas border region constitutes between 20% and 25% of the productive economy. If we include all individuals engaged in informal economic activities, the figure would be even higher because many individuals work in both the formal and the informal economy as well as engage in consumption informality. We base these estimates on some of the unique aspects of this and other border locations, aspects closely related to informality. These include the high incidence of self-employed persons along the border and in South Texas. This factor is even stronger for Mexican immigrants, a primary source of informality in the region. In addition, unemployment is relatively high in South Texas, motivating people to find alternative means to earn a living through informal channels. Finally, the higher incidence of undocumented residents promotes informality; lacking proper work authorization documents, these residents have limited access to formal employment. We present these factors as a data-based attempt to "measure the unmeasurable."

How Is the Informal Economy of South Texas Different?

Traits specific to informality in South Texas are the relative absence of day labor and the interaction between culture, ethnicity, and social capital. A brief examination of each will illustrate this relationship.

Relative Absence of Day Laborers

Compared to other parts of the country, day labor is not that prevalent in South Texas.[38] This may be due to the heavily interlaced social networks of the region, which leave little need for locations for impersonal market exchanges. Informal workers can easily be found by other means and through much more established informal networks. In other words, employers can easily find informal workers without having to go to a specific location to see who is available. Additionally, the presence of large numbers of Border Patrol agents may act as a deterrent for routine and predictable gatherings explicitly set aside for undocumented employment. Nonetheless, there is a small market for day labor that engages in project-specific tasks.

The Relation of Culture and Ethnicity to Informality

In the South Texas borderlands especially, but also elsewhere in the U.S., the informal economy is largely an ethnic economy. Light describes this type of situation as the result of doubly disadvantaged ethnic employment. He notes that it is a conundrum found in much of the research on ethnic economic initiatives.[39] The conundrum is essentially this: If disadvantage promotes formal self-employment, why do disadvantaged blacks, Mexicans, and Central Americans display low self-employment rates in the formal sector, whereas disadvantaged Asian immigrants display high formal self-employment rates? His response, based on resource constraint theory, is that doubly disadvantaged groups—those who not only lack economic resources but also lack essential human and cultural capital[40]—have less ability to undertake self-employment in the formal sector. As a result, doubly disadvantaged groups seek employment in the informal sector where slender resources will suffice. Some Asian immigrant groups who enjoy educational, capital, and cultural advantages (e.g., cultural orientations that promote highly productive use of community resources) are more likely to undertake self-employment in the formal sector.

Portes and Light examined different immigrant groups in the U.S. and found that successful immigrant communities offer newly arrived coethnics help in securing informal sources of credit, insurance, child support, English language training, and job referrals.[41] Less successful immigrant communities, in contrast, showed less commitment to one another and offered their members fewer important services. Korean immigrant communities, for example, are often characterized by high levels of trust and mutual offers of assistance and even the capital needed to start businesses. Those with resources lend to coethnics, reinforcing a strong norm that such help will be reciprocated to the community. This reciprocity not only requires strong cultural elements that bind the people in these communities to each other, but also some structural networks that help insure that such trust is not unreciprocated. This latter element is perhaps the key aspect of social capital—that networks of social relations may be more important than culture and rationality in shaping developmental outcomes (though culture is important in the formation of these networks).[42] Valdez adroitly adds, "Social capital may provide additional economic and noneconomic resources and support that, though not always essential, may improve Latino/as' market position."[43]

In the U.S economic system, Mexican and Central American immigrants also occupy a niche—but one not in the middle. Rather, the niche for these immigrants tends to be their willingness to labor in some of the most distasteful and dangerous occupations, a position that lands them at or near the bottom and frequently without capital or legal means to trade their labor in the formal market.

Leveraging Cultural Capital for Social Capital

Buying products in Mexico to resell in the U.S. may have another advantage for border informal traders—it can also help create and/or utilize social capital. Imelda Lara, for example, has always been known for making tamales. They are in such high demand that family and friends always ask for them. She never thought about charging for her tamales. They were a labor of love. Imelda, now in her 60s, found that "people would ask if I could make some *tamales* for a wedding, *quinceañera*,[44] or just a birthday. I never said no. I never charged for my services, but they always gave me some amount of money." Eventually, Imelda started charging for her *tamales* when she found she could no longer cover her bills with only her Social Security income. She earns $7 per dozen and prepares the tamales in advance, using a freezer and other time-saving tools that facilitate last-minute sales and make the process a bit easier. If Imelda could get more government assistance, she might cut down on how many orders she produces, but she would not stop making and selling tamales because, as she explains, "everybody needs some extra money." Over the years, Imelda has developed not only a clientele, but a group held together by a strong cultural bond. People drawn together by common culture and feelings of reciprocity often turn their cultural identity into social and even economic capital.

Often, ethnic products (especially those associated with holidays or special occasions) present an opportunity for seasonal employment. *Cascarones*, confetti-filled, decorated eggshells that are hurled against the ground (or upon the head of a friend or family member), usually by children, are a hallmark of the Easter season in South Texas. The Ornelas family from Laredo enjoys eating eggs year-round, and they save the emptied eggshells to make *cascarones*. The whole family of five pitches in, but the operation is lead by the mother. Some collect eggshells from neighbors throughout the year; others paint the eggs as Easter approaches; still others stuff confetti into the eggs, and others package the *cascarones* by the dozen for sale. Mrs. Ornelas organizes roadside sales of their product as Easter nears. All told, the family earns only about $200 for their year-long efforts, though most of the work is concentrated in the month leading up to Easter. This informal activity brings the family closer together and earns them a bit of spending money. And because friends and neighbors are also involved, social networks can be established or reinforced through an economic activity that emphasizes a common cultural heritage.

Other Factors Related to Informality in South Texas

Though we agree that ethnic ties and a double disadvantage do push Mexican immigrants and their families toward the informal economy, we believe that other factors are even more important in helping promote informality in the South Texas borderlands. Economic necessity and a scarcity of other resources form a foundation for informality here. Still, these are not necessarily the primary motivators at the micro-level. Family obligations may be one of the most powerful forces behind informal sector income-generating activities.

Poverty and family obligations combine in one form of informality not uncommon in South Texas—using child labor to help sustain a family. This was true for Denise Lopez, a fourteen-year-old high school student from Falfurrias. Not yet old enough to work legally on her own, Denise felt compelled to help her family make ends meet by working informally as a cashier in a sandwich shop. Denise wanted to contribute to the family finances after her father lost his job. She stated, "Now it seems they [my parents] are always worrying how they are going to pay the bills, and that's the main reason I started working." With the explicit approval of the shop owner, Denise, a U.S. citizen, was paid under the table in cash. The shop owner discounted Denise's wage below the mandated minimum wage; after all, he said, he was "doing her a favor." Of the money Denise earned at $4.95 per hour, she was able to keep some for small purchases such as cosmetics, but the remainder went to the family: "It is not like my parents want to take the money. They only use my money when they really can't pay the bills."

Informality is also a hedge against a life of uncertainty that the poor have to deal with—unemployment, seasonal employment, weather-regulated jobs, unforeseen medical and other major costs—all of which produce severe and unanticipated economic needs that cannot be met with a regular minimum-wage income and job conditions. Hector Sanchez is an occasional oil field worker. He earns good money when work is available, but he experiences frequent layoffs as oil prices go up and down. Since his most recent layoff, he has found ways of earning a living by doing carpentry and working on cars. He learned carpentry from his uncle and auto mechanics by working on his own vehicles. A friend who works for a contractor also helps him get work in spurts. If this friend's boss needs assistance for a job, he calls Mr. Sanchez and pays him cash for his work. When no jobs are available in the oil field or in construction, there are always clients with cars that need fixing. His family saves money when work is scarce by scrimping on water and electricity. The family receives financial assistance through Medicaid. After his wife got pregnant, they were able to obtain Medicaid for his wife and children. If he gets sick, however, he goes to the doctor in Mexico, where he also purchases necessities that are much cheaper there.

Poverty and the attendant forms of uncertainty that produce it are major factors that help explain the high level of informality in South Texas. Another important consideration is the state in its roles as a tax agent, report collector, and inspector. Indeed, it is this triple role of government that distinguishes formal from informal economic activity.

Governmental Factors Related to Informality

In a very broad sense, informality is economic activity that avoids governmental oversight, taxation, and regulation. The role of government in the informal economy, however, is subject to considerable debate. On the left, some neo-Marxist writers claim that the U.S. government is complicit in fostering informality. Vogel, for example, asserts

> It is political economics, not free markets, that shape global, national, and local economies. The movement of industrial and service production offshore to take advantage of cheap labor requires the compliance, or outright cooperation, of both home and foreign governments and is therefore a quintessentially political act. Also political is the widespread subversion of immigration and labor law for the sake of profits. These political machinations—not some mythical "invisible hand"—are the engines of the informal economy of the United States.[45]

Certainly, government regulatory agencies are subject to political maneuvering, though most observers would not see the U.S. informal economy as quite the result of politics that Vogel does. While a case might be made for governmental collusion in fostering dependent exploitation, we believe that this type of informality is less common in South Texas than survival informality. Some have argued, however, that the agribusiness sector benefits from having a large supply of migrant farm workers available that need not be supported year-round. They further argue that the farm block has influenced legislation to maintain this labor pool (the largest in the U.S.), both during the summer months of working up north and the winter months in South Texas when they largely depend on welfare and the informal economy to tide them over to the next growing season.

Neoclassical and neoliberal economists would more likely see the informal economy as an adjustment to market forces, with displaced labor from the U.S., Mexico, and Central America competing for scarce jobs in a postindustrial society and the government playing a main role as the enforcer of contracts. This view sees the informal economy as a small economic aberration, the result of governmental inability to oversee those at the fringes who cheat on taxes or avoid essential regulations.

Informality along the South Texas border is facilitated by some lack of governmental oversight at the level of state government. Texas does not have a state income tax. This means that informal workers and business owners do not worry about state income tax collectors, as they would in most other states. Many of those who operate on the economic margins are also not too concerned about the Internal Revenue Service. This federal agency seldom investigates informal workers or small business owners who live on the economic margins, not only because such workers can hide their meager incomes, but also because many earn so little that they would either not owe taxes or might even be eligible for the Earned Income Tax Credit.[46] In addition, for most informal workers the amounts that the federal government might collect would be so small as to make prosecution unproductive. As a result, subsistence informal enterprises that are not engaged in volume retail trade generally have little to worry about from tax collectors. And those involved in very small-scale retail trade (door-to-door or roadside stands) are also seldom investigated or prosecuted by the Texas Comptroller's Office.

Indeed, among those we interviewed who were engaged in survival informality, few expressed any concerns at all about governmental control of their enterprises or labor (other than the undocumented, who occasionally expressed fear of being deported). When we asked, "What difficulties do you experience in doing this (informal) work?", only 7.2%

of respondents mentioned being concerned about tax agents or inspectors.[47] Remarkably, few governmental enforcement problems were mentioned even though over half (54%) of respondents indicated that they knew they were breaking the law by being involved in informal work.

This situation underscores the primary limiting factors in preventing informality in any society—the regulatory *capacity* and the *will* of the state to enforce regulations. As Portes and Haller point out, strong regulation of the informal economy by the state not only requires that the state have the capacity (courts, regulators, inspectors, etc.), but also that it have the will to enforce these regulations.[48]

Factors Affecting the *Will* of the State to Enforce Regulations

There are a variety of factors that affect the will of the state to regulate and sanction legal violations by those in the informal economy. First, governmental agents need to consider the matter of efficacy—whether regulation will really reduce or control informality. Portes and Haller argue, "Official efforts to obliterate unregulated activities through the proliferation of rules and controls often expand the very conditions that give rise to these activities."[49] In other words, efforts to enforce ever more rules simply create more opportunities for individuals to make money by evading those rules. In Chapter 2 we saw this in underground economic activities: The more laws there are against drugs and the better the enforcement against drug smugglers becomes, the more profitable the drug trade becomes. Effective enforcement without a corresponding decrease in demand drives up the price of increasingly scarce drugs, leading to ever more profitable, daring, and inventive ways of evading drug enforcement. As a result, the state may feel that it is not in its best interest to step up enforcement of informal enterprises, especially those that operate at the economic margins of profitability on products that are otherwise legal.

A second factor that affects the will of the state to enforce regulations is another paradox described by Portes and Haller: The informal economy commonly yields a series of positive effects for the state, the very institution charged with its suppression.[50] In an area like South Texas, for example, where there are high levels of poverty, the informal economy provides social welfare benefits, of a sort, without requiring money from federal or state coffers. The "unemployed" can be gainfully employed, even though they may not be officially counted as such. The informal economy also absorbs and helps sustain large numbers of unemployed, underemployed, and irregularly employed, providing stability through recessions and seasonal layoffs. Individuals unable to find work in the formal economy can often find income in the informal sector. Indeed, one estimate of the informal economy's ability to take up slack from downturns in formal employment is based on research from 1980 to the mid 1990s, which showed that about one in five of the officially unemployed is really a disguised informal worker or entrepreneur.[51] It may be to the benefit of the state to not look too hard for informal enterprises since their actions could remove workers from jobs and increase social welfare costs.

A third factor affecting the will of the state to rigorously regulate the informal economy is the knowledge that the informal economy may actually lower the costs of doing business in the formal economy. Informality, for example, provides low-cost labor to formal enterprises and low-cost goods and services to consumers. A fourth factor is that, though tax revenue is lost through informality, the informal economy may return economic resources to the state through indirect taxes. Though informal workers or entrepreneurs may not pay taxes on their profits, they do pay rent (which helps subsidize property taxes), they do pay sales taxes on purchases, and they will begin to pay taxes when and if their informal microenterprise becomes large and profitable enough to join the formal economy.

Finally, at the micro-level, the will of the state to enforce regulations is weakened if the agents charged with enforcing the laws against informal economic activity find it distasteful to pursue very small-time or marginal informal operators, knowing that prosecution is unlikely, fines cannot be paid, and informals can easily abandon their enterprise and start another without much difficulty. In addition, officials may find themselves tempted to turn a blind eye when their own friends or relatives hire low-cost informal workers, such as nannies for their children, shade-tree mechanics for their auto repairs, and informal building tradesmen to remodel their homes.

This occasional tendency of officials to turn a blind eye to informality is illustrated by an interview with a twenty-three-year-old male who works for a local county government. His job with the county does not pay much, so when he needs extra "run-around" money, he participates in the informal economy by performing ranch work for friends, some of whom are high-placed local officials. He also does occasional welding jobs and builds and sells barbecue pits. His biggest profit in the informal economy, however, comes from selling animals for special occasions. He (informally) sells goats, chickens, and hogs. "There's a major increase in the amount of animals we sell during the holidays," he says. "During Christmas there's an increase in the amount of hogs [used to make pork *tamales*], and around Easter there is an increase in the number of young goats that I sell [for *cabrito*, a local delicacy]."

Factors Affecting the *Capacity* of the State to Enforce Regulations

Though most observers consider the U.S. a nation with a strong capacity to enforce regulations, the strength of the state enforcement apparatus varies considerably among geographic regions and among levels of government. Our system of government, with federal, state, county, and municipal levels, affects the regulatory capacity of the state in several ways. First, these levels may not be able or may not be willing to work in concert with one another, permitting informal economic actors to slip through, evade, or simply pit one level against another (e.g., when sanctuary cities protect immigration violators). In Texas, there is no income tax, so there is no state tax vehicle to aid the federal government in detecting informal businesses (and it probably would not be of value for the state to do so anyway because there would be so little in taxes to collect, unless sales taxes are an issue). So as far as an income tax, the federal government may be interested and capable, but the state may have no reason to cooperate. In this example, the federal government may wish to expand control by the IRS, but it will do so with little support from local or state authorities.

Another major issue in South Texas relates to the fact that the laws (and enforcement mechanisms) of one nation often do not match those of its neighbor. Texas, as we have said before, has little interest in enforcing gun laws for Mexico, while Mexico has little interest in preventing U.S. residents from purchasing prescription drugs in Mexico. Similarly, Mexico has no interest in preventing goods legally bought in Mexico (alcohol, for example) from being smuggled past Texas tax collectors. By the same token, U.S. and Texas officials have no interest in stopping articles legally purchased in Texas from being smuggled past Mexican authorities wanting to charge import duties.

The border also facilitates hiding income from government regulators. For example, Alfredo Loya sells cars. Many of his customers cross the border from Mexico to buy cars, use the Mexico license plates from their old cars to replace the Texas plates on the cars just purchased, and then cross the cars back into Mexico. All of these transactions take place in cash and outside the purview of the government. The fact that these car buyers will not register their automobiles in Texas makes it difficult for the government of Texas to know the transaction has taken place. Similarly, the Mexican government is unable to assess heavy import fees on the cars that Alfredo's customers bring into Mexico because they have no record of the sale. Hence, Alfredo pays no federal income tax on the money he makes selling cars to Mexicans, and the Mexicans pay no import duties in Mexico on the cars they buy from him. Alfredo mentioned, "After seeing one of my friends doing this sort of business, it looked so easy to not get caught and it brought in a lot more money so that I could provide better for my family." Still, for the cars he sells that remain in Texas, Alfredo declares his income and would be counted by the government as having a formal business.

Many informal entrepreneurs find ways to take advantage of the fact that there are many items that are legal in Mexico but banned in the U.S., such as freon for your air conditioner, pesticides, and steroids. This divergence of laws greatly expands the range of opportunities for using the laws of one nation or state against its neighbor. This diversity of laws, as well as the volume of individuals willing to break them, also affects the capacity of each state to enforce laws. U.S. authorities have largely given up trying to stop the importation of prescription drugs from Mexico. The demand and the volume have simply gotten too large to regulate. As a result, customs officials seldom demand to see a prescription for such prescription drug purchases; they are even less likely to ask for such paperwork if the amounts are reasonable for the person bringing them in.

This last example shows that increasing public acceptance of informality decreases the capacity of the state to enforce laws against informality. The more legitimate the informal market is perceived to be, the more it is accessed, utilized, and protected from official scrutiny or sanction. Farmers and ranchers in the border area are still able to hire undocumented workers because they are able to apply political pressure to prevent unannounced raids. The same is true of informal sales in flea markets. Though every vendor should be charging sales taxes on their sales, few collect such taxes. The capacity of the state to enforce regulations is reduced by widespread willingness to violate the law and to hide transactions by making cash payments.

It's not that the government cannot spot violations. Any drive through the *colonias* and fleas markets in South Texas would turn up many informal operations. But prosecutions are expensive and are not generally supported by the public unless major problems and/or complaints arise, such as food poisoning from unlicensed vendors, informal contractors taking big jobs from formal ones, or informal operations that become a public nuisance or a threat to public safety. In addition, because most border informality is survival informality, law enforcement operations to shut down informal enterprises have little (or even negative) effect. Prosecuting a convenience store owner for failing to report hundreds of thousands of dollars of unremitted sales taxes provides income to the state, while shutting down a taco stand nets almost nothing, and the operator can easily start up another enterprise because little capital or equipment is generally invested in such businesses.

The capacity of the state to enforce regulations against informality is also strongly affected by public attitudes. And attitudes regarding informality on the South Texas border tend to be much more tolerant than in other parts of the country. First, there are more informal enterprises in the border area, making them much more common. As a result, higher-income consumers experience enticements for informal purchases or services that do not exist (or are far more expensive) outside the borderlands. They also find informal services offered that can save them money and improve their lifestyle. In border cities, it is very easy to hire a maid to live in your home, care for your children, clean the house, and be available 24 hours a day, all for about $70–$100 a week. In addition, it is easy to hire someone to add a room to your house or pave your driveway without getting a building permit or having to go through formal contractors. Middle-income consumers on the border can get things from Mexico that are prohibited in the U.S. Because these informal purchases are so common (and so convenient to obtain), public attitudes do not support strong enforcement activities.

Formal enterprises also benefit from hiring an occasional informal worker. Thirty-six-year-old Sergio Gutierrez from Mexico lives in a trailer at construction worksites. Though Sergio believes his boss is magnanimous for allowing him to live rent-free at the construction site, Sergio also provides an invaluable security service which goes unnoticed and unpaid. Sergio works hard during the day doing the most menial construction tasks and then is expected to watch the work site at night. He earns $15,000 to $20,000 per year, most of which he sends to his family back home.

The Formalization of Informality?

What happens to informal businesses and to informal workers over time? Though we believe upward mobility may exist for some, the majority continue to struggle at the margins, making a bit more money, but unable to break out of survival informality. Many hope for a better future for their children in the formal world of work, seeing the informal sector as a means to help their children get there. Anecdotally, we see many examples of this from our interviews. Many of the students who conducted the interviews chose to interview family members engaged in informal enterprises while they themselves were getting a college education with the expectation of good jobs in the formal sector.

In our Informal and Underground Survey, we had many respondents who participated in both the formal and informal sectors. Indeed, slightly over half (51.5%) of the respondents to our survey worked in both the formal and the informal sectors.[52] Dual-sector participation allows workers to leverage aspects of their formal jobs—such as social benefits and business contacts—to reap further benefits from informal income opportunities. Some dual participants do not report informal income, for doing so would put their income in a range at which they could not maintain eligibility for welfare benefits, even though they still find it hard to make ends meet (this will be discussed in Chapter 8). The ability to access both sectors permits a higher standard of living than these households would obtain in one sector alone.

In the end, some informals perform quite well over time. A few make it into the formal economy. Others continue to struggle with their informal work. Some switch back and forth between formality and informality. And still others use informal operations as a fall-back when they get laid off or have unexpected expenses. Some return to Mexico because the life and lifestyle in the U.S. are too costly, both economically and socially. Lastly, most informals use their informal enterprises to provide hope for a better future for their children and for the next generation.

Consumption Informality

While we have primarily focused on the supply side of economic informality and underground activities up to this point, consumption, or demand, also deserves some explicit attention. In the summer of 2010, we conducted our Consumer Informality Survey of 357 consumers in South Texas to determine their purchase patterns with regards to over 120 select informal and underground goods and services. As these questions were sensitive in nature, we employed a purposive sampling design, utilizing embedded local interviewers to maximize respondent trust and response. Hence our findings are illustrative rather than definitive.

Nearly all our respondents (98.9%, or all but four) engaged in at least one form of consumption informality. We found high rates of at least one occasion of consumption participation for hiring someone to perform the following common household services: gardening (42.7%), housecleaning (34.9%), general home repair (43.1%), air conditioning repair (39.0%), and home remodeling (24.2%). Participation in underground activities, though less common, was widespread as well, including participation in gambling (16.5%), purchasing stolen goods (20.2%), visiting a house of prostitution (30.5%, men only), and using the services of a human smuggler or coyote (8.8%).

As we have argued, there is a widespread acceptance of informality that is reflected in the perceived morality of buying products "off the books." In our Consumer Informality Survey we asked, "How right or wrong is it to buy goods and services 'off the books'?" Only 31.8% felt it somewhat or completely wrong, leaving more than two-thirds with a positive or ambivalent view of buying informal products (see Figure 3.1). And even for the approximately one-third who believe it wrong to en-

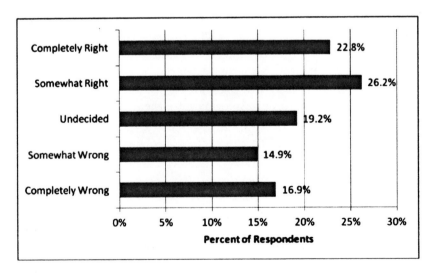

Figure 3.1. How right or wrong is it to buy goods and services "off the books"?

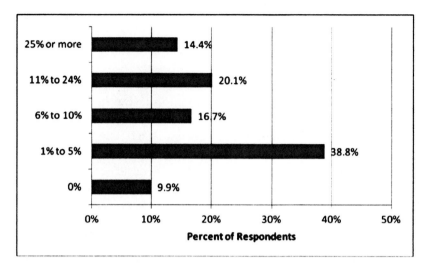

Figure 3.2. Percent of average weekly household purchases bought informally

gage in the purchase of informal products, 93.3% still admitted having purchased informal goods! Only four respondents of the 60 who indicated that buying "off the books" is completely wrong actually reported buying zero products informally.

We also asked about *regular* (at least weekly) household consumption and purchases of informal products. We found the volume of routine purchases to be considerable (see Figure 3.2). While fewer than 10% report they do not buy informally on a regular basis, over 90% report they do. And more than one-third of our respondents buy 11% or more of their household consumption through informal markets. Additionally, 49.9% of those surveyed reported frequently or occasionally initiating the process of buying "off the books." While consumers most often report using cash (89.5%) to facilitate their informal purchases, other cash substitutes are utilized—such as check (14.1%), barter (17.8%), credit/debit cards (12.3%), and food stamps/Lone Star card (10.3%). Together, these data suggest that consumption informality is an omnipresent feature of the South Texas economic landscape.[53]

Conclusion

In this chapter, we have examined the inordinate size of the informal economy of South Texas and have sought to explain why it is so large.

This has led us to examine both the micro-level factors that explain why individuals choose to engage in informal activities and the macro-level factors that produce so much informality in regions like the South Texas borderlands.

We contend that the push and pull factors that operate elsewhere are stronger in this border location, resulting in survival informality. People with their economic backs to the wall feel pushed out of the formal economy and pulled into informal activities, even if only for a time. But, as we pointed out in Chapter 1, factors that hold them in formal work or repel them from informality must also be considered at the micro-level. In this border environment (as during hard economic times everywhere), the usual hold and repel factors may be weakened.

Because of the large Mexican immigrant population and the greater acceptability in Mexico of using cash to hide informal transactions, for example, the negative stigma of informality is reduced. Likewise, when the investment needed to start an informal enterprise is low, one might feel less repelled by the prospect of having their enterprise closed or forfeited. Thus, though individuals everywhere go through push-pull and hold-repel decisions, we contend that the push-pull forces are stronger in the South Texas borderlands than in other regions of the U.S. and that the hold-repel forces are weaker here.

In addition, the South Texas border area has a multitude of factors that *facilitate* informality. Facilitating entrance into the informal sector is the widespread use of cash payments in the borderlands. Cash payments permit the skirting of government detection, whether for taxes, regulations, or work authorization. Additionally, fewer language barriers in the borderlands region ease communication between producer and consumer of informal goods and services. Also assisting in the prevalence of economic informality is the acceptance and long-standing nature of informality in Mexico as in South Texas through regular household consumption of informal goods and services. Nearly all consumers in the region engage in consumption informality, and the will of the government and government officials is correspondingly affected by this widespread violation of the law by the local population.

In this border environment, getting started in the informal sector is also facilitated by previously established social networks that can help one to find employment, get start-up tips, and even get low-cost start-up equipment through informal sources. Flea markets, which exist in large numbers throughout the South Texas borderlands, provide a source of informal sales and the low-cost equipment needed to start an informal business (e.g., lawn mowers).

In addition, the preponderance of informality in the area also facilitates even greater informality by straining the will and the capacity of government to control it. The high volume of *underground* activities (illegal drugs and immigration, especially) affects the ability of the state to enforce regulations against *informal* activities. When the area leads the nation in drug seizures, informal activities—especially those of the survival informality type—tend to be seen as less important and worthy of few resources. The courts especially are strained and overwhelmed. So even if the area had the power to thoroughly police informal activities, overwhelmed prosecutors would still lack the will to prosecute, resorting instead either to plea bargains or to simply dismissing cases.

The prevalence of informality is not just a function of the state's ability to enforce regulations. It also depends on the ability of individuals to leverage disparate regulations to their advantage. The federal government cannot depend on the state to help collect unreported income taxes because Texas has no state income tax and so no mechanism for collecting such taxes. Similarly, Texas gets little help from the federal government in apprehending or prosecuting individuals who fail to collect or pay state sales tax because there is, in most cases, no corresponding federal sales tax. To compound matters further, the laws and enforcement mechanisms of the U.S. frequently conflict with those of Mexico, creating a demand for prohibited goods or services in one country by legally obtaining these goods or services from the other.

The informal economy is also facilitated by the capacities of communities to organize to resist state controls and, simultaneously, to take advantage of the opportunities those controls create.[54] Undocumented informal workers in the area are often hidden by a sympathetic local— and mostly Mexican-origin—community. Even the local Anglo population becomes sympathetic to informal workers, especially undocumented workers, when they or their neighbors depend on them for child care and other services. This situation is particularly true on the border, not just because of the proximity of Mexico, but also because of the prevalence of so many additional regulations governing trade and cross-border exchange.

Informality thus provides a poverty-reduction "policy" by indirectly subsidizing the cost of living in one of the poorest sections of the country. The informal economy of South Texas absorbs and hides huge amounts of unemployment, underemployment, and irregular employment. All of these factors benefit the state by providing relative stability in an area of great economic need.

CHAPTER 4

Informality and Undocumented Workers

Within seven months of arriving in Laredo from Veracruz, Mexico, Abel Luna, an undocumented worker, was busy selling tamales door to door. His wife and sister-in-law made the tamales in a tiny apartment kitchen really too small for the business venture. Abel had come illegally with his wife, brother, and sister-in-law in search of a better life. At first, he tried securing an income by offering his labor as a gardener. That produced a few jobs mowing lawns for thirty-two-year-old Abel, though he could barely pay the rent and was afraid they would use up all they had saved for their new life. As Christmas arrived, Abel's wife Conchita wanted to make the family some tamales Veracruzana style. Abel asked one of his gardening customers if he could borrow some banana leaves from the family's small plot of banana trees. In the holiday spirit, Abel and Conchita shared their tamales with neighbors and were soon inundated with requests to buy these southern-Mexico-style tamales—and their tamale business was born.

When the tamales wrapped in banana leaves proved to be very popular and unique to the neighborhood, Abel exchanged a few dozen tamales every now and then with the tree owner. Over the two months since the tamale business started, the foursome has been able to generate sales of $300–$400 per week. This supplants but does not entirely replace the gardening business. Word-of-mouth promotion has helped their small informal enterprise as it continues to slowly grow. Though they fear being caught and deported or that others will prey upon their undocumented status, Abel and his family hope to one day regularize their immigration status and learn English.

Abel is one of the estimated 12 million illegal immigrants in the U.S., of whom two-thirds are thought to be from Mexico.[1] But unlike most of the undocumented Mexican workers who enter the U.S., Abel and his family are part of only 7–8% of this population who seek to remain in the border area.[2] Abel is also unlike many of the migrants who settle in the border area because he came without an embedded social network of family, friends, or contacts already living in the area. He may have chosen the border area because it is less expensive and ethnically more similar to Mexico than other parts of the U.S.[3] In addition, Laredo's proximity to Mexico allowed Abel and his family to come to South Texas with fewer start-up resources, though with greater opportunities of melting into the local environment, where 95% of the population is of Mexican origin.

But Abel and other immigrants who settle along the border pay a cost. Orrenius, Zavodny, and Lukens found an earnings penalty of $1.61 per hour (in 2006 dollars) for illegal Mexican immigrants who stop at the border rather than continue further into the U.S.[4] So the earning prospects for Abel and his family are not robust in the short term, given his border destination, educational background, lack of social network, and short time on the border. Nonetheless, if Abel and his family stick it out, within approximately 30 years they should expect to earn a modest living.[5] So, although Abel will struggle financially for some years to come, he has good reason to believe that he and his children will ultimately come out ahead for his decision to enter the U.S. illegally and work informally in a border location.

On the border, one runs into difficulties in precisely identifying who is undocumented and how their labor is informal. Officially, an undocumented worker is one who does not possess the proper entry and work authorization documents.[6] But as we discussed in Chapter 1, there are varying levels of documentation. The documentation continuum ranges from the polar ends of zero, or no documentation, to fully documented (i.e., U.S. citizenship). Some visas do not include work authorization, so, for example, those who come with a student or laser visa are unauthorized to work, but not undocumented. In this book, we refer to those who have such visas and work without authorization as "quasidocumented." To this category we might also add those who have documents that either are fraudulent or borrowed from a friend or relative.

Individuals who work with false or borrowed papers may report their income to the federal government, but they would still be considered informal workers because of their unauthorized work status. If they are apprehended, they may be charged not only with an immigration violation, but also with document fraud, possibly a felony. Similarly, those who knowingly hire workers with fraudulent documents may be prosecuted. Though it is difficult to prove that the employer had knowledge of a worker's undocumented status, the law still puts employers in the difficult position of having to judge whether an employee's papers are fraudulent, borrowed, or real. Though the law requires only that papers must *appear* to be legal, an employer could face legal difficulties if the Department of Homeland Security decides to prosecute.

For the wholly undocumented, regular trips back and forth across the border are not feasible. Backdoor arrangements such as "*un pasaporte negro*" (a black passport—border slang for an inner tube) to cross the Rio Grande/Bravo are utilized, and cross-border movement is highly restricted, not only by the Border Patrol, but increasingly by the Mexican cartels who demand a *plaza* (an extorted rent) for crossing their "territory." Yet once across, the undocumented, like the quasidocumented, find that their activities go largely unmonitored unless they draw attention to themselves. The complicated picture of informality, with its various categories of the undocumented/unauthorized, is shown in Figure 4.1.

Abel and other undocumented immigrants who settle along the border are not the only ones involved in undocumented informality. Employers who knowingly hire them are also part of this informal economy. Often, they benefit the most, paying very low wages and getting workers who will work hard at dangerous tasks for more than 8 hours a day and who can be otherwise exploited. Though there is some risk for these employers if caught, the rate of prosecution of employers is still very low.[7]

Many local employers benefit from the undocumented in a variety of jobs and work situations. Gilbert Maldonado, for example, is a farmer who hires illegal immigrants in South Texas. He sees undocumented workers as a win-win opportunity for himself and for his undocumented workers. He said, "I admit that I have them work from dawn till dusk. It's not about treating them like slaves; it's about keeping up with the competition." Gilbert receives hard-working and pliant workers at a very low cost. He continued, "They are good, hard workers, and I would gladly hire them over any American. Many of them are in desperate need of a job to help their starving families back in Mexico. I have sympathy for them because my great-grandfather was an immigrant from Mexico." Gilbert concluded by saying, "I think I treat them pretty fair. My wife cooks tacos of egg and beans for breakfast, and I even give them some rooms to stay in."

Though Gilbert does offer employment that enables undocumented workers to make a living, his motivation seems less altruistic than eco-

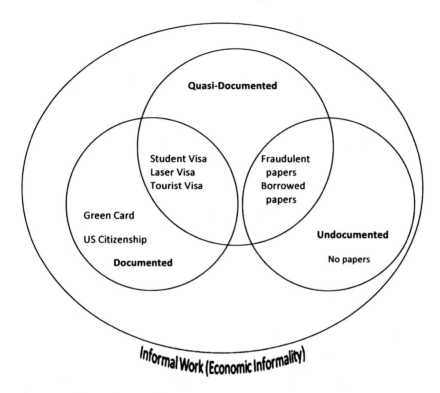

Figure 4.1. The confluence of documentation and economic informality
Notes:
1) The informal sector (or informal work or economic informality) describes a world of work performed outside the realm of government regulation. Yet informal work activity is not said to be criminal, in the sense that the work itself could be undertaken within the bounds of government regulation.
2) Undocumented = One does not possess papers to cross into *or* work in the U.S.
3) Documented = One possesses valid papers to cross into *and* work in the U.S.
4) Quasidocumented = One possesses papers to cross into *or* work in the U.S.
A laser, tourist, or student visa allows one to cross into the U.S. Fraudulent or borrowed papers may allow one to either cross into the U.S. (e.g., laser visa) or to live and work in the U.S. (e.g., green card).

nomic. He feeds his men "tacos of egg and beans for breakfast" but offers only very minimal housing. He provides an opportunity for workers on the economic margins to survive, but he gets workers who will work 15-hour days at less than the minimum wage. We propose that such treatment of undocumented workers, especially in agriculture, represents a form of dependent exploitation (see Chapter 3).

Undocumented Workers and the
Informal South Texas Border Economy

Actually, our research finds a wide mix of reasons for employing undocumented workers. Though we found many cases of clearly exploitative treatment, we also found many individuals who offer help to the undocumented without expecting disproportionate economic rewards. The story of María and Olivia Mariscal, two sisters who crossed the border illegally on a rubber inner tube and found work as undocumented maids with a supportive family, illustrates the nonexploitative network that many undocumented use in gaining employment and/or starting a business. Their story, as told by their interviewer, illustrates how family, friends, and employers often contribute to the success of undocumented workers.

> María, twenty-five, is a very beautiful person with a great laugh and a good personality. I first met María at a convenience store I manage. The employee who recommended María said that she was her neighbor's niece. I needed someone to look after my mom who had just had open-heart surgery and was confined to bed. María came to work for us for $60 per week, plus room and board. My mom, though, wasn't the only one needing her assistance. My younger brother Alex is mentally retarded. Alex is capable of doing most things for himself, yet there are some things he needs help doing.
>
> María worked out great with both my mom and with Alex. She was very helpful around the house and would always do what was asked of her. On Friday afternoon, I would take her back to her aunt's house. When Mom was in the hospital, María would work some weeks and not others. She needed a full-time job so she found one and asked if it was O.K. to stay with us on weekends. My mom told her that she would always have a place in her home and to never hesitate to call if she needed anything. María had a strong bond with my mom, and we always looked forward to her coming. She became more like a younger sister than a maid.
>
> María is intelligent and had attended secretarial school in Mexico. While she was staying with us, we helped her learn English, and she became assimilated in the ways of "The Valley." She must have changed jobs ten times because she always looked to move up. She found a guy in McAllen who she had known while working at the *maquiladoras* (global assembly plants) in Mexico. When they got married, she still kept in

touch with us. One day María called asking if her sister, Olivia, could stay with my mom until she could find a job. We helped Olivia find a job as a maid, but her first employer was mean, so we helped her find a job that paid even more money with kinder people. Recently, Olivia also moved up from this job when she purchased a portable sewing machine and began making belts from the tops of soft drink cans.

These sisters always surprised us with how daring they are. One day, for example, María called to ask me to take her shopping for a car. She didn't even know how to drive. She had been working for one hundred dollars a week and had managed to send money home to her mother and siblings in Mexico and still save enough money to pay $1,500 for a car. Even though she had no license and no insurance that are required to get the plates, she got her aunt to do everything she needed and drove the car home that evening.

With her car, María soon began taking bales of clothes back to Mexico whenever she visited her family there. Then she got a border crossing card that allowed her to cross legally, though not to work. María takes clothes to another sister, Elena, who lives in Reynosa. They set up a used clothing store in Elena's home. María and Olivia still visit my mom on the weekends, and we have set aside a room for them when they come. My mom always looks forward to seeing María and Olivia.

Ethnographic accounts like that of María and Olivia prompted us to examine the extent to which undocumented workers move up a ladder of mobility with increasing time in the U.S. borderlands. Though we do not have longitudinal data that would more adequately answer the question, a cross-sectional analysis strongly suggests a hierarchy that may be evidence of a ladder of increasing self-employment and rising income as one moves from undocumented immigrant to quasidocumented to resident and finally to U.S. citizen.[8] This is reflected in Table 4.1, which is based on our interviews of informal workers in South Texas.

The pattern shown in Table 4.1 is one of steady increase in the percentage who are self-employed as the level of U.S. legal status rises from completely undocumented to those who are U.S. citizens. Only 46% of the undocumented in our Informal and Underground Survey of informal workers were self-employed, compared to 83% of the citizens in the sample. Conversely, the *percentage* of income that informals earn from informal work decreases with each level from undocumented to U.S. citizen. Almost all of the income earned by the undocumented was from informal work, while U.S. citizens in our sample who were

Table 4.1. Self-employed informal activities (N = 526)

Immigration Status	% Self-Employed^	% Annual Income from Informal Work	Total Annual Income (U.S.$)
Undocumented	46.4	93.2	11,616
Quasidocumented (Other)	63.2	70.1	11,755
Resident Alien	71.3	66.9	18,892
U.S. Citizen	82.9	57.8	28,359

^Those not self-employed work for a wage or salary.
Difference between self-employment and wage and salaried employment: Pearson Chi-Square = 33.607; df = 3; p = .000.
Difference between percent of annual income earned in informal work: ANOVA, F = 11.076; p = .000.
Difference between Total Annual Incomes: ANOVA, F = 9.115; p = .000.
Source: Informal and Underground Survey.

involved in informal work relied on informality for only 58 percent of their income. This seems to suggest movement from informal to formal work as immigration status becomes regularized. Finally, Table 4.1 shows that with each increasing level of legal status, total annual income rises, more than doubling from the $11,616 earned yearly by the undocumented to the average of $28,359 earned by U.S. citizens involved in informal work.

The work history of Beto Perez (mentioned in Chapter 3) and others supports our hierarchical earnings ladder conceptualization. Beto began as a marginalized scavenger. He was able to raise his and his family's station in life after twenty years in the scavenging business. He now employs a few undocumented workers to help with the scavenging and makes enough money to occasionally help his son in medical school. His business is still informal, but it has helped his son move into the upper reaches of the formal economy.

Daniel Lozano, a middle-aged informal auto mechanic, also hopes to create a better life for his children. Daniel stated, "I've been working my whole life and will probably continue to work until the point when I cannot physically work anymore. That is why I tell my kids to do well in school, so they can have better opportunities than I had."

Those informals who are able to regularize their documented status over time find it easier to transition into the formal sector where pay and especially benefits are better. Pisani and Yoskwoitz found a relationship between earnings and degree of documentation that we believe is reflected in Figure 4.2.[9]

Figure 4.2 suggests that enhanced documentation permits higher earnings potential because the hazards associated with informality by compulsion leave fewer earnings possibilities. More specifically, those who are undocumented and who do not possess fraudulent or borrowed papers are subject to the whims of the employer and deportation authorities and remain vulnerable throughout their stay in South Texas. In contrast, those with the full right to work in the U.S. experience informality more as a choice: to earn supplemental income, to avoid the loss of social benefits, to evade government regulations, or to maximize income by avoiding taxes. Those in the middle (the quasidocumented), have papers allowing them to be in the U.S. but may lack the authorizations to work, lessening their fears of deportation but not of employer abuse.

Furthermore, we find that the amount of time spent as an informal on average is inversely related to documentation status. That is, the undocumented are primarily full-time informal economic participants while the fully documented may engage in informality more selectively. Lastly, we suggest those who engage in self-employment or entrepreneurial activities are better situated to enhance their earnings potential than informals without documentation who work for someone else.[10]

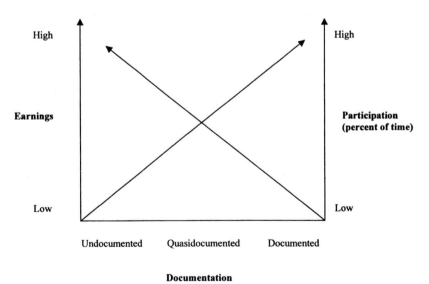

Figure 4.2. Earnings, participation, and documentation in informal markets

Though all work done by the undocumented should probably be regarded as informal, several respondents to the survey seem to have believed their work was informal only if they avoided paying taxes. Some undocumenteds who reported income from formal work are probably those working with false or borrowed documents, who have taxes and Social Security deducted[11] and, hence, who consider such employment formal work. In addition, some, like María, set up cross-border businesses using a laser visa (a permit for short shopping trips) to conduct a portion of their business on both sides of the border. Their work would be informal, not only because of their immigration status, but also because they skirt regulations and taxes on either or both sides of the border. On the border, these distinctions between informal and formal work are not quite so clear as they may be in other locations. Informality in border locations is complicated by high degrees of cross-border mobility and trade and the differing laws in the two neighboring countries.

Vignettes such as the preceding about María and Olivia help us better understand the precarious circumstances of, the resourcefulness of, and the networking used by undocumented workers on the South Texas border. They must find a way to make ends meet in a foreign land where customs, laws, institutions, and language are unfamiliar. Often, one family member gets a toehold by getting a job and establishing a good relationship with locals. Then they send money to family back home and also manage to help bring across family or friends and help them get established. Some, like María, even manage to start a business and to find a way to cross the border legally.

Social Capital and Informality among Undocumented Workers

Though some employers do take advantage of informal workers' vulnerable position, many, like María's employer, become part of an informal help network. In our 1994 Undocumented Mexican Workers Survey (which did not include live-in maids), we asked the 150 respondents to describe who helped them find their current job. Only 17% got such help directly from the employer or from a formal job announcement. Almost half (48%) said they got this help mainly from friends or relatives, while 25% relied on other undocumented workers. In María's case, we should recall that she obtained her job when María's aunt approached a neighbor, who in turn approached her own employer at the convenience store. And then María's employer (and the employer's mother) became part of a help network that enabled María to help her sister find work and help María get a car that she used to start a business.

Similar results were obtained in the Pew Hispanic Center's Survey of Mexican Migrants,[12] a survey of almost 5,000 Mexican migrants. This survey found that family networks played a key role in locating jobs for many migrants. For example, 45% of respondents reported that talking with friends and relatives in the U.S. was the most commonly used method of finding a job in the U.S. Respondents to the Survey of Mexican Migrants had very strong familial connections to the U.S. More than 75% of respondents had a relative other than a spouse or child in the U.S., even including respondents who had been in the U.S. for only two years or less. Most migrants (67%) reported that relatives lived in the same town as the respondent, and a majority (54%) of respondents indicated they lived in the same household as the relative.

These help networks are part of the social capital that undocumented informal workers find extremely important in finding work and in confronting the daily problems they face in a strange land. When we asked the undocumented workers in our 1994 Survey of Undocumented Mexican Workers to whom they turned for help when things were not going well, the largest response category (31%) was relatives and the second largest group (24%) was employers, followed by fellow workers (20%), friends other than fellow workers (20%), and others (5%). Social capital is an important resource for undocumented workers.

Some of the first mentions of the term "social capital" came from Jane Jacobs, Pierre Bourdieu and Jean-Claude Passeron, Glen Loury, James Coleman, Ronald Burt, Robert Putnam, and Alejandro Portes.[13] Portes and Sensenbrenner[14] argue that there are at least four different forms of expectations associated with social capital, each related to one of the major sociological theoretical traditions. The tradition that seems to best encapsulate our use of the term is Georg Simmel's focus on "reciprocity transactions," or norms and obligations that emerge from personalized networks of exchange.[15]

Portes[16] and Light[17] both examined different immigrant groups in the U.S. and found that successful communities offer new arrivals help with securing informal sources of credit, insurance, child support, English language training, and job referrals. Massey and Espinosa[18] examined Mexican immigration to the U.S. and showed that social capital is a far better predictor of where people will migrate, in what numbers, and for what reasons than the classical and human capital theories. Furthermore, Aguilera and Massey argue that wages of undocumented workers rise when they utilize embedded social networks, substantially more if the social networks are particularly strong and effective.[19] In other words, social capital may be a very strong pull factor or, conversely, when it is lacking, a strong repel factor in the decision of whether to migrate. Many researchers have found that social capital can promote common values and culture and help members band together for mutual benefit.

But social capital can also have its downsides. Networks that become too tight can limit contact with the outsiders who are needed to supply jobs and other resources. Communities can become exclusive, promoting the formation of gangs and even interethnic violence. The family, a major source of social capital, may also impose on entrepreneurs obligations that divert resources from potential investments. Portes and Sensenbrenner[20] looked at the difficulties some network members encounter in trying to leave a tight community in order to succeed economically. They found that some will anglicize their names and join outside groups (or religions) in order to free themselves from these tight networks.

By and large, however, social capital is seen as a positive resource for immigrant communities. Bourdieu[21] first used the term *social capital* in the 1970s to refer to the advantages and opportunities people gain through membership in certain communities. Their ethnic identity, their common language, and their strong norms of reciprocity promote trust and offers of reciprocal help. Trust makes many things possible. Trust generated by social capital can facilitate cooperation for the benefit of the entire ethnic community.

Though in María's case her employer became a friend and part of her help network, employers are often not part of this trust network and may be less than helpful. Over one-third (35%) of our survey respondents in the Undocumented Mexican Workers Survey said that their employer never treated them like a friend or a member of the family, though 26% did report frequently enjoying such treatment. Another 39% said that their employer sometimes treated them that way.

Depending upon one's social capital, finding work may be extremely difficult or relatively easy. For those with limited documentation, like María and Olivia, having embedded family and a social network of relatives, friends, and an extended community provides greatly increased access to job information and opportunities. Work may be found through employment in family enterprises or by having neighbors, family, or friends on the lookout for job opportunities. Those same individuals can then vouch for the person seeking work.

One of our subjects, Guillermo Martinez, found quick employment as a bricklayer when his cousin, an American citizen, hired him and provided Guillermo with a fraudulent Social Security number. Guillermo does not worry about being caught or questioned by others about his work status. We found other cases, however, in which the strong networks of social capital gave undocumented workers a false sense of security. Claudia Marroquin, for example, used family to integrate herself into her new country. She married an American citizen and they had two children. Even though Claudia could have filed her immigration paperwork to legalize her status, she chose to work as an undocumented worker for the first four years of their marriage. When she was finally caught and almost deported, Claudia decided to regularize her status. Since Claudia was embedded into the local environment, finding work was not too difficult even though she was undocumented. Claudia remembered, "Even when I was an undocumented worker and without the privilege of having a Social Security number, my employers most of the time would say, 'Don't worry,' and provided a false number themselves."

Twenty-six-year-old Ana María and her younger sister, twenty-year-old Luisa, both from San Luis Potosí, Mexico, crossed illegally using fake visas. They were helped by a lady who assisted them in finding their first jobs.[22] Ana María and Luisa are maids working on neighboring ranches for the same extended family. In securing employment as a maid, Ana María said "It is the easiest job to find without the hassle of claiming to be illegal. People just automatically understand that we are from Mexico and know that they don't have to spend a lot of money as they would with someone that is from here." Both Ana María and Luisa work hard five days a week, earning $85 per week. They are required "to clean the house and make sure dinner is ready." Ana María and Luisa have a nice place to stay, warm food, and earn a lot more than they did back home. For the next-door employers, hiring sisters helps stretch the length of time both maids are likely to remain, for the sisters' proximity to each other alleviates the loneliness of their live-in maid duties. It also allows Ana María and Luisa to be together on the weekends—a win-win situation. Thus, some employers become part of the networks of assistance because of advantages they perceive for themselves in doing so.

Those undocumenteds or quasidocumenteds who are not socially embedded find their search for employment much more difficult. They are more vulnerable to exploitation, as well as to deportation and may become disenchanted with the America they had dreamed about. Sergio Mata came to the U.S. in hopes of finding work, but he had no network of family or friends. He finally resorted to standing outside HEB (a major, privately-held Texas grocery store chain based out of San Antonio, with long ties to the border region and Mexico). He was approached by an elderly Anglo couple asking if he wanted a job. Sergio said yes and the Anglo couple took him to their home. At first, he mowed their lawn and maintained the outside of the house. He was pleased with his treatment. Then the couple wanted Sergio to do more. They asked him to build a deck, paint the inside of the house, and do other construction-like work. Sergio recalled, "They employed me to cut the yard and only paid me to cut the yard. I got upset but didn't want to say anything. The couple was good to me, but I just felt taken advantage of. I needed the work and the money so I kept my mouth shut. I worked with them for many years until I found something new."[23]

Without a network to provide a base from which to live and operate, finding (even informal) work once one crosses into the U.S. may be very challenging, as illustrated by Sergio's story. One alternative to finding employment that is often used by those with low social capital is self-employment. This option is used by some to overcome the lack of assistance in finding an employer and negotiating the obstacles associated with the lack of the proper work authorization credentials.

Self Employment

Though some undocumented immigrants may, like María and her sister Olivia, find self-employment as the end result of their quest to establish themselves in the U.S., other newly arrived undocumented immigrants use it when they become discouraged in finding an employer willing to hire them. Self-employment may form a viable option for gainful, first-employment for undocumented and the quasidocumented workers who lack social capital.[24] For many men, the most expedient self-employment returns come from landscaping or home gardening.[25]

Mario Mejía became a self-employed gardener in the McAllen-Edinburg area soon after his arrival. As an undocumented with only fraudulent crossing papers, Mario had difficulty finding work. After multiple job rejections due to his lack of proper work documentation, Mario decided to offer his services as a landscaper—mowing lawns at cut-rate prices. In essence, Mario gave up his search for informal wage employment and began a one-man lawn-care service in his effort to survive. Slowly, Mario built up a clientele as he differentiated his gardening service based on low prices. Mario noted that the work was hard and sometimes scarce (especially in winter months), though at least he created work that paid him somewhat better than he could find in his native Mexico. Though Mario feels it is better to accept low wages rather than going back to Mexico, he also understands he is barely hanging on in his new country. He added, "I know people [think] I'm just another dirty Mexican trying to cut their yard, but the money I make supports my wife and newborn baby back home. Work in Mexico is scarce; I have to be a man and support my family."

Mario was able to start his business with almost no start-up financing. In their study of self-employed gardeners in South Texas, Pisani and Yoskowitz found there were minimal start-up costs: 14% began with zero ($0) equipment (necessitating borrowing home owners' equipment), and nearly half began their businesses with equipment worth less than $100.[26] Many workers can find used equipment at bargain prices at local flea markets. Additionally, 75% of self-employed gardeners self-financed what equipment they did need, and more than 80% of gardeners worked informally. This high level of informality allows easy entry of the undocumented or quasidocumented into this occupational field because official work authorization is rarely required or asked for by homeowners or others seeking to hire these workers.

Other small business owners who are undocumented actually begin with the hope of turning their businesses into formal enterprises. The case of Cesar Tames illustrates the obstacles they encounter because of their undocumented status. Cesar is a forty-year-old undocumented man who completed the ninth grade in Mexico. He operates a company to install fences. He related,

> We started without any money and we're still in debt. We didn't even have any experience in building fences. We learned just by asking as we went along. We would ask for half the money down at the start of the project and the other half once we finished. We make between $200 to $300 per project. Right now I offer chain-link and cedar fences, but I would like to also offer iron-works, motorized doors, and different designs. That would increase my sales.
>
> If clients don't call you, you have to go out and find them. The key to success is your *ganas* (drive) to get ahead—also knowing your business (industry) and having patience to wait out the bad times. Right now

my business is not generating much profit. I know because I develop financial projections and account for all my expenses—water, light, gasoline—and then figure out how much I have to sell to generate a profit. I use Excel spreadsheets to do this.

I'm my only employee, but I subcontract part of my work to another small company. This company has three employees that come and do the work for me. I advertise in the yellow pages, but former clients [word of mouth] bring me most of my business. We also leave little signs on past projects (fences) with our name and phone number on them. People see these signs and then call us. I also go out and pass out my business cards. My advantage over the larger fence companies is that I can charge lower prices because I don't have as many expenses as they do. Their advantage is that they have been around for so long and they're well established. Also, they have more resources—larger inventories and better rates with suppliers.

I like to be honest. Right now, my business is registered with the court house, with the IRS, and with the sales taxes people (Texas Comptroller of Public Accounts). I've reported all my earnings since I first started my business. But because I am an undocumented immigrant, I can't receive any form of assistance. None. I report all my earnings. I also pay taxes on my property and pay sales taxes as well. Also, because of my immigration status nobody wants to lend me money. Just yesterday, Acción Texas told me, for the second time, that they would not lend me any money. The banks are even worse. They are simply not an option for me.

My main problem, though, is from government people who are not adequately prepared to deal with people like me. If the government is going to allow someone with an ITIN (Individual Tax Identification Number) to establish a business, then government officials who work with the public should be made aware of this. After I got my ITIN, I had a problem getting my Texas Sales Tax Permit. There was a huge line and the attendants there didn't want to listen to me. The first things they asked for were my Social Security card and driver's license. When I told them that I didn't have them, their response basically was, 'Whenever you have them, come back.' So, basically, I had to get my permit over the Internet. There I didn't have any problems.

When I went to the court house and explained my situation, they also asked for my driver's license and Social Security card. I tried explaining to them that I'm from Mexico—and that I already had my ITIN and sales tax permit. The first thing they said was, 'If you don't have your papers, there's no way you can have a business.' In truth, though, you can. It takes a lot of effort, but it can be done.

Many observers are surprised that the undocumented really can own businesses. In fact, by doing so, they avoid the necessity of having to present a Social Security number to a prospective employer. But as Cesar's case illustrates, the odds are greatly stacked against them. Some journalists and politicians accuse them of wanting welfare, cheating on taxes, and draining public resources. As a result, many who would comply with formal requirements give up on the formal route and move further into the shadows of informality (beyond their undocumented status).

Cynical observers would also be surprised to learn how many undocumented individuals pay taxes and how few use public services. Using data from the Mexican Migration Project, Catalina Amuedo-Dorantes and Cynthia Bansak found that during the 1986-2006 time period, 55% of undocumented migrants in border states had Social Security taxes withheld, and 52% had federal taxes withheld. In relation to the charge that the undocumented are predominantly on welfare, these authors found that only 5% received food stamps and only 10% used some form of public assistance to pay for their health care, even though 25% of them had visited a hospital.[27] They conclude, "In all instances, contrary to the general public perception, immigrants in U.S. border states appear more likely to pay government taxes and less likely to use public services."[28] So the net benefit resides with government and not with undocumented immigrants.

Erasmo Mendiola is another self-employed undocumented individual who works as a residential painter. When he first started five years ago, Erasmo worked for a friend. Soon, however, he realized that he could strike out on his own and earn more. Erasmo learned English, which helped him become independent. He now has an annual income of $20,000 and a small work crew to assist him. He says, "The work is hard and it is not always steady. Being undocumented is not always easy, especially when my customers refuse to pay me. There's not much I can do."

Table 4.2 below shows average hourly wages for several informal activities, based on responses from undocumenteds in our Informal and Underground Survey.[29] Most of the hourly rates are, on average, below the legal minimum wage. In Table 4.2, the informal activities marked by an asterisk (*) are those that tend to have high rates of self-employment.

Table 4.2. Informal activities and hourly earnings of undocumenteds (N = 110)

Informal Activity	Hourly Earnings in U.S.$
*General Buyer/Re-Seller of Goods	9.78
*Yard/General Repair	3.48
Fieldworker/Ranch Hand	3.85
Maid/Janitor	4.92
*Sells Products in Mexico	5.96
Construction/Skilled Manual Labor	4.61
*Food Vendor	2.98
*Retail (mom-and-pop outlets)	4.74
Other	5.05
Average (std. dev.)	5.52 (5.36)

Source: Informal and Underground Survey.
* = Generally self-employed.

Table 4.2 reveals no clear advantage for self-employed informal workers, except for those who buy and resell goods (which may require more capital). Often, such sales are done in flea markets or across the border. The earnings for all the other categories are not sufficient to bring these undocumented individuals above the poverty line. At the national level, the income figures are somewhat better, but still substantially lower than the figures for legal immigrants and U.S. citizen workers. The Pew Hispanic Center[30] estimated that 21% of undocumented workers earned incomes in 2008 that were below the poverty line, while the incomes of only 13% of legal immigrants and 10% of U.S. citizen workers were that low.

Wage and Paid Labor

The three informal activities in Table 4.2 that are not primarily self-employed workers are fieldworker/ranch hand, maid/janitor, and construction/skilled manual labor. Before we briefly describe these three categories, we need to point out how our local data correspond to data collected on undocumented wage earners at the national level. The

Survey of Mexican Migrants mentioned above used somewhat similar categories and found that at the national level 4 out of 5 Mexican migrants were employed in just five industries: agriculture (11%), hospitality (17%), construction (19%), manufacturing (19%), and cleaning/ maintenance/domestic service (14%).[31] They found that the predominance of any one of these categories varied considerably from one part of the U.S. to another. In addition, the weekly earnings for all respondents yielded a median of only $300 per week. Finally, over one-third of these workers (38%) experienced periods of unemployment lasting at least a month. The lowest earnings were found among women, those who speak no English, and those who do not have U.S. government-issued documentation.

Critics of undocumented workers often oppose granting them any form of "amnesty" that would allow them to legalize their status. They claim it would be unfair to legal immigrants who "stood in line" if those who came illegally didn't have to follow the same application process. This point of view ignores the fact that there is, practically speaking, no "line" for Mexican laborers who want to come legally. Only two of the sixteen employment-based visa categories for temporary immigrant status are available to low-skilled workers. One of these, the H2A, is restricted to agricultural workers, and the other, the H2B, is capped at 66,000 visas per year and is limited to "seasonal" or "temporary" work. In addition, only one of the five categories of visas for permanent immigration status is tailored to less-skilled workers, and it is capped at 5,000 visas per year. In other words, Mexican workers who want to come legally are crowded into categories that offer very few visas and often for only part of the year.[32]

Even Mexican workers lucky enough to have close family members who are U.S. citizens have a very long line to stand in. In the case of Mexican nationals, wait times for visas under the "family preference" system are currently 7 to 10 years for the spouse of a legal permanent resident and 10 to 12 years for an unmarried, adult child of a U.S. citizen.[33] Even if they manage to get to the head of the line, they need to show that they have guaranteed employment that will pay substantially above the poverty line, or show that they "will not become a public charge." Because formal channels are so restricted, many come the only way they can, as "illegal aliens," or undocumented workers.

Also, at the national level, some labor categories have very high rates of undocumented workers. According to Passel and Cohn,[34] 25% of all farm laborers in the U.S. are undocumented immigrants, as are 19% of building, grounds keeping and maintenance workers, and 17% of construction workers. Undocumented immigrants make up 40% of all brick masons in the U.S., and they make up nearly that high a share of drywall installers (37%). They also are 28% of dishwashers, 27% of maids and housekeepers, and 21% of parking lot attendants. With respect to industry shares, undocumenteds comprise 28% of workers in landscaping, 20% of those involved in dry cleaning and laundry, 13% of agriculture industry workers, and 10% of the leisure and hospitality workforce.

Fieldworker/Ranch Hand. At or near the bottom of wage earners are undocumented field and ranch hands. In a national study of 6,472 farm workers, the U.S. Department of Labor[35] found that 56% of respondents reported that their family income (from all sources) was less than $15,000 per year. Over 80% of respondents reported yearly family incomes of less than $25,000. Though this survey did not specify the legal status of these workers, it did find that 75% of them were born in Mexico.[36] The Survey of Mexican Migrants also found very low weekly earnings among agricultural workers, with 60% of them reporting earnings of less than $300 per week.[37]

At the national level, the Survey of Mexican Migrants[38] found that 11% of respondents were working in agriculture, with these about equally divided between men and women. This study found, however, that the percentage of undocumented who are employed as agricultural workers has declined from 17% among those who have been here 15 years or longer to only 9% of recent arrivals. At the same time, the percentage employed in construction and hospitality has increased from 23% to 42%.[39]

The higher percentage of our own sample in the Informal and Underground Survey who were engaged in farm and ranch work is most likely indicative of the importance of this occupation for the undocumented in South Texas. Farming and ranching are still a major part of the economy of South Texas, so the area attracts Mexican migrants with an agricultural background. South Texas is also the home base for the largest number of "follow-the-crops migrants" in the U.S.[40] Many undocumented immigrants, particularly those with a rural background, come to this area to join these migrant streams.[41]

Hoeing, irrigating, fence-making/mending, and harvesting are common jobs in farm or ranch work in South Texas. Carlos Mendoza remembered spending hours, days, and weeks digging holes for the poles and then threading barbed wire to the poles to construct fences. Carlos recalled that on one job he worked all day weeding and hoeing and then spent the early evening making fences. That lasted for three weeks. When the time to get paid came around, Carlos mentioned that "the *patrón* (employer) was going to pay us for cleaning the fields . . . but not for the fence work, claiming that he only had enough money to pay for clearing the field. I told the *patrón* that we worked very hard, but he only said that he was sorry and that there was nothing he could do. What could I do, being an undocumented worker? Who could I complain to? I had no rights." Like many undocumented workers, Carlos felt powerless because his informal status afforded him little recourse in the formal system, even when his employer violated their agreement.

One strategy of some undocumented workers is to gain experience within the system and learn how to outmaneuver those who would exploit the vulnerability of the undocumented. José Miranda began working the agricultural fields over a decade ago. When he first arrived as an undocumented worker he would not argue about the miserable pay the farmers gave him. After some time in the fields, he slowly noticed that those with papers were paid more than those without. José recalled, "At first I was afraid to even speak to the crew leaders. I knew that others working in the same fields were getting paid more than me simply because they had papers and I didn't." The crew chiefs would pocket the difference between what the farmer paid and what the crew chief doled out to the workers, preying on the undocumented's lack of legal recourse. Notwithstanding his lack of papers, José no longer works for crew chiefs who pay him less than other workers. With his ten years of experience in the industry, José stated, "I know many of the *mayordomos* (crew chiefs) lie to people about the pay so that they can keep the difference. But now I will argue with them to get my money even if they threaten to call *la migra* (Border patrol) on me." Though still undocumented, José is better able to navigate the thin line between exploitation and the need to work.

Children, too, are part of the story of undocumented informality. It is not uncommon to see children working in the fields, especially during harvest season.[42] Some undocumented families make the conscious choice of not involving their children, as is the case with Juan and María Ortega. María recalled, "We started working in the fields for about 75 cents to $1.00 per bucket (about $25–$30 per day). It was hard work that didn't leave us much time for our families. Sometimes, I would see people bring their children to help, but that didn't make much difference since kids were paid less and they tired quickly. No matter how bad we needed the money, never did we take our children to the fields."

The demand side of the equation is not often addressed. Employers are concerned with finding good help at the right price, getting rid of bad help while minimizing losses, and staying competitive in the business environment. Employers can be fair and compassionate or harsh and exploitative. One of our informants interviewed two rather detached ranchers, Ernie Miller and Tom Moon. Each employs undocumented workers who are jacks-of-all-trades on the ranch. Ernie said, "They do everything," and when they do not know how to accomplish a task then "they can learn or leave." Their interviewer noted the casualness with which they discussed undocumented labor, stating "Landowners talk to each other about the undocumented as if they were talking about a pickup or a tractor. They ask each other such questions as, 'How's that new Mexican of yours working out?' Or if one says that they have a job around the ranch that needs to be done but they don't quite feel like tending to it, the other will say 'Get a wetback' or 'My Mexicans are there if you need 'em.'" Neither Ernie nor Tom was worried about getting caught employing undocumented workers. They felt the worst that would happen to them was that their workers would be deported and they might possibly pay a small fine. In a dry, cost-benefit analysis, the $30 daily wage paid by Ernie and Tom would easily offset any potential levied fines.

Maid/Janitor. Though undocumented female immigrants are employed in a wide range of activities, domestic work is a primary occupation for female migrants. The Survey of Mexican Migrants reported that wages for women are well below those earned by men. Whereas 74% of female respondents earned less than $300 per week, only 38% of men earned less than that amount. In large part, this is related to the industry distribution of these workers: 82% of Mexican migrants employed in domestic service (almost all of whom are women) earned less than $300 per week.[43]

Dora Morales works as a maid. Though she has a husband and five children in southern Mexico, the twenty-six-year-old illegally crossed the border in order to provide for her family. Dora commented, "I work for this family because I have to help my husband support our family. He works too, but it isn't a lot of money, and we have five children to feed. The money I get here sure helps out. I send money every month with my brother, and I try to go home every few months, but then it's hard to say goodbye to my kids." While Dora is grateful for the opportunity to help provide for her own family, she lamented her treatment. "I have been accused several times of stealing from the families, but then they find what they thought was missing, and forget they said anything to me. It hurts my feelings that no one apologizes to me." Furthermore, Dora is treated as an "other" and is forced to eat separately from the family she labors for. Her employer does not call her by name, but rather by the more pejorative *"sirvienta"* ("maid"). Dora believes her fate is to always be a maid like her mother before her, as she does not have an education or papers to work legally in the U.S.[44]

Construction/Skilled Manual Labor. Construction work is a primary source of jobs for Mexican male migrants and is a male-dominated job market. Only 29% of Mexican migrants in the construction industry (the vast majority of them men) made less than $300 per week.[45] Antonio Moreno currently lives in McAllen, his home for the last four years. Though born and raised in Monterrey, Mexico, Antonio was encouraged to come to the U.S. by his American cousins who lived in McAllen. Still without proper work authorization papers, Antonio used his cousin's connections to land a job in construction. Though he regrets that taxes are taken out of his paycheck, he is generally happy with his earnings. He stated, "I like it here because I'm making a decent living. I get paid the minimum wage, and I only work eight hours a day." However, Antonio often relies on his cousins for housing, social networks, and protection. Periodically, Antonio does get picked up by the Border Patrol and taken back to Mexico. Antonio does not find this a big problem; he insists that he is easily able to return across the border bridge the same day by using his excellent command of English to answer immigration and customs officials appropriately.[46] Antonio hopes to one day legalize his residency; he really appreciates the U.S. But not everyone treats Antonio with respect. His coworkers call him names like 'mojado' ("wetback") and have fun at his expense by crying out 'Ahí viene la Migra' (the Border Patrol is coming)!

A Third Labor Market?

Where do these undocumented workers fit in the American labor market? As Cross and Johnson[47] point out, dual labor market theory in sociology differs from classical and neoclassical economic theory by positing two distinct labor markets in advanced postindustrial societies. The primary labor market offers high wages, easy access to upward mobility, and good job security to well-positioned workers. The secondary labor market provides much lower wages, weak job security, and poor chances of upward mobility, but it at least enjoys minimal government involvement and tax-related benefits. This split labor market is said to reproduce in the market the inequalities of society by marginalizing racial, ethnic, and gender minorities from access to the mechanisms of mobility, such as education, control over their workplace, and the credentials needed for advancement.

Cross and Johnson[48] posit that there is a third labor market—one made up of those unable to access either of these other two sectors. This is clearly where we see the vast majority of undocumented workers. Their work is not criminal (by most current definitions). And although they remain outside the protections of the law, they are subject to its penalties for the simple act of working without authorization. As a result, the labor market has a third and more distinct split that marginalizes the undocumented even further from the already minimal avenues of mobility open to the secondary labor market. Those in the third sector perform work normally avoided by the other two markets, and their labor often disproportionately benefits employers and workers in these other two markets. Often, for example, undocumented women watch the children of workers in the primary and secondary markets, allowing these parents to be employed and to obtain services for below-market prices. However, they are isolated from normal avenues of mobility and from the protection of government agencies. Often, they are scorned by other segments of society even as their marginalized position is condoned, promoted, or even enforced by government.

Public Attitudes about Undocumented Workers

This situation raises several important issues. Does the flow of informal labor in the form of undocumented immigrants respond more to the economic pull of jobs in the U.S. or to negative repel forces of public sentiment against the undocumented? In other words, can the ebbs and flows of undocumented immigration be best explained by changes in the economies of Mexico and the U.S. or by the cultural and legal maneuvers that try to prevent them from coming? Second, are these anti-immigration initiatives motivated more by economic or by cultural factors? Stated another way, is the stepped-up legislative and regulatory effort to "stop them at the border" driven by economic motives (e.g., preserving jobs for Americans) or by a cultural backlash against the perception that people who seem very different from us are "invading" our communities? Though we cannot provide definitive answers to these questions, we can propose some macro-level evidence relevant to the discussion.

According to a 2008 Gallup poll, a large majority of Americans (78%) favored some form of path to citizenship for illegal immigrants. The largest portion of this group was the 42% who favored requiring them to leave and then return if they meet certain requirements. The other 36% favored allowing them to remain in the U.S. and become legal. Among Republicans and those who lean Republican, 49% supported the "make-them-leave-and-then-return" approach, with 27% favoring letting them become legal without leaving. Among Democrats and those leaning Democrat, 36% supported making them leave before becoming legal, while 45% favored letting them become legal without leaving.[49] A more recent Gallup poll (August 2009) finds that 61% of Republicans now say they would like to see immigration decreased. This percentage is up from the 46% in 2008. At the same time, 46% of Democrats and 44% of independents would like to see immigration decreased; both figures represent a shift in the same direction, up from the 39% and 37%, respectively, who said the same in 2008.[50] According to the pollsters, this shift toward an increasingly tough stance seems to reflect the country's economic problems, since, as they note, Americans tend to become less pro-immigration during difficult economic times.

Groups that bitterly oppose undocumented immigrants have championed laws on a state-by-state level, on the claim that the federal government is not doing its job of enforcing the borders and that states have to step in. In 1994 Californians passed Proposition 187, which prohibited illegal immigrants from using social services, public health care, and public education in California. The proposition passed with 59% of the vote but was later found unconstitutional by a federal court. Soon after Proposition 187, similar bills were proposed in Illinois, New York, Arkansas, Colorado, Utah, Oklahoma, and Arizona. Ostensibly, these efforts were designed to limit illegal immigrants' access to state services, but many observers saw the proposed laws more as a means of forcing the undocumented to leave and/or discouraging new immigration to those states.[51]

Though the business community in Arizona has, in general, opposed the initiatives that punish employers and landlords for hiring or housing undocumented workers, it has not been strong enough to counter the anti-immigrant bias. As we showed earlier, though Republicans and Democrats show somewhat different patterns in how they view undocumented immigration, this issue also divides both parties, especially in the border states. Each party is trying to satisfy two competing interest groups. Economic conservatives (mainly Republicans) tend to favor the low-cost labor made possible by undocumented immigration (they also tend to promote free trade with Mexico and Latin America), while cultural conservatives (also mainly Republicans) tend to oppose admitting large numbers of immigrants who are racially and culturally different. Among Democrats, economic liberals want to keep out foreign labor that can weaken labor unions, while cultural liberals tend to favor human rights, especially the right of people to migrate to feed their family.[52]

Cultural conservatives and economic liberals, however, are often careful not to make the arguments just mentioned seem biased. Cultural conservatives are wary of being labeled racists for opposing immigration on racial or cultural grounds, and economic liberals are hesitant to sound too opposed to the rights of undocumented workers. As a result, the arguments made are often of a different nature. The undocumented are accused of being more criminal, of ruining American culture, or of being welfare cheats who come to the U.S. just to get on the public dole. As we point out in this and other chapters, such arguments are not only stereotypical, but are distorted and essentially untrue.

In Chapter 1 we showed that immigrants in general (and the undocumented in particular) actually have lower crime rates. They also exhibit strong family values and a strong work ethic, supposedly the backbone of the American culture that cultural conservatives say they want to promote. And, as we also showed, most studies of how much they consume in public benefits, in relation to how much they produce, reveal that they actually produce a net benefit to public coffers.

This latter point was the conclusion reached by the Texas Comptroller of Public Accounts, herself a Republican in a Republican administration. Her report, issued in December of 2006,[53] concluded that the absence of the estimated 1.4 million undocumented immigrants in Texas in fiscal 2005 *would have been a loss of $17.7 billion from the Gross State Product*. In addition, she estimated that state revenues collected from undocumented immigrants exceeded by $424.7 million what the state spent on services for them.

These findings are similar to those of other economists who have ex-amined the economic impact of the undocumented in the U.S. In an open letter sponsored by the Independent Institute to President Bush and Congress, more than 500 prominent economists, including five Nobel laureates, proclaimed that "immigration has been a net gain for American citizens." The letter adds that "while a small percentage of native-born Americans may be harmed by immigration, vastly more Americans benefit from the contributions that immigrants make to the economy, including lower consumer prices. As with trade in goods and services, gains from immigration were said to greatly outweigh the losses."[54]

Several years ago, a survey of the past presidents of the American Economic Association and the past chairs of the President's Council of Economic Advisers by the Cato Institute revealed that 80% of re-spondents agreed that immigration has had "a very favorable impact on the nation's economic growth." In addition, 70% said that even illegal immigrant workers "have a positive economic impact." In general, in-formed respondents agree that most immigrants do not displace native workers, depress wages, or abuse welfare.[55]

Public Attitudes in South Texas about the Undocumented

In 2002–2003, we conducted a survey of 424 residents of South Texas—The Perceptions of Deviance Survey. In it, we asked respondents to rate how good (from +1 to +5) or how bad (from −1 to −5) several forms of border-related behavior were.[56] We also included five items related to undocumented immigration. Data based on the responses to the five border-related items (shaded) and the five comparison items (unshaded) are listed in Table 4.3, with scores for different ethnic categories.

A review of Table 4.3 reveals some rather pronounced patterns in these responses. First, for the items related to undocumented immigra-tion, Mexican and Mexican American respondents were close to neutral about how good or bad they considered these actions to be. In contrast, Anglos (non-Hispanics) and those who chose to be called "American"[57] were more condemning of the behaviors associated with entering ille-gally into the U.S. (shaded cells). The greatest differences were found in responses to the first item, which asked how good or bad it was for Mexicans to enter the U.S. illegally to work. Mexicans rated that item slightly in the positive range, while Anglos and "Americans" saw it as significantly more negative. Still, when compared to the items related to

Table 4.3. Comparison of mean scores of various ethnic categories of South Texas respondents on how good or how bad they consider certain undocumented immigration-related (shaded) and other informal or underground activities to be; from 5 = very good to −5 = very bad

Item Description: How good or bad do you consider it for . . .	Total Sample Mean	Mexican Mean	Mexican American Mean	"American" Mean	Anglo/ Other Mean	F Score	Sig.
Mexicans to cross to work illegally in U.S.	−0.53	+0.64	−0.38	−2.10	−1.20	6.92	.000***
Mexicans to use a shopping visa to illegally work in U.S.	−0.47	−0.03	−0.25	−1.54	−1.06	3.12	.026**
Mexican women to give birth in U.S. to give child citizenship	−1.19	−0.83	−0.94	−2.16	−1.88	2.82	.039**
Valley residents to hire undocumented maid or nanny	−0.76	−0.12	−0.61	−2.00	−1.16	3.29	.021**
Mexican Americans to lend papers to Mexican family to enter U.S.	−2.16	−1.50	−2.05	−3.64	−2.30	5.12	.002***
Americans to not pay import duties on alcohol from Mexico	−2.08	−2.45	−1.99	−2.74	−1.77	1.51	.211
Americans to run drugs up North to support family	−3.15	−3.33	−3.06	−3.69	−3.01	0.98	.403
Mexicans to drive in U.S. without car insurance	−2.59	−2.28	−2.50	−3.51	−2.67	2.20	.088*
Mexicans to buy cars stolen from the U.S.	−3.36	−3.76	−3.27	−3.51	−3.25	0.98	.401
Americans to bribe Mexican police to avoid traffic fine	−1.05	−2.52	−0.70	−1.67	−0.80	6.20	.000***
N	426	58	260	39	69	—	—

Note: ***, **, * represent significance at the .001, .05, and .10 levels, respectively.
Source: Perceptions of Deviance Survey.

transporting drugs and buying stolen cars, it was not seen at the same level of deviance by any group.

Second, we can observe that each group seems more kindly disposed to "deviance" by members of its own group; this is especially pronounced with the item about Americans bribing police officers in Mexico and the item about Mexicans working illegally in the U.S. Mexicans condemn Americans for bribing a Mexican police officer, and Anglos and "Americans" condemn Mexicans for coming to the U.S. to work illegally. Though the pattern holds on the other behaviors, the differences are not statistically significant past the .05 level.

Finally, we should note that Mexicans and Mexican Americans who see items related to undocumented immigration in generally neutral terms did not let their tolerance for such behaviors carry over to other forms of cross-border deviance (the nonshaded cells). It would seem that tolerance for immigration violations does not carry over into general acceptance of other forms of lawbreaking related to the border. Nevertheless, South Texas is generally a very welcoming place for Mexican migrants, legal and undocumented.

Conclusion: "Escaping" the Undocumented World

Long-term, undocumented residents of South Texas keep hoping for some form of amnesty or another route to legalizing their status. Their children achieve it simply by being born here (though the anti-undocumented lobby opposes even that route). These children resent being labeled as "anchor babies" and must find ways to adjust to a world that calls their parents "illegal" for having come to the U.S. to give them a better life.

Leaving the undocumented world behind through broad amnesty offered by the Immigration Reform and Control Act (1986) permitted millions of the previous generation of Mexican illegal immigrants to legalize and regularize their status. Nevertheless, legalization does not necessarily mean work suddenly becomes formalized, but the rights of citizenship do allow for a more normal life that is free of the many threats—real and veiled—that routinely face undocumented immigrants. The structural characteristics of the South Texas economy remain difficult and will contribute to informality regardless of the results of the current drive toward immigration reform.

Amnesty is but one path toward legalization. Other paths include family reunification applications, marriage, temporary cross-border work visas, and regular application (with a normal wait time of more than ten years). Some Mexican migrants give up the struggle altogether and return to Mexico, while others migrate back and forth as a cyclical life-cycle strategy. For a fortunate few undocumented workers, good treatment from family, friends, and employers improves their opportunities and empowers them in their pursuit of the American dream. But these forms of help may ultimately fail to completely obscure the reality of their status as illegal immigrants.

The lack of documents to cross the border and/or work in the U.S. and the multibillion dollar wall built through the border region do not keep out those Mexicans wishing to come to live and work in South Texas. Life for the undocumented in South Texas is not easy, though with luck and embedded networks, even life in the shadows of the informal economy may be better than the economic situation they would face in Mexico. As long as Americans want cheap labor but don't want the country to get "too Mexican," undocumented Mexican workers will continue to work in the shadows of the informal economy.

CHAPTER 5

Informal Cross-Border Trade

Juanita Torres, born in Veracruz, Mexico, migrated to Texas at the age of five. After graduation from the University of Texas-Austin, Juanita got married and became a teacher in Laredo. She divorced and subsequently married a man from Nuevo Laredo, Mexico, where they made their new home. Happy with her life in Nuevo Laredo, Juanita stopped working and settled in as a housewife. Because she had become "naturalized" during her time in Texas, she was able to cross back and forth between Mexico and Texas seamlessly. Soon her Mexican family and friends began asking Juanita to bring back items from the U.S. on her trips. It was not long before she moved from fulfilling favors for her circle of family and friends to launching a full-scale used clothing resale operation out of her Nuevo Laredo home. She began small, making day trips to Laredo and San Antonio to acquire clothing at rock bottom prices (e.g., acquiring goods at yard sales, flea markets, and thrift-store outlets). From her start buying a couple of bags, to the hiring of her sister full-time, Juanita's enterprise grew so that she now purchases about $20,000 in clothing inventory a year, which she resells for $60,000 to Nuevo Laredoans who cannot easily cross the border. For those who can, her used clothing resale service reduces their time and hassle of traveling to the U.S. They find her selection impressive. Recently, it has become more difficult to pass through Mexican customs undetected, so she has set up a "payment plan" (*mordida*), or bribe to Mexican customs officials, to facilitate her passage back into Mexico. Now she crosses her goods virtually without incident.

Introduction[1]

Juanita, like many binational traders in the South Texas/Northern Mexico borderlands, has discovered how to leverage the border with informal activities that give her an advantage over those competitors who are limited to operating on only one side of the border. For informals like her who have the documentation to cross the boundary line freely, the border represents both opportunity and adversity. Informal entrepreneurs can buy things that cost less on one side and sell those things on the other side for a higher price.

These advantages, however, may come at a high cost in frustration and difficulty. For the undocumented, the border is a zone of adversity that can be crossed only at considerable peril. Those with documents find the loss of time in the complicated process of leaving one country and entering another a nuisance. Often, their informal goods are legal in one country but illegal in the other. In addition, they must deal with officials and laws, in two countries, that can be complex, arbitrary, and cumbersome. Most commonly, the laws that informal cross-border traders break at the border pertain to nondeclaration of goods and nonpayment of duties at customs.

We call these self-employed economic agents *cross-border informal traders* (or entrepreneurs). Juanita, from our opening vignette, is one such cross-border trader in the informal sector. She uses the border to acquire goods in the U.S. that she sells in Mexico. Because the border limits the ability of many consumers in Mexico to make purchases in the U.S., her possession of documents authorizing her to cross the border gives her market power among consumers in Mexico who depend on her for items from the U.S.

Other cross-border traders, like nineteen-year-old Alfredo Salazar, use the border to buy (or produce) in Mexico and sell for greater profit in the U.S. Alfredo uses fraudulent papers to cross from Mexico to South Texas in order to sell skateboards in parks. Alfredo's sales north of the border exemplify the bidirectionality of informal cross-border trade. From his middle-class home in Mexico, Alfredo takes the three-hour bus ride from Monterrey to the border about three times a month. Alfredo buys low ($1 to $5 per skateboard) in Mexico and sells high (up to $30 per skateboard) in South Texas. Though he does not bring skateboards with him on every trip north, his gross profits are adequate because he is able to save money by staying with an uncle in South Texas. Alfredo sells his boards without much interference from U.S. governmental authorities. He states, "All the money I make is mine; I don't report any of it. And that's great money for me since I am only nineteen years old." Alfredo avoids detection by federal and local officials as he crosses his boards into the U.S. and sells in public parks. He does worry that his cross-border business will eventually be discovered because he utilizes a fake visa to cross the border and carries a large number of skateboards (which he tells officials are for his family). Because he cannot be seen coming too frequently or with too many skateboards, he has to limit his business. His consumers have been good to Alfredo. Initially he thought American buyers would reject him or tell him to leave them alone. "Instead," he said, "they were interested in what I was selling. I sell the boards a lot cheaper than what they cost in the United States. I have my faithful customers. They know where to find me when they need more boards."

While the popular press has highlighted the rapidity of global economic interaction, or the flattening of the formal world,[2] globalization has also penetrated informal trade across national boundaries. Many of the same forces that drive globalization—increased connectedness,[3] mobility and place,[4] and institutions[5]—also facilitate small-scale informal cross-border commerce. *Financial Times* economics writer Martin Wolf[6] defines globalization as "the integration of economic activities, across-borders, through markets." This definition applies equally well to cross-border informal trade. Thus, cross-border informal traders are the "face" of informal globalization. This picture is sharpest at the border.

Oscar Martínez,[7] in his influential study of border people in the U.S.-Mexico borderlands, suggests "powerful transnational forces pull large numbers of borderlanders [Mexicans, Mexican Americans, and Anglos] into the orbit of the neighboring country, with a resulting array of cross-boundary relationships and lifestyles." Martínez categorizes those who actively cross the border and maintain strong cross-border linkages as transnational borderlanders. According to Martínez, transnational borderlanders come in many forms: commuters, binational consumers, (im)migrants, winter residents, biculturalists, and binationalists.[8] Transnational borderlanders who navigate the uncertain currents of the border require considerable socioeconomic, political, and cultural finesse. These skills are most prevalent among those who are biculturalists and binationalists. For Martínez, it is the act of binational consumption (in all of its manifestations) which binds the borderlands. And the transnational borderlander who buys on one side to sell on the other is at the nexus of binational exchange. We are most interested in those "transnational borderlanders" who utilize the border as a way to make a living primarily through informal means.

The State as Hedge

Cross-border informality exists as a phenomenon primarily because of state-sponsored regulatory control. For much of the history of human economic interaction, informality was the historical norm.[9] With the advent of the modern bureaucratic state and subsequent immigration controls, boundaries hardened, particularly along the U.S.-Mexico border, beginning in the early twentieth century,[10] a process that accelerated after 9/11.[11] Today, as theorized by Portes and Haller,[12] the state's attempt to serve as a hedge against informal activity actually spawns the very activity the state seeks to suppress. As discussed in Chapter 1 (and worth restating), "Official efforts to obliterate unregulated activities through the proliferation of rules and controls often expand the very conditions that give rise to these activities."[13] This concept is particularly relevant in cross-border activity.

Throughout this work, we have characterized the border as a line which allows for extensive arbitrage of informal cross-border goods and services. Juanita and Alfredo (described above) both find an opportunity in the border whereby each can buy low on one side and sell informally for a profit on the other. This informal cross-border entrepreneurship is facilitated by fraudulent crossing documents, family networks, facilitation payments, and a willing group of buyers who often seek to keep their purchases "off the record." It also requires that government officials on both sides of the border not inspect too closely or raise too many questions about this movement of merchandise. This detection failure is enhanced by the sheer volume of trade and movement of people and goods through border crossing routes. The volume usually ensures only a passing interest in Alfredo's seemingly innocuous activities. Over time, Juanita's movements have been detected by Mexican authorities, but she has made "arrangements" for safe passage of her goods into Mexico.

The state of Texas supports cross-border commerce through the timely rebating of sales taxes (known locally as *"manifiestos"*) to Mexican-domiciled consumers.[14] While U.S. residents are subject to the Texas sales tax (up to 8.25% in many tax jurisdictions), Mexicans are not because international trade comes under the constitutional purview of the U.S. federal government. States like Texas, nonetheless, could make the process of returning sales tax collections either cumbersome or effortless. Texas has chosen the latter, possibly as an enticement to Mexican shoppers.[15] This tax rebate procedure, however, offers opportunities for fraudulent collection of unauthorized rebates. It also allows cross-border traders the opportunity to buy U.S. goods in Texas without paying sales taxes, lowering their purchase price still farther, below that paid by American consumers.

Institutionally, the official U.S. customs requirements are less flexible than those of Mexico, though U.S. rules are not always enforced in an absolute manner. U.S. importation allowances are also more generous. U.S. residents may bring back $800 worth of goods from Mexico without paying duty.[16] For nonresidents, up to $100 of goods may be crossed into the U.S. duty-free. This $100–$800 window facilitates petty cross-border commerce for goods traveling into the U.S. for personal use or for resale. Small-time cross-border traders routinely avoid paperwork and fees as they pass prescription drugs and alcohol with minimal scrutiny.[17] Though NAFTA now permits most items from Mexico to cross duty-free, there is also an increased responsibility to produce the appropriate importation paperwork. Many informal traders take advantage of the more generous allowances while avoiding much of the paperwork that larger, more formal firms, must complete.

The Mexican customs process is more complex. There is an official $50 per person limit on goods brought back from the U.S.[18] For sure, this $50 restriction (reduced from $300) prompts more trips for regular Mexican cross-border shoppers and increases the demand for smuggling, camouflaging goods, or confusing officials by sending more people in the same shopping party.[19] Ultimately however, the customs process depends on daring, luck—pressing the button and getting a green light (signaling that one may proceed without inspection) or a red light (requiring a stop for inspection)[20]—or flexibility. This flexibility may be in the form of a cash payment requested from the customs agent to overlook the import violation, or something more elaborate, as a payment scheme to allow unimpeded entrance. A larger goods flow and/or frequent trips eventually leads to detection, which requires a fine or a payoff. Nevertheless, for the informal cross-border trader, because the risk of detection is low, as is the financial penalty, namely a small *mordida*, making these payments is simply a not-too-risky cost of doing business.

Bribery

Some Mexico-bound cross-border traders set up prearranged "understandings" with border customs officers. Others simply wait for the inevitable red light that will come about once every ten trips. The Mexican system of importation makes it almost mandatory for small-time importers to pay bribes to avoid the lengthy paper work or customs duties that larger firms routinely hire someone to take care of for them.[21]

In Mexico and many developing nations, the *mordida* has become part of the culture and the structure of cross-border enterprise. *Culturally*, most Mexicans do not like the corruption it represents, but it can save a lot of time (by not having to get permits, etc.) and money (almost always, those who pay it refer to it as a "service" the officer is doing and expect to pay less than the fine that would be charged). To the degree it gets institutionalized, however, it is a very difficult practice to eliminate because virtually all members of society become accomplices. Once it becomes an acceptable way to get out of trouble, it is easy to use it to fix ever more serious offenses. Drug traffickers, for example, will find it easier to buy off police, judges, and even top political figures when *la mordida* is winked at for traffic offenses. Over time, the choice to not participate may become increasingly more difficult.

The *mordida* is also part of a *structure* of corruption because the money derived from *mordidas* flows through a network of connected officials. Individuals wanting to become customs officers, for example, frequently have to "buy" their job and must regularly pay a portion of what they take in to higher-ups. This not only corrupts otherwise good individuals who cannot get the job without under-the-table payments, but also forces them to keep collecting *mordidas* to pay off higher-ups who, in turn, may be paying to keep their jobs. Thus, border officers often find it very difficult to resist the structural pressures to demand bribes in order to get or keep their job.

These pressures for bribes among Mexican customs officers are similar to those among Mexican police officers, which have been documented by Arteaga Botello and López Rivera.[22] According to their research, bribing behavior among police officers is reinforced throughout the hierarchy and by means of social networks that include access to privileged positions by paying *mordidas* to higher-ups. Novice police officers learn from veteran officers how to extort *mordidas*. In addition, as Arteaga Botello and López Rivera[23] point out, even when payoffs to higher-ups are not demanded directly, there is a subtle understanding that officers have to collect money and then pay up to the next one in the chain of command. It becomes understood among all ranks of police officers that the best neighborhoods (for the purpose of collecting bribes), patrol cars, and equipment are assigned according to the amount one is willing to pay his/her supervisor.

This situation, of course, presents an interesting twist on informality. Generally, we consider informal economic activities those that evade government oversight, inspection, or taxation. Cross-border trade into Mexico may also be seen as an under-the-table economic activity that is *pushed* by some government officials, or at least is done in collusion with them. It is not uncommon for many customs officials, for example, to make certain economic activities so difficult to handle in the prescribed formal manner that individuals are virtually forced to pay a bribe. Indeed, one notes with suspicion that the value of goods Mexican citizens can legally import into Mexico has been set so low (in spite of the tariff reduction NAFTA was supposed to implement) as to make the *mordida* a virtual necessity.

Diana Ríos, 44, lives in Reynosa, Mexico, and crosses into South Texas with her laser visa two to three times a week to sell Spanish-language Christian music. Diana enjoys the music and sees her enterprise as missionary work. While her microenterprise is small (Diana began with only a $400 investment), she believes her impact is important. Nevertheless, on one trip back to Reynosa with many unsold CDs, she pressed the customs light and it came up red. Diana recalled, "The Mexican Customs officials wanted to shake me down for a $100 fine . . . I refused to give them more than $50."

Claudia Ramos has had similar experiences. She is a middle-aged Mexican and informal cross-border trader who sells used clothing. On occasion, as Claudia returns in her vehicle from buying used clothes in South Texas, Mexican Customs take her inventory, threaten to impound her vehicle, or threaten to take away her U.S.-issued laser visa. Typically it costs Claudia upwards of $200 in bribes to pass through into Mexico, leaving her to lament, "Mexican officials are the absolute worst. They are always looking for a way to take your money."

Informal Entrepreneurship and Cross-Border Traders: Additional Perspectives

Few scholars have written on the cross-border nature of informality. A study from Sub-Saharan Africa highlights the border as a hedge and escape valve. In the previous decade (2000s), Duri[24] studied the cross-border informal economy between Zimbabwe and Mozambique at Mutare. He found that the extreme economic crisis in Zimbabwe, precipitated by the dictator Robert Mugabe, pushed many vulnerable groups, including Zimbabwean women and children, into cross-border survival activities. These activities include street vending, carting smuggled goods across the border, and engaging in the sex trade in neighboring Mozambique. Only a few borderlands Zimbabweans were able to escape starvation in Mozambique. Most were excluded by armed factions on both sides.

Joan Anderson was among the first to conduct economic studies on border informality twenty years ago. She focused on the Mexican side of the U.S.-Mexico border in two foundational studies: an empirical investigation into the causes of the growth of Mexican border informality[25] and a qualitative multi-case-based study focused on household survival strategies for the poor in Tijuana.[26] Anderson found that increased internal Mexican migration to the northern border increased the size of the economically active population engaged in informal economic pursuits. Her subsequent study with de la Rosa[27] was based on a qualitative assessment of eleven households in Tijuana. They found, among other things, that: 1) the informal sector acts as an employment sector of last resort for household survival; 2) poor families have a higher propensity for being participants in the informal sector; 3) households are bi-national and transnational actors in the cross-border or borderlands economy; and 4) the economy of U.S. discards is important to the Mexican side of the border.

In 2008, Anderson and Gerber's *Fifty Years of Change on the U.S.-Mexico Border*[28] was published. This work focuses on the longitudinal economic changes along both sides of the border. It includes a chapter on formal and informal labor, with several summary insights extracted from a career of studying the border economy. Of particular relevance are the following points: (1) recent declines in labor force participation rates on the U.S. side of the border may be in part explained by a growing informal sector; (2) there is still much to be learned about the informal economy, especially on the U.S. side of the border (where informal participation by choice may be as relevant as involvement by economic necessity); (3) an inverse relationship exists between income levels and informality—that is, as economies become more affluent, rates of informality decline; (4) immigration into the border zone, particularly to the U.S. border, fosters informality relative to the nation as a whole; (5) the informality along the U.S. border is more limited in scope than informality on the Mexican border, with informal employment on the U.S. side concentrated in construction, tourism, and domestic services; and

(6) heterogeneity (or tiers) exists within the informal sector, especially between entrepreneurs and wage employment.

In the only book-length treatment of informality on both sides of the U.S.-Mexico border, political scientist Kathleen Staudt[29] studied the El Paso–Ciudad Juárez metroplex. Staudt[30] suggests that "informal work is an omnipresent part of the reality on both sides of the U.S.-Mexico border." Utilizing standard research methods to obtain a representative sample of informals in six different housing divisions in core, old periphery, and new periphery neighborhoods, Staudt surveyed 600 households, 131 of which possessed informal businesses. Staudt notes "informality's legitimacy in Mexico contrasts with its illegitimacy in the United States."[31] Additionally, she argues that the border allows households to hide income, stretch consumption, maximize earnings, and find work. In essence, the border provides cross-border entrepreneurs the ability "to maneuver on both sides of the border, without calling official attention to themselves. They do so by taking advantage of the uneven enforcement of policies and regulations to lower their business costs, maximize opportunities, enhance incomes, and generate jobs through informal self-employment.[32]

More recent research reveals that informal workers and entrepreneurs along the border have the advantage of being able to easily buy ethnic products cheaply in Mexico and sell them to coethnics in the U.S. Using 2000 census data, Mora and Davila[33] found that Mexican immigrants in U.S. border cities more fully utilize the geographic advantages in international trade presented by the close proximity to Mexico than either non-Hispanic whites in border areas or Mexican immigrants farther from the border. Informal and/or undocumented laborers also have distinct advantages in the borderlands location, engaging in economic arbitrage between relative prices and wages on both sides of the border within the informal sector. Particularly important are business input costs, such as labor and intermediate goods, e.g., equipment, tools. For one tamale maker and vendor we interviewed, sourcing ingredients from Mexico makes more sense. "It's cheaper over there to get the red peppers and dried corn leaves for the *tamales*," he said. Cross-border traders also find it convenient that they have an ethnic market in South Texas which still demands these ethnic products from Mexico.

Medina[34] also studied the cross-national market, focusing on informal cardboard waste collectors in *Los Dos Laredos* (Laredo, Texas, and Nuevo Laredo, Mexico). The opportunities for the recycling of cardboard were closely associated with the discarding of cardboard in the booming formal retail and warehouse sectors in Laredo, in combination with the demand for recycled cardboard in industrial Mexican *maquiladoras* (border assembly plants). Medina found that the informal *cartoneros* (cardboard collectors/recyclers) of Nuevo Laredo were self-employed in a stable and relatively well-paying marketplace. Medina describes fully-employed and tenured (thirteen years in the business, on average) *cartoneros* earning three times the Mexican minimum wage and living in fair conditions. In order to participate, however, a would-be Mexican *cartonero* needed the legal ability (e.g., a laser visa) to cross into the U.S. to collect cardboard. They also needed tolerance for such collection activities from officials on both sides of the border. Medina argues that this type of cross-border recycling activity, or scavenging within the economy of discards, is the most lucrative because of its direct links to an industry that demands waste products such as metal, aluminum, glass, waste paper, plastics, and cardboard. He categorizes such informal labor as "recovery of materials for sale to industry."

The Laser Visa

Mexican cross-border entrepreneurs find the border crossing card, or laser visa, essential for entry into the U.S. This U.S. document is issued from consulates or the U.S. embassy in Mexico. The cost (in 2010) was $140 (or 1,890 pesos) for individuals 15 years of age and older, and the visa is good for a period of 10 years.[35] A Mexican passport is also required, as well as an interview with U.S. Department of State personnel. Typically, an interview appointment for a border consulate must be scheduled about one week in advance, with an additional two weeks for processing (if successful). The interview process seeks to reject those applicants who intend to migrate illegally to the U.S. and to ensure that: (a) the purpose of their trip is to enter the U.S. for such things as tourism, shopping, or medical treatment; (b) they plan to remain for a specific, limited period [and return to Mexico]; (c) they can show evidence of funds to cover expenses in the U.S.; (d) they have evidence of compelling social and economic ties abroad [Mexico]; and (e) they have a residence outside the U.S., as well as other binding ties that will insure their return to Mexico at the end of the visit.[36]

Nydia Soto, a day maid with a laser visa, carries a pristine $50 U.S. bill that she shows to U.S. immigration officials to demonstrate her intent and capacity to shop in South Texas. Carrying both the laser visa and the cash permits her to easily enter the U.S. to ply her trade. For immigration officials, it is nearly impossible to distinguish Nydia from the thousands of other regular (and legitimate) cross-border shoppers who contribute over $3 billion a year to the Texas economy.[37]

Entrance with a laser visa permits one to stay up to 30 days within the border zone before one must return to Mexico.[38] The laser visa, then, becomes an important cross-border facilitation document. The laser visa permits informal cross-border traders as well as cross-border workers to ply their trades (e.g., maids, gardeners, cement workers, drywallers, auto mechanics, etc.) in niche markets, based on tacit knowledge of the needs of their clientele.

The average income for maids (domestic servants) is related to their ability to cross the border frequently. Our own earlier research revealed that maids were paid average hourly rates of $3.44 for day maids and $2.61 for live-in maids.[39] Among maids who did not have work authorization, 91% of their employers did not report the wages paid to their maids.[40]

A further distinction between undocumented maids and those who are able to cross the border frequently is illustrated by the case of Irma Murillo, who illegally crossed the bridge from Reynosa when she was sixteen. She began working as a maid for the Martinez family in Harlingen. For fifteen dollars a week she did most everything. Irma recalled, "I had to clean the whole house from top to bottom. I was told to do the sheets from everyone's bed daily. There were five beds, meaning five different loads. I had to wash the dishes, sweep, mop, cook, and pick up constantly after the children. You name it, I did it."

Irma is a live-in maid, with no border-crossing card. She earns much less than day maids. Live-in maids typically live with the family they care for, are often on call 24/7, and do not possess the documents necessary to freely transit between Mexico and the United States. Many day maids generally start off as live-in maids and are able to switch to contracting their services as day maids. Day maids generally operate much more freely within the border environment than live-in maids.[41] Many day maids possess legal papers, ranging from U.S. citizenship, to resident aliens, to the laser visa which allows easy movement between Mexico and the U.S. Juanita Guevara crosses the border using her laser visa twice a week from Reynosa to clean houses in McAllen. As a day maid, she earns $40 per eight hour day ($4,160 per year), which she feels is plenty for her family of five in Reynosa. Juanita turns down extra work, satisfied with her twice-a-week routine and income, except when extra spending money is needed, such as for special events or for the holidays.

While the border-crossing card permits entry into the U.S., it is not without risks. Ever present is the possibility that U.S. officials will discover the card is being used to facilitate employment and will confiscate it. Yet for most cross-border informals, the opportunities outweigh the risks. For most cross-border informals, the laser visa serves as a ladder to higher earnings.

The Border as Opportunity

Norma Lucero began her cross-border trading odyssey informally and inauspiciously when she bought items such as radios, shoes, and clothes from Laredo flea markets and resold them in Mexican flea markets. The used goods market, or the economy of discards, provides a built-in advantage for cross-border informal entrepreneurs like Norma, who sell in Mexico. Used items[42] are in much greater demand in Mexico than they are in the U.S. After five years of earning a small but steady income selling discards, Norma decided to sell plaster (clay) figurines. One employee in Nuevo Laredo, where Norma lives, would make the plaster figurines; Norma would pick them up and paint them before selling them in Laredo. Two years later, she moved up the value chain into works of iron. Over the past two years, Norma's business has grown so that she now employs three workers in Nuevo Laredo to cut and weld the metal in the construction of roller chairs, tables, iron bars, barbecue bases, flowerpot holders, and house decorations.

Each successive business required successively larger amounts of capital, always obtained from the previous businesses. Her latest business ("*taller de fiero*," or ironworks) is only partially an informal enterprise. Norma's employees in Mexico are paid informally (about $400 a week). But the iron products are exported legally to the U.S. with minimal effort. Norma does not have a storefront in Laredo, so she delivers to Laredo wholesalers who sell to national wholesalers who visit Laredo. Though Norma earns about $500 a week on a revenue stream of $1,500 ($400 for help and $600 for materials), she believes she could earn more if she could set up a storefront in Laredo. That would allow her to augment her earnings by one-third through the elimination of the U.S. border-based wholesale broker. This move would certainly require a formal business setting for her in Laredo and that she adhere to some formal business practices, such as collecting sales tax and paying federal income tax, even while remaining informal in Mexico. It could still involve some U.S. informality, however, if Norma chose to accept cash payments off the books from some of her select U.S. customers.

Norma's story is illustrative of several important elements of cross-border businesses. Many, particularly those that are smaller, start out mostly informal. As they grow, they tend to combine formal and informal operations. They may also be mainly informal in one country and mostly formal in the other. As they grow in size, they find it increasingly difficult to hide their cross-border trade from government officials and tend to move increasingly toward formality. However, many, like Norma, may still handle off-the-books cash transactions for special customers.

At the smaller end of the scale, Mrs. Lorena Valenzuela from San Juan, Texas, earns $5,000 per year in flea markets in South Texas. Her specialty is Mexican candies. Serendipity played an important role in Mrs. Valenzuela becoming a regular flea market seller. One day she picked up some things lying around the house and sold them at a neighborhood flea market in Texas. With the help of her family, Mrs. Valenzuela, a retired florist, has been selling at *la pulga* (the flea market) ever since. In essence, South Texas flea markets are the region's precursors to, or substitutes for, eBay-type electronic marketing.

Pablo Leal, a U.S. citizen nearing retirement age, hurt his back and no longer has formal, full-time employment. Pablo says that he goes to South Texas flea markets and pawn shops and "buys [things] real cheap" and "then goes to Mexico [three times a month] to resell them" in order to avoid reporting any income. Similarly, thirty-six-year-old U.S.-born Arturo Peralta from Weslaco crosses into Mexico to buy pottery and returns home to sell it all on eBay. Occasionally, Customs officials question Arturo about his pottery when he is returning to the U.S., but he insists it is for his home. Arturo quipped, "It's simple and doesn't require too much time. Now I have extra money in my savings account. I haven't been able to do that in a while."

Above all, *la pulga* is the quintessential location for informal sales of used, cross-border items in South Texas. Here, buyers and sellers meet to exchange goods, often informally, to extend household consumption and earning activities. Typically, *pulga* consumers buy to lower their living costs, particularly for basic necessities and household goods, such as clothing, consumer electronics, furniture, and personal care products. *Pulga* sellers, by comparison, seek to enhance their earnings by reselling scavenged (and repaired) goods, hobby goods, foodstuffs, electronics, music, basic necessities, etc. *La pulga* may also offer stolen items at substantially reduced prices. Finally, *la pulga* can even serve as a place to network, including for the purpose of finding jobs, making it an important element of building social capital on both sides of the border.

Informal Cross-Border Traders: Survey Results

In our semi-structured Informal and Underground Survey, we briefly compared two groups engaged in informal economic activities—those who regularly cross the border and those who do not (as a reference group). Cross-border traders were deliberately oversampled, to yield 179 such respondents, or one-third of our survey respondents.[43] We found that women in our sample more frequently engage in cross-border informal commerce than men (see Table 5.1). This gender difference is significant and related to their unique niches. Women who engaged in cross-border activities are likely earning informal income by buying and selling goods (56.7%) or working as maids (14.4%) or cashiers (9.3%). While fewer men take on informal cross-border activities, those that do so find work as laborers (17.9%), buying and selling goods (39.8%), or as gardeners (10.3%).

The main difference between informal border crossers and noncrossers is their immigration status. A majority of noncrossers are either U.S. citizens or U.S. residents (65.9%). Cross-border traders in our survey were much more likely to be Mexican citizens with the ability to easily cross the border (e.g., 70.3% possess U.S. residency or a laser visa). These quasidocumented individuals tend to make the most of leveraging the border for informal economic gain. For example, we first introduced in Chapter 3 a group of Mexico-based sheetrock workers who cross the bridge each morning in Laredo using a laser visa. They are picked up by their supervisor not far from the bridge and are transported to their job drywalling new homes. Similarly, the buyers of discards in flea markets and used clothing warehouses cross the border daily, sorting and purchasing discards in Texas border cities and taking them to Mexico to sell.

Similar to immigration status, the generation scores (GS) of cross-border informals show much stronger and significant familial ties to Mexico than we found for non-cross-border informals. Though age does not separate informal cross-border actors from those tied to one side of

Table 5.1. Descriptive statistics for cross-border and non-cross-border groups*

Variable	Cross-Border		Non-Cross-Border	
Gender	%	N	%	N
Male	44.6	78	54.7	191
Female	55.4	97	45.3	158
	Cross-tab Pearson Chi-Square = 4.813, df = 1, p = .028**			

	Cross-Border		Non-Cross-Border	
Immigration Status	%	N	%	N
U.S. Citizen	20.0	35	44.4	151
U.S. Resident	20.6	36	21.5	73
Other (i.e., laser visa)	49.7	87	6.8	23
Undocumented	9.7	17	27.4	63
	Cross-tab Pearson Chi-Square = 135.700, df = 3, p = .000***			

	Cross-Border		Non-Cross-Border	
	Mean (std. dev.)	N	Mean (std. dev.)	N
Age	38.6 (12.4)	171	36.8 (12.4)	340
	ANOVA, F = 2.388, df = 1, p = .123			

	Cross-Border		Non-Cross-Border	
Generation Score	Mean (std. dev.)	N	Mean (std. dev.)	N
	1.2	175	3.2	349
	ANOVA, F = 34.877, df = 1, p = .000***			

*Includes both informal and underground participants.
Source: Informal and Underground Survey.

the border, cross-border informals tend to be in their prime earning years (ages twenty-four to fifty).

The documentation continuum in Table 5.1 ranges from the extreme of no documentation, to fully documented (i.e., U.S. citizenship). For the wholly undocumented, regular transit routes are unauthorized. So they use backdoor arrangements, such as false documents or swimming the river, to cross the Rio Grande/Bravo. In between are the quasi-documented who may utilize and access regular travel corridors (e.g., international bridges) and cross the border at will, though without authorization to work in the U.S. Yet once across, the undocumented, like the quasidocumented, find that their activities go virtually unmonitored unless they draw attention to themselves or attempt to move beyond the secondary inland checkpoints.

Because the quasidocumented and the undocumented have work restrictions, their earnings tend to be lower. Table 5.2 presents hourly wage data compiled from our survey for four categories: all informals; those informals working in South Texas only (non-crossers); cross-border informals; and underground participants (as a passive referent). For those without permanent rights to work in the U.S., cross-border informal activity enhances hourly earnings by 74 cents for undocumenteds[44] and $1.41 for those with laser visas. Informal cross-border entrepreneurs[45] generally earn more per hour than their domestic informal peers in South Texas, particularly for the undocumented (13.1% more) and quasidocumented (32.8% more). We conclude that the self-employment of most of our respondents would still fit within the category of survival informality.

As Table 5.2 shows, traversing the border augments informal earnings, yet at the cost of substantial difficulties and risks. For those with the ability to legally work in South Texas, the results are mixed. U.S. citizens earn more in their informal pursuits in South Texas ($11.80 per hour) than by crossing the border ($9.87 per hour). U.S. residents, on the other hand, earn more informally by crossing the border ($8.62 per hour) than by staying in South Texas ($7.93 per hour).

Our sub-sample of 179 informal cross-border traders had 166, or 92.7%, who were involved in informal activities. The remaining respondents (7.3%) were engaged in discernible cross-border underground activities (offered as a point of reference). This was based upon their reports of income-earning activities over the previous five years. The survey also distinguished between part-time and full-time pursuits and whether the respondent engaged in other economic activities. While our focus is on informal cross-border traders, we acknowledge that many more in the region do use legal means to conduct legitimate cross-border commerce.[46]

A demographic profile of the cross-border traders from our sample is shown in Table 5.3. Though our respondents ranged in age from seventeen to seventy-six, most were adults aged twenty-six to fifty. Residence

Table 5.2. Informal earnings and documentation (in U.S.$)

	Mean $/hour	Std. Dev.	N
All Informal Hourly Earnings			
Undocumenteds	4.99	5.53	81
Others (laser visa)	5.42	5.27	89
U.S. Resident	8.15	11.65	76
U.S. Citizen	11.29	21.82	91
South Texas Informal Hourly Earnings			
Undocumenteds	4.89	5.43	70
Others (laser visa)	4.30	4.12	18
U.S. Resident	7.93	9.97	52
U.S. Citizen	11.80	25.01	67
Cross-Border Informal Hourly Earnings			
Undocumenteds	5.63	6.38	11
Others (laser visa)	5.71	5.51	71
U.S. Resident	8.62	14.90	24
U.S. Citizen	9.87	7.99	24
Underground Hourly Earnings			
Undocumenteds	54.99	91.93	4
Others (laser visa)	9.59	10.61	2
U.S. Resident	21.79	12.69	2
U.S. Citizen	94.77	121.58	53

Source: Informal and Underground Survey.

was nearly evenly split between South Texas and Mexico, indicating a bidirectionality of economic activity. Homes of these cross-border traders contained an average of four family members with one dependent, a result of the life cycle of the respondents. Over half (55.1%) of our respondents had not completed high school, and fully one-third possessed just a grade-school education. Nevertheless, nearly one-third of our respondents had some postsecondary education, indicating informal activities may be a pull for some; for many others with lower educational attainment, they may find themselves pushed into informal activities. Mexico plays an overwhelming role in the education of our respondents, with more than eight in ten receiving the bulk of their education south of the border. This finding is concomitant with nativity, for approximately 82.0% of our respondents who were born in Mexico.

Individuals like Alfredo (mentioned in the beginning of this chapter)

Table 5.3. Cross-border traders—descriptive statistics

Demographic Variables	All (N = 179)	Informal (N = 166)	Underground (N = 13)
Mean Age (& std. dev.)	38.5 (12.5)	38.9 (12.5)	33.0 (11.3)
Current Residence (%)			
South Texas	46.9	44.0	83.3
Mexico	53.1	56.0	16.7
Household Size—Mean (& std. dev.)			
Number of Dependents (under 18)	1.3 (1.2)	1.3 (1.2)	1.6 (1.2)
Total Number of Members in Household	4.0 (1.4)	4.0 (1.4)	4.0 (1.5)
Education (%)			
0–4 years	6.8	7.3	0.0
4–8 years	25.6	24.4	41.7
9–11 years	22.7	2.6	25.0
12 years	14.8	14.6	16.7
12+ years	30.1	31.1	16.7
Where Educated (%)			
Mostly Mexico	81.4	84.1	36.4
Mostly U.S.	18.6	15.9	63.6
Birthplace (%)			
Mexico	82.0	85.6	33.3
U.S.	18.0	14.4	66.7
Immigration Status (%)			
U.S. Citizen	21.2	17.4	75.0
U.S. Resident & Green Card Holder	20.1	20.4	16.7
Undocumented	9.5	9.6	8.3
Other (laser visa)	49.2	52.7	0.0
Number of Years with Current Status—Mean (& std. dev.)	18.0 (13.7)	17.2 (13.5)	28.9 (12.3)

Source: Informal and Underground Survey.

come north from Mexico to sell their goods, while others like Monica Ojeda travel south to make an informal cross-border living. Monica is a resident of Nuevo Laredo and became the sole family breadwinner following her divorce in 1995. After a stint as a maid working in Laredo, she noticed the cross-border demand for sneakers. Monica recalled, "I would buy shoes for my kids at [Nuevo Laredo] flea markets because they were not expensive as in other places. That's when I saw that the customer could buy shoes at low prices that would also leave the seller a good profit." This picture stuck with Monica. As she took the bus to her work in Laredo and back again, Monica saw many of her fellow southbound travelers carrying items for resale across the border in Mexico.

Monica connected the dots. As her maid position became tenuous because of an abusive employer, Monica used her meager savings to purchase ten pairs of shoes in Laredo. She quickly resold all of the shoes in Nuevo Laredo to family, friends, and neighbors, recouping her investment of $45 with a $90 pay day, doubling her investment. Nowadays, Monica travels to Laredo to purchase many shoes. Monica rents a piece of land in the commercial sector of Nuevo Laredo for five dollars a day and also sells at the flea market during the weekend. Though she works seven days a week (Sunday being her busiest sales day), she earns about $100 each week on sales of 25–30 pairs of shoes. Monica's greatest competitive advantage is her border-crossing card, which permits her to legally cross into South Texas to obtain her inventory. She finds that a familiarity with foreign exchange rates is also a necessity, as she buys in dollars and sells in pesos.

Not all informal cross-border businesses are as small and as difficult to detect as Monica's. Marco Ocampo, age forty-five, operates on a much larger scale in Laredo, where he currently resides. Marco realized that he could purchase a pallet worth of damaged goods for as little as $150 from his employer, a big-box store. While these damaged goods were no longer suitable for sale at the big-box store, most of the damage was to the products' packaging, rendering about 85–90% in usable goods. Marco's wife Lidia (age forty) spends about one day per week sorting through the damaged goods. Marco employs one person (informally) to help transport and set up, which consumes about a half day's work. That setup occurs in a Nuevo Laredo flea market. Marco was raised and educated in Nuevo Laredo and understands the retail landscape of his hometown well. On a monthly basis, Marco and Lidia can sell $1,000 to $1,500 worth of goods, with a profit margin of 50–70%.

In essence, these damaged goods for resale in Nuevo Laredo are not declared upon entry into Mexico and are sold informally at one of the local flea markets. So far, luck has been on the side of Marco and Lidia, and Marco quipped, "I guess we could expect to 'pay-off' Mexican customs in case we are busted crossing the merchandise, but this has never happened." Marco had been engaged in this secondary informal cross-border activity for just under a year, but the probability of detection increases as he continues to cross more loads for resale in Mexico. His penalty, however, will likely be, as he said, a pay-off rather than the more severe institutional consequences he would face if he were selling in the U.S.

Most of our cross-border entrepreneurs access the border through formal crossing mechanisms, either by foot (26.8%), car (58.1%), or bus (5.5%). Tomás Matos used his small convenience store in Nuevo Laredo to arbitrage the border for a second business. His convenience store (established in 1979) already required him to cross the border into Laredo to acquire much of his inventory. While in the U.S., he would also pick up goods for friends and neighbors. Soon, many of these requests multiplied, with friends and more distant associates who didn't have the time or ability to cross the border requesting auto parts. Tomás then arranged to send a courier by car to Laredo on a daily basis to bring back auto parts exclusively. Eventually his on-the-side informal parts business grew to surpass earnings from his convenience store. Now Tomás specializes in commercial vehicle replacement parts, and he has store fronts on both sides of the border. Graduating from informality, Tomás' formal parts centers are located in both Laredo and Nuevo Laredo, employ eight workers, and generate business income over $150,000. His business meets the burgeoning need for replacement vehicle parts in this biregional transportation cluster. From humble and informal beginnings, Tomás has achieved business success through his ability to engage in cross-border trade.

We asked our respondents to identify the advantages and disadvantages associated with conducting business across the border. Three advantages claimed were (a) the ability to earn extra money at a higher rate of profit or pay; (b) the ability to access cheaper products; and (c) the ability to hide cross-border income. All three are areas clearly part and parcel of the ability to leverage the border for economic gains. The potential risks or disadvantages were more numerous and included the following: (a) the potential loss of one's visa status (or deportation for undocumenteds); (b) the time associated with either waiting to cross the border (e.g., long traffic lines at the bridge) or time away from family; (c) the difficulty in crossing products; and, for those on foot, (d) the oppressive heat. Some of our respondents attempted to ameliorate detection risk by getting business permits. However, none possessed business permits to operate on *both* sides of the border. A few (14.8%) held U.S. business permits. About one-third (32.7%) held Mexican business permits, and over half (52.1%) held no business permit at all—entirely expected in the cross-border world of informal and underground economic activity.

The type of work undertaken by our respondents is typical of cross-border entrepreneurship. The majority were engaged in the cross-border buying and (re)selling of goods (43.6%) and services (37.4%). For example, Jorge Galvez, age forty-nine, provides window glass repair informally on both sides of the border. Based in Laredo, Jorge first began the glass repair trade in 1987. By 1994, with seven years of glass work experience, Jorge was going through a difficult divorce and needed extra income to pay for the separation. Since he had already been doing some glass work for family and friends, Jorge sought to fill his nights and weekends with extra glass jobs. He utilizes glass discarded from his formal glass work, so most of his cost is his time. Since 1994, Jorge has operated informally in both Nuevo Laredo and Laredo, providing mostly home window repair and installation from which he earns about $600 extra monthly. As Jorge is originally from Mexico, he easily traverses the border and is familiar with the cultural environment on both sides of the border. The demand for his cross-border business has grown such that he cannot get to everyone who wants his glass services.

Alternately, Eduardo Garibay retails most anything that he can move (i.e., sell) from his small, informal store in Laredo: Mexican art, furniture, leather, medical supplies, and windshield wipers. Utilizing his cross-border network of friends, family, and business associates, he buys low in Mexico and Texas and sells for a modest markup, earning about $750 a week. Eduardo did not aspire to be a discount retailer, but he felt he could make a go of it after he was laid off from a formal job.

Another cross-border entrepreneur from Nuevo Laredo, Josué Solorio, invested $1,500 in a used inflatable castle that he rents to families throwing birthday parties that are replete with lots of kids, piñatas, and fun. Through newspaper advertising and word-of-mouth promotion, he rents out his inflatable castle on both sides of the border and charges what consumers are willing to pay (about 400 pesos for three hours in Nuevo Laredo (about $30) and $80 for five hours in Laredo. Josué's take is 50% of the sales, with the other 50% going to his family members who set up, care for, and take down the castle at the party. Josué quickly earned back his investment and purchased another inflatable castle to expand his business. He avoids government taxation on both sides and insurance payments in Texas as he capitalizes on doing business in two countries but is registered in neither country. He takes advantage of the Mexican penchant for celebrating children's birthdays in style.

Very few of our respondents became engaged in the informal cross-border economy by way of hobby (only 0.7%) or a formal training course

(10.2%). Most (84.3%) were introduced to the cross-border economic informal world by family, friends, or coworkers. As we have previously reported, having adequate social capital is an important consideration that facilitates cross-border trade, especially association with other persons already engaged in such activities. We also found that a receptive, or at least a nonpunitive, culture of acceptance of marginal economic activity was important. Finally, capital from family, friends, and personal savings allows for starting most informal cross-border entrepreneurial enterprises. Of these factors, personal savings is very important, as more than three-quarters of our sample (78.8%) reported having relied on additional income-generating jobs or enterprises to accumulate enough money to start their business.

As with other informal activities, informal cross-border activities must be hidden from government officials. This is easier when enterprises are kept small or are stretched out over time and space. Two-thirds (67.1%) of our respondents worked as cross-border informal entrepreneurs on a part-time basis. Most (61.9%) had held formal-sector employment at some point over the past five years, indicating the fluidity of movement between sectoral employment (informal, formal, and underground).[47] Informal cross-border survey participants who were able to work between sectors reported an average total annual income of $23,280—which includes formal earnings.

Enterprise size, as expressed by the number of employees, is also indicative of the small-scale operations of these economic activities. Nearly nine in ten (88.1%) informal cross-border enterprises had no paid employees, and 98.1% had two or fewer paid employees. Essentially, informal cross-border trade, as reflected by those we interviewed, takes place simply one microentrepreneur at a time. Further, such small-scale cross-border *informal* operations can remain hidden from officials because of the massive flows of *formal* trade crossing at the same transit points.

For example, Lilia Ulloa, a wheelchair bound elderly lady, does not conjure up suspicion of informal cross-border activity. Born in Nuevo Laredo in 1927 and crippled in a car accident at the age of nineteen in Mexico, Lilia tried as an adult to compensate her family for constant care. From her wheelchair, Lilia could still cook, so she began making and selling tamales. Lilia did this informally from her home in Nuevo Laredo until her mom died in 1982. She then moved to Laredo to live with other family members, and from there she still actively makes tamales for sale without government regulation. When Lilia first began selling tamales, many families still made their own tamales at home, so business was difficult. Slowly with the spread of modernity, families had less time and relied more on others to supply traditional (and time-consuming) foodstuffs. With the help of her family who donate sup-plies, transportation, and time during the holidays, Lilia is able to keep up with demand, please her customers, and contribute in a small way to her family. At the time of the survey, Lilia typically made on aver-age 200–250 dozen tamales in November, 250–275 dozen in December, and 30–50 dozen in the other months. At $4.25 per dozen, Lilia's annual sales hover around $10,000, with the informal endeavor perhaps netting $8,000. Due to her long stay in Nuevo Laredo, Lilia maintains a loyal customer base on both sides of the border: She has thirty devoted cus-tomers. With each sale, she still hands out a sales flier promoting fu-ture business. Her health has always been a challenge, and in her old age Lilia has arthritis in both of her hands. But Lilia has fulfilled a life-long determination to contribute to her family by sponsoring birthdays (she has thirteen grandchildren) and also to the culinary enjoyment of her many friends. The Mexican authorities pass Lilia through inspection without questions as she delivers to her Mexican customer base.

Few respondents indicated many challenges that hindered their in-formal cross-border trade. But for those who did face work-related chal-lenges, transportation, time, and the weather were presented as most bothersome. While most respondents in the group have held some form of formal employment, current levels of enrollment in social security are surprising. Only 12% of our cross-border entrepreneurs were en-rolled in social security, with half of those enrolled in the Mexican sys-tem. Clearly, short-term economic considerations trump long-term economic security plans. Nevertheless, there is a near universal feel-ing among our respondents that the current informal cross-border eco-nomic activity is the correct course of action, as 84.8% of them reported *not* having any regrets about their current line of work.

Underground Cross-Border Activity: Auto Theft

While the informal cross-border trader has been the focus of this chap-ter, we acknowledge other forms of extra-legal cross-border trade, such as underground activities, most notably the smuggling of drugs and people. As smuggling was covered in Chapter 2, we will limit our brief discussion here to another prominent example of cross-border under-ground activity—cross-border auto theft.

Gail Johnson recalled, "I have never felt as helpless as to find my car gone [when I was] walking out into the parking lot of HEB [a Texas grocery chain]. I have had two cars stolen since I took this nursing position in Brownsville. The last time I was even watching the 'scum' through my apartment window as they were driving away." As auto theft is a crime of opportunity, patrons at malls, hotels, and big-box stores are particularly prone to vehicle theft, especially from Thursday evening through Sunday. Auto theft in South Texas is a real concern; in 2009 Laredo led the state and nation in the rate of stolen vehicles (see Table 5.4). The border region as a whole is a very active area for vehicle theft, though the overall *number* of stolen vehicles pales in comparison to the number stolen in Houston, Dallas, and San Antonio (see Table 5.5).

Lack of cooperation by Mexican officials frustrates local police officers on the U.S. side of the border. A member of one police unit in South Texas received a report of two men breaking into a vehicle at a local mall. The men stole the car and headed toward Mexico. The officer recalled, "I chased the car to the bridge, and the vehicle ran the toll booth." On the Mexican side the "police just waved the car thieves through," laughing as it passed by. The officer lamented, "With police relations like that, how can you have any effect on auto theft?"

Actually, cross-border relations between police in Texas and Mexico work best through informal channels. Generally, when a car is stolen in the U.S. and taken to Mexico, the car's owner is reimbursed by his or her insurer, who writes it off as a loss—and then passes on higher rates to border residents. But some Texas law enforcement agencies are much better at recovering stolen vehicles from Mexico than others. In 2001, the Texas Department of Public Safety Motor Vehicle Theft Service recovered more than $25 million in stolen vehicles from Mexico. Much of the credit goes to the DPS Border Auto Theft Information Center (BATIC) investigators along the border, who invest considerable time in nurturing relationships with Mexican authorities. Before BATIC was created in 1994, fewer than 50 vehicles a year were recovered from south of the border.[48] Gallahan found that cities that had established good *informal* relations with Mexican police had a much higher recovery rate than those that relied primarily on formal recovery procedures or that had poor informal relations.[49] These relationships were typically built through a specially appointed local police department liaison who worked specifically in the area of auto theft and recovery with like counterparts in Mexico.[50] Of the Texas cities reporting more than 500 vehicles stolen in 1995, El Paso had a recovery rate of 52%, followed by Laredo with 41%, McAllen with 33%, and Brownsville with only 26%.

Table 5.4. National rank of 3 Texas MSAs (out of 361 MSAs) by rate of vehicle theft, 2002–2009

MSA*	2002	2003	2004	2005	2006	2007	2008	2009	Average
Laredo	49	30	23	32	22	8	2	1	22.0
McAllen-Edinburg-Mission	63	68	56	76	79	58	53	43	61.1
Brownsville-Harlingen-San Benito	116	112	105	119	99	91	114	75	103.8

*MSA = Metropolitan Statistical Area.
Source: National Insurance Crime Bureau (www.nicb.org)

Table 5.5. Texas MSAs top 10 for vehicle theft in 2009

MSA*	Texas Rank^	Number of Vehicle Thefts	National Rank^ (of 361)
Laredo	1	1,792	1
Houston-Sugarland-Baytown	2	25,655	25
El Paso	3	3,234	27
Dallas-Fort Worth-Arlington		25,685	39
McAllen-Edinburg-Mission	4	2,911	43
San Antonio	5	7,430	54
Longview	6	794	48
Brownsville-Harlingen-San Benito	7	1,122	75
Amarillo	8	752	76
Odessa	9	407	79
Beaumont-Port Arthur	10	1,072	88

*MSA = Metropolitan Statistical Area.
^By rate per 100,000 people.
Source: National Insurance Crime Bureau (www.nicb.org).

In the area of cross-border law enforcement, informal relations seem to work best, though they are not generally encouraged by the federal governments of the two countries.

No one knows for certain, but the best estimates suggest roughly 70% of cars stolen in South Texas end up on the Mexican side of the border. Again, the border is both a conduit for vehicle theft and a barrier to vehicle recovery. But what happens to these cars in Mexico? Some go straight to buyers who "ordered" the specific make, model, and year of the car. The car thief, driver, and lookout get their cut. The auto theft ring then sells the car to a Mexican national who gets a car at a much reduced rate. Some stolen cars are used by the drug cartels for transporting drugs and aliens. Part of the cost of the car goes to fixing the registration within Mexico, either through alteration of the origin markers on the car and/or "fixing" the paperwork at the appropriate Mexican agency.

For the fortunate, some stolen vehicles are recovered from Mexico. However, as might be expected, there is a much lower recovery rate of cars stolen in the U.S. and driven into Mexico than for cars stolen and recovered within the U.S.[51] But not all stolen cars are left whole; many are disassembled in chop shops where separated parts might bring in more money (and are much harder to trace) than the entire vehicle.

It is no surprise that underground cross-border activity reports a high remuneration rate, an expected consequence of the greater risk. What is more interesting is the higher hourly yield we calculated for those engaged in cross-border underground activities ($121.70) than for those engaged in underground activities in a single nation ($74.41). This is probably a reflection of the cross-border transportation of drugs, undocumented immigrants, and stolen vehicles.

The Complexity of Informal Cross-Border Participation

The U.S.-Mexico border presents a highly complex informal trade arena. This complexity is depicted in Figure 5.1, which shows the multiple two-way national and cross-border possibilities. This figure portrays the possibility of switching between formal, informal, and underground sectors, as well as simultaneous participation in all three sectors. In addition, participation may take place on either or both sides of the border. For example, a school teacher in South Texas may take an informal job as a gardener (point 4, Figure 5.1).

A common cross-border example might be Mexicans coming to the U.S. to purchase second-hand items (clothing, electronics, etc.) in either an informal or formal transaction (e.g., a flea market) and then selling those items formally or informally back in Mexico (points 24–29, Figure 5.1). One of our respondents, Marco, fits this profile. He owns a

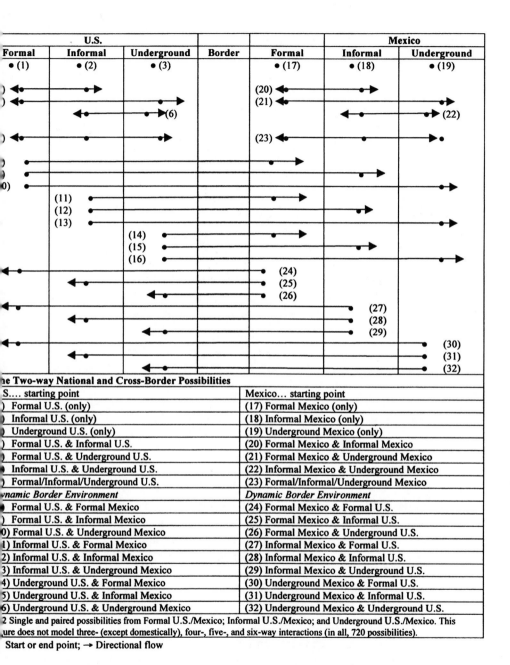

U.S.			Border	Mexico		
Formal	Informal	Underground		Formal	Informal	Underground

he Two-way National and Cross-Border Possibilities

S.... starting point	Mexico... starting point
) Formal U.S. (only)	(17) Formal Mexico (only)
) Informal U.S. (only)	(18) Informal Mexico (only)
) Underground U.S. (only)	(19) Underground Mexico (only)
) Formal U.S. & Informal U.S.	(20) Formal Mexico & Informal Mexico
) Formal U.S. & Underground U.S.	(21) Formal Mexico & Underground Mexico
Informal U.S. & Underground U.S.	(22) Informal Mexico & Underground Mexico
) Formal/Informal/Underground U.S.	(23) Formal/Informal/Underground Mexico
vnamic Border Environment	*Dynamic Border Environment*
Formal U.S. & Formal Mexico	(24) Formal Mexico & Formal U.S.
) Formal U.S. & Informal Mexico	(25) Formal Mexico & Informal U.S.
0) Formal U.S. & Underground Mexico	(26) Formal Mexico & Underground U.S.
1) Informal U.S. & Formal Mexico	(27) Informal Mexico & Formal U.S.
2) Informal U.S. & Informal Mexico	(28) Informal Mexico & Informal U.S.
3) Informal U.S. & Underground Mexico	(29) Informal Mexico & Underground U.S.
4) Underground U.S. & Formal Mexico	(30) Underground Mexico & Formal U.S.
5) Underground U.S. & Informal Mexico	(31) Underground Mexico & Informal U.S.
6) Underground U.S. & Underground Mexico	(32) Underground Mexico & Underground U.S.

2 Single and paired possibilities from Formal U.S./Mexico; Informal U.S./Mexico; and Underground U.S./Mexico. This
ure does not model three- (except domestically), four-, five-, and six-way interactions (in all, 720 possibilities).

Start or end point; → Directional flow

Figure 5.1. Dynamic economic activity in the South Texas borderlands environment*

small convenience store in Pharr, Texas. His regular inventory and sales are all reported formally. However, every two weeks, Marco, a U.S. citizen, crosses into Mexico and purchases specialty Mexican foods, statuettes, and piñatas. When he sells these specialty items for cash in his small store, he might not charge or collect sales taxes, thus becoming partially inserted into the cross-border informal economy. The main point of Figure 5.1 is the great range of permutations and combinations possible in this dynamic and complex cross-border environment.

Conclusion

Cross-border traders, prime examples of those Martínez[52] calls "transnational borderlanders," constitute an essential element of life on both sides of the South Texas/Northern Mexico border. Using informal networks and skirting governmental regulation, they provide essential goods and services to residents of both nations. They transport huge amounts of discards into Mexico, making it possible for the poor to afford basic necessities. They cross ethnic foods and other items into the U.S., allowing Mexican nationals living here to continue to enjoy their traditions and cuisine. And for the undocumented and those who cannot afford the cost of a passport, they provide low-cost alternatives to items and services beyond their reach. As such, they epitomize an informal version of free trade that is free only because governmental oversight is skirted or subverted.

This is not to say that the state has no impact on cross-border trade. It does, though its involvement can also create distortions. Intentionally or not, the U.S. government creates both wedges and opportunities in the arbitrage of informal activities across the border. The laser visa, for example, facilitates both legitimate cross-border shopping (the intended outcome) and informal cross-border activities (an unintended outcome). Thus it becomes a wedge that separates those who possess a laser visa from those who do not—creating potential winners and losers in the relatively easy access to the U.S. marketplace.

The Mexican government also creates wedges and opportunities, though perhaps more by the informality of its border officials than by the restrictions it enacts.[53] Illegal payments, or *mordidas*, given to Mexican officials to evade cumbersome rules and routines push many cross-border traders into informality in order to operate within a reconstructed institutional environment. Cross-border trade into Mexico may also be seen as under-the-table economic activities that are *pushed* by some government officials, or at least are done in collusion with them. Mexican officials also become a potential wedge to commerce even at the smallest levels of economic activity. Navigating the structure of corruption, and contributing to it, informal and underground operators manage to enhance their business opportunities and create a more predictable informal enterprise environment.

Many of the opportunities to arbitrage goods and services across the border result from long-standing inequality and poverty in the region. For example, cross-border maids and gardeners from Mexico serve as labor replacements in the U.S. because the cost of these household services is relatively low in comparison to their prices. That is, a cross-border maid may be employed informally to perform both cleaning and child-care duties for less than the cost of formal day care. These opportunities are possible due to the widespread poverty and low wages available for unskilled work in Mexico; also, these are part and parcel of the push-pull and hold-repel forces expounded on in Chapter 1. For those informals courageous enough to cross frequently, the border is a vibrant zone where one can make a living and arbitrage unique economic goods and services.

CHAPTER 6

Border *Colonias*: Informality in Housing

Irene Canales, a single mother, owns an older model mobile home in the rural part of Hidalgo County and is making payments to buy the lot that she has the trailer on. She said,

> Before I lived here, I was living with my mother, sister, and two broth-
> ers in my mother's small trailer. I left their house and went on my own
> because, with my children, it was difficult to have so many people in a
> small space. In addition, I didn't like my mother disciplining my children.
> When I left, she told me that I would be back in a week. I didn't know
> how I was going to make it, but I found a small one-bedroom add-on
> that a neighbor rented to me for fifty dollars a month. We had no furni-
> ture and the room had no kitchen, bathroom, water, or electricity. We
> had to share an outhouse with some people who lived there also. We
> slept on the floor until someone gave me a bed. I didn't know what to do
> for work. I had never made *tamales* before, but I decided to learn. On a
> small propane burner I started making tamales, and then we would go to
> the Wal-Mart parking lot to sell them. Little by little, I saved until I was
> able to get a small trailer house for $1,000. It took me a year to pay it
> off, but now we have our own place in this *colonia*. Now I split my time
> between working as a maid and making and selling tamales.

The informality of colonia housing permits some of the poorest of the poor, like Irene, to find housing—even if it's only a small trailer—and to engage in economic activities from their homes. Without colonias, Irene most likely would have ended up either homeless or evicted for overcrowding. By living out in the country, she was able to operate a small tamale-making business from her home. Had she been in the city, she would most likely have been closed down by a landlord or by health inspectors. Hidalgo County (and other South Texas counties) simply does not have the resources to police such activities in out-of-the way locations spread across the county's 1,570 square miles.

In both Mexico and Texas, informality is an important part of colonia housing. Colonias represent a great deal of informality in how homes are built or acquired (frequent lack of platting, unclear titles, informal lending processes, failure to enforce building codes, lack of zoning, etc.), and they are also a springboard from which residents can easily engage in informal economic activities. We will examine colonias as a form of informality and then will examine how they contribute to economic informality.

Colonias as Informal Housing

Initially, when colonias began to appear in Texas border counties in the 1960s, they were small collections of shacks outside city limits. Texas counties, however, had little authority to regulate the development of colonias and even fewer resources to do so. As colonia growth began to mushroom in the 1980s and as cities began to expand outward to include some colonias, the very poor living conditions of the colonias began to be seen as a major problem.[1] Some major border cities tried to avoid dealing with colonias by incorporating around the colonias. Others began to incorporate them within city limits and to blame (and try to pursue) the developers who had failed to bring in the minimal infrastructure usually required (paved streets, water, sewers, drainage, and electricity). Many colonias had not been platted. Few or no building regulations had been followed.

Most colonia lots were sold under a financing arrangement called "contract-for-deed." This arrangement, often offered at high interest rates, allowed developers and buyers to avoid banks and formal lending agencies. This was important because most low-income buyers either had no formal credit histories or very poor credit histories. Contract-for-deed, however, allowed the seller to retain ownership of the property until the last payment had been made. If the buyer fell behind in making payments, the developer could reclaim the property, often within 45 days, without going through a formal foreclosure process. Unlike deeds of trust, contract-for-deed arrangements were not recorded with the county clerk. In addition to making foreclosure easier, the less formal contract-for-deed made it more difficult for the county to enforce any commitments made by the developer to provide required infrastructure.[2] This arrangement opened the door to rather extensive abuse and exploitation of colonia residents.

In 1995, the Texas Legislature passed the Colonias Fair Land Sales Act designed to protect those who rely on contracts-for-deed. Developers were required to record the sales, and counties were required to record them. The bill also required developers to formally state what services they would provide and whether the property was located on a floodplain. They also had to provide buyers with an annual statement of the amount paid, the amount owed, the number of payments remaining, and the taxes paid on the purchaser's behalf. Despite the legislation, however, contract-for-deed buyers have found great difficulty in securing financing to build a house or to make improvements on the property. And because they will not legally own the land until they make the final payment, they cannot use the property as collateral when applying for a loan. Unlike a home in the formal housing market, a colonia home cannot be considered an asset for the home buyer.[3]

Victor Quiroga is one of the majority of colonia residents relying on a contract-for-deed to purchase his property. "The payments are cheap enough to afford," he says. "We pay no more than two hundred dollars a month for our half-acre lot. The man who sold these lots told us that with only a hundred dollars down, the lot would be 'ours.' Then we found out that because it is owner financed we will not really own it until we finish paying for it." Despite this difficulty, Victor really likes the idea of not having any restrictions on how or what he will build. "Someday," he says, "I will build our dream home on this lot. Right now we are just renting a nearby home. It is pretty run-down, and we don't even have a refrigerator. When it rains, we often get flooded."

Many colonia residents, like Victor, appreciate the informality of few or no building codes. It allows them to build their home themselves (often with the help of neighbors and family) and at their own pace (a seven-year completion rate is very common). While cities have the authority to enforce building codes, Texas counties have more limited authority. In 1993, the Texas Legislature sought to give counties the authority to enforce zoning and building codes, but the measure was defeated. The opposition came from counties who lacked financial resources to enforce codes, as well as from community groups representing the colonias who did not want to eliminate the opportunity for colonia residents to build their own homes.[4]

Though a lot of colonia homes are well built, many are not. Frank Davila, a student from the Rio Grande City area lives with his family in the small colonia of Garciasville. He describes how he and his family are building their home. "Since I was a little kid," he says, "we'd go to certain neighborhoods that are close and ask for discarded lumber, scrap metal, and materials. My dad, who works in home construction, sometimes brings home leftover pieces of lumber. Our house is not the prettiest house in the world, but we take pride in it. Our family does what we can with the little money we have to add to our home. *La casa de nosotros es mejor que las otras casas en la colonia* (our house is better than the other ones in our colonia)." Improvements to their home are made bit by bit, as their financial situation allows. But with time, their home has taken shape. Frank's sixteen-year-old sister, Gloria, who was present for the interview, added, "We only have two bedrooms and one bath to share between our parents and two younger siblings. It's hard to have the privacy every girl wants when you have to share a room with three *hermanos* (siblings)."

Though informality allows colonia residents to buy a lot that may not have been platted, to avoid inspectors and fees related to building codes, and to not worry much about zoning and title searches, such informality also makes them vulnerable to exploitation. Mrs. Rodriguez learned this the hard way when she and her husband bought a lot from the owner of a subdivision. He told them that the subdivision had paved streets, water, sewer lines, and light poles.

> It was 1987 when I decided to buy a lot in this subdivision. We liked the lower prices and good benefits the owner told us about. I was thrilled with the idea because the streets were paved and my children didn't have to get to school all muddy on rainy days. I was also thrilled with the idea because I didn't have to pay anything extra. Everything was included in the price of the lot. A year later, I found out that we had been tricked by the owner of the subdivision. The only thing this subdivision had was paved streets and water lines. We found out after he had sold all the lots that he had moved, and we are still unable to locate him. When the city of Pharr incorporated our colonia into its city limits, we talked to the mayor. He told us that all utilities should have been installed as soon as

the lots were put up for sale. Later on we found out that this was not the only subdivision where utilities were not fully installed. We're still trying to get help from a colonia support agency.

Though some observers see both advantages and problems related to colonia housing, reporters and government officials almost never say anything good about them. A report by the Federal Reserve Bank of Dallas, for example, stated that colonias are

unincorporated and impoverished subdivisions that flourish along the state's border with Mexico (where) 400,000 residents struggle daily with living conditions that resemble a Third World country—ramshackle dwellings, open sewage, lack of sanitary water and drainage, dusty un-paved roads, and no plumbing.[5]

Though such characterizations rightly point out that colonias often lack basic infrastructure and bypass many formal housing systems, they fail to recognize that the informality of colonia housing may actually meet many needs of impoverished border residents. Generally speaking, the official point of view ignores many additional positive aspects of colonia housing, including that they serve as a venue in which residents can develop social capital and financial capital, and they provide a place to live for many of the poorest of the poor.

Despite the problems, and despite massive state and federal efforts to improve or even eradicate colonias, this form of informal housing keeps expanding. Prior to 1970, only 10% of the Valley population was housed in colonias.[6] By 1990, 26% of the Valley population was living in colonia housing, even though the Valley population had doubled. A 1995 report by the Texas Water Development Board counted 1,436 colonias in Texas, with a total of 339,041 residents.[7] Hidalgo County alone contained over half of these colonias.

It has become difficult to count colonias and colonia residents, however, because the counting previously done by the Texas Water Development Board was merged with a system of the Office of the Attorney General of Texas. This new system was designed to count all economically distressed areas (EDAPs) in cities, in towns, and in some border counties not previously included. In 2003, this new system counted 2,333 distressed areas along the U.S.-Mexico border, with 484,892 residents, the vast majority of which were in Texas. Of these, 1,404 EDAPs were listed as having inadequate water or substandard wastewater treatment facilities. As we will show, the majority of colonias (now EDAPs) are in the Rio Grande Valley of South Texas.

Methodology for Our Study of Colonias

Though our Informal and Underground Survey did not include questions that allowed us to determine whether respondents lived in a colonia or not, our earlier Cultural Practices Survey contained a question about type of residence.[8] This allowed us to distinguish colonia residents from residents of low-income neighborhoods in South Texas cities. In this Cultural Practices Survey, we also asked how many were employed, either part-time or full-time. In this survey, 18% of colonia residents were self-employed, compared to only 2% of low-income city residents.[9] This self-employment participation gap would suggest that colonias facilitate self-employment, much of which seems to be informal.

The descriptions of colonia life in this chapter come primarily from four sources. The first is the Informal and Underground Survey described in preceding chapters. Second is a series of in-depth qualitative interviews conducted by University of Texas-Pan American (UTPA) students from 1995 to 2008 as part of the Borderlife Project in an effort to describe what it is like to live in a colonia. We name this data source Colonia Ethnographic Interviews, 1995–2008. The third source is the Cultural Practices Survey mentioned in the preceding paragraph. It was administered in 2000–2001 to 433 respondents. In addition to the question about type of neighborhood (including colonias), it included other items about crime and informal economic activities. Finally, we utilized data analyzed by the U.S. Geological Survey of Economically Depressed Areas (EDAPs) and the Office of the Texas Secretary of State, which assessed colonias in Texas with regard to health, infrastructure, and quality-of-life indicators.

Why Colonias? A Preliminary Analysis

Though we will explore the economic environment related to colonia development in greater detail later in the chapter, here we argue that colonias exist for three basic reasons. First, colonia residents are pushed into informality by the failure of formal systems (banking, municipal government, public utilities, etc.) to support low-cost housing for the poor. When formal systems fail, the poor respond with innovative informal methods that are off the books. Second, colonia residents are pulled into (or attracted to) informal housing because colonias make it easier to hide *economic* informality. And third, colonias are also attractive because of some of the cultural and social benefits they provide to Mexican-origin people in the South Texas borderlands. A brief examination of each of these factors follows.

1. Colonias as a Response to the Failure of Formal Housing Systems.

Mauro Granados, a migrant farm worker, describes how trying to follow formal systems often pushes low-income Valley residents into informality.

> I remember working very hard and staying long hours under the hot sun. I wanted something better for my family and thought I could get a loan to get a small business started. As I walked into the bank I felt my stomach turn and my ears burn. If looks could kill I'd be dead. I told myself it must be the old shirt, my second-hand slacks, and my working shoes. I didn't think it could be the color of my skin because most of the employees in the bank looked "Mexican" just like me. I proceeded to the loan department, where I was told to sit in the waiting area. I sat there for five hours. Finally, the janitor told me it was time to go home. I went early the next morning and sat there for three hours before they finally called me in. After only a minute or two of listening, the banker made me feel like a complete loser and told me my business ideas would never work. "You would never qualify for a loan with us," he told me. "Our requirements are very strict." I asked him what the requirements were and he said, "There are so many I don't have the time."

Typically, banks in the region require securitization for most types of loans. For example, a car loan is secured or collateralized by the vehicle. A business loan may be secured by recognized personal assets, such as a home or existing business. In Mauro's case, it was most likely assumed that he did not have any assets of value, or no assets with a formal value. That is, his assets were most likely owned in a nonrecognized or nonregularized manner (i.e., no legal or paper proof of ownership). From the perspective of the formal banking community, these assets are seen to be deficient. Hence, the bank officer did not even bother to inquire as to Mauro's assets.

This view by many in the banking community about South Texas colonia residents is common and sometimes appalling. In developing nations, innovative ways to overcome the many formal limitations low-income people face when trying to borrow money have been created, such as the introduction of microcredit (with the Grameen Bank of Bangladesh the most compelling example[10]). Few such options exist, however, for poor colonia residents in South Texas.

2. The Attraction of Colonias as a Place to Conduct Informal Economic Enterprise.

The second major "cause" of colonias, their advantages for economic informality, is illustrated by the story of Octavio Guerra. In 1985, he crossed the Rio Grande/Bravo without papers, seeking work to support his family. Though undocumented, he was able to find work as a migrant farm worker. In 1987, the Immigration Reform and Control Act (IRCA) legislation made it possible for Octavio to become a legal resident under its amnesty provisions. With his newly acquired legal status, he opened a *tapicería* (upholstery shop) and struggled to make a home for his wife and two children.

One day, a customer told Octavio he had a car in Reynosa that needed re-upholstering and asked Octavio to go with him to drive it back to Octavio's shop. As Octavio drove back into the U.S., he never dreamed of the problems that awaited him. The inspector at the bridge, seeing the rather beat-up vehicle, told him to take it to "secondary" for further inspection. An officer brought a dog to inspect the vehicle, and officers found 10 pounds of marijuana hidden in a compartment. Despite his explanations that he had been set up, they refused to believe him and threw him in the county jail. His court-appointed lawyer never came to see him until the day they went to court. Though the attorney plea-bargained ten years probation for pleading guilty to the drug charge, Octavio was immediately turned over to INS. They took away his residency card and deported him. Undaunted, he crossed again using *un pasaporte negro*, rejoined his family, purchased land in a colonia in the La Joya area, and started a business as a shade-tree mechanic and upholsterer. The colonia location allowed him not only to hide his illegal status, but to operate an informal business that provides a modest income, repairing vehicles for his low-income neighbors. In the sixteen years he has lived there, he has never been bothered by police or other government agents, largely because it is not obviously visible as a place of business.

3. Social and Cultural Advantages of Colonias.

The social, economic, and cultural benefits of colonias to low-income people of Mexican origin are the third factor that helps explain their growth and predominance in South Texas. One student who interviewed her colonia neighbors said

> I can count on my neighbors for help because most of us in the neighborhood are going through the same situations. Many of us women stay at home and tend to our children while our husbands go out and work. And we all speak Spanish. *La amistad* (friendship) is what gives me a sense of belonging in my neighborhood. Everyone that I interviewed agreed that there was a sense of shared identity among the neighbors. If one finds a solution to a problem, more than likely that person will share that solution with other neighbors. This then builds a sense of unity.[11]

Residents in many colonias help one another in building their homes, some knowing the basics of installing electricity, others knowing how to make and lay cement blocks, and still others knowing basic carpentry skills. Colonia neighbors also provide a network for finding bargains in food, clothing, and repair problems. If someone gets sick and cannot go to Mexico to purchase an antibiotic (or some other medicine) because of lack of papers to get back, someone who has such papers will often go. Thus, living in a colonia facilitates the development of a mutual-help network, much of it informal.

Colonias in Mexico

Part of the attractiveness of colonias to many of the Mexican-origin people of South Texas is their familiarity with colonias in Mexico. Mexican culture values home ownership, family solidarity, and communal help based on neighborhood association. Indeed, Mexico has a long history of unauthorized housing. Despite this history, the Mexican government for many years sought to limit or eradicate colonias as an unwanted blight or "cancer."[12] They were regarded as an aberration, a dysfunctional result of poverty and rapid urbanization. Often, the government resorted to eviction or herding people into large, formal housing projects. But rapid urbanization and limited governmental resources could only provide a fraction of the housing needed by low-income Mexicans.

Overwhelmed by this unmet need, the Mexican government in the 1970s began to regard colonias more positively, making efforts to legalize questionable or illegal land titles, provide essential services, and support colonia communities.[13] Since the 1990s, Mexico has followed a policy of incorporating colonias into the fiscal and regulatory structures of cities, stimulating the efforts of private home owners to produce their own housing, and providing governmental help in infrastructure development (water, sewers, and some streets). With the development of the *maquiladora* (border assembly plant) industry on the Mexican border (starting in the 1960s), colonias (both authorized and unauthorized) in or near Mexican border cities have become a major form of housing.

According to Ward many of the colonias in Mexico are built on land that was either illegally sold and developed or was seized by tenants and then regularized by governmental agencies.[14] In many cases the owners of the land collude with those who seize and build on the land, and the now-former owner is compensated twice—once by the tenant and again by the government, which "reimburses" the owner. In some cases colonias spring up on land that has been designated for other purposes, or land where no infrastructure exists. In such cases the colonia tenants often pressure the government to provide services once the colonia homes are built. It is also common for communal lands, called *ejidos* in Mexico, to be illegally sold by the communal owners and then regularized by the government. Thus, many of the colonias in Mexico are illegal and informal developments that are later formalized, even to the eventual point of acquiring deeds for the new owners. In most Mexican colonias, as in colonias in Texas, the homes are built by the colonia residents themselves with little help from formal lending institutions or builders. Many also are built with minimal attention to building codes, allowing inexperienced home owners to learn building skills as they piece together their new homes.

Some families are familiar with colonias in both countries. Rosalinda Tamez, a woman who lives in a Hidalgo County colonia, described how her present colonia home compares to her colonia home in Reynosa, Mexico. She said, "I have lived here in the United States for 4 years. I came here to follow my husband because he was able to get work on this side of the border. I don't mind living here because I know that my kids and I are better off here. You should have seen our house in Reynosa, if you think this house is bad. My husband and I both had to work when we were living in Mexico. I had to take my children with me selling sunflower seeds and peanuts. I hated those days."

Colonias: Push or Pull?

Though the preceding accounts suggest that colonia life provides some benefits to those who live in this informal setting, many of the forms of informality found in colonias result more from the push of poverty than the pull of advantages (such as culture or family). José Sauceda lives with his wife and five children in what we would consider a shack, made up of pieces of lumber that he finds or buys. An undocumented immigrant, José is self-employed, working in fields or cutting lawns for people. José lives in a larger colonia, on a half-acre lot. Of building his house, he said, "I try to use materials that people leave behind after constructing (or knocking down) a building. If I have enough money, I will buy what I can to build or repair our home. I have no other choice. I always have to be repairing something to keep my house up. Everything is so expensive, and the only thing that I can afford is something used or free." José makes about $9,000 a year. Given the poor condition his house is in, he and his family would be devastated by one of the hurricanes or strong tropical storms which periodically hit South Texas. José does not complain, however, because he knows he is here illegally. He also knows he does not qualify for any governmental assistance. He lives on a day-to-day basis, hoping that his children will have a better chance when they are older.

Another colonia resident, Alfredo Martinez, is in the U.S. legally but has similar problems. "We have no money left over from my check to fix the house," he says. "All of my money goes for gas or to fix my car which constantly breaks down. I work for a warehouse where they unload and load vegetables. It is not a stable job because they only call me when they need me. I recall a summer when it rained so hard that one part of our roof caved in. I had to take some cardboard boxes from work to patch it up. I couldn't believe I had to go to that extreme but I had no choice. I had no money to repair or rebuild the roof."

Colonias as a Springboard for Economic Informality and Underground Activities

As previously indicated, colonias not only represent informality in housing—they also facilitate other forms of informality. There is very limited quantitative data available on the number of informal activities in border colonias, and the data that are available are of limited applicability. In 1997, for example, the Office of Border Health of the Texas Department of Health conducted a survey of health and environmental conditions in colonias in which they asked about employment status.[15] They reported that 18% of colonia residents were unemployed, compared to 11% of noncolonia residents in the six Texas border counties they surveyed. Many colonia residents who reported being unemployed, however, were engaged in informal economic activities. Indeed, our qualitative research suggests that many colonia residents who might report being officially unemployed are, in reality, engaged in many informal or underground economic enterprises.

This is illustrated by several cases. Marcelo and Angela Saenz, a young couple with three very young children, live in a two-room house in Las Milpas (a large colonia now incorporated into the city of Pharr). Marcelo works as a handyman doing odd jobs, but Angela is unemployed. Although unskilled, she wants to work but can't find a job, and even if she could, she can't find or afford day care in the area. She also lacks transportation to go to and from work. Consequently, she generates a little income by selling food stuffs, things which her husband brings from Mexico, for 25 to 50 cents per item. Likewise, Francesca Reyna, who is about 65 years old, sells carbon firewood in front of her house north of Alamo. She says that she needed another source of income, and so she found out about the demand through friends from the colonia where she lives. She says that it helps out a lot because the only other income that she and her husband receive is from his monthly Social Security check. Isabel Rivas, her neighbor, has a husband who works in construction when he can find work. Or, when no construction work is available, he does yard work or odd jobs. To bring extra money, he also sells garden plants from his property. When work is especially scarce, he migrates up north with his family, though he considers migratory farm work his last resort.

Some colonias also attract individuals who want to hide underground activities. One colonia resident, Blanca Rivera, reported that most of her relatives who live in her colonia are involved in cockfighting. "Every weekend there is a group of people who not only fight roosters," she said, "but also drink and do drugs." Since she has two young daughters, she lives in constant fear. She continued,

> We don't dare go outside during these cockfights because the people there have money, drugs, and weapons. One time, the sheriff dropped in and chased a few men, with weapons drawn, as they ran across my

front yard. I was afraid. I always have to be on the lookout, and most nights I do not sleep well. Early one morning, before my husband went to prison, he ran inside the house yelling that we had to leave immediately because someone was going to do a "drive-by" (shooting). Me and my girls left with only the clothes we had on. I hate this lifestyle; I hate this colonia.

Advantages Associated with Texas Border Colonias

Cultural Advantages. Most of our respondents were more upbeat about their colonia homes. For many people of Mexican origin, colonias offer not only economic opportunities (formal and informal), but considerable cultural advantages as well. Mexican-origin people can live and easily communicate with virtually everyone even though they do not know English. Foods from Mexico are easy to obtain and celebrations are often very similar to those practiced in Mexico. Pablo Cordova, for example, says that when they throw birthday parties for the children, everyone in the block is invited and not just the children. Everyone shows up. When his wife throws bingo dinners, all the women gather to play, the men gather to drink, and the children play out in the streets from house to house. No one is a stranger and everyone interacts with each other. "People who live in colonias don't send out invitations in the mail and wait for an RSVP," he says. "The invitation is always informal, by word of mouth, and everyone is invited."

Family-Related Advantages. Another advantage offered by colonias is the possibility of family solidarity. Various adult members of a family can build multiple houses on one or two lots. Family members from Mexico can also come to stay for varying lengths of time, or can expect a base from which to get started with a job and a home by staying for an extended period of time with relatives. This, of course, would not generally be possible in an urban environment, where homes cannot be added or where landlords would object to adding extended family members to a household.

Family can also be relied on by many colonia residents to help build a colonia home. With the help of family members (and occasionally, neighbors), colonia residents are able to build their homes at their own pace, with whatever construction experience any member may have, and with mutual economic help until they achieve their ultimate goal of home ownership.

Social Capital Advantages. In the interviews, we saw a great deal of difference in the nature and extent of social capital in colonias. One interviewer, for example, said,

> I noticed how united and together this colonia was—how much they helped each other out. My last interview, for example, talked about how they help each other out in her colonia. She told me, 'I remember when Tencha Padilla, my neighbor, needed surgery. Her family is very poor and they don't have any medical insurance. So the colonia had a meeting and made several bingos and raffles to help Tenchita out. Thank God she is doing better now. Because of our unity, we have managed to get the county to put in better drainage systems and paved roads. That is what is so great about living in this colonia.'

Similarly, colonia residents often participate in *tandas*, an informal loan arrangement that allows people with emergency or major financial needs to draw from a pool of money to which all members regularly contribute. This custom, a round-robin savings pool more common in Mexico, is the only way many lower-income Mexicans who cannot get bank loans are able to purchase homes or meet other major financial obligations. When Carmen Vela's daughter was getting married, for example, Carmen encouraged friends in her colonia to start a *tanda*. From the money that came in, she was able to get nearly $2,000 to pay most of the wedding expenses. Now she continues to contribute, and other members occasionally draw upon the money accumulated when any of them experiences a major need.

Colonias also allow migrant workers and their colonia neighbors to help each other. Someone might be asked to keep an eye on the homes of migrant neighbors who are gone up north. Colonia resident Ana Reyes stated, "If we leave our house, I usually inform one of my neighbors about it. We usually keep watch for one another. You will not see any policemen coming into our neighborhood to keep an eye on things. That is why we have to count on each other." People also take turns keeping an eye on each others' kids after they come home from school. And they know who is good at certain tasks. For example, one colonia man said, referring to his neighbor, "Juana, the neighbor in number 3, makes excellent tortillas. Everyone comes to me when they need work done on their car. Carlos, the one in number 7, knows a little about electricity. We don't hesitate to help each other out if we are on good terms. Our colonia is like a little world of its own. We all help each other in any way we can."

Poverty creates unpredictability that the poor deal with through informality. Eliza Cruz is twenty-five and lives with her parents in a colonia that is just starting to form. Nevertheless, the bond with her neighbors started with the very first people who moved in. Eliza's parents are both sick and not able to work. She works very hard throughout the day and tries to fit in as much school as she can possibly handle without it affecting the number of hours she needs to put in to pay the bills. This hardly leaves time to tend to her parents' needs.

> But thanks to God we moved into a colonia, humble and poor, but full of helpful people that never stop giving. One day when my mother was tending to her tiny garden, she slipped and fell. It was in the morning, and the scorching sun had not hit its highest. I was at work and my father was inside watching TV. Thank God that the neighbor came home from the grocery store at about that time and saw her passed out from the pain. They got my mother to a doctor and back home by nighttime. They did not want to worry me, and so they decided to wait to tell me until I got home. By the time I arrived and found out, my mother was already back home feeling better. Since then, the ladies that stay home come over during the day to check up on my parents and phone them a few times during the day to see if they need something.

Eliza thanks God for moving her into what she calls a "colonia full of blessings." This closeness among neighbors is helped by the fact that the homes are often so close to each other that residents are in constant contact with one another.

Colonias: The Official Response

In developing nations, as Ward points out, public attitudes about informality in general and informal housing in particular have undergone a major shift that has not yet taken place to any appreciable degree in the U.S.[16] In the 1950s and 1960s, Latin American urbanization was already pushing people out of rural areas and into the shantytowns and squatter settlements of major urban centers. The initial response of most governments was to consider these areas a blight. Government policy, as a result, was intended to prevent or remove them. As these governments came to see that they were unable to provide a viable alternative, they adopted a more laissez-faire approach.

Starting around 1970, researchers and public officials began to see the positive functions of informal housing. Indeed, some came to see them as a solution to the housing crisis in developing countries.[17] As a result, self-help and self-built housing became not only acceptable, but a way of meeting the needs of the poor and a way to stimulate economic growth. Since the 1980s, the pattern has become even more oriented toward less government involvement in housing production and greater efforts to make the market work by providing adequate infrastructure and a better regulatory framework to prevent excesses. This has included such things as regularizing titles and even removing regulatory bottlenecks in the development of such housing forms. Indeed, as Ward points out, the conventional wisdom of international agencies today is that governments should intensify their efforts to make the market work more smoothly and to integrate informal housing settlements into property and tax structures in order to assure that services are provided and that consumers are not exploited by developers.[18]

Though the official response to colonias in Texas bears some similarities to the transformation that occurred in developing countries, there are important differences. Texas has gone from an earlier laissez-faire approach to colonias ("out of sight, out of mind") to trying to stop colonia growth through regulation. At the same time, however, Texas and federal officials have sought to provide needed infrastructure (water, wastewater disposal, platting, and making contract-for-deed more equitable) to existing colonias. In addition, while colonia development in places like Mexico was generally accomplished outside the law (squatting, land seizures, etc.), colonias in Texas developed largely within a legal structure of few regulations and/or lax enforcement.

In the 1960s, Texas colonias were not seen as much of a problem because there were relatively few of them and they were mainly well outside city limits. As cities began to expand outward and colonias began to rapidly multiply, however, the problems of poorly developed or missing infrastructure became increasingly hard to ignore. Colonias were expanding because there was little low-income housing, agricultural land could be easily subdivided, regulations governing land development were notoriously weak or nonexistent, and contract-for-deed offered a cheap (though exploitable) option to low-income buyers. This situation provided a cheap way for people with little or no credit to buy a lot and build a home, even though the subdivision may have been flood-prone; lacked water, sewers, and public utilities; and was virtually impassible after even a moderate rain storm.

As these infrastructure problems blossomed into a major public health issue, the state (and federal government) began to take action. In 1989, Texas began to enforce its Model Subdivision Rules more strictly in relation to county colonias. In 1995, House Bill 1001 was passed, requiring basic services in all newly sold colonia land in border counties. Also in 1995, Senate Bill 336 modified contract-for-deed transactions to give purchasers more protections against having their land easily confiscated without so much as a foreclosure process. Finally, a variety of bills and mechanisms provided funding that made it possible for counties to help provide water and other infrastructure utilities to colonias. Though all of this legislation helped existing colonia residents acquire basic services, the legislation was also intended to kill colonia development.[19]

This brief review reveals the somewhat ambivalent view Texas has had of border colonias. On the one hand, some observers (probably a small minority) see them as a form of free-market capitalism that facilitates the American dream of home ownership for even the poorest of the poor. On the other hand, colonias are simultaneously regarded by many as a form of blight, trapping the poor in third-world conditions and subjecting them to exploitation by unscrupulous developers.

Colonias as Free-Market Capitalism—
The Benefits of Minimal Regulation

An August 2008 article in *Texas Business Review* exemplifies the more positive view of colonias. It is entitled, "*Nuestra Casa* (Our House): A New Model of Self-help Improvement along the Texas/Mexico Border." It describes how Starr County, perhaps the poorest county in the U.S., whose residents average less than half the median household income of Texans generally and the rest of the nation and where over one-third of the population lives below the poverty line, has accomplished a home-ownership rate of 69%—a rate that is higher than the averages of the state of Texas (64%) and the nation (66%). These homes were constructed, the article reports, by the residents themselves, with the help of family, friends, and other colonia residents.[20]

This more positive view of colonias sees them as an economic necessity. Without them, it is reasoned, many of the poor would be homeless. It also acknowledges that the poor cannot afford to meet the standards of highly regulated housing or get commercial loans to buy or build a home. The South Texas borderlands are among the very poorest areas in the U.S. Over a million people live not only on the edge of America, but on the edge of poverty. It is widely recognized that housing is the single greatest expense of the poor.[21] So what would happen to the poor of South Texas without colonias? Even with a massive infusion of funds to support subsidized housing and rental assistance, large numbers of people would likely be homeless. So, in addition to other advantages of colonias, they help prevent homelessness. But many observers don't see that as much of an advantage, preferring to point out all their negative aspects.

Colonias as Blight—The Negative Consequences of Housing Informality

Though many public officials acknowledge at least some of the preceding benefits of colonias, by far the dominant view is that colonias are a blight that must be reduced, if not eliminated. A report by the U. S. Geological Survey, for example, characterizes colonias as a failure of formalized land administration systems, stating, ". . . in one of the richest countries in the world, the formalized land administration system was bypassed, which resulted in discrimination against the Hispanic migrant population, located in the poorest counties of the United States."[22]

Colonia residents, of course, see many of the problems of colonia life. One interviewer noted,

> When interviewing these families, I asked what was wrong with their homes. Juana Barrera responded that her plumbing did not work. Apparently when she bought the home it was not working, and since they are on a low budget they had to wait some time before fixing the plumbing system. The plumbing was backed up. They were also without water for the first two months of moving to their new lot. They had to walk four blocks to a family member's home to shower or go to the bathroom. Another woman, Lupita Zepeda, said that with the recent rains, the whole colonia was flooded. They had about two to three feet of standing water left from the rain. As a result, the school bus could not come all the way in to pick up her kids. They could not go to the store. They were pretty much isolated. All of Mary Alonzo's lot had turned into a pool, which had become infested with mosquitoes, creating many health problems.

Blight as Infrastructure Problem

As we have pointed out, colonias lack many forms of infrastructure that facilitate the health and well-being that most Americans take for granted. These include an adequate supply of potable water, sewage and drainage systems, satisfactory air quality, paved roads, and public transportation. Water problems are arguably the greatest problem of Texas colonias—not only getting potable water into colonias, but getting wastewater out. Ward argues that the issues of lack of water supply and of water disposal were so prominent that these water issues became, in the minds of many Texas officials, *the* defining characteristic of colonias.[23] Indeed, Ward alleges that the absence of adequate water and wastewater were such prominent problems that they overshadowed social, cultural, and economic issues. Some state officials concur, believing that if these problems could be solved the colonia problem would be solved and the colonia neighborhoods would no longer be colonias. Indeed, the new system of classifying colonias puts these water issues at the forefront, with "red" colonias (high health risk) being defined as those that are either unplatted, have an inadequate potable water supply, or have inadequate wastewater disposal.[24]

Figure 6.1 is based on data analyzed by the U.S. Geological Survey

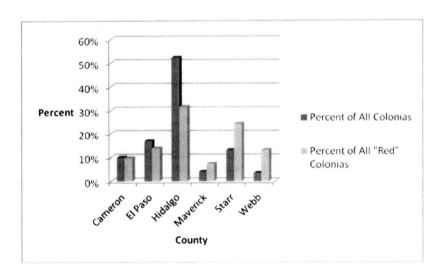

Figure 6.1. Distribution of colonias in six border counties, by percent of all Texas colonias and by percent of all "red" colonias in each county

with regard to Economically Depressed Areas (EDAPs). It shows that Hidalgo County has over half of all the colonias in the six border counties—counties that contain almost all of the colonias in Texas.[25] Because of the large number of colonias in Hidalgo County, it also has more red colonias (136) than any of the other counties, though Starr, Webb, and Maverick Counties have higher proportions of red colonias. Webb County (the Laredo area), for example, has fewer colonias (only 62, compared to Hidalgo County's 934), though its percentage of colonias designated as a health risk is much higher (see Figure 6.1).

Many of the residents of red colonias along the border get their drinking water from ground-water wells. Antonio Hinojosa, a colonia resident in this situation, described a recent incident.

> It was a hot, humid day. My little boy, Ernesto, was thirsty and wanted a drink of water. He asked me to get a pail of water from the water well, which provided all the water in the colonia. After I brought up the water, he gulped down the water. When I looked more carefully, it was brown and grainy looking. Apparently the water was contaminated with bacteria because little Ernesto became ill. The illness lasted several weeks and wasn't the only time this happened. My wife, Perlita, and I have also gotten sick from the water, which causes us to lose money on medical expenses and loss of work time.

Because South Texas has a heavy concentration of colonias, it has benefitted greatly from the infusion of state and federal funds to help resolve the water problems of colonias. Many colonias receive *potable water* from either a city or a water supply corporation (though water is not necessarily piped to each individual dwelling unit within colonias).

Unfortunately, the provision of *wastewater* facilities is not as positive, with the same report claiming that 73% of Hidalgo County colonias in 2003 did not have adequate sewer collection and disposal systems. A report by the Federal Reserve Bank of Dallas reported that 50.7% of colonia households in the Rio Grande Valley and El Paso use septic tanks, 36.4% use cesspools, 7.4% use outhouses, and 5.5% use other means to dispose of wastewater.[26]

Flooding (and standing water) is another major problem for colonias in the Valley. The region is very flat, and many of the colonias were built in flood-prone areas. Flooding in colonias is made worse by its contributions to health and sanitation problems. David Encarnación lives in a colonia north of Mission, Texas, in the Alton area. David said,

> I have been exposed to flooding all my life. One time when I was helping my family trying to get rid of floodwater around the house, I got sick. As the days went by I felt myself getting weaker and having a bad cough that never went away. It was to the point that I couldn't even get up, so my mom decided to take me to the doctor in Mexico where I found out that I had TB. I got a shot and some antibiotics and I got better. The doctor told me it was a good idea that I went to see him or I could have gotten really sick and possibly died.

Some colonia residents lack electricity because they were tricked into buying land that did not have adequate connections. Maria Hinojosa, now in her late forties, has three children. The colonia they moved into had only a few power lines running close to the main road. Those who lived off the main road of the colonia, like Maria, had to call the electric company to have electric lines run to their house. Maria said, "When we called the light company to install the line, I was astonished when I found out how much it would cost. I have not found a way to get that kind of money just to run lines to my house. Fortunately, the neighbors let me run a cord from their home until I could save the money needed. That has helped, but I worry what will happen when it rains and the electrical wire gets wet." Maria found out that only the homes in their colonia that were on the main road had electricity. Apparently, regulations required the seller to install at least those lines before he could sell any lots. The owner took advantage of the rest by selling them land without providing this basic service to the remainder of the homes in the colonia.

Social Problems Associated with Blight

Esperanza Godinez is a sixty-eight-year-old widow who lives near La Grulla in Starr County. She lives in a twenty-five-foot travel trailer with no electricity or running water. Her case illustrates how poor or missing infrastructure leads to social problems. She said,

> I live in a small travel trailer that I can proudly call 'mi casa!' One night, at about 2:00 A.M., I was awakened by a loud banging on my door; I was scared. I grabbed my purse with the little money it had in it and jumped out the window. I crawled over the fence and laid in the tall grass until I heard the boys leaving. Now every night I go to bed scared they will

come back and harass me once again. I know one of the boys. He is the son of my neighbor. I did not tell her what happened because I was afraid she would not believe me. Her son is always in and out of jail and always in trouble with the law.

Esperanza's problems with crime are not simply the result of one delinquent neighbor. Her location outside city limits, her isolation from her neighbors, and the fact that she has neither phone nor electricity make her more vulnerable to those who prey on the poor. As indicated earlier, residents of some colonias manage to ward off such problems by strong informal neighborhood associations. Residents of other colonias, however, have more problems with gangs and people who prey on them, with little well-developed social capital. Crime and delinquency are one of the problems that most plague residents of some colonias. Luis Aldape described the neighborhood where he lives:

> I live in a small house with my family. My dad is a hard worker and gives us the best he can. He encourages us to stay in school and do good so we can graduate and have a better life. Our house is not very well built, so when it rains the roof leaks. When the rain ends, our house fills with mosquitoes and all these other bugs. I really hate it, *pos que le hago* (but what can I do)? This neighborhood is filled with gangs, and they write graffiti on the "*tienditas*" (convenience stores) and street signs with their *símbolos de gangas* (gang symbols). They make the colonia look worse than it already is and take away our community pride. *Cuando yo cresca, mi vida va ser diferente; va ser mejor* (when I grow up, my life will be different; it will be better).

A mother lamented, "Drugs are everywhere, but these colonia kids are being pressured to sell and use drugs at a very early age. If they don't sell or participate, their lives can be threatened." Another lady said,

> Kids in this colonia don't have much hope. And since the police don't even care, what are we supposed to do? When there are problems, we call the city police, but they send us to the county sheriff's department since we live outside the city limits. When we call the sheriff about gang fights, they say they'll send help, but they don't show up until thirty or forty minutes later, after all the commotion has died down or when someone ends up dead in the middle of the street. If the gang mem-

bers ever find out who called, they will make that family's life a living hell. So [what] everyone mostly does is to not see or hear anything so they won't get into trouble.

Officer Padilla from the Hidalgo County Sheriff's Department acknowledges that they are spread too thin to patrol each colonia but that they respond as quickly as they can to calls for help. He related this story:

> I remember responding one weekend at a residence within a large colonia. The call was a disturbance call about someone playing the music too loud. By the time I got there, the people had already been drinking and most were too drunk to drive. I had been there before, because they frequently have loud weekend parties. I approached the residence carefully, asking the group in front of the house to please refrain from playing the music so loud. I remember that one gentleman was so intoxicated that he had passed out in a chair. I asked the owners of the residence to start wrapping things up or to go inside. I warned them that if I had to return, I would issue a citation for disturbing the peace and public intoxication to those in front. After an hour or so, we received another call. This time, gunshots had been fired and according to the caller, one man had been stabbed. As I arrived at the residence, one man was on the ground and another was on the sidewalk yelling. Both men had been drinking. Talking to them harshly was just going to make matters worse, so I put the man on the sidewalk in the car and began to question him. When I asked why he had done it, he simply replied, "You wouldn't understand."

In the Cultural Practices Survey, we asked a question that allowed us to determine whether respondents lived in a colonia, or in low-income, middle-income, or upper-income urban neighborhoods. We also asked them how often some of the preceding types of deviance or crime happened in their neighborhoods. The results of this analysis are presented in Figure 6.2.

An examination of Figure 6.2 shows a significant and consistent pattern on the first four variables, when responses are compared by neighborhood type. In each of these four forms of underground activities or deviance, colonia residents report higher levels of frequency than residents in middle- or upper-income neighborhoods but lower levels than residents in low-income urban neighborhoods. Indeed, pressure to buy

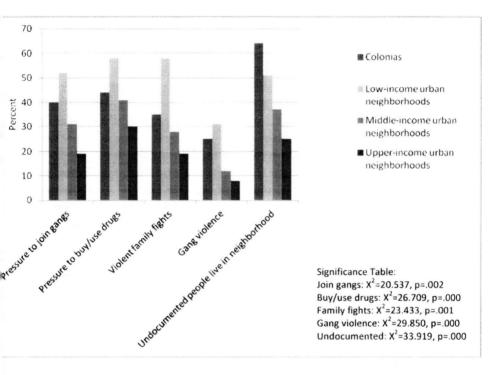

Significance Table:
Join gangs: X^2=20.537, p=.002
Buy/use drugs: X^2=26.709, p=.000
Family fights: X^2=23.433, p=.001
Gang violence: X^2=29.850, p=.000
Undocumented: X^2=33.919, p=.000

Figure 6.2. Reported frequency of five forms of deviance or informality in four categories of neighborhoods in the Rio Grande Valley, 2001–2002 (N = 418)

and use drugs was not much greater in colonias than in middle-class urban neighborhoods. Together, these findings support the proposition that, in terms of crime and deviance, colonias appear to be a better place to live than the alternative—low-income, urban neighborhoods.

The fifth variable, however, shows a considerably different result. The percentage who report undocumented residents living in their colonias is substantially higher than all the other neighborhood types, including low-income urban neighborhoods. This supports our contention that colonias facilitate informality, especially undocumented informality. They not only offer a relatively safe place to hide, but they also make it possible for undocumented residents to engage in informal businesses.

Poor Health Consequences. Health conditions in colonias are perhaps the major reason for considering them a form of blight. In the year 2000, the Office of Border Health of the Texas Department of Health published a study in which they compared health conditions for a random sample of 378 colonia residents in South Texas with a sample of 1,816 randomly selected noncolonia residents. A subsample of children from each of these two groups was tested to measure the prevalence of antibodies to Hepatitis A. Of the colonia children ten to twelve years of age, 30% were found to have antibodies to Hepatitis A, compared to only 10% of children of similar ages in the noncolonia sample. In addition, 9% of colonia children who were either 2 or 4 years of age reported experiencing diarrhea in the preceding two weeks, compared to less than 4% of the children of similar ages in the noncolonia sample. Colonia residents eighteen and older reported almost twice as many intestinal problems as individuals in the same age range from noncolonia areas. Such problems are likely linked to the issues of inadequate supplies of drinking water and inadequate disposal systems for wastewater, as well as other environmental concerns.[27] Additionally, because some colonias are remote, health emergencies are magnified due to extended travel time and the difficulty first responders have in finding specific residences.

Education-Related Problems. Inadequate education is another social problem endemic to colonias. Over half of the adults living in colonias have less than a high school education.[28] Some observers attribute this appalling lack of education to Mexican cultural attitudes.[29] We strongly disagree, finding it better explained by immigration and structural bias. The average educational level of Mexican immigrants into South Texas colonias is very low; perhaps as many as two-thirds of all immigrant colonia residents in the region possess less than a high school education.[30] Further evidence that these low rates of educational attainment are not based in Mexican culture can be found in the college enrollment levels in the Rio Grande Valley, 90% of the population of which is of Mexican origin. The motivation and demand for access to college is evidenced by the approximately 4.6% of the region's residents who were enrolled in Texas public universities and colleges in 2005. This is higher than the public statewide participation rate of 4.2% for the same year.[31]

Among colonia families, commitment to education was even more poignant. In one recent survey, over 69% of colonia parents agree with raising taxes to support the educational aspirations they have for their children (male and female). Also, 88% would volunteer in their child's school, and more than 90% would commit to volunteering up to 5 hours per week if it meant more students in their communities could go to college. In fact, over 75% of colonia parents would support longer school days, and more than 70% would support a longer school year if it meant their children would be well prepared to attend college.[32]

So for most colonia children and their parents, the problem is not traditional gender roles or lack of desire. The problems most colonia children encounter in school are due more to structural bias—unintentional consequences of their socioeconomic position—than to either cultural background or ethnic discrimination. They experience a problem of poor fit—the "fit" between colonia kids and others in their schools, as well as the "fit" between school and the other elements of society. Migrant farm work, for example, takes many of them out of school before the school year has ended and gets them back well after the school year has begun.

That colonias are located in rural areas presents another problem of poor fit. Delma Lopez said,

> Since my family and I live in a colonia about 15 miles away from school, our school bus is always late getting us to school. I can't even count the times when it would rain and, with our dirt roads, we'd get covered with mud. Well, even if we could get to school, of course, this was only the beginning of our problems. In high school, everyone makes fun of each other, especially of those of us from the colonias. Being from a border town, where almost everyone was Mexican American, we'd all get to school and drag mud all over the hallways. While on the intercom they'd say, "Please excuse the students from Hidalgo for being late." That would be so embarrassing. Everyone would later on just laugh and stare at us.

Many of our interviewers ran into this negative stigma of colonias. One said,

> Although colonias have their weaknesses, I came to understand that the women I interviewed saw their situation as an improvement over their life in Mexico. As I spoke to them, I noticed a sense of doubt and embarrassment in their faces. I asked them if they were ashamed of the situation they were living in, and their answer was no. They said they were only shocked that I would want to come into their neighborhood. One said, "No one like you ever comes out here. We always see the same people over and over again—just our family and our everyday neighbors. I am glad you came to speak to us."

Prospects and Conclusions

Colonias, a major form of informality in housing, facilitate an important alternative to slums and homelessness; they also provide a place where residents can launch life-sustaining informal economic enterprises that would be much more difficult in urban areas. The undocumented find them an excellent place to hide from immigration agents. They also find they can initiate very small informal enterprises, avoiding the problems of trying to get someone to hire them when they lack a Social Security card and other identification.

Colonia homes can facilitate informality in other ways. Being out in the county keeps them out of sight of many inspectors. Businesses can be run out of a home or a back yard without attracting the attention of landlords or officials. Paying by cash or even on credit is common and expected. Colonia residents often exchange services with no cash involved. They engage in informal lending practices. Generally, though not always, they watch out for each other and provide many informal services, such as child care, providing food in times of need, and multiple ways of tiding each other over during difficult times. Of course, the social cohesion of colonias is dependent upon the building up (or not) of social capital within the colonia community, typically a time-dependent and activist-dependent endeavor.[33]

Still, the informality of colonias creates serious problems for many residents. They must deal not only with the physical problems themselves, but also with a host of social consequences and negative public attitudes. Still, the informality that has produced colonias has given their residents an option besides homelessness or renting in slum housing. Though legislative efforts may have slowed colonia development, they have also brought substantial infrastructure to colonias. In 1989, the Texas Legislature passed the Model Subdivision Rules, which allowed county commissioners to establish and enforce minimal standards for water and wastewater in colonias that were previously unregulated. In addition, counties that accepted and enforced the rules were given access to funds for installing basic infrastructure. The Texas Water Development Board administered much of the funding. As a result, it is hard to find a colonia in Hidalgo County today without a potable water supply. Similarly, many formerly unpaved colonias now have paved streets, and the State Attorney General's Office has prosecuted some developers who failed to install promised infrastructure.

Many of the successes in getting the state to provide funds for colonia infrastructure came about as a result of fairly intense political pressure from local community coalitions. One of these, Valley Interfaith, is an Industrial Areas Foundation initiative modeled on the Saul Alinsky approach. One leader of this organization, Mrs. Anaya, has been living in Las Milpas (a colonia south of Pharr) for forty years and has seen many people living in bad conditions. She said,

> In 1983 I was first elected to the Executive Board of Valley Interfaith. Together we have worked for many years. So far we have gotten water, electricity, and sewer lines in Las Milpas. In 1987, Pharr incorporated Las Milpas into the city. I was very unhappy because after all the work that Valley Interfaith had done to get the main utilities for us, the city of Pharr decided to take over. Valley Interfaith, together with the residents, kept fighting to see more improvements, such as fire and police stations. We still need to do much more to finish the colonia projects, such as paving all the streets and closing the drainage canals.

Another local organization that promotes self-help and empowerment of colonia residents is Proyecto Azteca (started in cooperation with the United Farm Workers). Proyecto Azteca helps families earning between $6,500 and $10,000 a year who live in dilapidated housing to build their own homes. These residents, family members, and friends build the home off-site, with the help of Proyecto Azteca staff. The project also helps them to get full title to the lot so that it will not revert to a developer if a payment is missed. Once the homes are finished, they are moved to the lots of selected colonia residents.

A variety of other initiatives have been successful in providing decent housing for colonia residents. Some of these include a few local banks that have provided financing at low interest rates to colonia residents, helping them establish credit. Other agencies provide small grants from foundations and other sources to help colonia residents to help themselves. Some organizations simply help colonia residents organize themselves to pressure public officials to provide needed infrastructure for their colonias.

Guadalupe Garza described her involvement in such an effort:

> I have been living in the Valley all my life. I came to our colonia about two years ago. I have seen a few nice changes since I came here. The greatest necessity I saw when I moved here was to get the school district to have the bus enter our colonia to pick up my children for school. Sev-

eral of us went and talked to the officials at the school district, explaining the problem. Sure enough, the next day every student in our colonia was picked up inside the colonia. Other changes have not come as easily, but we are much more confident of ourselves now.

One of our student interviewers summarized the feelings of many of the students involved in the colonia interviews:

When I did these interviews, I was shy and embarrassed because I felt I might be invading the privacy of colonia residents. So, in order to get them to open up to me, I bought small angel figurines to give to each household. I figured the angel would symbolize "May God bless their home and their families." All of them were wonderful, but Julia Garcia was especially appreciative. When she saw that the angel figurines came in a religious gift bag, she cried. I could see that she was hurting and did not like living like this. Still, she was willing to keep trying . . . trying against great odds to do the work to succeed in America.

CHAPTER 7

The Informal Health Care Economy

WITH DEJUN SU

Marcos Segovia is a proud Mexican immigrant. He refuses to accept any welfare assistance. As a result of that choice and his low income, he and Dora, his wife, have no health insurance for themselves or for their children. This is one of Dora's major concerns. Speaking of how she worries whenever one of her children gets sick, Dora said,

> I just wait and pray for them to get better. Sometimes, I'll purchase over-the-counter drugs or use home remedies. If things don't get better, we take them to a doctor or a pharmacy in Mexico. At times even going to the doctor over there is expensive, but it's much less expensive than the cost of health care here in the Valley. I prefer to take my children to Mexico because I am more confident they will get better.

Lack of access to quality health care is a daily part of life for many residents of the South Texas border. This is especially true for those who live near or below the poverty line. Most would prefer to use conventional medical practices and practitioners but simply cannot afford to do so. Like Dora, they may turn to informal channels or just wait (and pray) that the illness will go away. For many, informal channels of health care are their only option. Such informal channels include going to Mexico to see health professionals or to buy prescription drugs (often without a prescription); using the prescription medications of a friend or family member; not claiming all their income so that their children, at least, can have Medicaid coverage; and using folk healing practices and/or practitioners.

To the degree that formal systems fail to meet the needs of a large segment of the population, no one should be surprised when they turn to informal means. This failure is particularly acute in Texas in general, and along the border, in particular. Texas, according to a 2005 U.S. Census report,[1] had the largest percentage (24.4%) of people without health insurance coverage of any state. The border states of New Mexico and Arizona were not far behind, with 21.9% and 19.6%, respectively. Even California, the remaining U.S.-Mexico border state, had a rate of 18.6%, just behind Mississippi, at 18.8%. By comparison, the U.S. average is 15.4% uninsured.

Not only are these border states at or near the top in the percentage of their citizens without health insurance, but the uninsured rates of one particular group—border Hispanics—have been especially high. In Texas, 38.5% of Latinos did not have health insurance in 2005, compared to 13.9% of Anglos and 26.2% of blacks/others. And within this group, those age sixty-five or less who are not covered by Medicare/Medicaid fare even worse. In one study of Texas border counties using a random sample, Bastida and other researchers[2] found that 65% of Latino respondents under sixty-five years of age reported having no health insurance.

Along with having an extremely high rate of uninsured people, Hidalgo County is also among the three or four counties in the U.S. with the lowest average household income. Yet ironically, the costs of health care here are among the highest in the U.S. as measured by average Medicare costs per person. According to a recent article in the *New Yorker*[3] magazine, Medicare spent an average of $15,000 per enrollee in Hidalgo county—or almost twice the national average—while the average income per capita was only $12,000. As the article states, "Medicare spends three thousand dollars more per person here than the average person earns."[4] One of the factors contributing to the high cost of health care in the area, according to Gawande, is that many prescribed treatment procedures are unnecessary, benefitting the hospitals and doctors financially more than they do the patients medically.

Informality in South Texas Health Care

As a result of these three factors (low rates of health insurance coverage, low income, and high costs of medical care), some South Texas residents often turn to informal options to meet their health care needs. Dora mentioned going to Mexico and using home remedies for some illnesses. In South Texas communities, folk medicine often coexists with

Western biomedicine, in part because standard health care is beyond the reach of many residents.[5]

Much more common than relying on folk medicine is the practice of many border residents (both Anglo and Latino) of crossing the border to buy prescription medication in Mexico. Generally, Mexican pharmacies do not ask customers to provide a prescription in order to buy prescription medication. One cross-border medical shopper, Laura Ortega, said, "Shopping for medicines in Mexico is much like grocery shopping in the United States. Some discount pharmacies have better prices than others." Another woman, Monica Calvillo, reported that the pharmacists in Mexico are very helpful, though not always knowledgeable. "Those that are very helpful," she said, "are those that want to make a sale. Even if a pharmacist does not know what the product they are selling will do, they will try to come off as convincing as possible so that the customer will feel a sense of security." Still another woman, Rosie Trujillo, has gone to the same pharmacy for years, and the pharmacist knows her and her family well. "Even the doctor whose office is around the corner knows who I am," she said. "He is our family doctor, and I trust him and the pharmacist."

As the preceding accounts illustrate, border residents do not always use conventional, or even formal, medical practitioners and facilities in the same way they are used in other parts of the U.S. This is perhaps even more true for those involved in informal economic activities. In our Informal and Underground Survey, we asked respondents what they used as their *main* way of meeting medical needs. Their responses are illustrated in Figure 7.1.

As Figure 7.1 shows, going to Mexico is the most common way these border residents who are involved in the informal economy respond to the difficulty of finding affordable health care in their own communities. Very few of them reported using emergency rooms. Indeed, noncitizen residents throughout the U.S. in general have low utilization of emergency rooms, and Hispanics throughout the U.S. make use of emergency rooms at about the same rate as non-Hispanics.[6] In South Texas, many medium- and low-income Latinos prefer the Mexican medical system to U.S. emergency rooms. Unfortunately, while undocumented individuals in South Texas might prefer the Mexican medical system, the difficulty they face in getting back into the U.S. from Mexico generally puts even that option out of their reach. For all others, however, proximity to the border and relatively low cost are major factors accounting for the preference for health care in Mexico.

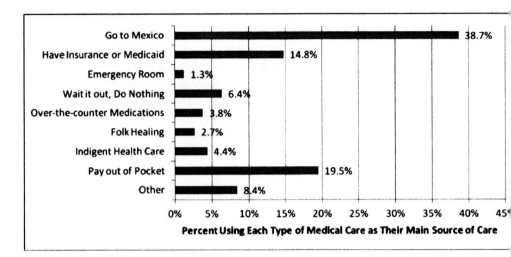

Figure 7.1. Percentages of South Texas participants in the informal economy who indicate specified types of medical care as their main way of meeting the medical needs of their family

What are the effects of extensive cross-border medical "shopping," especially when regulations are ignored or flouted in doing so? According to a report by the Texas Comptroller of Public Accounts,[7] "Health conditions on the Texas-Mexico border are among the worst in the United States." The U.S.-Mexico border has been defined as an area experiencing an "epidemiological transition," a condition in which areas of developed nations begin to acquire some of the health problems of developing countries.[8] Border communities suffer from much higher rates of some diseases than are experienced elsewhere in the U.S. For example, the mortality rate for diabetes in the McAllen area, the largest metropolitan area in the Valley, is about 1.5 times the state average. Women in the Rio Grande Valley are dying of cervical cancer at twice the national rate. Tuberculosis is more than twice as common on the border (13.3 per 100,000) as in other parts of the state (5.8 per 100,000).[9]

It would be easy to conclude that poverty, traditional medicine, and the poor quality of medical care in Mexico might explain these problems. That would ignore the fact that some health conditions are, in fact, better on the Texas border than in other parts of Texas. For example, only 6.2% of babies born in Hidalgo County had low birth weight in 2001, compared to 6.9% in the thirty-two border counties (i.e., counties within 62 miles of the U.S.-Mexico border) and 7.6% in Texas as a whole. Likewise, the rate of people who die from cardiovascular disease is 272.1 per 100,000 in Hidalgo County, 272.8 in other border counties, but 344.2 in Texas as a whole. Cancer death rates are also lower on the border: 138.9 in Hidalgo County, 159.3 for the border counties, and 192.7 for Texas as a whole. HIV and AIDS rates are also lower along the Texas-Mexico border (10.8 and 11.1, respectively) than in Texas as a whole (14.3).[10]

How does health care along the South Texas border differ from that found elsewhere in the nation and the state? How much of this care operates informally, or outside the purview of regulatory agencies? What are the consequences of such informality? We will utilize previously described quantitative and qualitative data to answer these questions. In addition, we will include data regarding cross-border health practices that was gathered in 2008 from a random sample of residents in the Texas borderlands from El Paso to Brownsville.

Informality and Border Health Care

The majority of the health care that takes place along the Texas-Mexico border utilizes practitioners and practices similar to those used elsewhere in Texas and the U.S. Nevertheless, unique aspects of the South Texas border present incentives and opportunities for informality unlike those outside this area. These unique aspects include (1) a large number of undocumented residents; (2) border residents who cross into Mexico for health care because of its low cost and cultural/geographic proximity; and (3) strong traditions of informal health care among the low-income Latino residents of South Texas.

1. Undocumented Immigrants and Informal Health Care

Undocumented Mexican immigrants affect the South Texas health care system in at least two major ways. First, a few are drawn to the U.S. in the hope of receiving health care they might not be able to access in Mexico. Second, undocumented immigrants who come for other reasons still have health care needs. When formal options are closed to them, many find it necessary to resort to informal means of meeting their health care needs.

Do the Undocumented Come for Public Health Care? The belief that undocumented immigrants come to the U.S. to get free health care does contain a small kernel of truth, as the case of Luis and Juana Benavides illustrates. After watching his wife Juana go through four miscarriages and stillbirths in Mexico because of the lack of money for proper medical attention, Luis knew he had to do something. Hearing that there was more advanced technology available in the U.S., they moved to the Valley. "When I heard this idea" said Juana, "I was willing to go along with it. I wanted to conceive children and to get away from Mexico's bad economy." Using a laser visa, they crossed the bridge at Hidalgo. "When we got to the inspection checkpoint," said Luis, "all they asked us was where we were headed to and for how long. I told the man we were going to see some relatives for the weekend." Luis and Juana moved in with some relatives, but were unable to find jobs. After three weeks, Luis started selling homemade foods. They borrowed money from relatives and borrowed a car from an uncle. Juana prepared the food, while Luis would drive around to sell it. During the first two weeks, they weren't selling enough food to make a profit. Luis continued,

> One day I sold food to some construction workers. A man came out of the house next door and bought a taco. He told me that if I wanted to sell more, I should look for people working in the fields, in construction, or any other work outdoors. He also suggested a greater variety of foods. After that, we started selling breakfast tacos, lunch tacos, fish, chicken, *gorditas*, and *pachucos*. Now we don't have to put up with anybody bossing us around, and we make enough to pay for necessities and a few luxuries. Most important, however, we earned enough money to be able to get help to have our two children.

In the end, Luis and Juana were able to successfully use the U.S. medical system to have their children in a hospital without problems. Yet they also worked hard informally to make their familial dream possible. Some media pundits would have us believe that the undocumented come for free services and constitute a huge drain on the nation's health care system. Those claims are grossly distorted and largely untrue. As we have pointed out elsewhere, the preponderance of evidence supports the conclusion that the economic benefits generated by undocumented immigrants generally exceed their costs.[11] That conclusion is reaffirmed in a 2007 Congressional Budget Office report[12] which states that "over the past two decades, most efforts to estimate the fiscal impact of immigration in the Unites States have concluded that, in aggregate and over the long term, tax revenues of all types generated by immigrants—both legal and unauthorized—exceed the costs of the services they use . . . However, many estimates also show that the cost of providing public services to unauthorized immigrants at the state and local levels exceeds what that population pays in state and local taxes."

The CBO report acknowledges that local governments in border states do have some basis for concern. The federal government collects more in taxes than it spends on programs for undocumented immigrants, though the reverse is true for municipal and county governments. The Texas Comptroller in 2006,[13] for example, estimated that while the *Texas* government collected $424 million more in revenue from unauthorized immigrants than it spent on health care, education, and law enforcement activities for that population, *local* governments incurred $1.4 billion in uncompensated costs for health care and law enforcement. Thus the problem is not too much demand for public services by undocumented workers but an unfair system of sharing both the costs and the revenues related to their health care services. We see this as yet another example of structural bias that negatively affects border locations.

County and municipal governments on the border with Mexico incur much greater costs for health care for undocumented immigrants than those entities further inland. According to a recent report commissioned by the twenty-four Southwest counties from California, Arizona, New Mexico, and Texas that border Mexico,[14] these county governments incurred almost $190 million in uncompensated costs in providing health care to undocumented immigrants. That amount, however, was only one-fourth of the uncompensated costs incurred by these counties during the year because the remaining three-fourths were not undocumented. At the national level, a Rand study concluded that health care provided to undocumented immigrants between the ages of 18 and 64 cost taxpayers only $11 per household for the year 2000.[15]

Alarmist (and exaggerated) statements by opponents of undocumented immigrants put pressure on state and local governments to curtail public health and other services to undocumented immigrants. Oklahoma, for example, led this effort in 2007, implementing a sweeping anti-immigration bill that denied benefits to undocumented immigrants. Yet, according to a Congressional Budget Office report,[16] the Oklahoma Health Care Authority spent only *one-third of 1%* of its budget for emergency Medicaid on undocumented immigrants. And since 2003, less than 1% of the individuals served and the dollars spent on Medicaid by the agency had been related to undocumented immigrants.

A recent article in the *Journal of American Physicians and Surgeons*[17] similarly exaggerates the image of Mexicans and other "illegals" coming for free benefits and flooding our clinics and hospitals. The author says, "Illegal aliens' stealthy assaults on medicine now must rouse Americans to alert and alarm . . . their free medical care has degraded and closed some of America's finest emergency medical facilities and caused hospital bankruptcies: 84 California hospitals are closing their doors . . . Polio was eradicated from America, but now reappears in illegal immigrants, as do intestinal parasites. Malaria was obliterated, but now is re-emerging in Texas."

Such articles spread a great deal of confusion and misinformation about the costs of health care delivered to undocumented immigrants and whether those costs can (or should) be paid for by state and local governments. The federal Consolidated Omnibus Budget Reconciliation Act of 1986 amended Medicaid law to authorize assistance to health care providers for services related to childbirth and emergency medical treatment delivered to undocumented immigrants. However, this "emergency Medicaid" covers only those services necessary to stabilize a patient; services delivered after a patient is stabilized are not covered. Writers like Cosman insist that emergency rooms are required to treat any "emergency," including such minor infirmities as ". . . cough, headache, and hangnail . . ." Cosman exaggerates. In reality, though, the law authorizes only enough health care to make sure undocumented immigrants don't die.[18] As a result, the costs of emergency Medicaid for the undocumented are surprisingly low.

The vast majority of undocumented immigrants do not come to the U.S. for publicly-funded health care, either for themselves or for family members in Mexico. Still, while living without documents in the U.S., health needs do arise. Angela Barragán is in this situation. She is in her early forties and is from Reynosa, Mexico. She and her husband were able to get the mica visa (a seventy-two-hour shopping permit). "Those seventy-two hours became fifteen years," she said. She is a domestic worker and knows she is illegal, but feels that she's helping people out. "We have had two children, but I had them in my own home, with the help of a *partera* (midwife). I can't even cross back to Mexico to buy medicine. We don't have health insurance, and we will never apply for government assistance unless we become legal citizens. We want to do it right."

Do the Undocumented Abuse Emergency Room Treatment? If Angela Barragán's children get sick, she calls her brother who is a doctor in Mexico, and he tells them what medicines to buy at a local pharmacy. Sometimes she has a family member cross over to Mexico to bring the medication. They only go to a doctor in Texas if it is an absolute emergency. She explained,

> One time we did have to take our daughter to a hospital because she had a very high fever. While I was waiting in the emergency room, a lady from the front desk asked if we had any type of aid to pay for the bill. I said we didn't. The woman told me to wait at the desk. Then someone from a local organization spoke to me, asking for our gross income. She said that her agency would pay for our daughter's bill. After that we never had to pay anything, and they never asked us to pay. She must have been an angel sent from God.

Angela, like many undocumented immigrants from Mexico and Latin America, uses hospital emergency rooms far less than U.S.-born Latinos, according to a 2005 report by researchers in California.[19] This report used the National Health Interview Survey of 18,398 U.S.-born persons and 2,843 immigrants. Using advanced statistical analysis, they determined that the "per capita total health care expenditures of immigrants were 55% lower than those of U.S.-born persons." They also found that expenditures of uninsured and publicly insured immigrants were approximately half those of their U.S.-born counterparts. Indeed, health care expenditures for immigrant children were 74% lower than those for U.S.-born children.

Most undocumented border residents go to a doctor or to an emergency room only in true emergencies. Many, like another interviewee, Rosa Perez, assume that they are not eligible for help and would risk deportation if they were to go to an emergency room. Rosa explained,

> I never realized how much I really needed emergency care till last year. I started getting sharp pains on my side and was uncertain what was wrong. I figured if I took some pain medicine, it would go away. The pain just got worse, but I was horrified to think of going to the emergency room and getting sent back to Mexico. My family dragged me to the emergency room saying that my life was more important than getting sent back to Mexico. The doctor who saw me said that it was my appendix and if I had waited any longer I would have died.

Rosa isn't the first Mexican immigrant who suffered from these types of problems because of their undocumented status and lack of health care coverage. Lack of insurance leads many immigrants to forego or postpone medical care, especially preventive care. This can cause their conditions to deteriorate, ultimately increasing the cost of treatment. As a result, some immigrants end up using hospital emergency departments—the most expensive source of health care—as their health care provider.[20]

Often, they are turned away after receiving little or no care. One undocumented man, Carlos Zuniga, said,

> I thought Mom was going to die. I went with her in the ambulance while my wife, Susan, drove the car to the hospital. She went to make arrangements for admission while I went with Mom into the emergency room. We were in the waiting room when Susan came back to tell me that the woman at the front desk said they could not admit Mom because she had no money and no insurance. I was mad, so I went to talk to her. She asked me also if we had any money or insurance and I told her that we didn't. She said that they could not admit her into the hospital. I asked, "How can anyone deny a very sick person medical attention? Are you telling me that you would let her die just because she has no money?" She said, "Don't try to make me feel guilty! It's not my fault. I'm just doing my job." I was bitter because we are so poor that my mother could die and we couldn't do a darn thing about it. After they stabilized her in the emergency room, they released her. We attempted to have her admitted into another hospital but they wouldn't take her there either. Finally, we took her to Harlingen to a hospital for indigent patients where they gave her Tylenol every four hours for the pain she was having. She is at home now partially paralyzed and with severe memory loss.

II. Crossing into Mexico for Informal Health Care

Had Carlos or his mom been legal, they could have taken her to Mexico where care would have been much less expensive. Several studies have explored why U.S. border residents utilize health care in Mexico.[21] A consistent finding from these studies is that the lack of health insurance is one of the greatest predictors of whether U.S. residents cross the border to use Mexican medical products and/or services. Border residents who cannot afford good health insurance use Mexican medical care as a main way of compensating for this lack. In essence, they substitute cash-based care in Mexico for insufficient and expensive medical insurance in the U.S.

Even people with U.S. health insurance often travel to Mexico to meet health-care needs, as revealed by our in-depth interviews with border residents. Guadalupe Treviño, for example, is a housewife whose husband is employed as a truck driver in San Benito. His wages are just $5.25 an hour. "With these earnings," she said, "it's difficult to support a family of six." When asked if her husband had medical insurance from his employment, she responded,

> Two years ago, my five-year-old daughter got sick and I took her to a doctor in San Benito. The doctor did a few lab tests on her. When I got ready to leave, I asked the secretary if she thought my husband's medical insurance would pay the fees. She answered, "Probably not, because the medical insurance would only pay if it was over a certain amount." She told me that the total fee for this consultation was "only $75.00." I thought that was a lot of money, but I had no choice but to pay it. Since that day, we take our children across the border to see a doctor or buy medicine over there whenever they get sick.

In a 2009 study of health insurance and cross-border health care choices in the region, Brown, Pagán, and Bastida found that 18.8% of South Texans *with* public health care had a regular doctor in Mexico and 29.6% had used a dentist in Mexico. For those South Texans *with* private health insurance, the instance of having a Mexican doctor and utilizing a Mexican dentist were even higher—25.1% and 36.9%, respectively.[22]

A recent study in selected Texas border counties found that 60% of residents under the age of 65 had no health insurance,[23] making them much more likely to turn to Mexico for their health care services. Often, these cross-border services are either informal or are under-regulated and under-enforced by U.S. standards, making them quasi-informal. A related study—a secondary analysis of a survey conducted in 2002–2003 among 1000 randomly selected adults in the El Paso/Ciudad Juárez area (500 on each side of the border)—describes the prevalence of cross-border purchase of health care and medications. That study found that 33% of El Paso residents reported purchasing prescription drugs in Mexico. The study also found that 9.4% of respondents had purchased dental services, 7.0% had made cross-border physician visits, and 1.4% had utilized a hospital in Mexico.[24]

From 2007 through 2010, we conducted our Cross-Border Healthcare Survey using a random sample of 1,605 border Texas residents[25] age 18 and older to determine what types of medical care they received from Mexico and their reasons for crossing the border for such care. Though this research was designed to measure both formal and informal cross-border health care, the data obtained are useful in helping us describe informal forms of cross-border health care. The results of this study will illuminate various forms of health care that South Texas residents cross into Mexico to utilize, such as pharmacies, doctors, and dentists in Mexican border cities.

Informal Cross-Border Prescription Drugs Purchases

South Texas residents frequently go to Mexico to purchase prescription drugs. Those who cannot go themselves often have someone else make prescription purchases in Mexico for them. Emilio, for example, sells prescription medicines that he brings from Mexico to customers in non-border towns. "I sell mostly antibiotics and diabetic medications," he said. "I usually make a trip to some larger cities two to three times a month. When I cross back from Mexico, the officers rarely give me any grief over the medication purchases. If they do, I tell them it is for me or my family." Emilio has little direct interaction with his customers, using a friend as an intermediary. Still, he knows something about why people make these purchases through him. "From what I have seen," he said, "most people who buy through me simply don't have health insurance or cannot afford medications here. Also, who has time to go to Mexico to get cheap medications when you live in Houston and Dallas?"

Though some South Texas residents might possibly obey all laws in purchasing medicine in Mexico, the majority clearly do not. When prescription drugs are purchased in Mexico and brought into the U.S., those who bring them are regulated by a host of laws, both in the U.S. and in Mexico. Officials with oversight in this area include Customs officers, FDA inspectors, DEA officers, and others. To bring the medications into the U.S., travelers technically are required to show a valid U.S. prescription to the inspector at the port of entry. In practice, however, Customs inspectors rarely ask for a U.S. prescription. Even if a person has a U.S. prescription, the law again technically requires that they have both a U.S. prescription and a Mexican prescription. Almost none do. Generally, U.S. Customs inspectors will allow U.S. residents to import a two- to three-month supply of a controlled medication without a valid prescription at an international land border. These medications must be declared upon arrival, be for one's own personal use, and be in their original containers. It is against the law to not properly declare imported medications to U.S. Customs agents.

In 2001, the FDA and other agencies conducted a spot check of pedestrians crossing into the U.S. at seven crossing points along the Texas, Arizona, and California borders with Mexico. Of those surveyed, 586 were in possession of prescription drugs, but only 56% of them had a prescription for the medication. Sixty-one percent of those with a prescription got it from a doctor in the U.S., and 39% had a prescription from a Mexican doctor. Almost none had a prescription from doctors on both sides of the border. The most common drugs purchased in Mexico were Amoxicillin (antibiotic), Premarin (estrogen), Claritin (allergy), Terramicinia (antibiotic), Ampicillin (antibiotic), ibuprofen (analgesic), penicillin (antibiotic), Vioxx (inflammation), Tafil (anxiety), Dolo Neuorobian (vitamin supplement), Glucophage (diabetes), Celebrex (arthritis), Naproxen (analgesic), Retin-A (acne), Ventolin (pulmonary disease), and Valium (controlled substance/nervous system depressant). Some of the drugs, however, were not approved for sale in the U.S.[26]

Even when U.S. residents obey U.S. laws in purchasing medications in Mexico, they are most likely in violation of Mexican laws. Technically, Mexican law prohibits Mexican pharmacies from honoring foreign prescriptions, though this law is routinely ignored or disobeyed. In addition, any drug classified as a controlled medicine cannot be purchased in Mexico without a Mexican prescription. This prescription must be written by a physician who is federally registered in Mexico. Furthermore, purchasing a controlled medicine without a valid prescription in Mexico is a serious crime for both the purchaser and the seller. Purchasing a controlled medicine with only a U.S. prescription is illegal, regardless of what the Mexican pharmacy may be willing to sell to the purchaser.

In Mexico, this means that medications such as Valium, Vicodin, Placidyl, Ambien, codeine, pseudoephedrine, Demerol, morphine, and Ativan cannot be legally sold over-the-counter without a valid prescription from a Mexican physician. If the purchaser succeeds in buying controlled medicines without a prescription, Mexican police can arrest the purchaser and vendor and charge them with possession or sale of a controlled substance. The sentence for possession of a controlled substance runs from ten months to fifteen years in a Mexican prison. Making such an illegal purchase also puts the buyer at risk for various extortion scams perpetuated by police officials (who sometimes work in league with the very pharmacy that sold the medication).

So, as U.S. residents trek to Mexico to buy prescription medicines (or purchase them over the Internet), they are almost certainly violating U.S. and/or Mexican laws. Border officials, however, have chosen not to fully enforce many of these laws. Under FDA guidance, border officials can use discretion to decide whether small supplies of drugs, even those not approved for importation into the U.S., can be allowed into the U.S. Thus, U.S. residents who declare their purchase and claim it is for personal use will generally not be stopped for importing prescription drugs into the U.S. unless they have more than a three-month supply or are importing a controlled substance.[27]

Even those who purchase over the Internet seldom have their purchases confiscated. Rarely does the FDA detain or refuse mail imports that are claimed for personal use. As a consequence, the FDA—counter to the Food, Drug, and Cosmetic Act—does not review tens of thousands of packages and eventually releases and sends them on to their addressees. This is due, in large measure, to the huge rate of packages coming into the U.S., which exceeds the FDA's capacity to manage. U.S. residents spend more than $1 billion annually at Mexican pharmacies. Consequently, it is likely that some of the controlled substances brought into the U.S., ostensibly for personal use, may be imported for resale and/or self-prescribed without oversight by a physician.[28]

This is not to say that all, or even most, prescription medicines purchased in Mexico are unsafe. Most pharmacological evaluations of drugs purchased over the counter in Mexico fall within an acceptable range of United States Pharmacopeia (USP) standards.[29] Nevertheless, the risks of getting an unsafe product are generally higher than for products purchased in the U.S. There are also risks related to getting medical advice from pharmacy attendants in Mexico, who may have little or no pharmaceutical training. Another study found that fewer than half the Mexican pharmacies studied had a licensed pharmacist on site.[30]

One of our student interviewers is a young woman who has some pharmaceutical training. She decided to see how many pharmacies had a licensed pharmacist on site. "When I attempted to talk to the pharmacists at some of the pharmacies in Nuevo Progreso," she said, "the result was the same in every pharmacy I visited. *'El farmaceutico no está. Regrese mas tarde'* (the pharmacist is not here. Come back later). Working at a pharmacy myself as a certified pharmacy technician, I will tell you, you

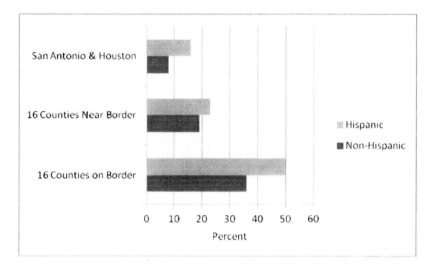

Figure 7.2. Percentage of Hispanic and Anglo respondents in each of three samples who say they have ever bought (or asked someone to buy for them) medications in Mexico

will never hear those words out of my mouth. A pharmacist in the U.S. is required to be in the pharmacy at all times it is operating."

In our survey of 1,605 South Texas residents, we asked respondents if they had ever bought medications in Mexico (or asked someone else to buy medications for them in Mexico). The responses shown in Figure 7.2 are for the 200 respondents in Houston and San Antonio, the respondents in sixteen Texas counties within sixty-two miles of the Mexican border (but not on it), and the sixteen Texas counties that share a border with Mexico. This figure also compares the responses of Hispanic respondents in these subsamples with those of Anglo (non-Hispanic white) respondents.

Figure 7.2 shows the importance of proximity to the border, as well as the importance of ethnicity. Very small percentages of Hispanics and non-Hispanics in Houston and San Antonio have purchased (or asked someone to purchase) medications in Mexico.[31] The figures rise considerably in the sixteen counties near (but not on) the border. And the numbers get close to 50% in the border counties. In addition, Hispanic residents in all three samples are more likely than their Anglo counterparts to use Mexico as a source for prescription drugs.

Besides geographic proximity to Mexico, we also identified several other important predictors of medication purchase in Mexico. Utilizing

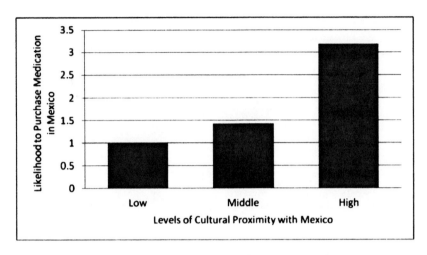

Figure 7.3. Ethnic proximity to Mexico and medication purchase in Mexico

logistic regression,[32] we sought to determine the relationship between purchasing medication in Mexico and age, gender, marital status, education, self-rated health condition, household income, and ethnic proximity with Mexico. As we have reported on and utilized in earlier chapters, ethnic proximity is measured by the generation score—an index constructed through the birth-nation calculation of three generations (grandparents, parents, and respondent). In this analysis, we divided generation scores of our respondents into three levels, "low," "middle," and "high." A low score reflects fewer birthright ties to Mexico, and a high score reflects a stronger birthright connection to Mexico.

Using generation score as a predictor of purchasing medication in Mexico, we found that those with closer generational ties (high generation scores) to Mexico were three times more likely to cross the border into Mexico to buy medication than those with fewer ties (low generation scores).[33] Those respondents with middle generation scores were 1.5 times more likely to purchase medication in Mexico than those with low scores (see Figure 7.3). Hence, a closer birthright tie to Mexico is a primary and significant predictor of crossing into Mexico to purchase medication, even when controlling for age, gender, marital status, education, self-rated health condition, and household income.

We also explored the link between health insurance and crossing the border to buy medication in Mexico. Consistent with what has been suggested in the literature, we found health insurance status to be a significant predictor of medication purchase in Mexico. Simply, those without health insurance are much more likely, 1.8 times in fact, to go to Mexico to purchase medication than respondents with health insurance (see Figure 7.4). Many report that they have been priced out of the American medical system. Cristela Silva perhaps best expressed the bind she feels she and others are in:

> My husband earns minimum wage. We just cannot afford to spend so much money. Even taking our children to the county clinics on this side is no longer an option for us. We have bills to pay, and we need to buy school clothes and supplies for our children. When my oldest son got a stomach infection, I took him to a clinic on this side and the doctors gave me a lot of prescriptions. I had to go back almost every other day. He did get better within a week. Then, when my daughter became ill with the same infection, we decided just to take her across the border. I told the pharmacist over there her symptoms and he gave me some pills. The next day my daughter was fine and I only paid six dollars.

Somewhat surprisingly, we did not find any significant effect of household income on medication purchase from Mexico. Intuitively, we would hypothesize that Texas border residents from wealthy households have little incentive to buy medications from Mexico since they can eas-

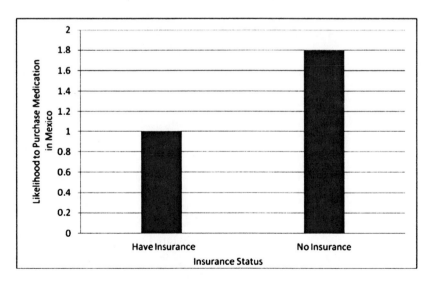

Figure 7.4. Health insurance and medication purchase in Mexico

ily afford to purchase U.S. medications. The findings from our analysis, however, do not support this hypothesis. In summary, cultural proximity and lack of health insurance (but not household income) both contribute significantly to the probability that a South Texan will cross the border into Mexico to buy medication.

For many who bring medications back into the U.S., the fear is how they will be treated by U.S. border officials, especially if they are purchasing a controlled medication. Art Canales, for example, stated, "My friends and I usually go on weekdays to avoid any suspicion from the U.S. Customs. We collect money and head to Mexico to purchase large quantities of Valium. We go once every three months to restock our supplies. It's like buying candy in a candy store. We request what we want and how much we want, and they sell it to us without any hassle or any questions. The tricky part is crossing it over to the United States. We've been doing it for two years now, and I haven't been caught yet."

But not everyone is lucky enough to cross without getting caught. Monica Sandoval's father overheard the interview with his daughter. He told the interviewer of an older friend who was detained because he was trying to cross the border with 600 Valium pills without a prescription. The friend had prostate cancer, and the Valium was to help ease the pain so he could sleep. He had been buying medication in Mexico for years because it was cheaper and easier than in the U.S. "He did not rob a bank, he did not kill anybody," explained the father, "but the risk was always there, and he just happened to get caught."

Individuals who purchase prescription medications from pharmacies in Mexico for themselves or family members seem to be aware of many of the risks involved. Lourdes Casas, for example, is a twenty-six-year-old single mother who lives in government housing and buys clothing and miscellaneous items here to sell in Mexico. "I visit a doctor in Reynosa and get the medications I need from local pharmacies," she said. "Most of these medications are sold over the counter in Mexico and anyone can buy them without a prescription. Sometimes I self-medicate, buying prescriptions over the counter. I know it is bad, but I still do it."

Some individuals who buy prescription medications without seeing a doctor find ways to minimize the risks. JR Rodriguez recalls one day his youngest son got very ill. He was frustrated because medications he had purchased in the U.S. didn't seem to be working. He decided to ask for information from an employee of a pharmacy he knew from his work as a deliveryman. The man cautioned JR about medications from

Mexico, but told him he could look for the same medication in a generic brand, perhaps with a stronger dosage. The friend also told him to make sure the box was still sealed and to make sure that it had not expired. Further, he explained that medications from Mexico generally lack the pharmacy-printed instructions that we are used to in the U.S. Mexican prescriptions usually come in the manufacturer's packaging that doesn't tell you how much medicine to take and how often to take it. Further, he explained, you will not know if a new medication will interact in a negative way with any medicine you are already taking. With some trepidation, JR purchased the medication in Mexico, and within three or four days his son was showing steady improvement.

Obviously, many individuals are able to find medications in Mexico that are less expensive. Without the proper precautions, however, wrongly prescribed medication can be dangerous. Gloria Guerra, for example, tells about a time when she was working at a call-response center and got sick from something that seemed to going around the group of employees.

> I couldn't afford to miss work because I was barely getting by as it was. I decided to go to Mexico and get some medicine so I could get over it quick. Well, I knew ever since I was a little girl that I was allergic to penicillin, so I talked to the guy at the Mexican pharmacy and told him what was wrong with me. He just handed me some pills and took my money. He didn't ask me if I had allergies or anything. I took the medicine and fell asleep and then I got really sick. My boyfriend took me to the emergency room because I got really bad. I ended up staying in the hospital for three days. That cost me a lot of money that I didn't have. The worst part is that I didn't have any more sick days at work because I had taken my baby to the doctor too many times, so I got fired. It turned out the man at the pharmacy had given me penicillin. Because of his negligence to ask me any history, I could have died.

The student interviewer with some pharmaceutical training (described earlier in this chapter) decided to see how people would be affected if she told them the risks involved in purchasing medications in Mexico. "Surprisingly," she said, "I got the same answer from every single person I interviewed. After showing my interviewees the material I had on Mexican pharmacies and sharing with them my prior knowledge working in the field, I asked: 'Will you continue going across the border for health care and prescription medication?' Short, sweet, and to the point—every single one of the seven people said, 'Yes.'" Their reasons were very similar. They could not afford treatment and medication from the American system. One of the seven people she interviewed, Maria Casas, described her reasons. "It's just too expensive here," she said. "I'm not a bad mom. I want the best for my kids, but because I work I don't qualify for help from the government. They say I make too much money. How can they say I make too much money? I barely make ends meet. Sometimes I just think it's better to quit my job and go on welfare."

The interviewer went on to say,

> This virtual open medicine cabinet might seem odd to Americans, who are used to doctors' visits, lab tests, and restricted access to prescription medications. But for many people on the border, this approach isn't odd at all. It represents what many feel should be a reality in the United States: affordable prescription drugs and doctors' visits, if needed. This is especially true for those people who have no prescription drug coverage and for those with inadequate private health insurance. Mexican medications are cheap and accessible. Just a simple trip across the border can mean hundreds of dollars per year in savings. Mexican doctors are easy to get an appointment with because you don't need one. It is health care at its simplest. And why shouldn't it be?
>
> Unfortunately the illusion is not always the reality. U.S. pharmaceutical manufacturers warn consumers against crossing the border, saying that since the regulatory systems are different in Canada and Mexico, consumers can never be sure what they are getting, even when the labels say that a reputable U.S. manufacturer makes the drug. The industry knows firsthand how easy it is for foreign renegade manufacturers to produce counterfeit drugs and replicate the original manufacturer's label.

Many residents of the Valley have mixed feelings about buying prescription drugs in Mexico, especially about doing so without a prescription. Many understand the need to economize when health costs have been rising so steeply. On the other hand, they also understand the need to avoid the risks and dangers of bad advice or products that people might get at Mexican pharmacies. This ambiguity is reflected by data collected in our Perceptions of Deviance Survey (administered in 2002–2003), some data from which are shown in Figure 7.5. This figure summarizes how 427 respondents from the Rio Grande Valley responded to

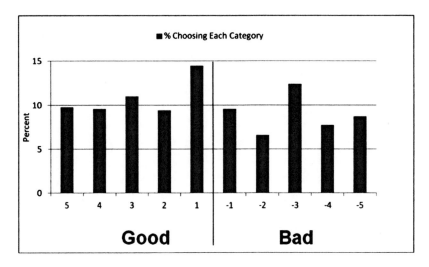

Figure 7.5. Percentages of South Texas respondents selecting each level of how good or how bad it is for Valley residents to buy prescription medicine in Mexico without a prescription (N = 427) *Source:* Perceptions of Deviance Survey.

the question about how right or how wrong it is for Valley residents to get prescription medicine in Mexico without a prescription.

As Figure 7.5 illustrates, the combined percentages of those who consider it bad for Valley residents to get prescription medicine in Mexico without a prescription was somewhat lower (45%) than the percentages of those who viewed it as something good (55%). When we calculated the average (mean) score responses for different ethnic categories, we found no significant differences between Mexicans, Mexican Americans, and Anglos (or similar groups), though those who insisted on calling themselves "white" or "American" had a slightly more negative view of this behavior than those who considered themselves Anglo, Mexican, Hispanic, or Mexican American. In essence, the results are mixed to slightly positive in terms of the morality of the pursuit of cross-border medications.

Some of the medicine purchased in Mexico has purposes other than curing an illness. Some high school kids go to Mexico to purchase steroids for themselves. One young high school senior said that he and his high school friends get steroids in Mexico in order to make it in high school sports. He and his friends cross the border in order to obtain a steroid that will improve their chances in making the cut for their varsity football team. Other individuals sell steroids and hormones purchased in Mexico to people in cities north of the Valley. "I buy in Mexico, and then I usually send them by mail," said Eddie Sauceda. "You would be surprised at the things people send using Fed-Ex and UPS. There's also a large market for female hormones as well. I sell them through a friend who owns his own store in a large city. He gets a lot of bodybuilders and transsexuals who need regular doses." When asked why he decided to pursue this line of work, he stated, "Hey, if some dude wants to look like Mr. Universe or start looking like a girl, why not make money off it? They're not hurting anyone."

Others buy similar products, but sell them locally. Roberto Dávalos, first introduced in Chapter 2, came up with this line of work five years ago when he noticed many people taking expensive supplements and steroids. "I would be working out at the gym," he said, "and people would complain about how expensive their supplements and steroids were." Roberto acquires nutritional supplements and steroids in Mexico and uses the border to buy low and sell high, in effect arbitraging price across borders.

Informal Cross-Border Use of Dental Services

Though some border residents actually prefer the care of Mexican dentists, it is clear that the primary reason for going to a Mexican dentist is economic. Joseph Acevedo believes Mexican dentists save him a lot of money. He regularly takes his daughter to Mexico to provide for her orthodontic needs. His daughter, Jessica, required braces. When he found that it would have cost well over $2,000 in order to get her teeth fixed in the U.S., Joseph found a good dentist in Mexico that is near the border in Reynosa. He takes Jessica every month in order to get her braces tightened for only $20 per visit. Jessica is supposed to wear braces for two years, at the end of which the total that he will have paid is $480 plus the $150 that it cost to put in her braces initially. This works out to a total cost of $630, a savings of over $1,370 (70%). "Not bad," said Joseph.

The Texas Department of Health has reported that all Texas counties that border Mexico have been federally designated as "medically underserved areas."[34] This means there are not enough doctors and other health care practitioners for the size of the local population. The thirty-two counties in Texas that are within sixty-two miles of the border, for example, had 855 persons per physician, compared to a rate of 661 in the rest of Texas. Similarly, these border counties have 1 registered nurse

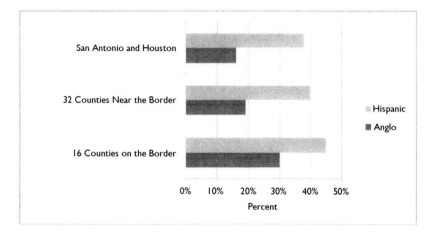

Figure 7.6. Percentage of respondents in each of three samples who say they have ever crossed the border to see a dentist in Mexico

for every 254 residents, compared to 1 nurse for every 156 residents for Texas as a whole. Even more striking is the number of dentists per resident: There is 1 dentist for every 6,535 residents in the border counties, compared to 1 per 2,820 residents for Texas as a whole.

As Figure 7.6 shows, proximity to the border is closely related to the use of dentists in Mexico by residents of South Texas, especially those living in the sixteen counties bordering Mexico. The figure also shows that this effect is especially pronounced for Anglo border residents. As one crosses into Mexican border cities, one is struck by the number of dental clinics within sight of the border. Equally surprising to see is the number of Anglos (especially retired "Winter Texans") who utilize these border dental clinics.

III. Traditional Forms of Health-Related Informality

Some South Texas residents engage in informal health care in ways other than buying and selling medication. Erasmo Silva's wife, for example, gives injections and birth control shots that she purchases in Mexico, though she has no formal training to do so. In Mexico she had to take care of her sick mother, so she learned how to give shots at a very young age. A neighbor near their current home in McAllen one day asked her if she knew someone who could give a birth control shot that the friend had purchased in Mexico. When others found out, they began asking her to give them shots and injections also, which she does for a small cash fee.

Much more common than those who might give shots or injections are folk medical practitioners. These can include several categories, including *curanderos* (folk healers), those who operate *hierberías* (folk pharmacies), and *parteras* (midwives). We have treated the first two categories in more detail in a previous work,[35] so we will discuss them only briefly here and give a bit more attention to parteras.

Curanderos are by far the least common of these three types in South Texas today. As we pointed out in *On the Edge of the Law*, most South Texas residents are suspicious of curanderos, even considering them to be practitioners of a form of witchcraft.[36] Don Artemio, a curandero, said,

> When I first came from Mexico, I brought with me the only thing I knew how to do—be a curandero. I grew up around four of the most well-respected curanderos in Reynosa, Mexico, so it seemed natural for me to carry on with what I learned over here since the majority of people here are from Mexico. Man, was I surprised. Some people are scared of me. I feel as if they walk in expecting to see a pot of boiling water and a black cat lying right next to a broom. My biggest problem, though, seems to be the fact that there are not enough hierberías (folk pharmacies) over here to conduct my job properly. So it's also very hard to find a loyal customer now-a-days. Most people are just looking to solve a one-time need.

Pablo Rendón is one of the few who occasionally visits a curandero. He sought medical help for ten years for his wife's infertility. He had searched for a cure with the best doctors in Mexico. However, none could tell him what was wrong, so he decided to take her to a curandera. The curandera told him that a jealous former girlfriend had put a curse on his wife to get vengeance on him for leaving her. "After that," he said, "my life was full of hope. The curandera did a spiritual cleansing that lead to my wife's recovery. Now we have four girls and four boys."

Some traditional Mexican-origin residents practice folk healing without the help of a curandero. José Yañez, for example, said,

> My parents were convinced that I was suffering from *susto* (traumatic fright). So they went and purchased an herb called *poleo*. I remember the taste was horrible, but I drank it anyway. That night my mother swept my

body with the branches of an herb. The next morning I really felt much better. From that day on, I thought it was amazing how one herbal plant can make a person feel so different. So I learned from my mother what different herbs are used for. And my mother learned from my grandmother. I am really glad that they didn't forget about healing with herbs. Herbs are a good, natural, and affordable medicine.

Hierberías. Those who practice traditional herbal healing on their own, as well as curanderos like Don Artemio, frequently utilize hierberías[37] as their source for traditional herbal medicines.

Ofelia Machado, for example, owns an hierbería and lives behind it. "A lot of times after I have closed the hierbería and have already gone to bed," she said, "people come to my home and get me out of bed because they need a certain herb for a baby or elderly person who is sick. I will get up and give them what they need even if they don't have any money to pay me for it."

Like curanderos, however, hierberías are often looked down upon by many of the Latino people of South Texas. One hierbería owner, Raúl Vasquez, said, "One time a man came in here and asked for some candles and oils. He also bought food items and told me, 'Put the candles on the bottom of the bag and the food on top. I don't want people seeing that I buy candles.' I told him I understood and did as he asked." Some hierberías, however, are doing good business. As prices for conventional medicine increase, more people are frequenting hierberías.

Often, owners of hierberías are suspected or accused of practicing medicine without a license. Since the FDA does not regulate herbal remedies in the same way they do drugs,[38] owners of hierberías are generally safe from prosecution, though some sell items that they claim can cure major medical problems. Mr. Garcia, who has a degree in education, recently had experiences that led him to seek help at a hierbería. He had grown up with parents who used herbs as remedies for ear aches, stomach aches, etc. Along with those remedies came prayers and candles also. Though he is well educated and economically stable, he still sees much that is positive in the folk medicine remedies that are part of his culture. He said,

> I was suffering from a great degree of pain in my upper spine, wrists, elbow, and shoulder. I couldn't sleep on a bed because the pain was unbearable. Lying down just made the pain worse. I slept on a recliner for about two months. Then I sought help at an emergency room. From

there I was referred to a family doctor. After getting no help from him, I was referred to a licensed physical therapist. I got no relief from any of them. I even went to a neurosurgeon who advised me to start proceedings to collect disability compensation because he said I would not be able to work again. I was determined not to continue like this. I wanted to keep on working and go on with my life. The surgeon wanted to fuse one of my vertebrae with a bone from my hip. I was ready to try anything. I was even ready to go to San Antonio to seek help from an acupuncturist. That's how bad I was hurting. I then turned to a hierbería. The faith healer there prescribed some herbs as well as rubbing an oil on my joints. I also saw a *sobador* (folk massage therapist). I finally started feeling much better. I attribute this to my faith in God, practicing mind over matter, and prayer. I know drinking the teas they gave me also helped.

Parteras. Another health-related practice on the South Texas border that is occasionally selected over conventional medicine for economic reasons is using parteras, or midwives. According to the Texas Midwifery Board, over 50% of all babies born in Texas in 1925 were delivered by midwives. By 2004, that percentage had dropped to 6.4%.[39] According to the National Center for Health Statistics, nearly 25,000 babies are born each year outside hospitals, with the largest rates of out-of-hospital births on the U.S.-Mexico border. Today, there are ten registered midwives in Hidalgo County, though there are other midwives registered as nurse midwives. In 1977, however, there were more than thirty midwives in Brownsville alone and similarly large numbers in other Valley cities. In 1983, Texas began implementing stringent restrictions on what midwives could do. As a result, many parteras either ceased practicing or went underground. Their numbers were further curtailed when Medicaid began making it possible for indigent and undocumented mothers to receive medical help and assistance from doctors and hospitals.

Though midwives are found elsewhere in the U.S., three factors make them more prevalent along the Texas border. First, the poverty of much of the local population leaves many unable to afford doctors, particularly when many Latino residents have, on average, more children per family than other population groups. Thus, parteras themselves may have very limited means with which to run their business. One student who conducted her interviews in an urban neighborhood on the south side of McAllen describes the home of the first partera she went to interview.

I walked into a little, two-roomed house used for a clinic by this partera. The partera had little to no educational background. Her income was basically a small percentage of the money released to her by her clients. The rest of her money went towards resources that the Texas Department of Health would fail to supply. A limited amount of cord clamps, towels, linens, and gloves were supplied by the Department of Health. Income and resources were low, and the physical environment did not seem suitable for a newborn baby.

Second, the border offers a setting where doctors who are trained in Mexico but who are not licensed to practice in Texas can have a limited practice as midwives. Not all midwives are women, however. The first midwife interviewed by another student was a male who had studied gynecology in Mexico. A friend influenced him to come to the U.S. and get certified as a midwife. Desperate to find a job, he agreed. He became certified, and he established a small clinic in a town in the Rio Grande Valley. His clinic has been operating for a year and a half; although his business has been prosperous, he plans to return to Mexico to begin practicing gynecology in the near future.

Lay midwives, on the other hand, are those who have learned their skills either from their mothers or through an apprenticeship with another lay midwife. They are quite different from the highly trained midwives who are graduates of Mexican medical schools. The average charge for a midwife to deliver a child is around $400. Some parteras even accept weekly or monthly installments during the pregnancy, so that when the child is born the labor is already paid for. Clearly, however, the parteras interviewed are not in this profession for money.

A third border-related factor is the desire of many women from Mexico to have a child born in the U.S., thus guaranteeing citizenship for the child. Because midwives can help provide birth certificates for the children they deliver, they are often popular among women from Mexico seeking to have a child born in the U.S. Though the birth certificates given by lay parteras are temporary, they still enable a child born under the partera's care to establish citizenship by birth in the U.S. One partera, Leti Cardoza, explained that the mother is responsible for sending the temporary certificate to Austin to exchange for a permanent birth certificate.

The ability to help get birth certificates gives parteras some leverage over those who are unable or unwilling to pay. Sandra Delgado said, "All five of my children were delivered by a partera who charged me one hundred dollars per child. I remember I had problems paying her for my two youngest children. So she withheld their birth certificates until I paid her. A year and a half later, after the birth of my youngest, I began looking for her so I could pay up and get their birth certificates. I needed those certificates so I could be eligible for food stamps and Medicaid for my children."

Because midwives can help establish birth in the U.S.—and thus automatic citizenship—they are subject to the temptation to falsify birth documents and, consequently, to suspicion by immigration agents. In the early 1990s, dozens of South Texas midwives were convicted of forging U.S. birth certificates for nearly 15,000 Mexican children as far back as the 1960s. The issue remained relatively dormant until 2007 when it was announced that by June of 2009 the Western Hemisphere Travel Initiative (WHTI) would require that all border residents be carrying a U.S. passport when returning to the U.S., even from a brief trip to a Mexican border city. When individuals from the South Texas border who were born with the help of a midwife applied, they were told their birth certificate was suspect and they could not get a passport.

This left thousands of Valley residents unable to travel to Mexico to see family. Others whose work involved cross-border trade were similarly unable to travel. The denials seemed to affect anyone in South Texas who had been born with the help of a partera. With the help of the ACLU and other organizations, a suit was filed against the State Department alleging discrimination on the basis of race and ancestry in violation of the Administrative Procedure Act, which safeguards against arbitrary and capricious government agency actions. In June of 2009, the State Department settled the lawsuit, promising that citizens would no longer be denied a passport solely because of their race or ancestry or because they happened to have been born at home with a midwife.[40]

Conclusion

The South Texas border, with its high rates of poverty and uninsured residents, leaves many residents without the resources to access formal medical care. As a result, many turn to informal medical services—both in Mexico and in the U.S. Though health care preferences in the South Texas borderlands are conditioned by Mexican cultural traditions, economic factors are the main reason large portions of the border population rely on informal systems of health care. Results from two congressional reports on drug-price differences between the U.S. and Mexico, for example, showed that the average cost of prescription drugs in Mexico is about half that in the U.S.[41] This substantial price gap and the greater ease of making drug purchases in Mexico pulls many U.S. border residents to Mexico to buy prescription medications. They find they don't need to pay a doctor to get a prescription for the medicine, and they can even get free "medical advice" at Mexican pharmacies.[42] As a result of such substantially lower costs, medical tourism in Mexico will continue to exert a strong pull for South Texans, especially the many low-income U.S. residents in the Texas border area.

Findings from our study described in this chapter suggest that the utilization of informal care services in Mexico and more traditional health practices in the South Texas borderlands is primarily an economic issue—especially for those who cannot afford health insurance. But cultural traditions and the lower price related to Mexican medicines and services are also important reasons borderlands residents give. Most of our respondents rated U.S. medical services as satisfactory but said that they simply could not afford them. Most used a combination of formal services in the U.S. and informal purchases in Mexico to meet their health care needs. We believe that these practices will persist, though perhaps at fluctuating rates, into the foreseeable future.

One strong hold factor that increasingly prevents this cross-border medical trade is the mounting regulation of the border by the U.S. government. As federal officials demand ever more documents from those who want to cross the border, informal use of Mexican health resources becomes progressively out of reach for low-income and undocumented people. The increasing costs of formal American medical care act to push many South Texas residents to use informal health care, either in Mexico (for those able to cross the border) or in South Texas. Those unable to access the Mexican health care market may be limited either to informal products and services in the U.S. or to already strained and underfunded emergency rooms in local hospitals. Most of those who utilize informal medicine recognize the risks involved. Most would probably prefer more conventional (formal) health care but feel they are being pushed out of that market.

As we have pointed out, individual risks are substantial for those who utilize informal medical care or products. There are also public health risks. So far, few studies have assessed the extent to which the utilization of informal forms of health care on both sides of the border contributes to some of the unique health issues in the South Texas borderland region. A large-scale de facto medical arrangement has evolved here without a clear understanding of its epidemiological consequences. Major medical consequences may be occurring at the macro-level, unrecognized by those who utilize the system. This would include the dangers of creating drug-resistant strains through mass over-utilization of antibiotics purchased without a prescription. It would also include the possibility that mass cross-border medical trade may contribute to the spread of a pandemic.

There is some hope that recent reforms will mitigate individual and public health risks. On April 15, 2010, President Obama signed health care legislation to reform health care in the U.S. Texas, with the highest number of uninsured residents in the nation, stands to gain the most, though most of its elected public officials have opposed the reforms. The legislation is still very new, so it remains unclear how well it will provide greater health care access for residents living in the South Texas border area.[43] For example, it is estimated that the new legislation will expand health insurance coverage to 32 million Americans who are currently uninsured. Potentially, most low-income residents in the South Texas border area will now be able to afford health insurance plans with governmental subsidies or tax credits. But are they willing to pay for it? If they get tax credits and governmental subsidies, will they cease to rely on Mexican doctors and pharmacies?

Prior to this legislation, we found that many individuals with health insurance still went to Mexico because that option is cheaper than meeting all their copays and deductibles. This suggests that these informal channels will persist. So in our 2010 Consumer Informality Survey we asked respondents what they would do if the government obliged them to buy health insurance and offered to pay for it. Well over half (68.5%) said they would get it and take care of most of their health care needs in the U.S. Nevertheless, 14.8% said they would buy the insurance but still go to Mexico for most medical needs, while 16.8% said they would avoid paying for it and would continue to go to Mexico for most medical needs. In other words, despite the prospect of government-backed health insurance, almost a third (31.6%) of our sample stated that they would still cross the border into Mexico to meet most of their health care needs whether or not the government helps them get American health insurance.

One group of border residents intentionally excluded from this legislation is undocumented immigrants. The legislation excluded them from accessing health insurance even if they were to pay for it themselves. In South Texas, this leaves a population about equal in size to that of Laredo totally cut off from most formal channels of health care. Since they do not have documents allowing them to get health care in Mexico, many will likely become a lucrative market for third-party informal health care vendors who will sell them medicine or practice medicine on them without a license. Others will have to rely on already over-utilized emergency rooms. The bottom line is that this system will get them some of the worst health care available, at the greatest possible cost to taxpayers, and at an increased risk to public health if diseases go untreated or only partially treated.

Finally, a word about how the state is complicit in the structural factors leading many to opt for informal health care. Much of the cost of formal health care is the result of government intervention in the market. Doctors and other conventional health providers enjoy a monopoly because of state licensing arrangements. Many well-trained Mexican doctors, for example, are unable to practice medicine in the U.S. because of immigration regulations and because they are required to pass exams that, according to many, are more rigorous than those required of U.S.-trained physicians. Similarly, state mandates allow drug companies to charge excessive prices for drugs that the state keeps free from competition, often for many more years than are needed to recoup research costs. The fact that American-made drugs are about half as costly in Mexico or Canada is evidence that U.S. consumers are operating in a very unfree and protected market.

While there are definite advantages to a highly state-controlled medical market, the benefits and the costs are often not evenly distributed. The poor, in general, get priced out of the market. The most vulnerable, the undocumented, are not even allowed to participate in it. So if those who bear the greatest costs and get the fewest benefits shop for medicine in a flea market or cross the border to access a more affordable (though more informal) option, we as a society ought to be more understanding and compassionate about their—and the entire region's—struggle to access quality medical care.

CHAPTER 8

Family and Welfare Informality

WITH AMELIA FLORES

Mario Marquez is an immigrant from Mexico with only a sixth-grade education. After Mario married Alma, a U.S. citizen, he became a legal U.S. resident. They lived in Houston until 1987 when Mario got laid off. They decided to move to the Valley, where Alma's family lived. Mario, who was just 29 at the time, found it difficult to find a job that paid as much as he had been earning in Houston. He was not about to rely just on the money that his wife was bringing in. He turned down a lower-paying job after a friend offered him $1,000 to transport drug money from Houston to the Valley. "It was really easy," he said, "so I started taking other jobs smuggling drugs and drug money. Even though I never mentioned anything to my wife, she suspected I was doing something illegal."

Alma recalled, "For four months, he had been hiding things from me. Every time I wanted to talk about it he would just ignore me or get angry. We had had a good relationship, so this was very difficult." After four months, Mario decided to get out of the business. But since he had spent a lot of money buying a few acres and building a house, he decided to do just one more job.

"They called me to see if I would take a few drugs to Houston," he said, "and I agreed. I was hooked on making easy money, and I didn't see any problem in doing one last job.

It was in December, and so I gathered up my family and told them we were going to have Christmas vacation in Houston with relatives."

Alma had a bad feeling, but since Mario kept insisting, they loaded the car and left. Everything was fine until they came to the La Sarita checkpoint [about sixty-five miles north of Harlingen]. "When the Border Patrol checked the car," he said, "they found a screwdriver that the men who loaded the drugs must have left just inside of the trunk. They got suspicious and sent us to secondary inspection."

Brianna, who was only eight years old, sadly remembers that day. "My dad was escorted away from our car and taken inside to be questioned. My mother had to wait outside with my nine-month-old sister, my five-year-old brother, and me. The Border Patrol started searching our car and tore it apart, inside and out."

Alma continued, "Although I was extremely afraid, I never broke down. I had to be strong for my children. After they took Mario away, I had to get my three children back home to the Valley. I had no money, no job, and I was in a new town. That was the saddest and worst Christmas ever. But on that day, I made a promise that this tragedy was not going to affect our love for one another."

Mario was sentenced to eleven years in prison. "I first turned to God, and started reading the Bible. Nothing changed, so I started believing in *brujería* (witchcraft). Several times, I even contemplated suicide by hanging myself. I had nothing but anger towards God, witchcraft, and myself. Eventually I remembered that I had a loving family waiting for me when I got out."

Alma recalled it as a very stressful time, but she knew she had to work hard for her family.

> I started off with help from food stamps and monthly welfare checks. The government also gave me help on how to find a job and do well on interviews. I got a job as a certified nurse's assistant in a nursing home. It was a very stressful job, but I needed to work hard for my family. I could not afford a babysitter, so Brianna had to take care of her little brother and sister.

Briana recalled, "Mom taught me how to cook when I was only eight years old, so I was able to feed them as well."

Alma worked as a nurse's assistant for several years until she fractured a disk in her lower back. After a month in bed, she found another job as a cafeteria clerk in the school her children attended. By then, Mario had decided to focus on being a positive role model for his family. Mario recalled, "The first thing I did was receive my GED. Next I got trained as a dental assistant." Alma insisted on visiting Mario every month. They didn't make enough to pay for the trips, so she made and sold tamales and bought artifacts from Mexico to raffle. Both Brianna and Ashley cannot remember ever seeing their mother buy anything new for herself. "Everything she wore was given to her or passed on from friends and family," recalled Briana. "Our greatest help was her faith in God."

In December of 1998, at the age of forty, Mario got out of prison after being incarcerated for eleven years. Alma was now thirty-eight-years old, Brianna was nineteen, Mike was sixteen, and their little sister Ashley was eleven years old. But then, even though their father was out of prison, he was not able to go home. He was turned over to immigration officials who revoked his status as a resident alien and deported him to Mexico. He got a job in Reynosa, Mexico (a border city), working for his sister in a store. The family crossed the border every weekend to see him, but it was still a struggle. One day, after going to a wedding in Reynosa, Alma and Mario told the children that their daddy was going home with them. Ashley recalled, "I remember feeling butterflies inside my stomach all the way to the border. We did everything we could to stay calm, and finally we all made it through."

Even though Mario was finally reunited with his family, he was now in the U.S. illegally. Mario recalled, "I felt as if I was literally in a bigger prison than before. I didn't have a driver's license and had to be careful never to get pulled over by a cop." Mario was able to start a cabinet business, but he believes he has to hide his income. He explained,

> There is no way I can report that to the government because I am not supposed to be here. I have to be extremely careful to avoid a paper trail that could lead the Border Patrol to me. I am the only one in the family that does not have health insurance, so it can get pretty tough. I got really sick one time and refused to go to the hospital because I did not want them to report me to the Border Patrol. I lay in bed for a few days at home until I couldn't take the pain anymore. I finally went into the hospital. Fortunately, they didn't report me and let me pay the bill in installments.

This account of the Marquez family helps illustrate the complexity of the underground and informal economy of the South Texas border. Both "good" and "bad" people get caught up in it. So-called "easy money" tempts, or pulls, individuals like Mario into the underground economy, while honest and hardworking people like Alma feel pushed toward informal economic activities as the only way they can find to support a family and sustain life. Families are pulled apart and spread across the border.

Welfare becomes a necessity for many, though if they claim even their meager informal earnings, they stand to lose government benefits, including health insurance and food assistance. In the struggle to stay alive and get ahead, informality increasingly becomes the way out. Even people who do not want to be on welfare or those who would really like to declare all their income find it difficult to live above board. As Mario found, however, as they use informality to escape their problems, they may only become more deeply drawn into informality and a life underground.[1]

Mario's case also helps us introduce two additional factors related to informality—family relationships and public welfare. As Mario's case illustrates, economic informality and underground activities can have a profound impact on the family. Often, they leave families dependent on welfare and, in some cases, underreporting income in order to be able to receive public assistance. In this chapter, we explicitly focus on informal and underground activities—sometimes separately, sometimes together—and how they can surround or even engulf families. We also make special reference to welfare and public assistance.

The Family in South Texas

Throughout the U.S., Hispanic children in low-income families are more likely to be living in a two-parent household than are low-income white or black children. According to the Urban Institute,[2] 53% of low-income Hispanic children are in married family households, compared to 43% of white low-income children and 18% of black low-income children.

Other factors, however, contribute to the strains on the family in South Texas. Many of these low-income families, for example, have at least one immigrant parent, many of them undocumented. In Hidalgo County, 57% of children live in a family with at least one immigrant parent, compared to 20% in other border counties and 11% in the rest of Texas. Nevertheless, because most of these children are born in the U.S., almost 90% of the children in these three areas are U.S. citizens. Despite the high rate of citizenship of these children, nearly one of every two Hidalgo County children (44%) lives in poverty. The same is true for children in other border counties (44%). However, the rate of children living in poverty in the rest of the state is only 21%.[3]

Census figures such as these help point out the complex relationship between family structure and informality in this border area. This is more clearly illustrated by our ethnographic profiles of informality, such as Mario and Alma's case. These ethnographic examples, taken together, illustrate how working in the informal and underground economy puts enormous strains on the family. They also show the reverse—that informality in the family (which we will discuss shortly) helps produce economic informality, even among honest and hard-working people.

The Impact of Informality and Underground Activities on the Family

Yolanda Garza, a forty-five-year-old mother of four boys, has experienced difficulties similar to those of Alma, though with less positive results. Her husband is currently in prison, but she prefers not to discuss what sent him there.

> It was very hard after he was arrested. I had never before had to support myself financially. I lost everything when he left, and even now I still feel as if I'm losing my children. My sons are twenty-one, eighteen, and sixteen years old. Ever since my husband was put in jail, my boys have suffered a lot. First we lost our house because I couldn't make the payments. My boys have ears, and they could hear everything that people would say about us. I think that made them act up even more. Since my husband's jailing, my boys have had problems with alcohol, drugs, and the police. Sometimes I feel they blame me for our situation. My three boys are all on probation, and CPS [Child Protective Services] is trying to take my youngest son away. My sons are taking this very hard, but I really can't do anything about it.

Family problems arising from informality are not limited to those resulting from family members sent to jail or prison. Informality, especially among the poor, puts many additional strains on the family. Lisa Chavez, for example, is a single mother who struggles to get by on an informal job taking care of an elderly woman.

> My job takes me away from my children. The lady I take care of needs more help at night now than she used to. Before, my hours were only during the day. But lately, she has needed me to stay overnight. Her family paid me for the extra hours, and the extra money helped a lot. Sometimes, I cannot get home until early the next morning. Recently, I came home one morning and found that my two older boys had been drinking with their friends in my house while I was gone. Their friends had even smoked marijuana in front of my younger kids. I found out that this had

been going on for several months. When I found out, I told my employer's family that I could not work nights anymore. They were angry because they said I didn't warn them with enough time. They fired me and only paid me a small part of what they owed me. But it didn't matter. My family is much more important.

Lisa's case illustrates that single parents involved in the informal economy are especially prone to difficulties in holding their family together. Often, they have to rely on an older child to be a surrogate parent while they are working. Roy Alamía remembered when his older sister took on his mom's role:

My oldest sister helped my mom raise us. She was sixteen years old and would sacrifice her Friday nights, weekends, and even homework hours to watch, care for, and feed us. She made sure she did more so Mom would have to do less when she came home. One time, when my brother and I were fighting, she spanked us. I remember crying, tears dropping down my face. Not because it hurt physically—but because I drove her to that point to where she needed to spank me. In a way, she was like another mother. At an early age, she had the responsibility of caring for three younger children while my mom was working.

Those who engage not just in informal activities (as Lisa Chavez did), but become involved in underground activities, create even greater risks for their family. Kathy Camacho is twenty-nine years old and is a single mother of two children. Kathy works as a bartender at a sports bar, earning minimum wage plus tips. Her mother takes care of her children while she works. In addition to that, she has found a way to bring home substantially more income. As she visits with her customers, she helps arrange drug deals between consumers and dealers. She is like the messenger and gets paid by a dealer for every customer she brings to him and gets larger amounts for larger deals. "I am afraid of getting caught," she said, "because I would automatically lose my children and my Medicaid insurance for them. Children get sick very easily, and I hardly have enough for even a doctor's visit."

The Impact of Family Informality on Economic Informality

At times, the relationship between informality and the family is reversed, with informal family relationships (those outside the parameters established by law or government agencies) stimulating economic informality. One of the most extreme forms of family informality is marriage fraud. Daniel Cardona, a U.S. citizen and college student from the Valley, recalled how he entered into a sham marriage for money. One day while waiting to wash his car at a car wash, he struck up a conversation with another man also waiting to wash his car. After a few minutes, the man asked Daniel if he would like to make some extra money. Daniel was always looking for "easy" ways to help pay his tuition. The man told Daniel, "All you have to do is get married with my friend who is here illegally. Once she obtains her citizenship, you get divorced. That's it." The price was $2,000. Daniel agreed, and before long he had "married for money." And before long, Daniel regretted his decision to earn some "easy" money. "It sounded so easy," Daniel said, "but now I feel trapped. Getting all of the paperwork filed and approved takes a long time. And I think the officials are suspicious." Knowing more now, Daniel stated, "I should have asked for more money or not have done it at all."

Daniel has good reason to worry. Conspiracy to commit marriage fraud is a felony punishable by up to five years imprisonment, a fine of up to $250,000, and three years of supervised release. In 2008, U.S. Immigration and Customs Enforcement (ICE) made 238 criminal arrests related to marriage fraud schemes and was successful in handing out convictions for 198 of those individuals. ICE also seized nearly $430,000 in assets related to these cases.[4]

As Daniel's story illustrates, individuals called coyotes seek out American citizens, hoping to get them to consent to a sham marriage. Ramón, a forty-two-year-old undocumented worker from Tamaulipas, Mexico, was brought over to the U.S. several years ago by a smuggler who promised to get him work. The coyote also agreed to help Ramón bring his wife and children here after he was settled, providing he was willing to enter into a sham marriage. Ramón and his wife have an agreement that he will hide the fact that they are married so that he can marry an American woman and eventually bring his family here. He has heard from several sources that there are women in the Valley who marry illegal aliens for a fee. "The fee is usually $800," he said. "These women marry for money, but not for a commitment."[5]

Another form of family informality is "deadbeat parents," or those who skip out on parental obligations. Luisa Estrada, for example, related this story: "My ex-husband forgot he has kids. I used to take him to court all the time for the child support. Legal aid, though, got tired of seeing me. It's not like he can't afford it; he has a good job. It's a struggle for us month to month, all year long. He has another family now. The only thing in my favor is that the law says that the first family comes first and the second is second. Still, I can't always afford to use the legal system, so often I have to make do with whatever I have."

Some deadbeat parents use informality to avoid their obligations by getting jobs that pay under the table, in cash. Anita Verdejo, for example, is a twenty-five-year-old woman on government assistance. She has three children and is currently unemployed. "I get housing assistance, food stamps, and medical services," she said. "I don't know where I would live if we didn't get food stamps or Medicaid. My children's father does not care for their well being. He married another woman and is somewhere up north. I think he works for cash so the police will not find him. I get nothing from him. Not even a phone call to check up on his kids."

Juanita Cuellar also had to deal with a deadbeat dad who pushed her into informality. Because she is not a citizen, she has fewer options. While she was living in Mexico, she started dating a U.S. citizen. In order for them to be together, he had her come illegally to the U.S., promising to marry and legalize her after the baby was born.

> The first months in the U.S. were like heaven. I thought I was the happiest girl ever. My boyfriend would buy me everything. Three months after my child's birth, however, he just left. One day, I went back to the trailer where we lived and there was no sign of him. I had no family to turn to. There was no point in returning to Mexico because my family there was having a really hard time. My neighbors sometimes helped me by giving me milk or a few dollars. It was a miracle my son and I survived. I had to face the world on my own in a country where I had no idea how the laws worked. I was terrified, not knowing how I was going to support myself. I came to the U.S. because of love, not to take advantage of anyone. Now, I'm working as a maid in my neighbor's house and taking care of their four children. It's difficult, but I've managed to overcome some problems. Sometimes my son comes from school and tells me that the kids hit him or call him a *mojado* (wetback), even though he was born here just like them.

Family problems also pressured Mari Espinoza into economic informality. Although she has a full-time job as a beautician, she has her own customers on the side that she sees in her home or theirs.

> When my husband left me for another woman, I was devastated, emotionally and financially. My ex-husband had taken many loans out using

my credit card to help his family start a business in Mexico City. When he left, he returned to Mexico. During the divorce, I learned that I had to pay off the cards since they were under my name. Altogether, he left me owing $56,000. I also had to make payments on the mortgage on our new home, our furniture and appliances, and payments on our car. All of this doesn't include my utilities, gas, work expenses, food, or the help I give my family. I was sinking in bills and needed help with day care, so I underreported my income so that I could qualify for CCMS [Child Care Management Services] services. I get paid mostly in cash, so it's like being a waiter and underreporting your tips. I also qualified for Medicaid by underreporting. One month when I was in the middle of the divorce and really depressed, I messed up. I claimed having paid more bills than I had income. The CCMS worker cut off my childcare services and said that I could reapply but I would have to start all over and show better documentation regarding my finances. I haven't reapplied yet. I was really devastated and embarrassed. How could I explain to this worker how desperate I was? I couldn't, so I didn't. I earn about $1,200 dollars extra each month that I do not report to the government. I underreport my finances not to get rich or for luxuries. I only do it because I need the assistance in order to survive.

Welfare and Informality

Families struggling to survive often have to turn to welfare assistance, but they often meet with less than desirable results. Texas has a philosophy of minimal governmental expenditures for the poor. This is reflected in a state constitutional provision that until 1970 limited welfare expenditures to 1% of the state's budget. This contributes significantly to the fact that Texas has the highest rate in the U.S. of children lacking health insurance. Indeed, based on 2007 Census data, it is estimated that one-sixth of all uninsured children in the U.S. live in Texas.[6] Texas has no general relief program, and in 2000, its Temporary Assistance for Needy Families (TANF) benefit was the fifth lowest among the fifty states.[7] In part, this is because Texas has no state income tax but does have the fifth most regressive state and local tax system in the U.S.[8] In 1998, TANF in Texas covered only 21% of poor children, compared to the national average of nearly 50%.[9] Between 1996 and 2006, however, Texas pushed many of the very poor off TANF assistance with a 73% decline in TANF support, the tenth largest decline in the nation.[10]

Mary Vergara has experience with TANF and other programs for the poor. She is a thirty-six-year-old single mother of three: a sixteen-year-old daughter and two sons, one eleven and the other a one-year-old toddler. The father of her one-year-old abandoned them when the baby was only three months old. She started receiving TANF, but only until her baby's father could be tracked down to provide child support. Mary does not like the program because she receives only $224 a month, which is not nearly enough for her expenses. She is also required by the TANF program to get a job in order to continue receiving her benefit checks. She has great trouble doing so, however, because she does not have a car and lives in a rural area, isolated from most job opportunities. She survives by helping her sister clean houses, for which she receives some cash that she has to hide from the program.

Mary also receives food stamps, public housing, and Medicaid for her children. She explained that she had to show a lot of bill receipts and other paperwork in order to get her food stamps. She remembers the food stamp process was a long one. "The caseworkers reviewed the case several times," she said. "They had to make sure that I was, in fact, eligible for those services. I like the program, but it is really hard to go in for appointments every six months just to keep getting benefits." Because Mary does not have a car, she must rely on family members and friends to take her everywhere she needs to go. She said that her daughter wants to look for a part-time job to help her. Her daughter is looking for work and has submitted applications at local supermarkets and fast-food restaurants.

As Table 8.1 shows, approximately 23% of the participants in our Informal and Underground Survey indicated that they or someone in their family had applied for and/or were receiving food stamps and 24.1% had applied for and/or were receiving Medicaid or Medicare (some were receiving both). Almost 60% of our informal/underground respondents, however, had not applied for and were not receiving any forms of governmental welfare assistance.

In 2008, the food stamp program was renamed the Supplemental Nutrition Assistance Program (SNAP). As before, families must still pass an assets test and two income tests to qualify, and benefits are issued through an electronic benefits transfer card (known in Texas as the Lone Star Card). In 2007, the monthly benefits for a family of three were $408.[11] National standards in 2009 required that applicants be below the federal poverty line of $18,310 for a family of three.[12]

For years, Texas has made qualifying for food stamps difficult and

Table 8.1. Type of welfare applied for or received by respondents in the Informal and Underground Survey in preceding 12 months

Type of Welfare Applied for or Received	Number	Percent
None	313	59.3%
Medicaid/Medicare	127	24.1%
Food Stamps (Lone Star Card)	120	22.7%
WIC	31	5.9%

Note: No total is given since many respondents reported multiple forms of assistance.
Source: Informal and Underground Survey.

time-consuming. Applicants have to show countless documents, wait for hours in highly bureaucratized offices, and experience long delays in finally getting approved. This seems hard to understand given that Texas, like other states, is only administering federal benefits. The state is responsible for administering the program and even receives federal funding for half the administrative costs. Bruce Bower of Texas Legal Services, whose agency sued the state because of excessive delays, comments, "All the state had to do was add personnel. Instead, they starved the program."[13]

The recession of 2008 and 2009 greatly increased the problems of people receiving welfare. Texas food stamp applications soared from 38,000 in 2008 to more than 65,000 by October 2009. Two-thirds of applicants had to wait longer than the federally mandated thirty days, and nearly half had to wait more than sixty days. By adding 500 new employees, requiring overtime of existing employees, and assigning veteran employees to tackle the oldest cases, the state managed to decrease its pending cases to 62,000.

This backlog had been building for six years, having begun with a disastrous privatization effort that was cancelled after two years because of massive foul-ups.[14] At the same time, large numbers of existing employees of the Texas Health and Human Services Commission (which runs the federal program) quit, believing they were going to be laid off. Overworked staff, misplaced applications, and low morale contributed to another problem—a high "negative error rate," or the number of people denied who in reality were eligible for the benefits. This rate is estimated to be one in five according to reports to the state legislature. And this error rate does not even include the number of "lost" applications. Until recently, applicants in Texas had to go back through the very arduous process of going to the agency to requalify for the program every six months.

Many people we interviewed stated that the application procedures are extremely frustrating, especially the time it takes to apply. A 2001 General Accounting Office (GAO) report stated that, on average, applicants spent nearly five hours and made at least two trips to the local food stamp office to apply for food stamps.[15] Guadalupe ("Lupe") Esquivel is married and has six children. She and her husband both work but still cannot make ends meet. She is grateful for the food stamp program and believes that without it her family might be homeless. "Without it," she said, "we would have no money after paying for food to pay our housing payments and utility costs." In spite of her appreciation for the program, however, she hates the long waits, both at the office and in waiting to be qualified. "I have to wait most of a day at the food stamps office until my number finally gets called," she says. "I have to ask for the entire day off from work, and it makes it especially hard because I am a part-time worker and I don't get paid when I'm not working. I get no paid time off, no sick pay, and no benefits such as health insurance for me or my family. That's why I have to depend on welfare."

The requirement to produce work-related documents creates other problems. Claudia Soto's husband works full-time, but she is a thirty-three-year-old stay-at-home mother of four boys. She has had jobs in the past, but now she has a three-year-old and a two-month-old at home, so it has been difficult for her to go back to work. Her family receives food stamps and Medicaid. Claudia also receives Women, Infants, and Children (WIC) benefits for her smaller children.

> I have no concerns with the WIC program. The food stamp program, though, is much more complicated and strict. They demand a lot of proof of employment, bill receipts, car expenses, and property ownership. The food stamp and Medicaid people ask a lot of questions. They make a lot of demands, take forever to qualify you, and are sometimes rude when we go in for interviews. What is really irritating, though, is that they make us involve my husband's employer. They require that he verifies that he employs my husband and shows how much they pay him each month. My husband feels embarrassed that he must go through that every six months. Many employers look down on their employees if they are receiving public assistance. If I tried to get off welfare and help my

husband, I would not qualify for childcare. I guess that's OK because I'm protective of my kids, and I really don't want some stranger at a day care center watching them.

Melinda Castro is also frustrated with the food stamp program. She is twenty-four years old, married, and has two small children. She does some work as a temporary employee of the school district. Her husband does not work because he is taking college classes. Melinda has been receiving welfare for about four and a half years. She believes that the people at the Medicaid office are helpful, but she dislikes the food stamp program. She says that the food stamp program asks too many questions. Also, having to meet with a caseworker every six months was a waste of time because there had not been any changes in her income or such personal information as her place of employment or her address. Even though her information doesn't change, she says that the amount of food stamps that she receives seems to always be changing. She dreads having to show check stubs, rent receipts, and utility bills and answering all the questions she is asked.

Many of the people interviewed believed that the eligibility requirements of the food stamp program are too burdensome. Any change in income has to be reported within a few days, which is hard for people whose work is part time or temporary. In addition, if someone's income increases even slightly past a certain ceiling ($16,608 for a family of three in 2007), they could lose this important source of food support for their family.[16] Esther Dominguez explained that she has very little time to go down to the food stamp office since she works and goes to night school:

> Also, the agency will make a federal case if I forget to report any changes on my income, address, telephone number, or place of employment. I recently got a raise at my job and I was earning a little bit more money, and they sent me a letter saying that if I did not report the changes at a proper time, they would not give me food stamps for the following months. I wasn't trying to hide anything. It's just hard to remember or find time for telling them every time something changes.

Many low-income people, however, do hide income. In addition to working part-time at Walmart, Cristela Fuentes has an informal job taking care of some elderly people on weekends and nights. Also, one of her daughters babysits on weekends and after school. But neither of them reports their informal income so that the family can keep their meager benefits. They fear that if they are found out, the government will take away their benefits and they will go hungry. Cristela said, "Even if I work the extra job, we will all go hungry if we do not get food stamps. One time I couldn't make it to the meeting with my caseworker because our car was broken. They took away our food stamps, and we had to struggle for those months. We ate rice and beans a lot, and there were days when we only ate once a day. It is really hard for us, even though we get help to buy food."

Many of the people we talked to stated that they hated not reporting all their income but that it was necessary to do so to keep food stamps or other benefits. A thirty-three-year-old single mother, Alicia Delgado stated,

> I have four children, and I cannot afford to have my Lone Star card reduced. I have been cleaning houses for a couple of years now. If all my earnings as a housecleaner were to be reported, my food stamps would be greatly reduced or eliminated. Besides, the amount I get each month always changes, depending on how many requests I get for cleaning. Luckily I have some understanding families that pay me decently and help me get home when my children get out of school.

Welfare Fraud and Informality

Failure to report all of one's income in order to maintain benefits is a form of welfare fraud. Because it is a form of shielding income from the government, it also constitutes a form of informal economic activity, in the same way that shielding income to avoid paying taxes is an informal economic activity. One Texas report stated that in 1995 Texas spent $523 million on Aid to Families with Dependent Children (AFDC) and received $2.3 billion in federal food stamp benefits. As much as $222.4 million was spent in error, and approximately 36% of this erroneous spending was attributed to recipient fraud.[17] A 1997 GAO report stated that the biggest form of fraud was the underreporting of income. Using figures from the GAO report, we calculate that only 3.4% of the total spent on food stamps was attributable to fraud. Since 1997, Texas and other states have tightened restrictions, and the losses due to error and fraud are thought to have been cut to less than half the previous portion.[18]

Locally, employees of the food stamp program see cases of hiding income as both a protection of meager benefits and, in the case of some, outright fraud to steal from the government. One caseworker, Jaime Escobar, stated, "Some clients fail to report income because they are faced with extreme economic circumstances or emergencies. Others lie just to cheat the system. I have had some clients who applied in two states just to get more food stamps or Medicaid." Another worker, Juan Flores, said that some clients who are employed in good jobs claim that they are not employed so they can get benefits. A third worker, Dora Garza, described a woman who applied for financial assistance and food stamps, claiming she was a single mother with four children whose husband left her a year ago and who had no other source of income. "In reality," she said, "the husband never left the household and works as a truck driver making $70,000 to $80,000 a year."

Another of our respondents, Cindy Gomez, described a case of welfare fraud involving her own brother and his wife. She said they receive every type of benefit the government allows.

> My brother works for my father, but he gets paid *por debajo de la mesa* (under the table). He tells the people where he applies for aid that he doesn't work much. He ends up receiving around $600 a month in food stamps. Even though they make a good income from my father, they never have to spend any of their own money on food. When they submit their taxes, my father also lies and reports only a small portion of what he has paid them for the year. They also receive WIC and have been getting Medicaid for their children for the past ten years.

There are other individuals who not only earn good income that goes unreported, but do so in underground economic activities. Cynthia Gonzalez is a thirty-five-year-old U.S. citizen with post-high school training who is currently not officially employed. In the past year, she has applied for or renewed assistance for health care, food, housing, and disability. Only the application for disability was denied. Cynthia is not disabled, but she is hoping to establish a claim for disability so that she can increase her benefits without having to work. In order to make money, she often goes to Mexico to purchase medication, alcoholic beverages, and cigarettes, which she then resells in the U.S. She has even engaged in selling some drugs that are illegal in the U.S. She has been doing this for about seven years. When asked why she does something that is clearly dangerous and illegal, she responds, "Why not? Everyone else does it."[19]

Other individuals engage in welfare to maintain a particular lifestyle. One student who interviewed her friend Samantha Guajardo was surprised when Samantha told her that she receives food stamps, Medicaid, and childcare assistance. The interviewer knew her friend was making good money as a stripper and liked to party a lot. Samantha said,

> I hated applying for welfare, but I have had a hard life. I never could count on anyone but myself. My father was in prison, and my mother had problems similar to mine. I guess I followed in her footsteps. My aunt took me in with all my kids, and I've been with her for two years now. For a time, I worked in a fast-food chicken restaurant and even started going to nursing school. But I never saw my kids. My boyfriend got thrown in jail, and I didn't want to add to his problems by reporting him for not giving me child support. My kids even started calling my aunt "Mom." They didn't miss me or even bother to hug me. I know I've made mistakes, but I'm trying to change by working where I am. Now I make good money and work less. But it's too late. My little ones don't want me anymore. Where I work, I get paid in cash so I don't have to report it. It's better for me. Otherwise I would lose the help I get. When I worked at the chicken place, I couldn't get much in food stamps because I was working. Now I say that I'm not working. I get more. It's better this way.

Though some of those engaged in fraud or underreporting income did so even when they had no economic need to do so, the vast majority of those we interviewed felt pushed into it by regulations that cut the benefits needed to survive.

According to our own Informal and Underground Survey, those most likely to receive public assistance are those with the strongest legal ties to the U.S. One-third or more of respondents who are U.S. resident aliens or U.S. citizens received some form of public assistance, while a much smaller percentage of the undocumented and quasidocumented received public assistance, most likely through a U.S.-born family member. Regardless of immigration status, household incomes of those receiving public assistance are meager to very modest (see Table 8.2).

In our Informal and Underground Survey, 59% of respondents did not receive any welfare at all, 17% had been denied welfare, and 20.6% said they had felt compelled to hide income or property in order to receive welfare benefits. Among this group that hid income, the average declared yearly family income was nearly $10,000, while their actual *total* income, including informal income, was nearly $30,000. To put this in a context, the National Center for Children in Poverty calculates that

Table 8.2. Informality, immigration status, public assistance, and household income

Immigration Status	Percent of Each Category Who Report Receiving Some Form of Welfare Assistance	Mean Annual Household Income (U.S. $)
Undocumented	18.3% (n = 28)*	$8,873
Quasidocumented	11.8% (n = 18)	$10,756
Resident Alien	36.6% (n = 56)	$15,407
U.S. Citizen	33.3% (n = 51)	$34,251
Total	100.0% (n = 153)	$22,539

*Welfare assistance to this category is most likely allocated for U.S.-born citizen children.
Source: Informal and Underground Survey

the average family of four needs a yearly income of at least $44,100 to meet their basic needs.[20] Those below this level are regarded as "low income." Thus, to the extent that our sample describes participants in the South Texas informal economy, the majority of those who do hide income in order to maintain welfare benefits seem to do so because they live so close to the edge: Their choosing to not report informal income is a strategy to survive rather than a means of cheating the system.

The average number of individuals living in the homes of our 524 respondents was 4.1. In 2009, the official poverty line for a family of four was $22,050. This means that the undocumented respondents who were receiving some form of welfare (most likely for their U.S.-born citizen children) earned less than half the official poverty rate for a family of four. Resident aliens were only slightly above the official poverty line. However, informals who were U.S. citizens and who received some form of welfare had an average income that was 180% of the 2009 official poverty rate for a family of four. Still, even their average income was below the $44,100 level reported above as needed to meet the basic needs of a family of four. So welfare fraud does exist, even among the few who make substantially more than they need to meet basic needs. But contrary to most stereotypes, U.S. citizens are far more likely than those in the other (immigrant) categories to be engaging in welfare fraud by failing to report informal income. And even their average total income is substantially lower than the amount needed to sustain basic family needs.

Other Forms of Welfare Informality

Another form of welfare fraud is "trafficking" in food stamps. Some respondents reported using their food stamp allocations to buy things
other than food or even trading the benefits for money. One respondent
said, "In the city of Alton, if you know the right people, anything can
be gotten with your food stamps." The same lady continued, "My son's
birthday was a couple of weeks ago. I didn't have any money, but the
young lady accepted my food stamps to buy a board game and a stuffed
animal."

Unlike failure to report income in order to obtain benefits, trafficking does not involve fraud to get benefits. Rather, it involves getting
merchants to allow users to purchase items other than those officially
allowed. Often, the merchant takes a significant cut for allowing unauthorized purchases (generally reported to be about one-half of the
amount charged). This practice was much easier when food stamps were
actually stamps. Now that Texas uses the Lone Star Card, the practice
is more difficult but certainly not impossible if merchants are willing.

Two adult females who traded stamps for other purchases described
how the process worked. Each of them would sell three-fourths of their
food stamp allotment to a regular monthly customer. The buyer would
give them $5 for every $10 worth of food coupons, an exchange rate of
2 to 1. Often, the money gained from the trade would be used to pay
rent or items not authorized for purchase with food coupons. These two
women even used money derived from the trade to pay their utilities.

Alma Herrera is fifty years old, divorced, a high school dropout, and
the mother of four children. Though her children are grown and gone,
she remembered the struggles to feed and provide for them as children on her meager salary as a teacher's aide: "There was never enough
money to feed and clothe my children. I was on food stamps then and
still have the Lone Star Card today. Many times, I have had to trade my
food stamps for money, even though it was illegal. Sometimes I would
pay people I owed with food stamps. It was the only way that I could get
money for things like gas for my car or other necessities. I hated doing
it, but I simply could find no other way."

A USDA study in 2006 estimated that between 2002 and 2005, food
stamp trafficking nationwide diverted an estimated $241 million from
food stamp benefits. Overall, however, such trafficking involved only
1.1% of each benefit dollar, since the benefits given during that period
were $24 billion. The study estimated that about 7% of all active, autho-

rized food stamp-receiving stores engaged in the trafficking. Though large stores and supermarket chains redeemed 90% of the food stamp benefits during that period, they were responsible for only 21% of the benefits trafficked. Most trafficking was done by small neighborhood stores that accounted for only 3.5% of redemptions but made up 45.5% of all benefits trafficked. The USDA study further estimated that the amount of trafficking has been cut back to only about one-third the amount trafficked in the 1999–2002 period, due mainly to the use of electronic banking cards such as the Lone Star Card and to an increase in investigations of retailers.[21]

When many taxpayers think of welfare fraud, they imagine freeloading, able-bodied people who refuse to work and who cheat to get welfare benefits. Another major stereotype is that of the illegal aliens who are draining huge amounts of resources meant to help U.S. citizens. As the preceding data and stories show, however, much of the fraud that occurs is done by people hiding the few extra dollars they make in order to not lose the benefits they desperately need. In addition, the beneficiaries of trafficking are not just the recipients, who might lose up to half of their benefits in the trade, but merchants who profit by allowing food stamps to be used for purposes other than those for which they are intended.

Food stamps are often a dire necessity. Minerva Hinojosa is a farmworker who remembers arriving at a farm where her family was contracted to work. But having just paid for repairs to their truck, the family had no money to live on.

> That was because on the way, our truck broke down. We had to fix it in order to get to work. My parents went to ask for food stamps at the local office. The caseworker wanted my parents to return on Monday to do some more paperwork. She didn't want to help us even though my mom kept telling her that we had no money to buy food for us four children waiting in the car. Finally, my mom called the food stamp supervisor here in Edinburg. He talked to the caseworker over the phone. She finally authorized us to get food stamps. That day was a very long and scary day for me and my brothers.

We tend to forget that food stamps also benefit farmers and growers. This was one of the main reasons they were initiated by the Department of Agriculture. Juanita Valdez Cox, an organizer of migrant farmworkers, remembered her own life as a farmworker:

Welfare, even though it was not wanted, helped us get by and pay *los bi-les* (the bills). These programs were necessary to get by, but they detracted from our sense of pride, of being self-reliant by being able to provide for our family and give them something better than we had. We want work rather than get welfare. But it is often scarce and totally undependable. In truth, welfare helps the farmer or grower more, because it keeps workers available so that he does not have to keep workers on the payroll year round.

The Perceived Illegitimacy of Many Welfare Policies

Marcelina Juarez felt that the requirements for food stamps foster dishonesty:

> When I went to apply for food stamps I was living with my boyfriend, but he didn't help me pay my bills or support my two little boys. The application took forever to fill out, and the questions they ask are real personal. After many hours of waiting, they gave me an appointment for the next week. When I went for my interview the man told me that I couldn't have the stamps because I was living with a man and he should be responsible for me and my boys. I told him that he didn't help me and that I needed to buy food. He just said "Sorry." I got smart and decided that the only way I could get the help I needed was to lie. I went to McAllen this time to apply again. I put on the application that I lived alone, and this time I qualified. Now I always think that one of these days they're going to find out and I'm going to be in trouble. But I have to have food for my little boys, you know?

Teresa Salmon did get caught. She is currently serving five years probation for theft by deception. She, her husband, their two daughters, and a nephew live together in Mission. Her husband assists a local crew leader to head a group of farmworkers in the area. When they left for Las Cruces, New Mexico, to work harvesting onions, Teresa said she didn't close her case in Texas because it was too much trouble to get off the roll and then get back on the benefits again. When she returned to the Valley and went in for her recertification interview for food stamps and Medicaid, she didn't get her story straight and was flagged for an investigation. She said that somehow the food stamp office was able to get information about them working, with whom, and where. Within two weeks she was sent a letter to appear before the Justice of the Peace in Mission. There she was arraigned, sent to the county jail, fingerprinted, and booked for fraud. As she spoke, she seemed deeply humiliated.

> I thought it wouldn't matter to close my case because we were only going to be away for eight weeks to harvest onions. Now I have to pay back all the benefits I got during that time, pay court costs, attorney fees, and probation and other fees that I don't understand. All these costs are way more than what I used in benefits at the time. I tell everyone what happened to me to keep them from going through the same thing I did. Even if you know you wouldn't get caught, it is better not to put yourself at risk in the first place.

Many migrant farmworkers, like Teresa, find the regulations for federal assistance confusing and demeaning. Some refuse to put themselves at risk, avoiding welfare altogether. According to a 2000 survey by the Department of Labor, the median family income for farmworkers was $16,250.[22] Even though most farmworkers fit the eligibility profile for assistance programs such as Medicaid, Aid to Families with Dependent Children, and Social Security Insurance, many actually do not seek or obtain these benefits. This is because enrollment and eligibility standards are not designed to accommodate people who must move frequently to find work or whose income may fluctuate dramatically, even though their annual wages are well below the poverty level.

It is ironic that the farmworkers who produce much of the food provided by food stamps suffer from these stereotypes and myths about welfare. Julia Figeroa, for example, worked for many years as a migrant farmworker, travelling every year to farms in the Midwest. She stated, "They would call us 'stupid Mexicans' and would say we just came to steal their land and their food, all because the government provided us with food stamps. I always wanted to tell them, if they don't like for us to come and steal their land and their food, why don't they go work their own stupid fields. Up north was the only place that we would receive government help because down here my husband still works during our months here, even though he is sixty-four years old."

Though Teresa Salmon, like many informal workers, is willing to acknowledge her dishonesty in failing to report her income, some are not. Antonio Moreno blamed government and society. "Here in the Valley, things are very tough. I went to the employment office looking for a job, and there wasn't any. I had to support my wife and myself. I was desperate until a friend introduced me to this line of work" (he steals cars and sells them in Mexico). When asked if he considered what he was doing to be morally wrong, he answered,

> Morals! Don't talk to me about morals. People today don't have any morals. If they did, I would not be where I am today. A couple of years ago my family was really in the dumps. I mean we had to beg our friends for money in order to eat. We went to apply for welfare but were refused because of a problem with alcohol that I had back then. My neighbors, who were a lot better off than we were, went to apply for welfare as well. The difference was that their application was accepted. The reason being that they had children. Can I help it if I couldn't afford to have children? How was I supposed to raise a kid when we could barely survive ourselves? So don't talk to me about morals.

Another respondent, Lourdes Romero, felt that many welfare regulations work at purposes counter to their intent.

> When they found out at DHS [Department of Human Services] that I had enrolled at college, they cancelled my benefits. They said that I did not inform them about my Pell Grant, which they said put my income above my need. How the hell do they know what I NEED anyway?! I have to pay back three months of checks. It may not be a lot to you but $141 a month is a fortune to me. I was so angry. How can I get myself off welfare if I'm not allowed to get my education at the same time? I cry a lot and pray that my little girl will never have to go through this.

The situation described by Lourdes seems to exemplify the paradox of state control[23] that we discussed in Chapter 1. As outlined there, this paradox holds that official efforts to obliterate unregulated activities through the proliferation of rules and controls often expand the very conditions that give rise to these activities. In other words, as officials increasingly regulate welfare to prevent cheating, they expand the conditions that lead welfare recipients to believe they cannot survive without breaking the rules. So, at the macro-level we find in South Texas more and more regulations that contribute to informality.

The micro-level process by which we see this taking place in bureaucratic agencies has been described as "goal displacement."[24] Observers of bureaucratic organizations have long described how bureaucratic rules seem to end up working against the very purpose for which programs within the bureaucracy were created. This condition occurs when bureaucratic regulations originally conceived as a means become transformed into the end in themselves. Rules designed to keep welfare recipients from cheating come to replace the fundamental goal of welfare—to help individuals and families become self-sustaining. This happens because the functionaries who administer welfare are not given discretion regarding how the rules should be administered. So enforcing the rules becomes their goal. They will enforce the rules even if doing so contradicts or subverts the basic purpose of the agency. Even though they may clearly see what is happening, they are not empowered to make exceptions. That power is left to politicians. And in places like Texas, elections are not won by understanding and adjusting to the needs of welfare recipients. Indeed, some Texas politicians seem to see bureaucratic red tape, long waiting periods, and insensitive functionaries as a good way of saving tax dollars by discouraging welfare applicants—even those that might be deserving.

The proliferation and confusion of welfare policies and rules leave many border residents confused and unable to understand or feel that they can comply with welfare regulations. Elena Badillo is a thirty-six-year-old U.S. citizen who survived a major car accident. The accident left her disabled and unable to hold a job. She is currently receiving Supplemental Security Income (SSI), Medicare, Housing, and food stamps. Elena laughs because she qualifies for only $10.00 a month in food stamps due to her SSI and Medicare allotments. When she spoke to the Social Security Office about getting a part-time job, they told her that she could but that her housing payment would increase and that her SSI check would probably decrease. She was confused because she did not understand why they would discourage her from getting a job. So, if she has some unexpected expenses, then she sells newspapers on weekends, making approximately $50 a weekend. But she does not report the extra income. Other times she "dog sits" for her friends and their family pets. She stated that the extra money helps and any extra goes into a savings account which she keeps under her sister's name. She says that she will continue to do this as long as she can, but there is no way she will report any of this income.

The frustration informals experience is illustrated by Perla Cifuentes and her husband. They each work, and their combined income leaves them barely within the CHIP income guidelines. Still, they cannot afford the $20 copayment for each of the three medications their teenage daughter needs each month for epilepsy episodes and high blood pressure. This is due in part to other debts that Perla's husband has accumulated due to his own illness and his unpaid hospital bills. Perla admitted, rather vaguely, "I do what I have to in order to get my children the health care they deserve."

Conclusion

Many welfare recipients in South Texas would like to comply with welfare regulations and report all their income. They come to believe, however, that many program guidelines fail to take into account their extenuating circumstances and that no one is willing to grant any exceptions, no matter how compelling. So, if the formal system does not work, they increasingly turn to the informal economy as a way to meet basic needs. If reporting extra income would take away health care for their children (but still leave them unable to buy private insurance), they do not report the income. As they find others in the same situation, they develop networked communities accustomed to relying on each other and informal devices for survival. They also come to share a common definition of the system as generally operating unfairly. Suspicious of official intervention, they increasingly see informal activities as a necessary part of life and willingly facilitate community-wide informality by accepting cash transactions, bartering food stamps, and participating in other informal activities.

Years ago, sociologist Robert Merton proposed that "social structures exert a definitive pressure . . . to engage in non-conforming, rather than conforming, conduct."[25] We certainly find evidence for that in attempting to explain welfare informality in South Texas. The structure of the welfare system in Texas, with very stingy income guidelines and other qualifying and reporting requirements, puts enormous pressure on migrant farmworkers, undocumented individuals, low-wage laborers, and others to hide income in order to receive or maintain even minimal benefits.

Basically, Merton proposed that in societies like that of the U.S., the structural position of many marginalized populations leaves them without the institutionalized means to accomplish the culturally sanctioned goals of society. This, he asserted, led to deviant behavior. Merton says, "On the one hand, they are asked to orient their conduct toward the prospect of accumulating wealth and on the other, they are largely denied effective opportunities to do so institutionally." The consequences, he says, are psychopathological personality, and/or antisocial conduct. He says that people like Al Capone represent the triumph of amoral intelligence over morally prescribed failure, especially in a society that places a high premium on economic affluence and social ascent for all its members.[26]

We strongly reject such a characterization of most of the informals described in this chapter, and indeed throughout the book. It is for this reason that we believe it very important to distinguish between behavior that is criminal (underground activities) and that which is informal. As illustrated in Figure 1.2, the Legal/Informal sector is very different from the Illegal/Informal one, though both would be classified as "deviant" in Merton's dimensions.

Individuals involved in underground activities, especially those with high risk and high potential earnings, do come much closer to Merton's description of individuals who innovatively find ways to break the law to attain prestige, wealth, and power. But informals, especially those who "fudge" on reporting income in order to maintain scarce benefits, do not. Those we interviewed have not internalized values that demand wealth and power, nor do they choose criminal means to achieve such aims. They simply want to survive, and they reluctantly break or skirt some of the rules to do so. Though we do not condone (nor do we condemn) the breaking of welfare regulations, we acknowledge that the structure of welfare assistance in Texas, particularly on the border, produces enormous strains on individuals, creating pressure to not report all their earnings in order that they may continue to receive meager benefits.

Conclusion

Melissa is involved with the informal sale of liquor. She is not employed, and the only formal income she and her husband receive is the $975 disability check that he receives every month. Melissa previously had a job but quit because the department of human services found out that she was working. "They denied food stamps and Medicaid for me and my family," she said. "I was not making enough to cover food and health services for my children, so I decided to quit. It's not like I was making a lot. I think that it's better now because we have food, health insurance for our children, and I get to spend more time with my children."

In the neighborhood where she lives, everyone knows that she sells bottles of liquor.

> I have a cousin that works at a bar. When she makes up drinks, she dilutes the drinks with water. The owner knows about how many bottles are consumed weekly, but he doesn't know that she mixes water in with the alcohol or that she keeps the bottles of alcohol that she saves. Since he only shows up once a week, she is able to get like three bottles every week before he comes around. She brings them to me and I sell them. She knows that we [Melissa's family] are not doing so great, so most of the time I keep all the money that I make from the sale.
>
> I know that my cousin could get in big trouble for stealing the bottles, but I don't think I could get in trouble because I am not the one stealing the liquor. I only sell it. If the government finds out that we are getting money from somewhere, they would take away my benefits. I do get scared of having my benefits taken away because that's all we've got. When we lost our benefits before, I had to go to the Rio Grande Valley food pantry to ask for food.

When asked what happens if she doesn't sell her three bottles a week, she replied, "I take the bottles to Mexico and my sister can sell them there."

The Uniqueness of the South Texas Borderlands

Melissa works in both the informal and the underground economies on both sides of the South Texas-Northern Mexico border. Throughout this book, we have focused on the borderlands from Laredo to Browns-ville, formerly known as the Nueces Strip. At times, our discussion has included the adjoining Mexican territory, particularly the state and border communities of Tamaulipas. As we have proposed from the beginning of the book, the Nueces Strip in South Texas is unique not only historically, but in contemporary U.S. society. Most obvious is the large preponderance of Mexican-origin peoples in the region. Nowhere else in the U.S. is there such a dense concentration of Hispanics over so large a swath of territory as in South Texas. Hence, the intersection of ethnicity and culture makes South Texas unique where extralegal economic activities may leverage the vast well of cultural and social capital for economic gain.

Distinctive informal ethnic and labor markets have also developed in South Texas. Because of the relative ease of obtaining informal labor there, as well as the widespread acceptance of informal consumption, markers of enclave informal markets elsewhere, such as day labor centers, are mostly absent in the region. The incidence of cross-border informality is relatively high. High rates of poverty, inequality, and a large presence of undocumented individuals in South Texas together produce and reproduce informality. For example, high levels of poverty induce many South Texans to find creative methods to stretch incomes. In our Consumer Informality Survey we found those with lower incomes more likely to consume informal repair services (e.g., auto repair, air conditioning repair) and purchase (suspected) stolen goods as a strategy to lower the costs of necessary expenditures. Those with higher incomes are more likely to substitute own account or household labor for hired help around the home (e.g., maids, gardeners, and elder care). The high incidence of undocumented peoples in South Texas funnels income earners primarily into the informal sector. Only 1.9% of our undocumented respondents were enrolled in Social Security (an indication of formal work), and those few were probably enrolled through the use of fraudulent or borrowed papers. As part of staying hidden from public view because of the high risks involved, 96% of our undocumented respondents participated in the informal sector rather than the underground sector.

The Paradoxes of Informality

In Chapter 1, we introduced four paradoxes of informality proposed by Portes and colleagues. Throughout the book, the essence of these paradoxes has been developed, so we only briefly address them here. We have argued that highly evolved social capital is a key facilitator of informality. Entering an informal network and staying hidden from government detection requires social capital that is well developed, with expectations of reciprocity. We have argued that structural bias is inherent in the state's attempt to exercise control in the name of reducing informality (and underground activities) and that this structural bias may lead to serious unintended consequences. Furthermore, the state, at its various levels, often has neither the capacity nor the will to effectively suppress the widespread and accepted informality in South Texas.

While modern state agencies at all levels collect and report voluminous amounts of economic information, these governmental entities are virtually silent on the subject of economic informality. Since informal activity is outside the purview of government, there is no appropriate mechanism to track such economic activity. Though official policy does not include what it cannot measure, we have demonstrated that indirect measurement is possible.

There are both intended and unintended effects of informality. Unintended effects include poverty-reduction that benefits the state. For example, self-built *colonia* housing permits the poor to live in housing unsupported by government social agencies (for which they may otherwise be eligible). By failing to enforce mandated infrastructure development and construction practices, the state benefits from reduced social outlays. A similar picture emerges for health services for South Texans when Mexico is used as a primary health care option. In sum, the four paradoxes reflect the ways in which the actions of government actually distort the economy and perpetuate informality.

Changes in the Status of Informal Workers over Time

Juan Jose Flores, a former migrant farmworker, has been a U.S. citizen for sixty-five years. He told this story:

> When I was eighteen I swam across the border and made it safely to Hidalgo without getting caught by immigration. I found a job quickly working in the fields here in the Valley. I was very excited because I was going to make some money for my family in Mexico, and they were going to be very proud of me. I worked from sunup until sundown in those fields. I was told I was going to be paid a dollar an hour by my employers. When payday came around, I only got 80 cents an hour. I was being treated unfairly and lied to by these people. It seemed like they would just pay us whatever they wanted because we were just all wetbacks from Mexico who couldn't understand any English. I remember one of my bosses was an Anglo from Chicago. He used to call us names like "dirty wetbacks," "spics," "low class bums," and many other names I would like to forget. It was my first job in America, and I didn't want to let down my family, so I decided to carry on for a year or two until I had enough money to buy a car and look for a new job. I still sometimes look back at the days where I was treated like the scum of the earth and pray my grandchild will never get treated the same way. I am now an American citizen and glad I made the decision to migrate here because now my family has a chance to live a better life. I just hope they never have to experience what I did when I was working in the fields.

Though Mr. Flores clearly experienced racism and exploitation, his situation was considerably better than that experienced by South Texas Mexicans during much of the preceding 50 to 100 years. In the early 1900s, Mexican immigrants could be shot by Texas Rangers for simply being Mexican. Our interviews with other undocumented workers indicate that some abuse continues, but perhaps with less racism than Mr. Flores experienced (at least in South Texas).

Like most other South Texas Mexican Americans, he is proud of his American citizenship. Despite the repression and dispossession experienced by nineteenth-century South Texas Hispanics, today there is no visible effort afoot to secede from the U.S. Some scholars and talk show hosts, however, would have the public believe otherwise. Samuel Huntington,[1] for example, states, "Mexican-Americans . . . argue that the Southwest was taken from them by military aggression in the 1840's, and that the time for *la reconquista* (reconquest) has arrived . . . Conceivably, this could lead to a move to reunite these territories with Mexico."

Racism vs. Structural Bias

Though we argue that much of the harm experienced by Mexican-origin peoples in the borderlands in previous decades was motivated by rampant racism, we allege that today the inequality and difficulties they experience stem mainly from structural bias. We understand, however, that while racism by Anglos and whites against racial minorities has declined, it was largely responsible for setting in place the institutionalized system of unequal power that today produces structural bias. In addition, racism continues to motivate some of the discrimination that Mexican-origin border residents experience. Nevertheless, we believe it is useful to analyze the role of structural bias and racism as somewhat competing explanations of the harsh conditions and treatment experienced by the individuals presented in the preceding chapters.

Joe R. Feagin is a leading proponent of racism as the primary cause of inequality and discrimination in America today. In his book *Racist America*,[2] Feagin argues that beginning early in American history, white males set in place a deeply entrenched system of racism against blacks that continues today, affecting not only black-white relations, but also relations of whites with other "peoples of color." Systemic racism, he proposes, remains a deeply entrenched part of the culture and structure of American society today.

Fundamental to this racism is the idea that individuals enjoy rights and/or privileges based not on the fact that they are human but that they belong to a particular group or niche. The rights set forth in the Declaration of Independence were not really to be extended to all individuals, he points out, but were intended for those of a privileged class, namely, white males. Black slaves, Indians, and women were to be ruled over and kept in their "natural" position.

This mind-set was fomented by the twin forces of capitalism and colonialism. European and American elites accepted their economic, military, and political ascendency as proof that they were brighter, stronger, and destined to rule "lesser" peoples. This racial framing included racial stereotypes, racial interpretations, race-based emotions, and strong inclinations to discriminate against "inferior races." In these colonial and capitalistic systems, conquered peoples were relegated to the lowest rungs of society. As such, they could be dominated and exploited with little remorse. The resources and labor extracted from them within the U.S. and elsewhere in the world could be used for the benefit of the white masters, though it was often excused or legitimized as being "for their own good" or for the greater good of society.

White racists found supposedly scientific support for controlling darker races in early interpretations of the theory of evolution. Social Darwinists argued that the white race was superior to darker races. Whites saw themselves as the primary architects of the great wealth accumulated through capitalism and colonialism. As a result, they believed they were entitled to greater wealth and power. Racism, as a deeply entrenched belief, afforded them a superior social position as the "natural" outcome of their supposed superiority or their "manifest destiny." They could exploit and dominate weaker groups with a generally clear conscience.

Still, white, male slave owners and colonizers invested considerable energy in making racism seem morally "right" to themselves and to others. They set in place not only an American system of apartheid, but a deeply ingrained collective mind-set that legitimized exploitation, making it seem the natural order of things—even God's will. This apartheid system manifested itself in all major institutions—the economy, the government, education, religion, and even the family. Thus, *systemic racism* included not only recurring and grossly unequal structural relationships (master-slave; owners-workers; men-women; rulers-ruled), but also a culture that laid out how each race should interact with others and a complex explanation of why such things must be.

Even when slavery was ended by the Civil War and the racist Jim Crow segregation system followed and was challenged by the civil rights movement, racism continued to dominate the culture and structure of American society. Blacks today, Feagin argues, are still segregated and economically marginalized by systemic racism. In the minds of whites— and for many people of color—light skin is still deemed to be a mark of superiority. Though systemic racism today is less blatant, he proposes, it still accounts for much of the discrimination, segregation, and inequality suffered by blacks and other people of color. Though systemic racism may not be as easily accepted or as brutally enforced, it continues to reproduce racial inequality, racist behavior, and racist beliefs, largely to the benefit of white males, especially those at the top.

Feagin points out a number of deeply ingrained beliefs in American culture that today flow from this racist mind-set. He suggests that whites in general believe that racism no longer exists except in the minds of a few "sick" people. In addition, many whites believe that blacks enjoy opportunities equal to (or, with affirmative action, even greater than) whites. Likewise, whites generally believe that the privileges that many of them enjoy are based on merit rather than racism past or present. Similarly, many whites believe that the problems blacks and other minorities experience are related to a culture of poverty or undesirable ethnic characteristics. Some whites point to "model minorities" (Japanese Americans, for example) who have achieved greater equality in American society as evidence that racism is ended. Blacks and Latinos, they assert, should emulate those minorities and European immigrants to achieve similar results.

Feagin proposes that systemic racism thrives today alongside a denial of its existence. Whites can enjoy the benefits while blaming blacks and other minorities for the problems they continue to experience. Systemic racism not only affects black-white relations, he alleges, but applies equally well to Anglo-Latino relations. Mexicans (and other Latinos) in Feagin's view are still seen by Anglos/whites as an inferior racial group. He presents evidence that whites tend to think of minorities in terms of a racial continuum that runs from whites to blacks, with Latinos somewhere in between the two poles. Some whites regard Latinos as belonging to a category that could be described as "honorary whites," but still a notch or two below whites. Whites, according to Feagin, still think of Latinos mostly in racist terms, regarding them, like blacks, as biologically, intellectually, and culturally inferior.

Feagin proposes that racism is behind the belief that periodically emerges among white Americans that the country is being taken over by inferior people with an inferior culture. This belief often results in harsh countermeasures since it combines racist fears with nationalistic anxiety about losing "our American way of life." Recent reports of the greatly increasing size of the Latino population and projections that they and other nonwhites will soon outnumber whites fuel these fears. Such anxieties contribute to the anti-immigrant backlash recently seen in many parts of the U.S., including draconian anti-immigrant laws, rapid increases in the number of hate crimes, and even efforts to change the Constitution to deny citizenship to U.S.-born children of undocumented parents.

Conservative Anglos/whites who vehemently denigrate undocumented Latinos or demand their deportation claim that their opposition is based not on racism but on the illegal status of undocumented

Latinos. Likewise, they often justify racial profiling by police and extensive background checks by landlords and employers as simply being extra vigilant—claiming that undocumented Latinos bring with them a higher crime rate, which, as is explained elsewhere in this volume, is grossly exaggerated and erroneous. Their refusal to alter their views in the light of strong counterevidence leads us to believe, with Feagin, that their animosity is racist.

Feagin asserts that anti-Latino racism is simply an expansion of the antiblack racism that permeates U.S. history. It is not a separate racism, but the same as that directed against blacks. We agree that racism has historically dominated Anglo-Hispanic relations in Texas, as illustrated by the Cortina story and discussion in the Introduction. Whites in South Texas did indeed treat Mexicans and Mexican Americans much like they treated blacks, regarding them like blacks, as inferior. We propose, however, that this has changed dramatically in South Texas today. Racism still exists, but in a greatly reduced form, with far fewer occurrences today of outright racist treatment.

Is Systemic Racism Still the Major Problem for Latinos in the U.S.?

Juan Chapín is originally from Guatemala. When asked if he had ever felt discrimination, he told his interviewer with a laugh, "Look at me, of course I have. I'm short and I look indigenous." Juan said that the worst treatment has been by Hispanic people here in the Valley. "The whites in Michigan aren't as racist," he claimed. "Up north they need our labor, and here there are too many immigrants to choose from. If an employer abuses his workers they could be reported to human rights groups and they will quickly take action."

Juan has worked in many types of jobs. He currently sells tacos in a small community in the Valley, at a local stand. "It's the worst job I ever held," he said. "My boss makes me work long hours and only pays me $20 a day, even though he makes more than $3000 a month in profits. I decided to quit, but he accused me of stealing money from the cash machine and refused to pay me for that week. He told me I needed to pay him back what he said I had stolen. There was nothing I could do because I am afraid of being sent back to Guatemala."

Feagin sees even brown-on-brown discrimination like that described by Juan as simply another aspect of the antiblack racism that characterizes much of U.S. history. Minorities, he proposes, live in a racist society, receiving racist images from the media and from personal interaction. So the Mexican American children we observed who call Mexican immigrant children *mojados* (wetbacks) are simply reflecting racist images that they have internalized from exposure to long-standing racism in American culture.

South Texas Mexican Americans today are remarkably loyal to the U.S., with few expressing perceptions of racism on a daily basis. As a group, they identify with and feel much greater loyalty to the U.S. than to Mexico. Indeed, in our Cultural Practices Survey, only 19% of Mexican-origin respondents said they liked the lifestyle of Mexico; only 26% claimed to like Spanish-language TV; and only 18% identified themselves as "Mexican."

Many of the Latinos we interviewed had some experience with racist whites, but the frequency of these experiences decreased significantly from the 1970s through the 2000s. Many had a story or two about harsh treatment in areas north of the Valley, but at least an equal number reported, like Juan, that the majority of their experiences with whites up north were positive.

In support of the systemic racism argument, Feagin presents research showing that most whites still see Latinos in racial rather than ethnic terms. In his sample of 151 college students, a majority of white respondents categorized Mexican Americans and Puerto Ricans as not white, though a majority of the same individuals regarded Italian Americans, Japanese Americans, and Chinese Americans as white. He presents survey data from a 2002 Pew Center survey[3] to show that a majority of Mexican Americans also tend to see their own group as nonwhite.

A 2006 nationwide survey of 8,634 Latinos by the Inter-university Consortium for Political and Social Research (ICPSR)[4] similarly showed a substantial majority of Latinos/Hispanics (66%) consider themselves to be of a race other than white. Nevertheless, this survey also presents evidence that a relatively small portion experience treatment that could be described as racist. Only 6% reported ever having been prevented from moving into a neighborhood because the owner or landlord refused to rent or sell to them; only 14% felt that they had been treated unfairly by police (though 39% believed police did not treat Latinos in general fairly)[5]; only 16% believed they had been unfairly fired or denied a job or a promotion; and only 16% felt they had ever been treated unfairly or badly in a store or restaurant. Such data do not support the proposition that Latinos today experience the pervasive racism that they experienced prior to the 1960s.

Feagin argues that Latinos, particularly first- or second-generation immigrants, downplay the discrimination they experience because they are trying to establish a toehold in the U.S. In addition, they may fail to see their treatment as discrimination because their status in the U.S. is generally far better than it was in their homeland. Though we did see some evidence of this in our interviews, our South Texas Hispanics report racist treatment much less frequently today than they did in previous decades.

As indicated earlier, we agree with Feagin that systemic racism has been a primary factor in the treatment of the Latinos we have described in this volume. Our view, however, is that racism, once the dominant cause for harmful treatment, *directly* accounts for much less of the inter-ethnic inequality today. Racism and racist thinking still exist, though in greatly reduced manifestations. So how do we explain the continuing inequality between Anglos and Latinos, especially those in South Texas?

We propose that anti-Latino discrimination today has become more indirect—that it now exists in the forms of ethnocentrism and (especially) structural bias. Racism may have declined, but it has left in place systemic inequality (structural bias). Latinos and blacks are not on a level playing field, though whites proceed as if they are. Laws and regulations are imposed through "democratic action" that may, intentionally or unintentionally, hurt the poor and powerless. But unlike their middle- or upper-class contemporaries, minorities lack the power to block such rules or policies. Minorities often cannot block such laws, etc., even though they may (in some areas) outnumber the upper and/or middle class.

Throughout the book, we have argued that structural bias has become the primary means by which South Texas as a geographical and political entity and South Texas Hispanics as minority-group individuals experience inequality of treatment. We would like to extend and illustrate this point with a return to the types of discrimination discussed in the Introduction and summarized below in Figure C.1. As this figure illustrates, bigotry and exploitation (both very common in the time of Cortina) have given way in recent decades to cultural bias/ethnocentrism and structural bias. The difference between the forms on the left and those on the right, as shown in this figure, is the degree of intentionality of the harmful treatment.

Harsh bigotry and exploitation were very common in the times of Cortina and the nineteenth-century Texas Rangers. Most nineteenth-century Anglos and Mexican elites had no qualms about stating and pur-

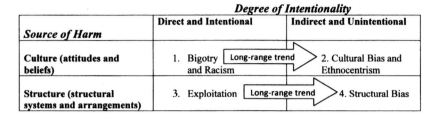

Figure C.I. Long-range trends in the types of discrimination experienced by South Texas Hispanics

	Degree of Intentionality	
	Direct and Intentional	Indirect and Unintentional
Form of Reaction to Discrimination	1. Revolt and Withdrawal Long-range trend	2. Informality

Figure C.2. Long-range trends in the form of reaction to discrimination by South Texas Hispanics

suing their supposed superiority over low-income Mexicans, Mexican Americans, and Native Americans of the area. Bigotry, racism, and exploitation were not only common, but were seen as morally justified by those who perpetrated them. Anglo Texans had no problem with stealing land and cattle from Mexicans, but they reacted with racist hostility when Cortina dared do the same to them.

But as the forms of discrimination have experienced a long-term change, so also have the reactions to them. Cortina responded to bigotry and exploitation with rebellion and violence. But to a large degree, low-income South Texans today respond to structural bias against them with informal economic activities, as illustrated in Figure C.2.

We are not proposing that this reaction is necessarily a conscious choice. Indeed, we see it as an indirect and largely unintentional response. Most Mexicans do not choose to respond to harsh immigration policies by deliberately thumbing their noses at the system. As the American economy draws Mexican people northward (over the border), poverty and harsh regulations push them into the shadows. Many engage in the only form of economic activity possible—survival informality (or working "around" the laws and regulations). They do not come to violate laws, but to work hard, to be (otherwise) law-abiding, and to make do as best they can. For this reason, we believe that they and most other Mexican-origin people of the region see their actions as morally legitimate.

Despite the change in reactions, the process of external actors exerting control in the South Texas borderlands region has a long history. When distant power centers become active in the region because of national policy issues—from territorial adjustment and military encounters in the nineteenth century to immigration, national security, globalization, and drug interdiction in the twenty-first century—the local population is forced to cope and adapt. Some locals may eventually give in and become co-opted. Others, like Juan Cortina, may lay out a more independent course and directly confront the system. But most will respond to directives from Washington, D.C., Austin, or Mexico City by skirting over, under, and around these policies.

Some, particularly those who operate in the underground economy, do more than eke out a living. For the most part, their criminality is not simply a reaction to discrimination. Most (especially the smuggling organizations) are opportunists who flout the laws, engage in violence, exploit underlings, and risk the lives and well being of their families for personal gain. We do not see structural or cultural bias as the main motivation for their underground activities.

Structural Bias

Though racism and exploitation continue to push events along the border, we see structural bias (and to a lesser degree, cultural bias) as the most important macro-level factor promoting informal and underground activities. Within the political environment of both state and federal government, South Texas and the adjoining regions in Mexico are often excluded from the debate over most policy matters. As a geographically distant land, the region is often overlooked, occasionally mystified, and mostly ignored unless a conflagration takes hold in or through the region. Today, unauthorized immigration, drug violence, and national security are the primary flash points that capture national attention about the region.

Racism's darkest legacy in South Texas, we propose, is its creation of structural bias. Today, privileged white males, acting democratically, can muster the political power and influence to block arrangements that negatively affect them, even if such negative side effects were not intended to harm them. In contrast, weaker groups, such as the general border population in South Texas, have much less ability to block adverse side effects. While far-off elites may express pity for those on the border, they can always point out that these effects were not deliberately intended to harm and can thus escape both blame and shame. Those in power can say, "We all have to sacrifice," though they seldom make any significant sacrifices.

Our discussion of health insurance in Chapter 7 is illustrative. By a rather large margin, Texas leads the nation in the number of uninsured residents, with greatly disproportionate numbers of them along the Mexican border. Texas politicians rail against health care legislation, even seeking to block the program in Texas. Border residents who stood to benefit from this legislation were virtually sidelined from the debate, though probably less for racist reasons than for an inability to promote their own interests with any real power.

In the not-so-distant past, free trade, trade clearance, environmental health (i.e., water), and contagious disease were the issues du jour. Regardless of the contemporary issue of concern to far-off power centers in Washington, D.C., Mexico City, and Austin, structural bias and some elements of racism promote policies often detrimental to borderlanders while giving them little say in formulating or implementing these policies. Rather, the inequality compels locals to "make do" or "survive" within the chaos directed from outside the region.

One example concerning immigration is illustrative. The specters of immigration and crime have haunted and confounded the immigration debate for generations, and this debate has intensified of late. While isolated cases of immigrant crime are emphasized and wrongly generalized, the preponderance of empirical evidence suggests that communities with large immigrant flows are safer because of immigration. Wadsworth's recent study using a decade of annual census and crime data from 1990 to 2000 found, as did previously cited research by Robert J. Sampson, that an infusion of immigrants into American cities reduced homicides by 9.3% and robberies by 22.2%.[6]

Nonetheless, the debate in Washington, D.C., is dominated by the erroneous (and sometimes racist) link between immigration and crime, with (generally) unintended consequences for borderlanders. In our own survey, as reported in Chapter 2, we found that most underground activity was conducted, cumulatively, by persons born in the U.S. (77.7%), those who are now U.S. citizens (88.0%), or those who reside in the U.S.

legally (92.2%). So it is a huge red herring to assert that underground participants in the borderlands are disproportionately immigrants (legal or undocumented).

In addition, there is an insensitivity to (or a tremendous lack of understanding of) the unique problems of the border area. Informality exists alongside a desire to be law-abiding, but there is widespread selective disobedience of the law. As partisan politics and catering to anti-immigrant and antiwelfare elements dominates policy-making in Washington and Austin, informality on the border increases. And as it increases, respect for and obedience to the law are undermined. In essence, Washington, Austin, and Mexico City do more to create Third World conditions in the borderlands than low-income Mexican immigrants who illegally cross the border do.

Other Major Structural and Cultural Forces that Facilitate or Foster Informality

While we identified social and cultural forces in the Introduction and have employed these divisions throughout the book, we would like to summarize (in Table C.1) many of the specific factors and forces operating within the South Texas borderlands. The structural forces involve the web of relationships among populations at the margin—the undocumented, the unprotected, the uninsured, the uneducated, the uninvited, the unrepresented—who utilize the informal economy as a path to survival. Cultural forces involve understandings that emerge among a population and direct their behavior. Cultural factors also bind borderlanders together and not only facilitate informality but help foster it. The interplay of these structural and cultural factors in the region is summarized in Table C.1. While the table does not provide an exhaustive list, the structural and cultural factors presented summarize many of the forces that characterize informality in South Texas and distinguish it from informality in other regions of the U.S.

Push-Pull/Hold-Repel

Early on, we introduced a push-pull/hold-repel model of micro-level decision-making for individuals considering entry into the informal sector. While the model is based on cost-benefit analysis, we propose that

Table C.1: Structural and cultural forces favoring informal and underground activities in the South Texas borderlands

Structural Factors	Cultural Factors
Large numbers of undocumented people who cannot utilize formal economic or public channels	Cross-national culture (e.g., language, common place of origin) facilitates cross-national informal/underground activities
Reporting choices within the market exchange ("I won't report this transaction if you don't report it.")	Strong family bonds that protect, encourage, or hide informal and underground activity
Different laws and/or enforcement of laws in U.S. and Mexico that create informal and cross-border economic opportunities	Forms of consumption informality that are not regulated or enforced (e.g., prescription drugs from Mexico)
Readily accessible facilitation mechanisms for informality (e.g., the cash economy, willing consumers)	Human capital (knowledge of how to work informally) widely available
Regulations that push needy people off government assistance (i.e., food stamps and Medicaid for children)	Informality becomes "standard business practice" (e.g., cash transactions, mutual protection norms)
High volume of illicit trade keeps small operators from being prosecuted	History and legacy of informality and underground activities
Poverty, low education levels, high unemployment	Perceptions among some of inequity or illegitimacy of laws
Easy availability of informal labor pools	Cultural traditions in Mexico that are illegal in the U.S. (i.e., prostitution, cockfighting)
Lax housing and land regulatory enforcement allowing for *colonia* development	Extensive social capital networks among informals
High demand for cheap labor without sufficient guest-worker provisions	Bilingualism and binationalism facilitate informal cross-border exchange
Large migratory (nonnative) populations	Cultural traditions from Mexico that legitimize informality
Welfare regulations that disallow assistance for recipients with incomes just above the poverty line and create alternate paths for meeting basic human needs (e.g., accessing health care in Mexico)	Cultural nationalism and racism in the U.S. that opposes legalizing vast numbers of undocumented workers

such a model is necessary to overcome the tendency to consider only push and pull factors. We believe that informality cannot be understood solely in terms of what motivates it, but that one must also take into account the factors, if present, that might prevent it. The breakdown of these hold-repel factors may be just as important in promoting informality as the presence of push-pull factors.

For Texas residents participating in the formal South Texas economy, one cost of remaining formal may be the loss of governmental benefits if one reports all income. That is, for households living on the economic margin, government benefits may determine access (or not) to critical household needs such as health care and nutrition. By participating in the informal sector, a rational decision is being made between adding income while maintaining social services rather than trading formal income while reducing social services. In this case, reporting formal earnings may produce a net loss to those living on the economic margins.

Other border residents may periodically assess whether to informally access the other side of the border in order to acquire cross-border employment, prescription medication, or other goods and services. Throughout the book, we have pointed out how the interplay between these push-pull and hold-repel forces has impacted the creation and continuation of informality in South Texas.

Why Informality Is Greater in the South Texas Borderlands

While extralegal activities in the region would exist without the border, the scope and scale of activities are certainly magnified by the border and add to the uniqueness of South Texas. The border acts in two ways in the extralegal economic environment in the South Texas borderlands. On the one hand, it acts as a hard line limiting movement and access. On the other, it acts as a lever of opportunity for those who understand how to overcome the constraints and access the opportunities. For example, human smugglers (*coyotes*) utilize their knowledge of the hard border and its policing to smuggle people across from Mexico into the U.S. From a cottage industry in early years to one dominated by powerful cartels today, human smugglers have become better organized in response to decisions in Washington, D.C., to harden the border against illegal drug shipments, undocumented workers, and national security threats.[7] Because of this federal action, the costs to clandestinely cross the border have soared, facilitating profiteering, organized crime, and a widening underground economy—though all of these are unintended consequences.

More innocuous are the laser visa and the ability to bribe (mainly Mexican) border officials. These two elements facilitate a host of cross-border informal activities flowing both northward and southward across the border. The laser visa facilitates the legal movement of people northward from Mexico into the U.S., ostensibly to engage in cross-border shopping. While more than two-thirds of individuals crossing northward into Texas report shopping as their primary purpose,[8] others, once across, may engage in common informal trades such as domestic service, construction, cross-border commerce, and gardening.

The Legal-Criminal/Formal-Informal Dimensions Summarized

Discussion of the underground and informal sectors requires nuance and the recognition that economic participation in these two sectors is not just a simple continuum. In Chapter 1, we developed a dynamic typology based on a legal-illegal continuum and a formal-informal continuum. The result was a four-quadrant classification table of (in)formality and (il)legality: (1) Legal/Formal (the formal economy); (2) Legal/Informal (the informal economy); (3) Illegal/Formal (the false formal economy); and (4) Illegal/Informal (the underground economy).

We have demonstrated throughout the book that informality takes on many shades and that participants may be inserted into formal *and* informal markets simultaneously or that they may simply reside primarily on one end of the continuum or the other. Each quadrant carries a commensurate level of risk associated with the degree of (il)legality and (in)formality. We believe our Informal and Underground Survey respondents understand and are fully aware that participation in activities other than those which are fully formal and legal carries associated risks. We found that 84.4% of those who participate in the informal sector report having no regrets about doing so; 59.6% of underground participants feel likewise. When reported by immigration status, more than eight in ten have no regrets about their chosen economic path; and this was unrelated to the level of acculturation.

Continually adapting to local circumstances, the extralegal economy in South Texas is a vibrant response to the many challenges to and opportunities (structural, cultural, geographic, governmental, entrepreneurial) for survival and, occasionally, prosperity. Approximately one-third of the population engages the extralegal sector as a means of earning or saving income. Nearly all consumers participate at some level in the consumption of informal goods or services. As we have seen from the historical profiles presented, this pattern in the region is not new.

Conclusions

Out of the political chaos of Mexico in the 1850s, José Maria de Jesús Carvajal, a transnational borderlander (using Martínez's typology) proposed, much like the leaders of the Republic of the Río Grande a decade earlier, that there be a special zone for the Mexican border adjacent to Texas.[9] While Carvajal's movement was ultimately unsuccessful, his leadership of what is known as the Merchant's War sought in part to facilitate in Mexico the duty-free movement of goods within a twelve-mile zone of the river, from Laredo to Brownsville. By the end of the 1850s, the *zona libre* in Mexico became a reality, initiated by the governor of Tamaulipas. Even the Treaty of Guadalupe Hidalgo (1848) that ended the Mexican War permitted free trade along the border so long as U.S. troops were present.[10]

Since the 1840s, free trade between Mexico and the U.S. has continued to rely on informal as well as formal channels. Though we argue that informality often grows as governments pass more and more laws (and informal entrepreneurs find more ways to circumvent them), we also assert that informality thrives when governments refuse to formalize informal trade realities. The classic example of this is the presence of over 12 million undocumented individuals working illegally in the U.S. because they have almost no access to legal channels. In 1994, Robert D. Kaplan reflected a similar reality related to illicit drugs, stating that "Drugs constitute the economic subsoil of Mexico—the subterranean part of North American free trade that doesn't require treaties or congressional approval."[11]

In that same year, Mexican author Carlos Fuentes said that it was inevitable that there should be a highly mobile labor market between Mexico and the U.S. "It is happening," he said, "but nobody knows how to deal with it, or they do not want to deal with it . . . The U.S.-Mexico border is going to be one of the great hubs of an interdependent culture . . . for the 21st Century, if we do not drown in blood and intolerance . . . This border is the most exciting border in the world . . . I have always said it is a scar, not a border. But we don't want the scar to bleed again. We want the scar to heal."[12]

Since 1994, unfortunately, the scar has begun to bleed profusely. Drug wars in Mexican border cities have cost more lives than the number of Americans killed in our wars in Iraq and Afghanistan combined.[13] The rhetoric—and the associated hate crimes—against undocumented Mexicans continues to escalate. Americans are in denial that our insatiable appetite for cheap Mexican labor can somehow be satisfied by keeping Mexicans in Mexico. Even as the American work force ages and the birthrates needed to replace workers decline, many continue to believe that Mexicans only come to steal American jobs.

Along the South Texas border, however, low-income people quietly go about overcoming life's challenges by finding informal solutions to problems created either by formality or by the failure to formalize economic realities. If these South Texans can't afford American health care, they find an informal substitute in Mexico. If they can't get medical care and food for their kids by declaring all their income, they fail to report the small amounts that would disqualify them. If they can't afford formal housing, they build their own out in the county where they can skirt or ignore regulations. If they can't get legal authorization to work, they get false documents or start a business, careful to avoid licenses and taxes that might alert government agents to their unauthorized status.

Most importantly, however, they learn to leverage the border to earn a living. A few go deeply *under* the law in enterprises that risk lives, destroy character, and exploit associates. Most, however, just go *over* and *around* the maze of regulations, hoping that if they cannot escape the need for economic informality, they can at least make it possible for their children to do so.

Borderlife Survey Research Projects Utilized in This Volume

As reported in the Introduction, the bulk of the data focused on the informal and underground economy in South Texas comes from our informal and underground surveys conducted 2006–2009. Some of the data reported herein comes from previously reported Borderlife projects (see Table A.1). One is our Cultural Practices Survey (described in the 2006 volume, *On the Edge of the Law*), which was administered to 432 Mexican-origin residents of the Rio Grande Valley in 2001. We use it to assess how frequently respondents participated in certain cultural and economic practices and how they felt about keeping these practices. We also occasionally report results from two other previously reported surveys—our 1994 Undocumented Mexican Workers Survey of 150 undocumented Mexican respondents; and our Perceptions of Deviance Survey (administered 2002–2003), which had 424 respondents rate how good or how bad 48 specific forms of border-related behavior were. This allowed us to not only compare the relative perceptions of "deviancy" of items related to informal activities, but also to show how specific population groups felt about such practices.

In 2008, Dejun Su (coauthor of Chapter 7 in this book) and Chad Richardson, with the help of UTPA colleague Dr. José Pagán, received a $300,000, three-year federal grant from the Agency for Healthcare Research and Quality to conduct a survey on the use of health care in Mexico by South Texas residents. We were able to utilize this telephone survey of 1,605 randomly selected Texas adults in South Texas border counties to determine their frequency of cross-border visits to obtain various forms of Mexican health care (prescription drugs, consultations with doctors or dentists).

Throughout the last decade (1995–2008), we were also able to acquire 150 in-depth ethnographic interviews of Lower Rio Grande Valley *colonia* residents. These insights into their daily lives help inform Chapter 6.

Finally, as we worked on completing this book in 2010, we developed and administered our Consumer Informality Survey of 372 South Texas adults. We helped students develop a broad sample of consumers in South Texas. Student interviewers were encouraged to solicit interviews with a wide range of con-

Table A.I. Projects utilized in this volume

Project Title	Year(s) Conducted	Sample	Size (N)
1. Cultural Practices Survey	2001	Mexican-origin residents	432
2. Undocumented Mexican Workers Survey	1994	Undocumented workers	150
3. Perceptions of Deviance Survey	2002–2003	All Lower Rio Grande Valley ethnic groups	424
4. Informal and Underground Survey	2006–2009	Informal/underground participants	526 (835)
5. Healthcare Utilization in Mexico	2008	Texas border counties	1,605
6. Colonia Ethnographic Interviews	1995–2008	Colonia residents	150
7. Consumer Informality Survey	2010	Lower Rio Grande consumers	372

sumers and to include those who they did not believe were likely to be making informal purchases. The intent of the survey was to determine the types of informal purchases South Texas residents make, the frequency of such purchases, and the beliefs and feelings they have about making purchases of informal goods and services.

Names of Students Who Contributed Ethnographic Accounts

Note: Each of the following student researchers authorized and contributed to the anecdotal accounts cited in this volume. If a student contributed more than one account, a number in parentheses follows his or her name and indicates how many anecdotal accounts that student contributed. We do not cite students' names alongside their respective anecdotal accounts in order to preserve the anonymity of the individuals they interviewed.

Águilar, Laura
Alaníz, Magdalena (2)
Álvarez, Joelda (2)
Ayala, Alma
Ballejos, Marie (2)
Barajas, Stephanie Ruiz (2)
Barrera, Vania
Benavides, Juan
Buenrostro, Yadira
Cano, Adriana
Cano, Nellie
Cantú, Nadia
Cantú, Nidia
Cantú, Rebecca J. (4)
Carmena, Graciela (2)
Carrío, Adriana
Castillo, Miriam (2)
Cervantes, Areceli
Chapa, Robert
Corona, Mary
Cruz, Eric M.
Del Toro, Irene
Escamilla, Maritza (6)
Escobar, Carlo (4)
Escobar, Clarissa

Felix, Esmeralda
Flores, Luis (2)
Flores, Priscilla
Fonseca, Judy
Gallegos, Eunice S.
García, Celina
García, Elda
García, Humberto (4)
García, Ramona (2)
Garza, Blanca E.
Garza, Carlos
Garza, Erica M.
Garza, Marisa
Gómez, Rubén
Gonzales, Celina
González, Celina
Gonzales, Celina Rae
González, Eliza (2)
Gonzales, Jovita
Guajardo, Becky (4)
Guerrero, Teresa (2)
Gutiérrez, Christina
Gurrusquieta, Anna (2)
Harrison, Rebecca (2)
Hernández, Claudia (2)

Hernández, Isabel
Hernández, Kristina
Hernández, Lilyana (2)
Hinojosa, Mariano
Huerta, Ana María
Juárez, Jesús
Lares, José
Lazo, José I.
Leal, José
Leuders, Lois
Leyva, Nancy (2)
López, Javier, Jr.
Maldonado, María
Maldonado, Nadia (2)
Maldonado, Ramón (2)
Mariscal, Armando
Márquez, Rosa
Martínez, Abel, Jr.
Martínez, César (3)
Martínez, Robert
Martínez, Roland (4)
McGuffin, Lamar
Mirales, Areceli
Mireles, Norma
Monsivais, Pablo (2)
Montalvo, José Miguel
Morales, Alex, Jr.
Morán, Eloy
Muñiz, Juan
Muñoz, Cynthia
Naranjo, Hector (2)
Orozco, Jorge
Ortega, Rosa Anna
Peña, Liza (2)
Peña, Priscilla
Pérez, Linda Ann
Pérez, Magali
Perkins, Josephine

Ramírez, Deana
Rendón, Melissa (5)
Reyes, Graciela (2)
Rodríguez, Eliza
Rodríguez, Juan
Rosales, Diorica A.
Rosales, Margarita
Rosas, Cindy
Salinas, Alfredo
Salinas, Élida (3)
Samaniego, Abelardo, Jr.
Sánchez, Ana
Sánchez, Cynthia
Sepúlveda, Sergio (2)
Sifuentes, Richard (2)
Smith, Brian
Sylva, Connie
Tafolla, Andrea
Tafolla, Imelda
Tobías, Gregorio
Torres, Blanca E. (2)
Trejo, Ricardo A.
Trejo, Richard
Trujillo, Blanca María Guadalupe
Trujillo, Brenda
Ureste, Joanne (2)
Valadez, Eduardo
Valdez, Mayra
Valladares, Eduardo
Vallejos, Marie
Valles, Nancy
Villarreal, Ignacio, Jr.
Villarreal, Jovelle (2)
Villarreal, Yvonne (2)
Villegas, Mayra (3)
Womack, Aaron
Zarske, Gregory E.
Zúñiga, Norma

Notes

Preface

1. Dr. Richardson first came to UTPA in 1977 and retired in 2010. He is Professor of Sociology-Emeritus at UTPA.

2. The Borderlife Project was inspired by the Firefox experiment initiated in Appalachia. Chad Richardson engaged the collaboration of Dorey Schmidt (English Department) to help students publish their research in the local McAllen, Texas, newspaper, *The Monitor.* Nearly fifty articles were published (and later republished in *Border Life in the Rio Grande Valley* by the Hidalgo County Historical Society). Later, Dr. Richardson developed the Borderlife Project into a research initiative and an archive for a myriad of research endeavors.

3. Dr. Van A. Reidhead, Dean of the College of Social and Behavioral Sciences, University of Texas-Pan American, personal communication to the author, January 30, 2007.

Introduction

1. Wanda Falding is a pseudonym. Likewise throughout the book, we employ pseudonyms for all of our informants.

2. Mexicans have long referred to this river as the Río Bravo ("mean or dangerous river"). We use the name by which it is more commonly and officially known in the United States, mainly to avoid confusing those not familiar with the region. In this volume, we use several geographical markers—South Texas, the Valley, the Lower Rio Grande Valley (LRGV). By South Texas, we refer to our entire study area, from Laredo to Brownsville and including the areas just to the north, typically up to the second border inspection checkpoint. The Valley, or LRGV, more specifically refers to the counties of Starr, Hidalgo, Willacy, and Cameron. When we include border environments in Mexico, we specifically mention Mexico.

3. Jerry D. Thompson, *Juan Cortina and the Texas-Mexico Frontier,* 2.

4. John S. Ford, *Rip Ford's Texas,* ed. Stephen B. Oates, 261–262.

5. James R. Douglas, "Juan Cortina: el Caudillo de la Frontera" (M.A. thesis, University of Texas, 1987).

6. Jerry Thompson, *Juan Cortina and the Texas-Mexico Frontier*, 11, 12.

7. Ibid., 11, 12.

8. Ibid., 19.

9. The key battle that turned the tide of the war was the Battle of Santa Gertrudis (near Cortina's birthplace in Camargo). In this battle, which took place on June 16, 1866, 1,800 Imperialist soldiers (many of them Hungarians) were defeated as they were escorting 200 carts of supplies from Matamoros to Monterrey. Following this defeat (and the subsequent fall of Matamoros), Napoleon III withdrew French troops from Mexico, leading to Emperor Maximilian's defeat and execution.

10. As this incident shows, Colonel Ford could himself be a fierce opponent while still manifesting a "clemency worthy of emulation." His influence in South Texas history is impressive. At times a doctor, newspaper publisher, Confederate colonel, explorer, captain in the Texas Rangers, Mayor of Brownsville, and politician, he commanded Confederate troops in the last battle of the Civil War, the Battle of Palmito Ranch (near Brownsville) in May of 1865. This battle (which Ford won) occurred two weeks after Lee had surrendered and was instigated, many believe, by a Union commander trying to advance his postwar career.

11. Though Max Weber's main emphasis was on the need for legitimacy of the state, we extend his analysis to the need for legitimacy of the formal economy. For a discussion of Weber's concept of legitimacy, see Randall Collins, *Weberian Sociological Theory*.

12. James A. Irby, *Backdoor at Bagdad: The Civil War on the Rio Grande*. Today we see a similar situation with the (illegal) export of guns to Mexico to fuel the drug wars there.

13. We will use the term *Anglo* throughout this text (as it is used in South Texas) to indicate non-Hispanic whites.

14. Cultural geographer Daniel D. Arreola (*Tejano South Texas: A Mexican American Cultural Province*) states, "What is clear from the documents is that the region generally south of the Nueces River was, from the mid-eighteenth century, a separate administrative unit of colonial New Spain and later the Republic of Mexico, despite claims to the contrary by the Republic of Texas" (31).

15. Ibid., 2.

16. Throughout the book, we use the terms *Hispanic* and *Latino* interchangeably.

17. Real Estate Center at Texas A&M University, "Market Report 2010—Laredo," 1, http://recenter.tamu.edu/mreports/Laredo.pdf (accessed July 12, 2010).

18. U.S. Census Bureau, 2006/2007/2008 American Community Survey, http://www.census.gov/acs/www/ (accessed June 20, 2010).

19. Real Estate Center at Texas A&M University, "Market Report 2010—Laredo," 11, http://recenter.tamu.edu/mreports/Laredo.pdf (accessed July 12, 2010).

20. U.S. Census Bureau, "American Fact Finder," http://factfinder.census.gov/servlet/ACSSAFFFacts?_event (accessed May 2, 2010).

21. Ibid.

22. U.S. Department of Labor, Bureau of Labor Statistics, "May 2008 State Occupational Employment and Wage Estimates—Texas," http://www.bls.gov/oes/2008/may/oessrcma.htm (accessed July 12, 2010); Real Estate Center at Texas A&M University, "Market Report 2010—Laredo," 11, 14, http://recenter.tamu.edu/mreports/Laredo.pdf (accessed July 12, 2010).

23. Alberto Dávila and Marie T. Mora, "English Skills, Earnings and the Occupational Sorting of Mexican Americans Working along the US-Mexico Border." *International Migration Review* 34, no. 1 (2000): 133–157, 146.

24. Michael J. Pisani, "Why Do Seasonal Unemployment Patterns in the Middle and Lower Rio Grande Areas Differ from the Rest of the State?" *Texas Labor Market Review* (February 2003): 13–14.

25. The TAMIU undergraduate student interviews took place between 1998 and 2002. In all, about 500 ethnographic interviews (using a semistructured interview guide) of border businesses were collected. Each student conducted an interview with a business in either Laredo or Nuevo Laredo, with a stated focus on and preference for very small, informal enterprises.

26. Student research generally takes place as a class assignment. Students are given a choice to either work on several ongoing border-related projects or to work on a project related to their own interests, many of which are not directly related to border issues. Students are given training in conducting interviews (particularly in guaranteeing anonymity of their subjects). When they submit their work, they are given a grade and then asked whether they wish to authorize all (or portions) of their work for possible publication. They are clearly informed that a decision to do so (or not) will not change the grade they have received.

27. For an ethnographic look at the informal and underground economy in an urban and Midwestern setting, see Sudhir A. Venkatesh, *Off the Books: The Underground Economy of the Urban Poor*, a study of a poor neighborhood in Chicago's Southside.

28. Many of these interviews dealt with such topics as drug and human smuggling, undocumented workers, and other topics that will be dealt with in subsequent chapters.

29. Much of the following is based on an excellent history of this era, Charles H. Harris and Louis R. Sadler, *The Texas Rangers and the Mexican Revolution: The Bloodiest Decade 1910 to 1920*.

30. Ibid., 260.

31. Tim Johnson, "Mexico Rethinks Drug Strategy as Death Toll Soars," *McClatchy Newspapers*, August 12, 2010, http://www.mcclatchydc.com/2010/08/12/99089/mexico-rethinks-drug-strategy.html#ixzz0zVu56cpz (accessed August 20, 2010). According to this report, Mexico's intelligence chief said in early August 2010 that as many as 28,000 people had been killed since Mexican president Felipe Calderón came to office in late 2006.

32. See Gabriel Arana, "The Border Violence Myth," *The Nation*, May 27,

2009, http://www.thenation.com/article/border-violence-myth (accessed July 24, 2010).

Chapter One

1. This and other names are all fictitious and are used simply to reference them in further discussion of their cases.

2. This discussion of informality is related to our article, Michael J. Pisani, Chad Richardson and J. Michael Patrick, "Economic Informality on the U.S.-Mexican Border: A (Re)View from South Texas," *Journal of Borderlands Studies* 23, no. 2 (2008): 19–40.

3. Alejandro Portes and Richard Schauffler, "Competing Perspectives on the Latin American Informal Sector," *Population and Development Review* 19 (March 1993): 33–60.

4. This discussion of culture and structure parallels the usage of these terms in the two preceding volumes on social life in South Texas. See Chad Richardson, *Batos, Bolillos, Pochos, & Pelados: Class & Culture on the South Texas Border* and Chad Richardson and Rosalva Resendiz, *On the Edge of the Law: Culture, Labor & Deviance on the South Texas Border.*

5. This has resulted in a rather widespread sex trade in child prostitution in some border communities.

6. Christopher Bajada and Freidrich Schneider, eds., *Size, Causes and Consequences of the Underground Economy: An International Perspective.*

7. Though we use the term *underground economy* in this book, other terms, such as the *shadow economy, hidden economy, black economy, gray economy, parallel economy, clandestine economy, illegal economy,* and even the *informal economy* have been used by others, oftentimes confusing the topic. See for example, Matthew H. Flemming, John Roman, and Graham Farrell, "The Shadow Economy," *Journal of International Affairs* 53, no. 2 (2000): 387–409.

8. Christopher Bajada and Freidrich Schneider, "Introduction," in *Size, Causes and Consequences of the Underground Economy: An International Perspective,* eds. Christopher Bajada and Freidrich Schneider, 1.

9. Ibid.

10. Jessica Rocha, "The Underground Economy Business: Informal Economy Turns Brownsville's Economic Engine," *The Brownsville Herald,* January 27, 2003. The best empirical estimate of informality for a specific region of the United States is 16% for the city of Los Angeles. See Kevin Klowden and Perry Wong, *Los Angeles Economy Project.*

11. Jan L. Losby, John F. Else, Marcia E. Kingslow, Elaine L. Edcomb, Erika T. Mal, and Vivian Kao, "Informal Economy Literature Review," The Institute for Social and Economic Development and The Aspen Institute, December 2002, http://www.ised.org/ (accessed May 5, 2007).

12. In Figure 1.1, the estimate of informality in the border region is based solely on estimates of informal production and sales.

13. Keith Hart, "Small Scale Entrepreneurs in Ghana and Development Planning," *Journal of Development Planning,* 6 (April 1970): 104–120.

14. Alejandro Portes and Kelly Hoffman, "Latin American Class Structures: Their Composition and Change During the Neoliberal Era," *Latin American Research Review* 38, no. 1 (2003): 41–82.

15. See Bajada and Schneider, eds., *Size, Causes and Consequences;* Sudhir A. Venkatesh, *Off the Books: The Underground Economy of the Urban Poor;* and Bruce Weigand, *Off the Books: A Theory and Critique of the Underground Economy.*

16. Manuel Castells and Alejandro Portes, "World Underneath: The Origins, Dynamics, and Effects of the Informal Economy," in *The Informal Economy: Studies in Advanced and Less Developed Countries,* eds. Alejandro Portes, Manuel Castells, and Lauren A. Benton; Miguel A. Centeno and Alejandro Portes, "The Informal Economy in the Shadow of the State," in *Out of the Shadows: Political Action and the Informal Economy in Latin America,* eds. Patricia Fernandez-Kelly and Jon Shefner, 23–48; Alejandro Portes and William Haller, "The Informal Economy," in *The Handbook of Economic Sociology,* 2nd edition, eds. Neil J. Smesler and Richard Swedberg, 403–425; John C. Cross and Bruce D. Johnson, "Expanding Dual Labor Market Theory: Crack Dealers and the Informal Sector," *International Journal of Sociology and Social Policy* 20, nos. 1/2 (2000): 98–136; John C. Cross and Sergio Pena, "Risk and Regulation in Informal and Illegal Markets," in *Out of the Shadows: Political Action and the Informal Economy in Latin America,* eds. Patricia Fernandez-Kelly and Jon Shefner, 49–86.

17. John C. Cross and Bruce D. Johnson ("Expanding Dual Labor Market Theory: Crack Dealers and the Informal Sector," *International Journal of Sociology and Social Policy* 20, nos. 1/2 (2000): 98–136) suggest that intermediate or "grey areas" exist in between products and processes. They argue that a continuum of (il)legality and (in)formality intersects generating four quadrants in which labor may participate. That is, some activities may be reconstructed to be illegal in some circumstances, yet legal in others. Cross and Johnson argue "sexual activity outside of marriage is not considered illegal in most states, but payment for such sex is," indicating that prostitution may be classified as semi-legal (Ibid., 105). Cross and Johnson (2000) also suggest some activities may be in part formal and part informal, such as a small workshop that is a registered business but does not abide by government-mandated occupational safety regulations. Though Cross and Johnson fail to adequately distinguish between activities and goods, we build upon their work and offer a revised typology inclusive of exemplars from South Texas.

18. Helen Thorpe, "The Great Hand-Me-Down Heap," *The New York Times Magazine,* October 15, 2000.

19. Alejandro Portes and William Haller, "The Informal Economy," in *The Handbook of Economic Sociology,* 2nd edition, eds. Neil J. Smesler and Richard, 42.

20. Indeed, one of our informants told us that the greatest difficulty of this type of operation today does not come from federal officials in Mexico or the U.S. but from the Mexican drug cartels that patrol the border to collect their "plaza" (or toll) for smuggling anything into the U.S.

21. Miguel A. Centeno and Alejandro Portes, "The Informal Economy in the Shadow of the State," in *Out of the Shadows: Political Action and the Infor-*

mal Economy in Latin America, eds. Patricia Fernandez-Kelly and Jon Shefner, 26–27.

22. Ibid., 34.

23. See Chad Richardson, *Batos, Bolillos, Pochos, & Pelados: Class & Culture on the South Texas Border* and Chad Richardson and Rosalva Resendiz, *On the Edge of the Law: Culture, Labor & Deviance on the South Texas Border.*

24. John Sharp, "Bordering the Future: Challenges and Opportunities in the Texas Border Region," http://www.window.state.tx.us (accessed April 19, 1999).

25. Tim Slack, Joachim Singelmann, Kayla Fontenot, Dudley L. Poston, Jr., Rogelio Saenz, and Carlos Siordia, "Poverty in the Texas Borderland and Lower Mississippi Delta: A Comparative Analysis of Differences by Family Type," *Demographic Research* 20, no. 15 (2009):353–376.

26. Sharp, "Bordering the Future," http://www.window.state.tx.us (accessed April 19, 1999).

27. Ibid.

28. Michael V. Miller, "Vehicle Theft Along the Texas-Mexico Border," *Journal of Borderlands Studies* 2, no. 2 (1987): 12–32.

29. Carole Keeton Strayhorn, "Undocumented Immigrants in Texas: A Financial Analysis of the Impact to the State Budget and Economy." Special Report from the Texas Comptroller, 2006, http://www.window.state.tx.us /specialrpt/undocumented/undocumented.pdf (accessed June 20, 2007).

30. Ibid.

31. U.S. Department of Homeland Security, *Yearbook of Immigration Statistics: 2005*, http://www.dhs.gov/files/statistics/publications/yearbook.shtm (accessed May 13, 2006).

32. Strayhorn, "Undocumented Immigrants in Texas," 17–19, http://www .window.state.tx.us/specialrpt/undocumented/undocumented.pdf (accessed June 20, 2007).

33. The "laser visa" is more formally known as the border crossing card. Since October 2008, the laser visa has also doubled as a B1 [business visitor]/B2 [pleasure, tourism or medical treatment visitor] visa for Mexicans. According to the U.S. Department of State, the laser visa came into being April 1, 1998. See U.S. Department of State, "Visitor Visas—Business and Pleasure," http:// travel.state.gov/visa/temp/types/types_1262.html (accessed July 22, 2010).

34. Michael J. Pisani, Chad Richardson and J. Michael Patrick, "Economic Informality on the U.S.-Mexican Border: A (Re)View from South Texas," *Journal of Borderlands Studies* 23, no. 2 (2008): 19–40; Michael J. Pisani, Carlos Sepulveda, and Amelia Flores, "Consumer Power Asymmetries: Stretching Household Consumption via Consumption Informality in South Texas," (paper presented at the Association of Borderlands Studies Annual Conference, Salt Lake City, Utah, April 14–16, 2011).

35. Ellwyn Stoddard (in *U.S.-Mexico Borderlands Issues: The Bi-national Boundary, Immigration and Economic Policies*, El Paso: The Promontory, 2001) says in his introduction, for example, "While local residents and institutions rely upon informal frontier networks to resolve their common border problems, federal bureaucrats wrestle with preserving national sovereignty by means of tightly-controlled mechanisms."

36. Described by Chad Richardson, *Batos, Bolillos, Pochos, & Pelados.*

37. Another possible solution would be to transform NAFTA to a common market (as modeled by the European Union) whereby Mexicans and Canadians (and Americans) could work across the region without government interference. At this point in time, U.S. public opinion, unfortunately, does not support deeper integration with Mexico. Hence, integration is incomplete, benefiting industrialists but pushing many of the costs of unfinished integration upon workers.

38. Though some push factors might just be the opposite of pull factors (e.g., no jobs at home versus many jobs in new location), there are many factors (e.g., death of a loved one) that are not simply opposites. The same is true of hold-repel factors, as we will show elsewhere in the book.

39. Edwin G. Nelson and Erik J. De Bruijn, "The Voluntary Formalization of Enterprises in a Developing Economy—The Case of Tanzania," *Journal of International Development* 17, no. 4 (2005): 575–593, 576.

Chapter Two

1. In the introduction, we indicated that a pilot (mainly qualitative) survey of 307 participants was administered to informal and underground operators prior to developing a longer survey form administered to an additional 528 persons. Because questions about some of the demographic variables were identical in both surveys, we occasionally combine the two samples to get 835 respondents; for other questions, we use only the final sample of 157 underground operators who were involved mainly in underground activities. Also, throughout this chapter slightly different sample sizes are reported in the tables. This is a reflection of some missing data for particular variables of interest. We believe the missing data does not skew our findings.

2. Auto theft and chop shops (where autos are stripped and parted out) are also major underground activities in the region. We briefly discuss auto theft and chop shops in Chapter 5 and at more length elsewhere, so we have omitted these activities from the discussion here; see also Chapter 7, "Property Crime," in Chad Richardson and Rosalva Resendiz, *On the Edge of the Law: Culture, Labor & Deviance on the South Texas Border.*

3. Though some human smugglers do pressure undocumented aliens to carry drugs, many do not, perhaps fearing the greater risks of also being involved with drug smuggling. The drug laws are more strictly enforced and carry heavier penalties.

4. Houston Chronicle, "80 Fighting Cocks Seized in Houston," as reported in the *Laredo Morning Times*, January 25, 2007, 9A, http://airwolf.lmtonline .com/news/archive/012507/pagea9.pdf (accessed March 23, 2008).

5. The Humane Society of the United States, "The Ranking of State Cockfighting Laws," http://www.hsus.org/acf/fighting/cockfight/state_cockfighting _laws_ranked.html (accessed April 12, 2008).

6. John C. Cross, "Passing the Buck: Risk Avoidance and Risk Management in the Illegal/Informal Drug Trade," *International Journal of Sociology and Social Policy* 20, nos. 9/10 (2000): 69–70.

7. This issue could be classified under the *market risks* proposed by John Cross (Ibid.).

8. John C. Cross and Bruce D. Johnson, "Expanding Dual Labor Market Theory: Crack Dealers and the Informal Sector," *International Journal of Sociology and Social Policy* 20, nos. 1/2 (2000): 96–124, 117.

9. Chad Richardson and Rosalva Resendiz, *On the Edge of the Law: Culture, Labor & Deviance on the South Texas Border*, 154.

10. Chad Richardson, *Batos, Bolillos, Pochos, & Pelados*, 73.

11. John C. Cross and Sergio Pena, "Risk and Regulation in Informal and Illegal Markets," in *Out of the Shadows: Political Action and the Informal Economy in Latin America*, eds. Patricia Fernandez-Kelly and Jon Shefner, 55.

12. Jeremy Roebuck, "Sheriff Indicted," *The Monitor*, October 15, 2008.

13. Houston Chronicle, "Brownsville," *Houston Chronicle*, March 4, 2009.

14. Robin Emmott, "Drug Smugglers Bribing U.S. Agents on Mexico Border," *Reuters*, July 15, 2008.

15. Andrew Becker, "Southwest Border Corruption Cases Continue to Rise," *Center for Investigative Reporting*, November 20, 2009.

16. The most common forms of pirated goods in the "open" underground market are DVDs and clothing. If you ask most folks in South Texas where you can buy a pirated DVD, they will most likely point you to the nearest flea market or high school.

17. For an expanded discussion of *curanderas* and other cultural practices, see Chad Richardson, *Batos, Bolillos, Pochos, & Pelados* and Chad Richardson and Rosalva Resendiz, *On the Edge of the Law*.

18. For another description of such cult-like practices in Mexico, see Alma Guillermoprieto, "Mexico's Shocking New Saints," *National Geographic* 217, no. 5 (2010): 54–73.

19. Miguel Timoshenkov, "Adios, 'Santa Muerte'," *Laredo Morning Times*, March 25, 2009.

20. The rate of *property* crime in Texas border cities, however, is closer to the rates found in the larger Texas cities.

21. Rubén G. Rumbaut and Walter A. Ewing, "The Myth of Immigrant Criminality and the Paradox of Assimilation: Incarceration Rates Among Native and Foreign-Born Men," in *Border Battles: The U.S. Immigration Debates*, Immigration Policy Center special report.

22. Ibid., 3.

23. George W. Bush, "President Bush Addresses the Nation on Immigration Reform," White House, Office of the Press Secretary, May 15, 2006.

24. After Chad Richardson and Rosalva Resendiz, *On the Edge of the Law*, the Generation Score is computed at three generation levels, with a possible total score ranging from 0 to 12, as follows: (a) respondent (4 if born in the U.S., otherwise 0); (b) respondent's parents (4 if both parents born in the U.S., 2 if one parent is born in Mexico [and the other in the US], and 0 if both parents were born in Mexico); and (c) respondent's grandparents (4 if all born in the U.S.; 3 if three grandparents were born in the U.S.; 2 if two grandparents were born in the U.S.; 1 if one grandparent was born in the U.S.; and 0 if no grandparents were born in the U.S.). The generation score or acculturation scale may

be modified for groups other than Mexicans by recording birth dichotomously: U.S. or outside U.S.

25. Edward E. Tellas and Vilma Ortiz, *Generations of Exclusion: Mexican Americans, Assimilation, and Race.*

26. Brian Duncan, V. Joseph Hotz, and Stephen J. Trejo, "Hispanics in the U.S. Labor Market," in *Hispanics and the Future of America*, eds. Marta Tienda and Faith Mitchell, 263.

27. Tellas and Ortiz, *Generations of Exclusion*, 154.

28. Robert J. Sampson, "Rethinking Immigration and Crime," *Contexts* 7, no. 1 (2008): 28–33.

29. Ibid., 33.

30. Fred Burton and Ben West. "The Barrio Azteca Trial and the Prison Gang-Cartel Interface," STRATFOR *Global Security and Intelligence Report*, November 19, 2008.

31. See G. V. Corbiscello, "Border Crossings: A Look at the Very Real Threat of Cross Border Gangs to the U.S.," *Journal of Gang Research* 15, no. 2 (2008): 33–52.

32. Burton and West, "The Barrio Azteca Trial."

33. U.S. Department of Justice—National Drug Intelligence Center, *National Drug Threat Assessment 2010.*

34. Burton and West, "The Barrio Azteca Trial."

35. Cross and Johnson, "Expanding Dual Labor Market Theory," 96–124, 114.

36. Alejandro Portes and William Haller, "The Informal Economy," in *The Handbook of Economic Sociology*, 2nd edition, eds. Neil J. Smesler and Richard Swedberg, 409.

Chapter Three

1. Edgar L. Feige, "Defining and Estimating Underground and Informal Economies: The New Institutional Economics Approach," *World Development* 18, no. 7 (1990): 989–1002.

2. Texas Comptroller of Public Accounts, "Convenience Store Owner Arrested for Tax Fraud Under New Law," Criminal Investigation Division—Case Spotlight, 2009.

3. Alejandro Portes and William Haller, "The Informal Economy," in *The Handbook of Economic Sociology*, 2nd edition, eds. Neil J. Smesler and Richard Swedberg, 409.

4. See Ivan Light, "The Ethnic Economy," in *The Handbook of Economic Sociology*, 2nd edition, eds. Neil J. Smesler and Richard Swedberg. Usually, self-employment among immigrants to these countries is limited to those who have lived there (even if on welfare) for six years, undertake formal apprenticeships, pass examinations, satisfy authorities that their enterprise is in the public interest, and, once in business, adhere to detailed regulations for labor standards, wages and hours, social security payments, and product safety. The price of such extensive regulation is that the unemployed are treated much more generously.

5. Michael J. Pisani and David W. Yoskowitz, "Grass, Sweat, and Sun: An Exploratory Study of the Labor Market for Gardeners in South Texas," *Social Science Quarterly*, 86, no. 1 (2005): 229–251; Michael J. Pisani and David W. Yoskowitz, "*Por Necesidad*'—Transnational Labor Movements, Informality and Wage Determination: An Exploratory Study of Maids on the U.S.-Mexican Border," *The Journal of Borderlands Studies* 16, no. 1 (2001): 67–82.

6. Pisani and Yoskowitz, "*Por Necesidad*,'" 77.

7. Michael J. Pisani and David W. Yoskowitz, "Opportunity Knocks: Entrepreneurship, Informality & Home Gardening in South Texas," *Journal of Borderlands Studies* 21, no. 2(2006): 59–76.

8. Ibid.

9. Pisani and Yoskowitz, "*Por Necesidad*,'" 77.

10. Chad Richardson, *Batos, Bolillos, Pochos, & Pelados: Class & Culture on the South Texas Border*, 76.

11. Pisani and Yoskowitz, "*Por Necesidad*,'" 79.

12. Apparently, this practice is fairly common in South Texas. Many customers, familiar with the practice, develop friendships with workers in auto dealerships, repair shops, and other skilled labor enterprises and then approach them about working "on the side." This is another form of consumer-led informality we discuss elsewhere.

13. See Martin Medina, "Scavenging on the Border: A Study of the Informal Recycling Sector in Laredo, Texas and Nuevo Laredo, Mexico" (PhD diss., Yale University, 1997) for the only comprehensive study of scavenging in the South Texas borderlands. Medina focuses on the borderplex community of Los Dos Laredos. Though his study reflects scavenging in the early 1990s, we believe his findings are illustrative of the present South Texas scavenging context. Medina estimated that there were over 3,378 scavengers in Los Dos Laredos, 94.9% of whom were part-time scavengers (like Sandra) mainly interested in scavenging for aluminum cans. In "Informal Transborder Recycling on the U.S.-Mexico Border: The *Cartoneros* of Nuevo Laredo," *Journal of Borderlands Studies* 16, no. 2 (2001): 19–40, Medina found 173 full-time scavengers, of which 48 scavenged for cardboard and 125 for aluminum cans. The cardboard scavengers— these were cross-border recyclers—earned a premium of three times the Mexican minimum wage for their work. In "Scavenging on the Border," Medina used a sample of 100 informal-sector scavengers from Los Dos Laredos and found a strong, positive correlation between capital inputs (e.g., truck and *tricicleta* ownership) and income from scavenging. In all, Medina found South Texas scavengers picking up the following goods: cardboard; aluminum cans; iron, steel and copper scrap; car components (e.g., batteries); discarded furniture, appliances, and construction materials (e.g., wood, windows and frames, toilets); clothing; and date expired but otherwise edible food.

14. Alejandro Portes, Manuel Castells, and Lauran Benton, eds., *The Informal Economy: Studies in Advanced and Less Developed Countries*.

15. Perhaps the closest form we found in South Texas is the *tanda*, a joint money-raising system among friends who each contribute a set amount each month, allowing the individual most in need to withdraw a large amount for special occasions (such as weddings, starting a business, or a health crisis).

Trust and a long-term relationship are obviously required so that individuals who have taken a large portion of these communal funds will continue contributing so that others will have similar opportunities.

16. In her study of the informal economy of the El Paso, Texas/Ciudad Juárez, Mexico, metroplex, *Free Trade: Informal Economies at the U.S.-Mexican Border*, Kathleen Staudt found that on the U.S. side of the border, informality is often only supplemental. That is, many informals access the informal sector when extra money is needed. However, Staudt argues that on the Mexican side of the border the informal economy often saves the participants from absolute deprivation and poverty.

17. Marx defined exploitation as a ratio: $P/(P + W)$, where P = Profits and W = Wages, as reported in Light, "The Ethnic Economy," 667.

18. Portes and Haller, "The Informal Economy," 413.

19. Marta Tienda and Rebecca Raijman, "Immigrants' Income Packaging and Invisible Labor Force Activity," *Social Science Quarterly* 81, no. 1 (2000): 291–310.

20. Light, "The Ethnic Economy," 654.

21. Jimy Sanders, Victor Nee, and Scott Sernau, "Asian Immigrants' Reliance on Social Ties in a Multiethnic Labor Market," *Social Forces* 81, no. 1 (2002): 281–314.

22. U.S. Census Bureau, "Hispanic-Owned Firms: 2002–2002 Economic Census, Survey of Business Owners."

23. Marie T. Mora and Alberto Dávila, "Mexican Immigrant Self-Employment Along the U.S.-Mexico Border: An Analysis of the 2000 Census Data," *Social Science Quarterly* 87, no. 1 (2006): 91–109. See also Light, "The Ethnic Economy," 651. Light states, "In point of fact, the rate of immigrant self-employment is higher in the informal sector than in the formal sector, and both rates increase drastically when multiple job-holding is considered."

24. Mora and Dávila, "Mexican Immigrant Self-Employment," 103.

25. Alberto Dávila, Marie T. Mora, and Alma D. Hales, "Earned Income along the U.S.-Mexico Border," in *Labor Market Issues along the U.S.-Mexico Border*, eds. Marie T. Mora and Alberto Dávila.

26. Mora and Dávila, "Mexican Immigrant Self-Employment," 104.

27. Ibid., 103.

28. Barry Molefsky, "America's Underground Economy," in *The Underground Economy in the United States and Abroad*, ed. Vito Tanzi.

29. Mora and Dávila, "Mexican Immigrant Self-Employment," 100.

30. Ibid., 103.

31. Sharif suggests this situation forces a fire sale for labor, or in his words the "distress sale of labor." Sharif writes: "I contend that involuntary unemployment means wage-unemployment which relates to the working poor only, and that its generation along with a downwardly rigid wage rate is the result of distress sale of labor and workers' participation in nonwage self-employment as an alternative to wage-unemployment. To these workers, the wage rate is exogenously given, and they accept the employment available at this wage rate. However, if the level of employment is not sufficient to generate minimum subsistence for the worker and his family, the worker would try to supplement his

wage-income by self-employment, generally at low productivity" (Mohammed Sharif, *Work Behavior of the World's Poor: Theory, Evidence and Policy*, 115).

32. Michael J. Pisani, "Why Do Seasonal Unemployment Patterns in the Middle and Lower Rio Grande Areas Differ from the Rest of the State?" *Texas Labor Market Review* (February 2003): 13–14.

33. Madeline Leonard, *Invisible Work, Invisible Workers: The Informal Economy in Europe and the U.S.*

34. Peter M. Gutmann, "Statistical Illusions, Mistaken Policies," *Challenge* 22, no. 5 (1979): 14–17.

35. Pew Hispanic Center, "Mexican Immigrants in the United States, 2008," Fact Sheet, 2009.

36. While they are informal in one sense (working without authorization), they simultaneously may be formal if they report their income for tax purposes or have it automatically deducted when working with false or borrowed documents.

37. Kathleen A. Staudt, *Free Trade: Informal Economies at the U.S.-Mexican Border*, 71.

38. Abel Valenzuela, Jr., Nik Theodore, Edwin Meléndez, and Ana Luz Gonzalez, "On The Corner: Day Labor in the United States," working paper.

39. Light, "The Ethnic Economy," 653.

40. The term "cultural capital" has come to have different meanings in sociology and economics. Sociologists often follow Pierre Bourdieu ("Cultural Reproduction and Social Reproduction," in *Power and Ideology in Education*, eds. J. Karabel and A. H. Halsey), who argues that parents from all social classes endow their children with somewhat unique cultural elements. He emphasizes that the elite make their culture into a form of capital, however, by controlling the definition of their culture as "superior" and then by restricting access to it (through elite schools, for example). While this concept is useful, we will use the term *cultural capital* to refer to any culturally acquired competencies that can be leveraged to obtain economic benefits, no matter how these competencies are valued or restricted. This usage is more common in economics.

41. Alejandro Portes, ed., *The Economic Sociology of Immigration: Essays on Networks, Ethnicity, and Entrepreneurship*; Ivan Light and Carolyn Rosenstein, "Expanding the Interaction Theory of Entrepreneurship," in *The Economic Sociology of Immigration: Essays on Networks, Ethnicity, and Entrepreneurship*, ed. Alejandro Portes.

42. In South Texas, we find that these networks are highly class-specific, with low-income Mexican immigrants getting little help from wealthy Mexican immigrants. Though we have not researched this phenomenon past our ethnographic accounts, we attribute what we do see to the well-entrenched and highly segregated class system found in Mexico.

43. Zulema Valdez, *The New Entrepreneurs: How Race, Class, and Gender Shape American Enterprise*, 5.

44. The *quinceañera* in Latin culture represents a woman's formal coming-of-age party, similar to a "sweet sixteen" or debutant.

45. Richard D. Vogel, "Harder Times: Undocumented Workers and the U.S. Informal Economy," *Monthly Review* 58, no. 3 (2006): 29–39.

46. The Earned Income Tax Credit is a refundable federal income tax credit for low- to moderate-income working individuals and families. Congress originally approved the tax credit legislation in 1975 in part to offset the burden of Social Security taxes and to provide an incentive to work. When the EITC exceeds the amount of taxes owed, it results in a tax refund to those who claim and qualify for the credit.

47. Twenty-nine percent indicated that they had experienced no difficulties in their informal work.

48. Portes and Haller, "The Informal Economy," 409.

49. Ibid., 410.

50. Ibid., 419.

51. Leonard, *Invisible Work, Invisible Workers*.

52. After excluding participants in the underground economy, we had 261 respondents (out of 625) who were only informal and 322, or 51.5%, who worked in both formal and informal economic activities.

53. As we are in the beginning stages of analyzing this consumer informality data, we will be sharing more extensive findings in subsequent publications.

54. Portes and Haller, "The Informal Economy," 410.

Chapter Four

1. Jeffrey S. Passel and D'Vera Cohn, "A Portrait of Unauthorized Immigrants in the United States," http://pewhispanic.org/files/reports/107.pdf (accessed April 30, 2009).

2. Pia M. Orrenius, Madeline Zavodny, and Leslie Lukens [in "Why Stop There? Mexican Migration to the U.S. Border Region" (working paper 08–03, Federal Reserve Bank of Dallas, 2008) http://www.dallasfed.org/research/papers/2008/wp0803.pdf (accessed January 15, 2009)] found through the examination of data from the Mexican Migration Project housed at Princeton University that only 7.4% of migrant trips ended at U.S. border cities.

3. David Spener, *Clandestine Crossings: Migrants and Coyotes on the Texas-Mexico Border*, 29.

4. Orrenius, Zavodny, and Lukens, "Why Stop There?" 15.

5. George J. Borjas and Lawrence F. Katz, "The Evolution of the Mexican-Born Workforce in the United States," in *Mexican Immigration to the United States*, ed. George J. Borjas, 35.

6. The Pew Hispanic Center frequently uses the term "unauthorized immigrants," though it notes that the term "undocumented immigrant" can be used interchangeably. [See Jeffrey S. Passel and D'Vera Cohn, "Trends in Unauthorized Immigration: Undocumented Inflow Now Trails Legal Inflow," v, http://pewhispanic.org/files/reports/94.pdf (accessed November 5, 2008).]

7. Until recently, few employers were investigated or prosecuted. Recently, however, the Obama Administration has indicated a greater willingness to prosecute or fine employers who knowingly hire illegal workers. Still, of the more than 6,000 arrests related to worksite enforcement in 2008, only 135 arrests were of employers. See U.S. Department of Homeland Security, "Fact Sheet,"

April 30, 2009, http://www.ice.gov/doclib/pi/news/factsheets/worksite_strategy .pdf (accessed May 12, 2009).

8. Michael J. Pisani, Chad Richardson and J. Michael Patrick, "Economic Informality on the U.S.-Mexican Border: A (Re)View from South Texas," *Journal of Borderlands Studies* 23, no. 2 (2008): 19–40.

9. Michael J. Pisani and David W. Yoskowitz, "Grass, Sweat, and Sun: An Exploratory Study of the Labor Market for Gardeners in South Texas," *Social Science Quarterly*, 86, no. 1 (2005), 229–251; Michael J. Pisani and David W. Yoskowitz, "'*Por Necesidad*'—Transnational Labor Movements, Informality and Wage Determination: An Exploratory Study of Maids on the U.S.-Mexican Border," *Journal of Borderlands Studies* 16, no. 1 (2001): 67–82.

10. Michael J. Pisani and David W. Yoskowitz, "Opportunity Knocks: Entrepreneurship, Informality & Home Gardening in South Texas," *Journal of Borderlands Studies* 21, no. 2 (2006): 59–76; Pisani, Richardson, and Patrick, "Economic Informality on the U.S.-Mexican Border: A (Re)View from South Texas."

11. The IRS issues Taxpayer IDs to both documented and undocumented workers to enable them to pay taxes. A significant but unknown number of the 8.6 million Taxpayer IDs are to undocumented workers.

12. Fieldwork was conducted at Mexican consulates in Los Angeles, New York, Chicago, Atlanta, Dallas, Raleigh and Fresno from July 12, 2004, to January 28, 2005. A total of 4,836 individuals responded to a twelve-page questionnaire in Spanish. See Rakesh Kochhar, "Survey of Mexican Migrants: Part Three," Pew Hispanic Center, http://pewhispanic.org/files/reports/58.pdf (accessed December 13, 2005).

13. For a review of the origins and uses of the term, see Alejandro Portes, "Social Capital: Its Origins and Applications in Modern Sociology," *Annual Review of Sociology* 24 (1998): 1–24.

14. Alejandro Portes and Julia Sensenbrenner, "Embeddedness and Immigration: Notes on the Social Determinants of Economic Action," *American Journal of Sociology* 98, no. 6 (1993): 1320–1350.

15. The other forms of expectations related to sociological theoretical traditions were value introjection (from Durkheim and Weber), bounded solidarity (based on Marx), and enforceable trust (based on Weber).

16. Alejandro Portes, ed., *The Economic Sociology of Immigration: Essays on Networks, Ethnicity, and Entrepreneurship*.

17. Ivan Light, "Immigrant and Ethnic Enterprise in North America," *Ethnic and Racial Studies* 7, no. 2 (1984): 195–216.

18. Donald Massey and Kristin E. Espinosa, "What's Driving Mexico-U.S. Migration? A Theoretical, Empirical, and Policy Analysis," *American Journal of Sociology* 102, no. 4 (1997): 939–999.

19. Aguilera and Massey note the fully embedded wage premium for embedded social networks may be upward of 34.5%, generating greater margins for the undocumented over the documented in the use of social capital. They also find that undocumenteds with English-speaking ability are less likely to use embedded social networks in finding a job; these same undocumenteds also increase their earnings through English language acquisition. See Michael B.

Aguilera and Douglas S. Massey, "Social Capital and the Wages of Mexican Migrants: New Hypotheses and Tests," *Social Forces* 82, no. 2 (2003): 671–701.

20. Portes and Sensenbrenner, "Embeddedness and Immigration."

21. Pierre Bourdieu, "The Forms of Capital," in *Handbook of Theory and Research for the Sociology of Education*, ed. John G. Richardson, 241–258.

22. Their contact most likely had an embedded network with the family in San Luis Potosí.

23. Chad Richardson, *Batos, Bolillos, Pochos, & Pelados: Class & Culture on the South Texas Border*, describes how the work of the undocumented is often so open-ended that any number of duties can be added without negotiation for additional pay.

24. Ivan Light, "The Ethnic Economy," in *The Handbook of Economic Sociology*, 2nd edition, eds. Neil J. Smesler and Richard Swedberg.

25. Michael J. Pisani and David W. Yoskowitz, "Opportunity Knocks: Entrepreneurship, Informality & Home Gardening in South Texas," *Journal of Borderlands Studies*, 21, no. 2 (2006): 59–76.

26. Ibid., 65.

27. Catalina Amuedo-Dorantes and Cynthia Bansak, "How Do Mexican Migrants Affect Public Coffers? Changes in the Utilization of and Contribution to Public Benefits of U.S. Border States," in *Labor Market Issues along the U.S.-Mexico Border*, eds. Marie T. Mora and Alberto Dávila, 160–174.

28. Ibid., 174.

29. The survey did not specifically ask for hourly wage figures, but we calculated these averages from reported income and reported time spent in informal and formal activities.

30. Passel and Cohn, "A Portrait of Unauthorized Immigrants in the United States," 17.

31. Kochhar, "Survey of Mexican Migrants: Part Three."

32. Rob Paral, "No Way In: US Immigration Policy Leaves Few Legal Options for Mexican Workers," http://www.ilw.com/articles/2005,1123-paral.shtm (accessed August 3, 2010).

33. Ibid.

34. Passel and Cohn, "A Portrait of Unauthorized Immigrants in the United States," 16.

35. U.S. Department of Labor, "A Demographic and Employment Profile of United States Farm Workers," http://www.doleta.gov/agworker/report9/toc .cfm (accessed March 21, 2010).

36. According to the 2003 American Community Survey, Mexicans comprised 30.7% of all foreign-born workers in the U.S., but amounted to 88.8% of the foreign-born labor force in farming, fishing, and forestry; 60.2% in construction and extraction; and 51.6% in building and grounds cleaning and maintenance. See U.S. Census Bureau, 2003 American Community Survey, http://www.census.gov/acs/www/ (accessed June 20, 2007).

37. Kochhar, "Survey of Mexican Migrants: Part Three."

38. Ibid.

39. Ibid.

40. Though this category embodies the popular stereotype of farm work-

ers, it represents only about 10% of the entire labor force of crop farm workers (USDA, Rural Labor, 2008: 5), with the other 90% living year round at or within commuting distance of their places of labor. See William Kandel, "A Profile of Hired Farmworkers, A 2008 Update," http://www.ers.usda.gov /Publications/ERR60/ERR60.pdf (accessed November 2, 2009).

41. Douglas Massey ["The Settlement Process Among Mexican Migrants to the United States: New Methods and Findings," in *Immigration Statistics: A Story of Neglect*, eds. Daniel B. Levine, Kenneth Hill, and Robert Warren] found that 91% of undocumented immigrants from rural areas became migrant workers during their first year in the U.S. Though this category represents a very large part of the jobs obtained by undocumented workers in the U.S., it has been declining in recent years.

42. According to the Child Labor Coalition, "The most antiquated aspect of the federal child labor laws is the division of the employment of youth into two categories: agricultural and non-agricultural labor. The result is that minors working in agriculture are less protected from exploitation and more exposed to hazardous employment than minors in non-agricultural employment. Children working as hired farm workers may work at younger ages, work in more hazardous occupations at younger ages, and work for more hours than other employed youth. Estimates of youth farm workers run as high as 800,000 in the $25 billion dollar agriculture industry." See Child Labor Coalition, "Weak and Inadequate State and Federal Child Labor Laws," http://www.stopchildlabor .org/USchildlabor/weaklaws.htm (accessed March 22, 2010).

43. Kochhar, "Survey of Mexican Migrants: Part Three," 23.

44. For a more comprehensive treatment of maids in South Texas, see Chapter 3 of Richardson, *Batos, Bolillos, Pochos, & Pelados*.

45. Kochhar, "Survey of Mexican Migrants: Part Three," 23.

46. In 2009, the Western Hemisphere Travel Initiative made crossing into the U.S. much more difficult. It was no longer as simple as declaring oneself an American citizen; the initiative required would-be crossers to show a U.S. passport or a passport card.

47. John C. Cross and Bruce D. Johnson, "Expanding Dual Labor Market Theory: Crack Dealers and the Informal Sector," *International Journal of Sociology and Social Policy* 20, nos. 1/2 (2000): 96–124.

48. Ibid.

49. Jeffrey M. Jones, "Fewer Americans Favor Cutting Back Immigration: Public as Likely to Favor Status Quo as to Favor Decreased Immigration," Gallup Poll, July 10, 2008, http://www.gallup.com/poll/108748/Fewer-Americans -Favor-Cutting-Back-Immigration.aspx (accessed February 1, 2010).

50. Lymari Morales, "Americans Return to Tougher Immigration Stance: More Want Immigration Decreased than Kept the Same or Increased," Gallup Poll, August 5, 2009 http://www.gallup.com/poll/122057/Americans-Return -Tougher-Immigration-Stance.aspx (accessed February 15, 2010).

51. Bryan J. Balin, "State Immigration Legislation and Immigrant Flows: An Analysis" (working paper, The Johns Hopkins University School of Advanced International Studies, 2008), https://jscholarship.library.jhu.edu/bit stream/handle/1774.2/32826/State%20Immigration%20Legislation%20and

%20Immigrant%20Flows%20032008.pdf;jsessionid=D0AA4490CF664C01C
D5D7CCA1D214FD9?sequence=4 (accessed on February 3, 2010).

52. Though not all Republicans are conservative and not all Democrats are liberal, of course, the tendency for these associations is quite strong.

53. Carole Keeton Strayhorn, "Undocumented Immigrants in Texas: A Financial Analysis of the Impact to the State Budget and Economy," Special Report from the Texas Comptroller, December 2006, http://www.window.state.tx.us/specialrpt/undocumented/undocumented.pdf (accessed July 13, 2007).

54. This letter is particularly interesting in that it is signed by economists from different fields, political affiliations, and ideologies.

55. Editorial, "Immigration Consensus," *The Wall Street Journal*, June 20, 2006.

56. For a further discussion, see Chad Richardson and Rosalva Resendiz, *On the Edge of the Law: Culture, Labor & Deviance on the South Texas Border*, especially Chapters 6 and 7.

57. This group was found to consist of Mexican Americans who had assimilated (or were trying to do so) into Anglo society and of Anglos who didn't want to be labeled as anything except "American." Both groups were clearly very conservative in their opinions and rejected traditional Mexican culture.

Chapter Five

1. An earlier (and considerably different) version of this chapter appears as Michael J. Pisani and Chad Richardson, "Cross-border Informal Entrepreneurs Across the South Texas–Northern Mexico Boundary," in *Entrepreneurship & Regional Development* within the special issue "Cross-border Entrepreneurship and Economic Development in Border Regions. " In this paper we explore the determinants of informal cross-border entrepreneurship through multivariate statistical analysis. We encourage those readers interested in a more advanced statistical treatment of the topic to consult this resource.

2. See, for example, Thomas L. Friedman, *The World Is Flat: A Brief History of the Twenty-First Century*.

3. Manfred B. Steger, *Globalisms: The Great Ideological Struggle of the Twenty-First Century*, 3rd Edition.

4. Harm De Blig, *The Power of Place: Geography, Destiny, and Globalization's Rough Landscape*.

5. Jagdish Bhagwati, *In Defense of Globalization*.

6. Martin Wolf, *Why Globalization Works*, 14.

7. Oscar J. Martínez, *Border People: Life and Society in the U.S.-Mexico Borderlands*, 59.

8. Briefly, Martínez (Ibid., 61) defines these groups as follows: 1) commuters are "people who cross the border on a daily basis to work in the neighboring nation"; 2) binational consumers are "people who do a substantial amount of shopping and/or consume numerous services in the neighboring nation"; 3) (im)migrants include a range of people, from those who pass by to those who settle; 4) winter residents or snow birds are those who winter in the region

while maintaining a residence in the interior U.S.; 5) biculturalists are "people whose lifestyles and mind-sets reflect two cultures"; and 6) binationalists are "biculturalists whose lives are deeply enmeshed in the societies of the two nations and who consequently have a strong international outlook." See Martínez for comprehensive coverage of the topic.

9. Donald W. Light, "From Migrant Enclaves to Mainstream: Reconceptualizing Informal Economic Behavior," *Theory and Society* 33, no. 6 (2004): 705–737.

10. Oscar J. Martínez, *Troublesome Border*, 52.

11. Peter Andreas and Thomas J. Biersteker, eds. *The Rebordering of North America: Integration and Exclusion in a New Security Context*, 1.

12. Alejandro Portes and William Haller, "The Informal Economy," in *The Handbook of Economic Sociology*, 2nd edition, eds. Neil J. Smesler and Richard Swedberg, 409.

13. Ibid., 412.

14. John W. Mogab, Michael J. Pisani, Kay E. McGlashan, Sharon Welkey, and Beth E. Wuest, "*Manifiesto*—The Texas Sales Tax Rebate and Cross-Border Mexican Shoppers: A Profile of Mexican Consumer Behavior at an In-land Texas Retail Center," *Texas Business Review* (October 2005): 1–5.

15. This rebate may be akin to the short sales tax holiday Texas offers to all shoppers in August, on specified back-to-school themed products. See John W. Mogab and Michael J. Pisani, "Shoppers' Perceptions of the State Sales Tax Holiday: A Case Study from Texas," *American Journal of Business* 22, no. 2 (2007): 45–56, for a fuller exploration of the topic.

16. This was increased from $400 in 2003. The period of time for this import limit is meant to be 30 days, but this is almost always ignored by customs agents, especially since it is difficult to keep track of each individual's imports.

17. Typically, if a U.S. Customs agent becomes aware of purchases of alcohol in Mexico, the buyers in automobiles will be instructed to declare it at a point as much as several hundred feet beyond the checkpoint. Since the declaration must be made to Texas state officials, however, most agents pay little or no attention to whether the shopper actually stops to make the declaration.

18. Occasionally, a tax holiday is declared and may last for a specific period of time; for example, winter *paisanos* or those Mexicans returning to Mexico for the Christmas holidays may be permitted to bring back goods beyond the specified duty-free amount, or some goods ranging up to $4,000 or more in value [e.g., computers] may be exempted.

19. Víctor Dávila, Nader Asgary, Gilberto de los Santos, and Vern Vincent, "The Effects of Government Restrictions on Outbound Tourist Expenditures," *Journal of Travel Research* 37 (February 1999): 285–290.

20. Perhaps, on average, one in ten entrants into Mexico receives a red light.

21. For north-bound traders, however, bribing a U.S. Customs officer is very risky. Those who attempt to do so may be subject to prison, fines, and confiscation of property.

22. Nelson Arteaga Botello and Adrian Lopez Rivera, "'Everything in this

Job Is Money': Inside the Mexican Police," *World Policy Journal* 17, no. 3 (2000): 61–70.

23. Ibid., 66.

24. Fidelis P. T. Duri, "Informal Negotiation of the Zimbabwe-Mozambique Border for Survival by Mutare's Marginalized People," *Journal of Developing Societies* 26, no. 2 (2010): 125–163.

25. Joan B. Anderson, "Causes of Growth in the Informal Labor Sector in Mexico's Northern Border Region," *Journal of Borderlands Studies* 3, no. 1 (1988): 1–12.

26. Joan B. Anderson and Martin de la Rosa, "Economic Survival Strategies of Poor Families on the Mexican Border," *Journal of Borderlands Studies* 6, no. 1(1991): 51–68.

27. Ibid.

28. Joan B. Anderson and James Gerber, *Fifty Years of Change on the U.S.-Mexico Border: Growth, Development, and Quality of Life.*

29. Kathleen A. Staudt, *Free Trade: Informal Economies at the U.S.-Mexican Border.*

30. Ibid., 88.

31. Ibid.,68.

32. Ibid., 73, 157.

33. Marie T. Mora and Alberto Dávila, "Mexican Immigrant Self-Employment Along the U.S.-Mexico Border: An Analysis of the 2000 Census Data," *Social Science Quarterly* 87, no. 1 (2006): 91–109, 99.

34. Martin Medina, "Informal Transborder Recycling on the U.S.-Mexico Border: The *Cartoneros* of Nuevo Laredo," *The Journal of Borderlands Studies* 16, no. 2 (2001): 19–40.

35. Minors under 15 applying for a border crossing card at the same time as their parents are charged only $14 (as of 2010).

36. U.S. Department of State, "Visitor Visas—Business and Pleasure," http://travel.state.gov/visa/temp/types/types_1262.html (accessed July 22, 2010).

37. Suad Ghaddar and Cynthia Brown. "The Cross-Border Mexican Shopper: A Profile," *Research Review* 12, no. 2 (2005): 46–50.

38. Prior to 2005, this visa was good for only 72 hours. Currently, if one travels beyond the secondary inspection port (station) and outside the borderlands "float zone", an additional visa is required (typically a form I-94).

39. Michael J. Pisani and David W. Yoskowitz, "'*Por Necesidad*'—Transnational Labor Movements, Informality and Wage Determination: An Exploratory Study of Maids on the U.S.-Mexican Border," *Journal of Borderlands Studies* 16, no. 1 (2001): 67–82, 75, 77.

40. Ibid., 79.

41. Live-in maids are much more restricted to a single home environment and so are more vulnerable to abuse and open-ended expectations.

42. Other popular used items in Mexico include electric clothes washers and dryers, televisions, window-mounted air conditioning units, and cars.

43. The results of the survey are illustrative rather than definitive because of the purposive nature of the sampling design.

44. Until 2009, undocumented individuals who could speak good English and maintain the correct "presence" were able to cross into the U.S. without having to show documents, simply by stating they were U.S. citizens. Since 2009, they need an official U.S.-issued passport or passport card.

45. After David G. Blanchflower and Andrew J. Oswald ["What Makes an Entrepreneur?" *Journal of Labor Economics* 16, no. 1 (1998): 26–60], we define entrepreneurship as individuals who work for themselves for a profit. Also, throughout the book we use entrepreneurship and self-employment interchangeably, as suggested by Ken Clark and Stephen Drinkwater in "Recent Trends in Minority Ethnic Entrepreneurship in Britain," *International Small Business Journal* 28, no. 2 (2010): 136–146.

46. For a fuller discussion of cross-border interaction, see Anderson and Gerber, *Fifty Years of Change on the U.S.-Mexico Border*, and Marie T. Mora and Alberto Dávila, eds., *Labor Market Issues along the U.S.-Mexico Border*. Additionally, even the mostly legal cross-border trade may resort to some elements of informality.

47. Typical formal-sector positions include food service, child care, manual labor, retail/customer service, *maquiladora* work, and medical assistant.

48. Texas Department of Public Safety—Public Information Office, "Recovery of Stolen Vehicles from Mexico Rises," January 30, 2002, http://www.txdps.state.tx.us/director_staff/public_information/pr013002.htm (accessed October 1, 2010).

49. Russell L. Gallahan, "Vehicle Theft and Recovery in Texas Cities along the United States-Mexico Border" (M.A. thesis, Texas State University, 1997), 24.

50. Ibid., 38.

51. Michael V. Miller, "Vehicle Theft Along the Texas-Mexico Border," *Journal of Borderlands Studies* 2, no. 2 (1987): 12–32; Russell L. Gallahan, "Vehicle Theft and Recovery in Texas Cities along the United States-Mexico Border," (M.A. thesis, Texas State University, 1997). According to Gallahan, the recovery rate within the United States in 1995 was 62%.

52. Martínez, *Border People*, 61.

53. In reality, of course, these two cannot be separated. Even though Mexico officially became part of a free-trade system, state-mandated restrictions that keep Mexicans from importing more than very small purchases make it possible for officials to solicit bribes.

Chapter Six

1. Peter M. Ward, *Colonias and Public Policy in Texas and Mexico: Urbanization by Stealth*, 90.

2. Colonia Initiatives Program of the Office of Texas Secretary of State, "Tracking the Progress of State-funded Projects that Benefit Colonias" (Final Report in Response to Senate Bill 827 by Senator Judith Zaffirini and Representative Ryan Guillen 79th Regular Session, Texas Legislature), http://www.sos.state.tx.us/border/forms/sb827_111706.pdf (accessed May 28, 2008).

3. Ibid., 16.

4. Ward, *Colonias and Public Policy*, 105.

5. Ariel Cisneros, "Texas Colonias: Housing and Infrastructure Issues," *The Border Economy*, 19–21.

6. Kingsley E. Haynes, *Colonias in the Lower Rio Grande Valley of South Texas: Summary Report*, 9.

7. Federal Reserve Bank of Dallas, "Texas Colonias: A Thumbnail Sketch of the Conditions, Issues, Challenges and Opportunities."

8. Actually, the use of the Cultural Practices Survey has the advantage of being more inclusive of the Valley population, since our survey of informal and underground activities included only people involved in informal or underground activities.

9. Only 4% of these self-employed colonia residents held second jobs in the formal sector. For another 14%, their self-employed colonia occupation represented a second job, outside of their full-time regular formal sector job. In the main, self-employed colonia residents were primarily informal sector participants.

10. See, for example, Alex Counts, *Small Loans, Big Dreams: How Nobel Prize Winner Muhammad Yunus and Microfinance Are Changing the World.*

11. We found that some colonias have a great deal of unity and social capital, while others do not. Those lacking in it have problems with gangs and vandalism. We suggest that the reasons behind this difference in colonia unity would make an excellent research topic.

12. Ward, *Colonias and Public Policy*, 7.

13. Ibid., 7.

14. Ibid.

15. Ronald J. Dutton, Minda Weldon, Jackilen Shannon, and Cheryl Bowcock, "Survey of Health and Environmental Conditions in Texas Border Counties and Colonias," June 2000, http://www.dshs.state.tx.us/borderhealth/pdf/EXECSUM.pdf (accessed August 12, 2002).

16. Ward, *Colonias and Public Policy*, 7, 8.

17. Peter Lloyd, *Slums of Hope.*

18. Ward, *Colonias and Public Policy*, 67.

19. Ibid.

20. Cecilia Guisti, *"Nuestra Casa* (Our House): A New Model for Self-help & Improvement along the Texas/Mexico Border," *Texas Business Review* (August 2008), 1–5.

21. One recent USDA report concluded that the cost of shelter plus utilities makes up 44% of the budget for a poor person. See Dean Jolliffe, "The Cost of Living and the Geographic Distribution of Poverty," *Economic Research Report* 26 (September 2006), http://www.ers.usda.gov/publications/err26/err26.pdf (accessed October 8, 2008).

22. Jean W. Parcher and Delbert G. Humberson, "CHIPS: A New Way to Monitor Colonias along the United States–Mexico Border," Open-File Report 2007–1230, http://pubs.usgs.gov/of/2007/1230/pdf/OFR2007-1230.pdf (accessed April 14, 2009).

23. Ward, *Colonias and Public Policy*, 99–100.

24. Parcher and Humberson, "CHIPS: A New Way to Monitor Colonias."

25. According to the Colonia Initiatives Program's report, "Tracking the Progress of State-funded Projects that Benefit Colonias," 90% of all Texas colonias can be found in these six counties.

26. Federal Reserve Bank of Dallas, "Texas Colonias," 8.

27. Dutton, Weldon, Shannon, and Bowcock, "Survey of Health and Environmental Conditions," 19.

28. Ibid., 14.

29. Lawrence E. Harrison, *Who Prospers? How Cultural Values Shape Economic and Political Success.*

30. Derived from the American Community Survey 2007–2009 3-year estimates (U.S. Census Bureau, http://www.census.gov), we find that 60.5% of the foreign born living in Cameron, Hidalgo, Starr, Webb, and Willacy counties possess less than a high school education. Another 17.6% of the foreign born in the same counties possess a high school education, so nearly 80% of the foreign born have educational attainment levels of high school or less. We believe that educational attainment rates are generally low in colonias because immigrants constitute a large proportion of the residents in colonias.

31. These data are available from the Texas Higher Education Coordinating Board (THECB), http://www.txhighereddata.org/.

32. Engaging Communities for College Readiness (ENCORE), "College Readiness in the Rio Grande Valley," 11–15.

33. Basic infrastructure typically follows well-organized colonias because well-organized residents understand how to apply political pressure to public officials.

Chapter Seven

1. U.S. Census Bureau, "Income, Poverty, and Health Insurance Coverage in the United States: 2004," 2005, http://www.census.gov/prod/2005pubs/p60 -229.pdf (accessed May 12, 2009).

2. Elena Bastida, H. Shelton Brown III, and José A. Pagán, "Persistent Disparities in the Use of Health Care Along the US–Mexico Border: An Ecological Perspective," *American Journal of Public Health* 98, no. 11 (2008): 1987–1995.

3. Atul Gawande, "The Cost Conundrum: What a Texas Town Can Teach Us about Health Care," *The New Yorker*, June 1, 2009.

4. According to Robert Pear ("Health Care Spending Disparities Stir a Fight," *The New York Times*, June 8, 2009), this article was used by President Obama as evidence of what was wrong with health care in the U.S. In addition, the article prompted a Texas congressman to call for an investigation by the GAO.

5. Jeiny Zapata and Raelene Shippee-Rice, "The Use of Folk Healing and Healers by Six Latinos Living in New England: A Preliminary Study," *The Journal of Rural Health* 10, no. 2 (1999): 136–142.

6. Derek DeLia and Joel Cantor, "Emergency Department Utilization

and Capacity," Robert Wood Johnson Foundation, http://www.rwjf.org/files /research/072109policysynthesis17.emergencyutilization.pdf (accessed October 2, 2009). On page 3, this report concludes that "Non-citizen residents of the United States use the ED [emergency department] at a rate that is much lower than the national average. Hispanic residents (regardless of citizenship) have ED utilization rates similar to the non-Hispanic white population." See also, Larry Ortiz, Lydia Arizmendi, and Llewellyn J. Cornelius, "Access to Health Care Among Latinos of Mexican Descent in Colonias in Two Texas Counties," *The Journal of Rural Health* 20, no. 3 (2004): 246–252.

7. John Sharp, "Bordering the Future: Challenges and Opportunities in the Texas Border Region," http://www.window.state.tx.us (accessed June 2, 2001).

8. Federico G. de Cosio and Andrés Boadella, "Demographic Factors Affecting the U.S.-Mexico Border Health Status," in *Life, Death, and In-Between on the U.S.-Mexico Border: Así Es La Vida*, ed. Martha O. Loustaunau and Mary Sanchez-Bane, 1.

9. James Pinkerton, "Health Care: Crisis at the Border. Poverty, Lack of Doctors Cloud Area's Future," *Houston Chronicle*, May 5, 2002.

10. Texas Department of State Health Services, "Demographic and Health Profile of Hidalgo County, 2001," Selected Fact Sheets, 2001, www.dshs.state. tx.us/borderhealth (accessed July 19, 2008).

11. Even the Heritage Foundation, a staunchly conservative organization, recognizes that the undocumented pay more in taxes than they receive in benefits. Robert Rector (in "Amnesty and Continued Low Skill Immigration Will Substantially Raise Welfare Costs and Poverty," http://www.heritage.org /research/reports/2006/05/amnesty-and-continued-low-skill-immigration -will-substantially-raise-welfare-costs-and-poverty [accessed September 12, 2008]), argues, "Overall, immigration is a net fiscal positive to the government's budget in the long run: the taxes immigrants pay exceed the costs of the services they receive."

12. Congressional Budget Office, "The Impact of Unauthorized Immigrants on the Budgets of State and Local Governments," http://www.cbo.gov /ftpdocs/87xx/doc8711/12-6-Immigration.pdf (accessed May 8, 2008).

13. Carole Keeton Strayhorn, "Undocumented Immigrants in Texas: A Financial Analysis of the Impact to the State Budget and Economy," http://www .window.state.tx.us/specialrpt/undocumented/undocumented.pdf (accessed July 13, 2007).

14. MGT of America, "Medical Emergency: Costs of Uncompensated Care in Southwest Border Counties," http://www.bordercounties.org/vertical /Sites/%7BB4A0F1FF-7823-4C95-8D7A-F5E400063C73%7D/uploads /%7BFAC57FA3-B310-4418-B2E7-B68A89976DC1%7D.PDF (accessed October 13, 2007).

15. Dana Goldman, James P. Smith, and Neeraj Sood, "Immigrants and the Cost of Medical Care," *Health Affairs* 25, no. 6 (2006): 1700–1711.

16. Congressional Budget Office, "The Impact of Unauthorized Immigrants on the Budgets of State and Local Governments," 9.

17. Madeleine Pelner Cosman, "Illegal Aliens and American Medicine," *Journal of American Physicians and Surgeons* 10, no. 1 (2005): 6–10.

18. The Emergency Medical Treatment and Active Labor Act passed by Congress in 1986 requires hospitals to provide emergency medical care to *anyone* needing emergency treatment.

19. Sarita Mohanty, Steffie Woolhandler, David U. Himmelstein, Susmita Pati, Olveen Carrasquillo, and David H. Bor, "Health Care Expenditures of Immigrants in the United States: A Nationally Representative Analysis," *American Journal of Public Health* 95, no. 8 (2005): 1431–1438.

20. DeLia and Cantor, "Emergency Department Utilization and Capacity," 3.

21. See, for example, Michael Seid, Donna Castañeda, Ronald Mize, Mirjana Zivkovic, and James W. Varni, "Crossing the Border for Health Care: Access and Primary Care Characteristics for Young Children of Latino Farm Workers along the US-Mexico Border," *Ambulatory Pediatrics* 3, no. 3 (2003): 121–130; Luis G. Escobedo and Victor M. Cardenas, "Utilization and Purchase of Medical Care Services in Mexico by Residents in the United States of America, 1998–1999," *Revista Panamericana de Salud Pública* 19, no. 5 (2006): 300–305; Eduardo P. Macias and Leo S. Morales, "Crossing the Border for Health Care," *Journal of Health Care for the Poor and Underserved* 12, no. 1 (2001): 77–87; Leticia Fernández and John Amastae, "Transborder Use of Medical Services among Mexican American Students in a U.S. Border University," *Journal of Borderlands Studies* 21, no. 2(2006): 77–87; Bastida, Brown, and Pagán, "Persistent Disparities in the Use of Health Care"; José O. Rivera, Melchor Ortiz, and Victor Cardenas, "Cross-Border Purchase of Medication and Health Care in a Sample of Residents of El Paso, Texas, and Ciudad Juarez, Mexico," *Journal of the National Medical Association* 101, no. 2 (2009): 167–173.

22. H. Shelton Brown III, José A. Pagán, and Elena Bastida, "International Competition and the Demand for Health Insurance in the US: Evidence from the Texas-Mexico Border Region," *International Journal of Health Care Finance and Economics* 9, no. 1 (2009): 25–38.

23. Bastida, Brown, and Pagán, "Persistent Disparities in the Use of Health Care," 1987.

24. Rivera, Ortiz, and Cardenas, "Cross-Border Purchase of Medication and Health Care," 167.

25. This study ran from 2007 to 2010, with Drs. José Pagán, Dejun Su, and Chad Richardson as co-principal investigators. The study was funded by the Agency for Healthcare Research and Quality to assess the use of health care in Mexico by South Texas residents. For comparison purposes, we also included 200 residents from Houston and San Antonio. Winter Texans were not purposely sought out for this survey; hence we do not explicitly discuss this subgroup. But this group is discussed at length in Richardson's *Batos, Bolillos, Pochos, and Pelados: Class and Culture on the South Texas Border*, and we refer interested readers to this resource.

26. William P. Bro, "Importation of Prescription Drugs and Risks to Patient Safety," *California Western International Law Journal* 36, no. 1 (2005): 105–116.

27. Tom McGinnis, director of pharmacy affairs for the FDA, as quoted in Kathleen Doheny, "Think Twice Before Buying Prescription Drugs in

Mexico," *Los Angeles Times*, August 8, 2004, http://www.latimes.com/features /health/medicine/la-tr-healthy8aug08,1,2053803.column (accessed August 24, 2007).

28. The interstate shipment, including importation, of unapproved new drugs is prohibited in the U.S. ("Unapproved" new drugs are any medicines that have not received the FDA's approval and include foreign-made versions of U.S.-approved drugs.) See Marvin Shepherd, director of the Center for Pharmacoeconomic Studies at the University of Texas at Austin, as cited in John M. Taylor, "Imported Drugs," Testimony before the U.S. Senate Committee on Health, Education, Labor and Pensions. http://www.fda.gov/NewsEvents /Testimony/ucm113825.htm (accessed August 23, 2007). Taylor is Associate Commissioner for Regulatory Affairs, U.S. Food and Drug Administration.

29. The United States Pharmacopeia (USP) is an official public standards-setting authority for all prescription and over-the-counter medicines. See Kelly L. Karlage and Paul B. Mydral, "Comparison of Three Pharmaceutical Products Obtained from Mexico and the United States: A Case Study," *Drug Development and Industrial Pharmacy* 31, no. 10 (2005): 993–1000.

30. A.N. Turner, C. Ellertson, S. Thomas, and S. Garcia, "Diagnosis and Treatment of Presumed STIs at Mexican Pharmacies: Survey Results from a Random Sample of Mexico City Pharmacy Attendants," *Sexually Transmitted Infections* 79, no. 3 (2003): 224–228.

31. Our survey did not request information about purchasing drugs from Mexico through the Internet, so we are unable to include such individuals in these figures.

32. This statistical procedure predicts the likelihood of an event occurring, in this case, the odds of purchasing medication in Mexico.

33. In this logistic regression model, "low" is the referent category.

34. Sharp, "Bordering the Future," 105.

35. Chad Richardson and Rosalva Resendiz, *On the Edge of the Law: Culture, Labor & Deviance on the South Texas Border.*

36. Richardson and Resendiz (*On the Edge of the Law*) found that only 17% of Valley residents reported that they, their friends, or their family members would use a *curandero*, and then only if regular doctors were unable to help.

37. In other parts of the U.S., these "folk pharmacies" are often called *botánicas* or *boticas*. Alternative medical treatments found in hierberías are often used to treat such conditions as diabetes, arthritis, and menstrual pain. They also sell products designed to attract love, bring good luck or wealth, and deflect jealousy or other "evils."

38. The FDA regulates dietary supplements under the Dietary Supplement Health and Education Act of 1994 (DSHEA). The FDA is responsible for taking action against any unsafe dietary supplement product after it reaches the market. Generally, manufacturers do not need to register their products with the FDA or get FDA approval before producing or selling dietary supplements. A call (August 7, 2009) by one of the authors to the FDA about *hierberías* was met with the response, "They are not within the purview of the FDA."

39. Kevin Seiff, "Midwives Struggle against New Fears and Horror Stories among Patients," *The Brownsville Herald*, August 23, 2008.

40. Castelano, et al. v. Clinton, et al., 1, http://travel.state.gov/_res/docs/pdf/Castelano_Final_Notice_English_3.pdf (accessed November 5, 2011).

41. U.S. Congress (House), "Prescription Drug Pricing in the 7th Congressional District of Maryland: An International Price Comparison," Minority Staff Report, Committee on Government Reform and Oversight, August 10, 1999, http://cummings.house.gov/pdf/intl.pdf (accessed January 7, 2008).

42. Rivera, Ortiz, and Cardenas, "Cross-Border Purchase of Medication and Health Care," 167.

43. For a good overview of the implications of this policy, see Anne Dunkelberg, Stacey Pouge, and Kymberlie Quong Charles, "What Every Texan Should Know: Health Care Reform Law," Center for Public Policy Priorities, http://www.cppp.org/files/3/2010_09_June_WhatsIntheLaw.pdf (accessed June 2, 2010).

Chapter Eight

1. Here we use the term *underground* to mean both illicit economic activities and those hidden from government purview.

2. Margaret C. Simms, Karina Fortuny, and Everett Henderson, "Racial and Ethnic Disparities Among Low-Income Families," http://www.urban.org/uploadedpdf/411936_racialandethnic.pdf (accessed November 18, 2009).

3. Frances Deviney and Florencia Gutierrez, "Texas Kids Count: Our Border, Our Future," http://www.cppp.org/files/KC/BorderFamilies%28Scrn%29.pdf (accessed December 6, 2009).

4. U.S. Immigration and Customs Enforcement, "50 Indicted as Part of National Marriage Fraud Scheme—Individuals Entered into Sham Marriages to Gain Citizenship," news release, August 11, 2009, http://www.ice.gov/pi/nr/0908/090811cincinatti.htm (accessed August 9, 2010).

5. This account also appears in Chad Richardson and Rosalva Resendiz, *On the Edge of the Law: Culture, Labor & Deviance on the South Texas Border*, 147.

6. Carmen DeNavas-Walt, Bernadette D. Proctor, and Jessica Smith, "Income, Poverty, and Health Insurance Coverage in the United States: 2007," 25, http://www.census.gov/prod/2008pubs/p60-235.pdf (accessed August 9, 2010).

7. In 2008, 750,959 U.S. families with one adult were receiving TANF. Of these families, 15,978 (only 2.1%) were in Texas. See U.S. Department of Health and Human Services, Administration for Children & Families, "Table 6—Temporary Assistance for Needy Families—Active Cases Percent Distribution of TANF Families with One Adult by Number of Recipient Children, October 2007–September 2008," http://www.acf.hhs.gov/programs/ofa/character/FY2008/tab06.htm (accessed May 28, 2010).

8. Center for Public Policy Priorities, "Who Pays Texas Taxes?" http://www.cppp.org/files/7/POP%20284%20taxincidence.pdf (accessed August 26, 2008).

9. Randolph Capps, Nancy M. Pindus, Kathleen Snyder, and Jacob Leos-Urbel, "Recent Changes in Texas Welfare and Work, Child Care, and Child

Welfare Systems," The Urban Institute, http://www.urban.org/UploadedPDF/TX_update.pdf (accessed August 25, 2008).

10. Janet Elliott, Terri Langford, and Chase Davis, "The State of Texas: The Cost of Cutting Welfare," *The Houston Chronicle*, January 28, 2007.

11. National Center for Children in Poverty, "Texas: Food Stamps," www.nccp.org/profiles/TX_profile_29.html (accessed September 24, 2009).

12. Shelia R. Zedlewski and Ei Yin Mon, "Many Low-Income Working Families Turn to the Supplemental Nutrition Assistance Program for Help," http://www.urban.org/UploadedPDF/411938_snapforhelp.pdf (accessed September 22, 2009).

13. Brian Thevenot, "Bureaucratic Delays Create Huge Food Stamp Backlog," *The Texas Tribune*, December 7, 2009, http://www.texastribune.org/texas-issues/food-stamps-program/bureaucratic-delays-create-huge-food-stamp-backlog/ (accessed January 14, 2010).

14. According to Anne Dunkelberg ("Texas Medicaid and CHIP Enrollment Update," Center for Public Policy Priorities, http://www.cppp.org/research.php?aid=575 [accessed November 25, 2006]) of the Center for Public Policy Priorities, the limited use of public benefits in Texas is due, in large part, to the fact that Texas currently contracts with private companies to perform various, discrete functions related to the administration of public benefit programs (including designing computer systems, operating employment and training programs, and processing Medicaid claims). While the state claims that outsourcing increases efficiency, reduces costs, and improves client services, critics argue that outsourcing reduces accountability for the use of public funds and increases the potential for fraud, financial conflicts of interest, and cost overruns.

15. Robert E. Robertson, "Food Stamp Program: Program Integrity and Participation Challenges," http://www.gao.gov/new.items/d01881t.pdf (accessed August 23, 2009).

16. This generally means that even a family with an income under the poverty line can be disqualified for making "too much money"—even if their total income might still leave them below the official poverty line. In 2009, the official poverty line for a family of three was $18,310; see U.S. Department of Health and Human Services, "The 2009 HHS Poverty Guidelines," http://aspe.hhs.gov/poverty/09poverty.shtml (accessed August 4, 2010).

17. See the Texas Department of Human Services, "Texas Food Stamp Corrective Action Plan," www.window.state.tx.us/tpr/tpr4/c6.fr/c601.html (accessed March 12, 2007). It is very difficult to determine from more recent reports how much welfare fraud is detected in Texas. Often, the figures include Medicaid fraud and vendor fraud, almost all of which is perpetrated by medical businesses and stores rather than by low-income recipients of welfare.

18. U.S. General Accounting Office, "Illegal Aliens: Extent of Welfare Benefits Received on Behalf of U.S. Citizen Children," http://www.gao.gov/archive/1998/he98030.pdf (accessed December 10, 2008).

19. In our Informal and Underground Survey, 58.1% of *underground* participants earning a household income of over $40,000 a year reported receiving

some form of government assistance, making them (as a category) not only the best paid, but also the most abusive of welfare.

20. National Center for Children in Poverty, "Texas: Demographics of Low-Income Children," http://www.nccp.org/profiles/TX_profile_6.html (accessed November 18, 2009).

21. Richard E. Mantovani and Carol Olander, "The Extent of Trafficking in the Food Stamp Program, 2002–2005," http://www.fns.usda.gov/ora /MENU/published/SNAP/FILES/ProgramIntegrity/Trafficking2005.pdf (accessed November 11, 2009).

22. U.S. Department of Labor, "A Demographic and Employment Profile of United States Farm Workers," http://www.doleta.gov/agworker/report9/toc .cfm (accessed March 21, 2010).

23. Alejandro Portes and William Haller, "The Informal Economy," in *The Handbook of Economic Sociology*, 2nd edition, ed. Neil J. Smesler and Richard Swedberg, 409.

24. Robert K. Merton, *Social Theory and Social Structure*, 213; Peter M. Blau and Marshall W. Meyer, *Bureaucracy in Modern Society*, 120.

25. Robert K. Merton, "Social Structure and Anomie," in *Deviant Behavior: A Text-Reader in the Sociology of Deviance*, 3rd edition, ed. Delos H. Kelly, 132.

26. Ibid., 138.

Conclusion

1. Samuel Huntington, *Who Are We? The Challenge to America's National Identity*, 246.

2. Joe R Feagin, *Racist America: Roots, Current Realities, and Future Reparations*.

3. Pew Hispanic Center, "2002 National Survey of Latinos," 31–33, http:// pewhispanic.org/files/reports/15.pdf (accessed March 2, 2011).

4. Luis R. Fraga, et al., "Latino National Survey (LNS), 2006." Interuniversity Consortium for Political and Social Research/Resource Center for Minority Data, http://www.icpsr.umich.edu/icpsrweb/RCMD/studies/20862 (accessed March 5, 2011).

5. We suspect that this difference results from the greater propensity of young Latino men to experience problems with the police, rather than from a perceived mistreatment across all age groups.

6. Tim Wadsworth, "Is Immigration Responsible for the Crime Drop? An Assessment of the Influence of Immigration on Changes in Violent Crime Between 1990 and 2000," *Social Science Quarterly*, 91, no. 2 (2010): 531–553.

7. David Spener, *Clandestine Crossings: Migrants and Coyotes on the Texas-Mexico Border*.

8. Suad Ghaddar and Cynthia Brown, "The Cross-Border Mexican Shopper: A Profile," *Research Review* 12, no. 2 (2005): 48.

9. Jerry Thompson, *Cortina: Defending the Mexican Name in Texas*, 23.

10. John A. Adams, Jr., *Conflict & Commerce on the Rio Grande: Laredo, 1755–1955*, 85–86.

11. Robert D. Kaplan, "History Moving North," *The Atlantic Monthly* 279, no. 2 (1997): 22.

12. Carlos Fuentes, "Perspective on Immigration: Why Damn a Great State Resource?" *Los Angeles Times*, September 28, 1994, http://articles.latimes.com/1994-09-28/local/me-43798_1_united-states (accessed September 16, 2010).

13. See *Los Angeles Times*, "How Many Have Died in Mexico's Drug War?" June 7, 2011, http://latimesblogs.latimes.com/laplaza/2011/06/Mexico-war-dead-update-figures-40000.html (accessed November 6, 2011); U.S. Department of Defense, "U.S. Casualty Status," November 3, 2011, http://www.defense.gov/news/casualty.pdf (accessed November 6, 2011).

Bibliography

Adams, John A., Jr. *Conflict & Commerce on the Rio Grande: Laredo, 1755–1955.* College Station: Texas A&M University Press, 2008.

Aguilera, Michael B., and Douglas S. Massey. "Social Capital and the Wages of Mexican Migrants: New Hypotheses and Tests." *Social Forces* 82, no. 2 (2003): 671–701.

Amuedo-Dorantes, Catalina and Cynthia Bansak. "How Do Mexican Migrants Affect Public Coffers? Changes in the Utilization of and Contribution to Public Benefits of U.S. Border States." In *Labor Market Issues along the U.S.-Mexico Border.* Edited by Marie T. Mora and Alberto Dávila, 160–174. Tucson: The University of Arizona Press, 2009.

Anderson, Joan B. "Causes of Growth in the Informal Labor Sector in Mexico's Northern Border Region." *Journal of Borderlands Studies* 3, no. 1 (1988): 1–12.

Anderson, Joan B., and James Gerber. *Fifty Years of Change on the U.S.-Mexico Border: Growth, Development, and Quality of Life.* Austin: University of Texas Press, 2008.

Anderson, Joan B., and Martin de la Rosa. "Economic Survival Strategies of Poor Families on the Mexican Border." *Journal of Borderlands Studies* 6, no. 1 (1991): 51–68.

Andreas, Peter, and Thomas J. Biersteker, ed. *The Rebordering of North America: Integration and Exclusion in a New Security Context.* New York: Routledge, 2003.

Arana, Gabriel. "The Border Violence Myth." *The Nation,* May 27, 2009. http://www.thenation.com/article/border-violence-myth (accessed July 24, 2010).

Arreola, Daniel D. *Tejano South Texas: A Mexican American Cultural Province.* Austin: University of Texas Press, 2002.

Arteaga Botello, Nelson, and Adrian Lopez Rivera. "Everything in this Job Is Money: Inside the Mexican Police." *World Policy Journal* 17, no. 3 (2000): 61–70.

Balin, Bryan J. State Immigration Legislation and Immigrant Flows: An Analysis. Working Paper, The Johns Hopkins University School of Advanced

International Studies. https://jscholarship.library.jhu.edu/bitstream/handle
/1774.2/32826/State%20Immigration%20Legislation%20and%20Immigran
t%20Flows%20032008.pdf;jsessionid=D0AA4490CF664C01CD5D7CCA1
D214FD9?sequence=4 (accessed February 3, 2010).

Bajada, Christopher, and Freidrich Schneider, eds. *Size, Causes and Consequences of the Underground Economy: An International Perspective.* Aldershot, U.K.: Ashgate, 2005.

———. "Introduction." In *Size, Causes and Consequences of the Underground Economy: An International Perspective.* Edited by Christopher Bajada and Freidrich Schneider, 1–11. Aldershot, U.K.: Ashgate, 2005.

Bastida, Elena, H. Shelton Brown III, and José A. Pagán. "Persistent Disparities in the Use of Health Care Along the US–Mexico Border: An Ecological Perspective." *American Journal of Public Health* 98, no. 11 (2008): 1987–1995.

Becker, Andrew. "Southwest Border Corruption Cases Continue to Rise." *Center for Investigative Reporting*, November 20, 2009. http://www.centerforin-vestigativereporting.org/blogpost/20091120southwestbordercorruption casescontinuetorise (accessed December 12, 2009).

Benería, Lourdes. "Subcontracting and Employment Dynamics in Mexico City." In *The Informal Economy: Studies in Advanced and Less Developed Countries.* Edited by Alejandro Portes, Manual Castells and Lauren A. Benton, 173–188. Baltimore, Md.: The John Hopkins University Press, 1989.

Bhagwati, Jagdish. *In Defense of Globalization.* New York: Oxford University Press, 2004.

Bienefeld, Manfred. "The Informal Sector and Peripheral Capitalism: The Case of Tanzania." *Bulletin of the Institute of Development Studies* 6 (February 1975): 53–73.

Blanchflower, David. G., and Andrew J. Oswald. "What Makes an Entrepreneur?" *Journal of Labor Economics* 16, no. 1 (1998): 26–60.

Blau, Peter M., and Marshall W. Meyer. *Bureaucracy in Modern Society*, 3rd edition. New York: Random House, 1987.

Borjas, George J., and Lawrence F. Katz. "The Evolution of the Mexican-Born Workforce in the United States." *In Mexican Immigration to the United States*, ed. George J. Borjas, 13–55. Chicago, Ill.: The University of Chicago Press, 2007.

Bourdieu, Pierre. "The Forms of Capital." In *Handbook of Theory and Research for the Sociology of Education*, ed. John G. Richardson, 241–258. New York: Greenwood, 1985.

———. "Cultural Reproduction and Social Reproduction." In *Power and Ideology in Education.* Edited by J. Karabel and A. H. Halsey, 487–511. New York: Oxford University Press, 1977.

Brannon, Jeffrey T., Wilke D. English, and Patricia Kriner. "Commercial Banking on the U.S.-Mexico Border." *Journal of Borderlands Studies* 2, no. 1 (1987): 17–35.

Bro, William P. "Importation of Prescription Drugs and Risks to Patient Safety." *California Western International Law Journal* 36, no. 1 (2005): 105–116.

Brown III, H. Shelton, José A. Pagán, and Elena Bastida. "International Competition and the Demand for Health Insurance in the US: Evidence from the Texas-Mexico Border Region." *International Journal of Health Care Finance and Economics* 9, no. 1 (2009): 25–38.

Burton, Fred, and Ben West. "The Barrio Azteca Trial and the Prison Gang-Cartel Interface." *STRATFOR Global Security and Intelligence Report.* http://www.stratfor.com/weekly/20081119_barrio_azteca_trial_and_prison_gang_cartel_interface (accessed January 14, 2009).

Bush, George W. "President Bush Addresses the Nation on Immigration Reform." White House, Office of the Press Secretary, May 15, 2006. http://georgewbush-whitehouse.archives.gov/news/releases/2006/05/20060515-8.html (accessed March 8, 2007).

Capps, Randolph, Nancy M. Pindus, Kathleen Snyder, and Jacob Leos-Urbel. "Recent Changes in Texas Welfare and Work, Child Care, and Child Welfare Systems." The Urban Institute. http://www.urban.org/UploadedPDF/TX_update.pdf (accessed August 25, 2008).

Castelano, et al. v Clinton, et al., "Notice of Final Settlement Agreement in a Class Action," Civil Action No. CA M08057 in the U.S. District Court for the Southern District of Texas (2009). http://travel.state.gov/_res/docs/pdf/Castelano_Final_Notice_English_3.pdf (accessed November 5, 2011).

Centeno, Miguel A., and Alejandro Portes. "The Informal Economy in the Shadow of the State." In *Out of the Shadows: Political Action and the Informal Economy in Latin America.* Edited by Patricia Fernandez-Kelly and Jon Shefner, 23–48. University Park: The Pennsylvania State University Press, 2006.

———. "World Underneath: The Origins, Dynamics, and Effects of the Informal Economy." In *The Informal Economy: Studies in Advanced and Less Developed Countries.* Edited by Alejandro Portes, Manuel Castells and Lauran Benton, 11–37. Baltimore, Md.: The Johns Hopkins University Press, 1989.

Center for Public Policy Priorities. "Who Pays Texas Taxes?" http://www.cppp.org/files/7/POP%20284%20taxincidence.pdf (accessed August 26, 2008).

Child Labor Coalition. "Weak and Inadequate State and Federal Child Labor Laws." http://www.stopchildlabor.org/USchildlabor/weaklaws.htm (accessed March 22, 2010).

Cisneros, Ariel. "Texas Colonias: Housing and Infrastructure Issues." The Border Economy, 19–21. Dallas, Tx.: Federal Reserve Bank of Dallas, June 2001.

Clark, Ken, and Stephen Drinkwater. "Recent Trends in Minority Ethnic Entrepreneurship in Britain." *International Small Business Journal* 28, no. 2 (2010): 136–146.

Collins, Randall. *Weberian Sociological Theory.* Cambridge, Mass.: Cambridge University Press, 1986.

Colonia Initiatives Program of the Office of the Texas Secretary of State. "Tracking the Progress of State-funded Projects that Benefit Colonias" (Final Report in Response to Senate Bill 827 by Senator Judith Zaffirini and Representative Ryan Guillen, 79th Regular Session, Texas Legislature). http://www.sos.state.tx.us/border/forms/sb827_111706.pdf (accessed May 28, 2008).

Congressional Budget Office. "The Impact of Unauthorized Immigrants on the Budgets of State and Local Governments." http://www.cbo.gov/ftpdocs /87xx/doc8711/12-6-Immigration.pdf (accessed May 8, 2008).

Coppock, Mike. "The Republic of the Rio Grande." *Wild West*, December 2005: 3. http://www.historynet.com/the-republic-of-the-rio-grande.htm/3 (accessed September 27, 2010).

Corbiscello, G. V. "Border Crossings: A Look at the Very Real Threat of Cross Border Gangs to the U.S." *Journal of Gang Research* 15, no. 2 (2008): 33–52.

Cosman, Madeleine Pelner. "Illegal Aliens and American Medicine." *Journal of American Physicians and Surgeons* 10, no. 1 (2005): 6–10.

Counts, Alex. *Small Loans, Big Dreams: How Nobel Prize Winner Muhammad Yunus and Microfinance are Changing the World.* Hoboken, N.J.: John Wiley & Sons, Inc., 2008.

Cross, John C. "Passing the Buck: Risk Avoidance and Risk Management in the Illegal/Informal Drug Trade." *International Journal of Sociology and Social Policy* 20, nos. 9/10 (2000): 68–91.

Cross, John C., and Bruce D. Johnson. "Expanding Dual Labor Market Theory: Crack Dealers and the Informal Sector." *International Journal of Sociology and Social Policy* 20, nos. 1/2 (2000): 96–136.

Cross, John C., and Sergio Peña. "Risk and Regulation in Informal and Illegal Markets." In *Out of the Shadows: Political Action and the Informal Economy in Latin America*, ed. Patricia Fernandez-Kelly and Jon Shefner, 49–86. University Park: The Pennsylvania State University Press, 2006.

Dabla-Norris, Era, Mark Gradstein, and Gabriela Inchauste. "What Causes Firms to Hide Output? The Determinants of Informality." IMF Working Paper, August 2005, no. 160.

Dávila, Alberto, and Marie T. Mora. "English-Language Skills and the Earnings of Self-Employed Immigrants in the United States: A Note." *Industrial Relations* 43, no. 2 (2004): 386–391.

———. "English Skills, Earnings and the Occupational Sorting of Mexican Americans Working along the US-Mexico Border." *International Migration Review* 34, no. 1 (2000): 133–157.

Dávila, Alberto, Marie T. Mora, and Alma D. Hales. "Earned Income Along the U.S.-Mexico Border." In *Labor Market Issues Along the U.S.-Mexico Border*, ed. Marie T. Mora and Alberto Dávila, 107–120. Tucson: The University of Arizona Press, 2009.

Dávila, Víctor, Nader Asgary, Gilberto de los Santos, and Vern Vincent. "The Effects of Government Restrictions on Outbound Tourist Expenditures." *Journal of Travel Research* 37 (February 1999): 285–290.

De Blig, Harm. *The Power of Place: Geography, Destiny, and Globalization's Rough Landscape.* New York: Oxford University Press, 2009.

De Cosio, Federico G., and Andrés Boadella. "Demographic Factors Affecting the U.S.-Mexico Border Health Status." In *Life, Death, and In-Between on the U.S.-Mexico Border: Así Es La Vida*, edited by Martha O. Loustaunau and Mary Sanchez-Bane, 1–22. Westport, Conn.: Bergin & Garvey, 1999.

DeLia, Derek, and Joel Cantor. "Emergency Department Utilization and Capacity." Research Synthesis Report, No. 17, Robert Wood Johnson Foundation. http://www.rwjf.org/files/research/072109policysynthesis17.emergency utilization.pdf (accessed October 2, 2009).

DeNavas-Walt, Carmen, Bernadette D. Proctor, and Jessica Smith. "Income, Poverty, and Health Insurance Coverage in the United States: 2007." U.S. Census Bureau, Current Population Reports, 25. http://www.census.gov /prod/2008pubs/p60-235.pdf (accessed August 9, 2010).

De Soto, Hernando. *The Other Path: The Informal Revolution.* New York: Harper & Row, 1989.

Deviney, Frances, and Florencia Gutierrez. "Texas Kids Count: Our Border; Our Future." Center for Public Policy Priorities, http://www.cppp.org/files /KC/BorderFamilies%28Scrn%29.pdf (accessed December 6, 2009).

Doheny, Kathleen. "Think Twice Before Buying Prescription Drugs in Mexico." *Los Angeles Times,* August 8, 2004. http://www.latimes.com /features/health/medicine/la-tr-healthy8aug08,1,2053803.column (accessed August 24, 2007).

Donato, Katherine M., and Evelyn Patterson. "Women and Men on the Move: Undocumented Border Crossing." In *Crossing the Border: Research from the Mexican Migration Project.* Edited by Jorge Durand and Douglas S. Massey, 111–144. New York: Russell Sage Foundation, 2004.

Douglas, James R. "Juan Cortina: *el Caudillo de la Frontera.*" M.A. Thesis, University of Texas. 1987.

Duncan, Brian, V. Joseph Hotz, and Stepehn J. Trejo. "Hispanics in the U.S. Labor Market." In *Hispanics and the Future of America.* Edited by Marta Tienda and Faith Mitchell, 228–290. Washington, D.C.: The National Academic Press, 2006.

Duncan, Brian, and Stephen J. Trejo. "Ethnic Identification, Intermarriage, and Unmeasured Progress by Mexican Americans." In *Mexican Immigration to the United States,* ed. George J. Borjas, 229–267. Chicago, Ill.: University of Chicago Press, 2007.

Dunkelberg, Anne. "Texas Medicaid and CHIP Enrollment Update." Center for Public Policy Priorities, October 24, 2006. http://www.cppp.org /research.php?aid=575 (accessed November 25, 2006).

Dunkelberg, Anne, Stacey Pouge, and Kymberlie Quong Charles. "What Every Texan Should Know: Health Care Reform Law." Center for Public Policy Priorities. http://www.cppp.org/files/3/2010_09_June_WhatsIntheLaw.pdf (accessed June 2, 2010).

Duri, Fidelis P. T. "Informal Negotiation of the Zimbabwe-Mozambique Border for Survival by Mutare's Marginalized People." *Journal of Developing Societies* 26, no. 2 (2010): 125–163.

Dutton, Ronald J., Minda Weldon, Jackilen Shannon, and Cheryl Bowcock. "Survey of Health and Environmental Conditions in Texas Border Counties and Colonias." Office of Border Health, Texas Department of Health. http://www.dshs.state.tx.us/borderhealth/pdf/EXECSUM.pdf (accessed August 12, 2002).

Ellard, Charles J., and Jerry Prock. "A Comparison of Border and Non-Border Banks in Texas." *Journal of Borderlands Studies* 5, no. 2 (1990): 69–80.

Elliott, Janet, Terri Langford, and Chase Davis. "The State of Texas: The Cost of Cutting Welfare." *The Houston Chronicle*, January 28, 2007.

Emmott, Robin. "Drug Smugglers Bribing U.S. Agents on Mexico Border." *Reuters*, July 15, 2008. http://www.reuters.com/article/idUSN15311994 (accessed January 18, 2010).

Engaging Communities for College Readiness (ENCORE). "College Readiness in the Rio Grande Valley" (An ENCORE Research Report to the Bill & Melinda Gates Foundation & Texas Valley Communities Foundation). Edinburg, Tx.: ENCORE, 2008.

Escobedo, Luis G., and Victor M. Cardenas. "Utilization and Purchase of Medical Care Services in Mexico by Residents in the United States of America, 1998–1999." *Revista Panamericana de Salud Pública* 19, no. 5 (2006): 300–305.

Feagin, Joe R. *Racist America: Roots, Current Realities, and Future Reparations.* New York, Routledge, 2010.

Federal Reserve Bank of Dallas. "Texas Colonias: A Thumbnail Sketch of the Conditions, Issues, Challenges and Opportunities." n.d. http://www.dallas fed.org/ca/pubs/colonias.pdf.

Feige, Edgar L. "Defining and Estimating Underground and Informal Economies: The New Institutional Economics Approach." *World Development* 18, no. 7 (1990): 989–1002.

Fernández, Leticia, and John Amastae. "Transborder Use of Medical Services among Mexican American Students in a U.S. Border University." *Journal of Borderlands Studies* 21, no. 2 (2006): 77–87.

Flemming, Matthew H., John Roman, and Graham Farrell. "The Shadow Economy." *Journal of International Affairs* 53, no. 2 (2000): 387–409.

Ford, John S. *Rip Ford's Texas.* Edited by Stephen B. Oates. Austin: University of Texas Press, 1963.

Fraga, Luis R., John A. Garcia, Rodney Hero, Michael Jones-Correa, Valerie Martinez-Ebers, and Gary M. Segura. "Latino National Survey (LNS), 2006." Inter-university Consortium for Political and Social Research/Resource Center for Minority Data. http://www.icpsr.umich.edu/icpsrweb/RCMD/studies/20862 (accessed March 5, 2011).

Friedman, Thomas L. *The World Is Flat: A Brief History of the Twenty-First Century.* New York: Farrar, Strauss and Giroux, 2005.

Fuentes, Carlos. "Perspective on Immigration: Why Damn a Great State Resource?" *Los Angeles Times*, September 28, 1994. http://articles.latimes.com/1994-09-28/local/me-43798_1_united-states (accessed September 16, 2010).

Gallahan, Russell L. "Vehicle Theft and Recovery in Texas Cities along the United States–Mexico Border." M.A. thesis, Texas State University, 1997.

Gawande, Atul. "The Cost Conundrum: What a Texas Town Can Teach Us about Health Care." *The New Yorker*, June 1, 2009. http://www.newyorker.com/reporting/2009/06/01/090601fa_fact_gawande?currentPage=all (accessed September 23, 2009).

Ghaddar, Suad, and Cynthia Brown. "The Cross-Border Mexican Shopper: A Profile." *Research Review* 12, no. 2 (2005): 46–50.

Goldman, Dana, James P. Smith, and Neeraj Sood. "Immigrants and the Cost of Medical Care." *Health Affairs* 25, no. 6 (2006): 1700–1711.

Guillermoprieto, Alma. "Mexico's Shocking New Saints." *National Geographic* 217, no. 5 (2010): 54–73.

Guisti, Cecilia. "*Nuestra Casa* (Our House): A New Model for Self-help & Improvement along the Texas/Mexico Border." *Texas Business Review* (August 2008), 1–5.

Gurtoo, Anjula, and Colin C. Williams. "Entrepreneurship and the Informal Sector." *Entrepreneurship and Innovation*, 10, no. 1 (2009): 55–62.

Gutmann, Peter M. "Statistical Illusions, Mistaken Policies." *Challenge* 22, no. 5 (1979): 14–17.

Harris, Charles H., and Louis R. Sadler. *The Texas Rangers and the Mexican Revolution: The Bloodiest Decade 1910 to 1920*. Albuquerque: University of New Mexico Press, 2004.

Harrison, Lawrence E. *Who Prospers? How Cultural Values Shape Economic and Political Success*. New York: Basic Books, 1992.

Hart, Keith. "Informal Income Opportunities and Urban Employment in Ghana." *Journal of Modern African Studies* 11, no. 1 (1973): 61–89.

———. "Small Scale Entrepreneurs in Ghana and Development Planning." *Journal of Development Planning* 6, (April 1970): 104–120.

Haynes, Kingsley E. *Colonias in the Lower Rio Grande Valley of South Texas: Summary Report*. Austin: The University of Texas at Austin, the LBJ School of Public Affairs, 1977. http://www.eric.ed.gov/PDFS/ED147055.pdf.

Houston Chronicle. 2009. "Brownsville." March 4. http://www.chron.com/CDA/archives/archive.mpl?id=2009_4707373 (accessed September 12, 2009).

———. "80 Fighting Cocks Seized in Houston." As reported in the *Laredo Morning Times*, January 25, 2007, 9A, http://airwolf.lmtonline.com/news/archive/012507/pagea9.pdf (accessed March 23, 2008).

The Humane Society of the United States. "The Ranking of State Cockfighting Laws," http://www.hsus.org/acf/fighting/cockfight/state_cockfighting_laws_ranked.html (accessed April 12, 2008).

Huntington, Samuel. *Who Are We? The Challenge to America's National Identity*. New York: Simon & Schuster, 2004.

Instituto Libertad y Democracia (ILD) [Institute of Liberty and Democracy]. "A Reply." *World Development* 18, no. 1 (1990): 137–145.

Irby, James A. *Backdoor at Bagdad: The Civil War on the Rio Grande*. El Paso: Texas Western Press, 1977.

Itzigsohn, José. *Developing Poverty: The State, Labor Market Deregulation, and the Informal Economy in Costa Rica and the Dominican Republic*. University Park: The Pennsylvania State University Press, 2000.

Johnson, Tim. "Mexico rethinks drug strategy as death toll soars." *McClatchy Newspapers*, August 12, 2010. http://www.mcclatchydc.com/2010/08/12/99089/mexico-rethinks-drug-strategy.html#ixzz0zVu56cpz (accessed August 20, 2010).

Jolliffe, Dean. "The Cost of Living and the Geographic Distribution of Poverty." United States Department of Agriculture, Economic Research Report, no. 26. http://www.ers.usda.gov/publications/err26/err26.pdf (accessed October 8, 2008).

Jones, Jeffrey M. "Fewer Americans Favor Cutting Back Immigration: Public as Likely to Favor Status Quo as to Favor Decreased Immigration." Gallup Poll. http://www.gallup.com/poll/108748/Fewer-Americans-Favor-Cutting -Back-Immigration.aspx (accessed February 1, 2010).

Kandel, William. "A Profile of Hired Farmworkers, A 2008 Update." U.S. Department of Agriculture. http://www.ers.usda.gov/Publications/ERR60 /ERR60.pdf (accessed November 2, 2009).

Kaplan, Robert D. "History Moving North." *The Atlantic Monthly* 279, no. 2 (1997): 21–31.

Karlage, Kelly L., and Paul B. Mydral. "Comparison of Three Pharmaceutical Products Obtained from Mexico and the United States: A Case Study." *Drug Development and Industrial Pharmacy* 31, no. 10 (2005): 993–1000.

Klowden, Kevin, and Perry Wong. *Los Angeles Economy Project*. Santa Monica, Calif.: The Milken Institute, 2005.

Kochhar, Rakesh. "Survey of Mexican Migrants: Part Three." Pew Hispanic Center. http://pewhispanic.org/files/reports/58.pdf (accessed December 13, 2005).

Leonard, Madeline. *Invisible Work, Invisible Workers: The Informal Economy in Europe and the U.S.* New York: St. Martin's Press, 1998.

Light, Donald W. "From Migrant Enclaves to Mainstream: Reconceptualizing Informal Economic Behavior." *Theory and Society* 33, no. 6 (2004): 705–737.

Light, Ivan. "The Ethnic Economy." In *The Handbook of Economic Sociology*, 2nd edition. Edited by Neil J. Smesler and Richard Swedberg, 650–677. New York: Russell Sage Foundation, 2005.

———. "Immigrant and Ethnic Enterprise in North America." *Ethnic and Racial Studies* 7, no. 2 (1984): 195–216.

Light, Ivan, and Carolyn Rosenstein. "Expanding the Interaction Theory of Entrepreneurship." In *The Economic Sociology of Immigration: Essays on Networks, Ethnicity, and Entrepreneurship*, edited by Alejandro Portes, 166–212. New York: Russell Sage Foundation, 1995.

Lloyd, Peter. *Slums of Hope*. New York: St. Martin's Press, 1979.

Lopez, Joaquin, and Keith Phillips. "Banking Industry Evolution Along the Texas-Mexico Border." *Southwest Economy* 4 (July/August 2007): 11–13.

Los Angeles Times, "How Many Have Died in Mexico's Drug War?" June 7, 2011. http://latimesblogs.latimes.com/laplaza/2011/06/Mexico-war-dead-update-figures-40000.html (accessed November 6, 2011).

Losby, Jan L., John F. Else, Marcia E. Kingslow, Elaine L. Edcomb, Erika T. Mal and Vivian Kao. "Informal Economy Literature Review." *The Institute for Social and Economic Development and The Aspen Institute*. http:/www.ised. org/ (accessed May 5, 2007).

Macias, Eduardo P., and Leo S. Morales. "Crossing the Border for Health Care." *Journal of Health Care for the Poor and Underserved* 12, no. 1 (2001): 77–87.

Mantovani, Richard E., and Carol Olander. "The Extent of Trafficking in the Food Stamp Program, 2002–2005." The Office of Analysis, Nutrition, and

Evaluation, U.S. Department of Agriculture, Food and Nutrition Service. http://www.fns.usda.gov/ora/MENU/published/SNAP/FILES/Program Integrity/Trafficking2005.pdf (accessed November 11, 2009).

Martínez, Oscar J. *Border People: Life and Society in the U.S.–Mexico Borderlands.* Tucson: The University of Arizona Press, 1994.

———. *Troublesome Border.* Tucson: The University of Arizona Press, 1988.

Massey, Donald. "The Settlement Process Among Mexican Migrants to the United States: New Methods and Findings." In *Immigration Statistics: A Story of Neglect.* Edited by Daniel B. Levine, Kenneth Hill, and Robert Warren, 255–292. Washington, D.C.: National Academy Press, 1985.

Massey, Donald, and Kristin E. Espinosa. "What's Driving Mexico-U.S. Migration? A Theoretical, Empirical, and Policy Analysis." *American Journal of Sociology* 102, no. 4 (1997): 939–999.

Medina, Martin. "Informal Transborder Recycling on the U.S.-Mexico Border: The *Cartoneros* of Nuevo Laredo." *Journal of Borderlands Studies* 16, no. 2 (2001): 19–40.

———. "Scavenging on the Border: A Study of the Informal Recycling Sector in Laredo, Texas and Nuevo Laredo, Mexico." PhD diss., Yale University, 1997.

———. *The World's Scavengers: Salvaging for Sustainable Consumption and Production.* Lanham, Md.: AltaMira Press, 2007.

Merton, Robert K. "Social Structure and Anomie." In *Deviant Behavior: A Text-Reader in the Sociology of Deviance,* 3rd edition, ed. Delos H. Kelly, 132–142. New York. Saint Martin's Press, 1999.

———. *Social Theory and Social Structure,* revised and enlarged edition. New York: Free Press of Glencoe. 1957.

MGT of America. "Medical Emergency: Costs of Uncompensated Care in Southwest Border Counties." http://www.bordercounties.org/vertical/Sites/%7BB4A0F1FF-7823-4C95-8D7A-F5E400063C73%7D/uploads/%7BFAC57FA3-B310-4418-B2E7-B68A89976DC1%7D.PDF (accessed October 13, 2007).

Miller, Michael V. "Vehicle Theft Along the Texas-Mexico Border." *Journal of Borderlands Studies* 2, no. 2 (1987): 12–32.

Mogab, John W., and Michael J. Pisani. "Shoppers' Perceptions of the State Sales Tax Holiday: A Case Study from Texas." *American Journal of Business* 22, no. 2 (2007): 45–56.

Mogab, John W., Michael J. Pisani, Kay E. McGlashan, Sharon Welkey, and Beth E. Wuest. "*Manifiesto*—The Texas Sales Tax Rebate and Cross-Border Mexican Shoppers: A Profile of Mexican Consumer Behavior at an In-land Texas Retail Center." *Texas Business Review* (October 2005): 1–5.

Mohanty, Sarita, Steffie Woolhandler, David U. Himmelstein, Susmita Pati, Olveen Carrasquillo, and David H. Bor. "Health Care Expenditures of Immigrants in the United States: A Nationally Representative Analysis." *American Journal of Public Health* 95, no. 8 (2005): 1431–1438.

Molefsky, Barry. "America's Underground Economy." In *The Underground Economy in the United States and Abroad,* ed. Vito Tanzi, 47–67. Lexington, Mass.: Heath & Co., 1981.

Mora, Marie T., and Alberto Dávila. "Mexican Immigrant Self-Employment Along the U.S.-Mexico Border: An Analysis of the 2000 Census Data." *Social Science Quarterly* 87, no. 1 (2006): 91–109.

Mora, Marie T., and Alberto Dávila, eds. *Labor Market Issues along the U.S.-Mexico Border.* Tucson: The University of Arizona Press, 2009.

Morales, Lymari. "Americans Return to Tougher Immigration Stance: More Want Immigration Decreased than Kept the Same or Increased." Gallup Poll. http://www.gallup.com/poll/122057/Americans-Return-Tougher -Immigration-Stance.aspx (accessed February 15, 2010).

National Center for Children in Poverty. "Texas: Demographics of Low-Income Children." http://www.nccp.org/profiles/TX_profile_6.html (accessed November 18, 2009).

———. "Texas: Food Stamps." http://www.nccp.org/profiles/TX_profile_29 .html (accessed September 24, 2009).

National Insurance Crime Bureau website. http://www.nicb.org (accessed July 7, 2010).

Nelson, Edwin G., and Erik J. De Bruijn. "The Voluntary Formalization of Enterprises in a Developing Economy—The Case of Tanzania." *Journal of International Development* 17, no. 4 (2005): 575–593.

O'Day, Patrick. "The Mexican Army as Cartel." *Journal of Contemporary Criminal Justice* 17, no. 3 (2001): 278–295.

O'Day, Patrick, and Angelina López. "Organizing the Underground NAFTA." *Journal of Contemporary Criminal Justice* 17, no. 3 (2001): 232–242.

O'Day, Patrick, and Rex Venecia. "Cazuelas: An Ethnographic Study of Drug Trafficking in a Small Mexican Border Town." *Journal of Contemporary Criminal Justice* 15, no. 4 (1999): 421–444.

Orrenius, Pia M. "The Effect of U.S. Border Enforcement on the Crossing Behavior of Mexican Migrants." In *Crossing the Border: Research from the Mexican Migration Project.* Edited by Jorge Durand and Douglas S. Massey, 281–298. New York: Russell Sage Foundation, 2004.

Orrenius, Pia M., Madeline Zavodny, and Leslie Lukens. 2008. "Why Stop There? Mexican Migration to the U.S. Border Region." Working Paper 08–03, Federal Reserve Bank of Dallas. http:// www.dallasfed.org/research /papers/2008/wp0803.pdf (accessed January 15, 2009).

Ortiz, Larry, Lydia Arizmendi, and Llewellyn J. Cornelius. "Access to Health Care Among Latinos of Mexican Descent in Colonias in Two Texas Counties." *The Journal of Rural Health* 20, no. 3 (2004): 246–252.

Paral, Rob. "No Way In: U.S. Immigration Policy Leaves Few Legal Options for Mexican Workers." *Immigration Daily*, The Immigration Policy Center, 2005. http://www.ilw.com/articles/2005,1123-paral.shtm (accessed August 3, 2010).

Parcher, Jean W., and Delbert G. Humberson. "CHIPS: A New Way to Monitor Colonias along the United States–Mexico Border." Open-File Report 2007–1230, U.S. Department of the Interior, U.S. Geological Survey. http:// pubs.usgs.gov/of/2007/1230/ (accessed April 14, 2009).

Passel, Jeffrey S., and D'Vera Cohn. "A Portrait of Unauthorized Immigrants in the United States." Pew Hispanic Center. http://pewhispanic.org/files /reports/107.pdf (accessed April 30, 2009).

———. "Trends in Unauthorized Immigration: Undocumented Inflow Now Trails Legal Inflow." Pew Hispanic Center. http://pewhispanic.org/files /reports/94.pdf (accessed November 5, 2008).

Patrick, J. Michael. "Small and Mirco-Enterprise Development in *Colonias* and Urban Barrios in Webb County and Laredo, Texas." Paper presented at the Annual Meeting of the *Rio Bravo* Association and Conference on *Campo y Ciudad*: Borderlands in Transition, March 30-April 1, 2000, Texas A&M University-Kingsville, Kingsville, Texas.

Pear, Robert. "Health Care Spending Disparities Stir a Fight." *The New York Times*, June 8, 2009. http://www.nytimes.com/2009/06/09/us/politics /09health.html (accessed October 19, 2009).

Pew Hispanic Center. "Mexican Immigrants in the United States, 2008." Fact Sheet. http://pewhispanic.org/files/factsheets/47.pdf. (accessed March 30, 2010).

———. "2002 National Survey of Latinos." http://pewhispanic.org/files /reports/15.pdf (accessed March 2, 2011).

Pinkerton, James. "Health Care: Crisis at the Border. Poverty, Lack of Doctors Cloud Area's Future." *Houston Chronicle*, May 5, 2002. http://www.chron .com/CDA/archives/archive.mpl?id=2002_3542344 (accessed November 23, 2009).

Pisani, Michael J. "The Negative Impact of Structural Adjustment on Sectoral Earnings in Nicaragua." *Review of Radical Political Economics* 35, no. 2 (2003): 107–125.

———. "Nicaraguan Self-Employed Women under Neoliberalism: Characteristics and Determinants." *Latin American Business Review* 7, no. 1 (2006): 89–106.

———. "Why Do Seasonal Unemployment Patterns in the Middle and Lower Rio Grande Areas Differ from the Rest of the State?" *Texas Labor Market Review* (February 2003): 13–14.

Pisani, Michael J., and José A. Pagán. "Sectoral Queuing in a Transitional Economy: The Case of Nicaragua in the 1990s." *LABOUR: Review of Labour Economics and Industrial Relations* 17, no. 4 (2003): 571–597.

———. "Sectoral Selection and Informality: A Nicaraguan Case Study." *Review of Development Economics* 8, no. 4 (2004): 541–556.

———. "Self-Employment in the Era of the New Economic Model in Latin America: A Case Study from Nicaragua." *Entrepreneurship & Regional Development* 16, no. 4 (July 2004): 335–350.

Pisani, Michael J., and J. Michael Patrick. "A Conceptual Model and Propositions for Bolstering Entrepreneurship in the Informal Sector: The Case of Central America." *Journal of Developmental Entrepreneurship* 7, no. 1 (2002): 95–111.

Pisani, Michael J., and Chad Richardson. "Cross-border Informal Entrepreneurs Across the South Texas–Northern Mexico Boundary." *Entrepreneurship & Regional Development* 24, nos. 3–4 (2012): 1–17.

Pisani, Michael J., Chad Richardson, and J. Michael Patrick. "Economic Informality on the U.S.-Mexican Border: A (Re)View from South Texas." *Journal of Borderlands Studies* 23, no. 2 (2008): 19–40.

Pisani, Michael J., Carlos Sepulveda, and Amelia Flores. "Consumer Power Asymmetries: Stretching Household Consumption via Consumption Informality in South Texas." Paper presented at the Association of Borderlands Studies Annual Conference, Salt Lake City, Utah, April 14–16, 2011.

Pisani, Michael J., and David W. Yoskowitz. "Grass, Sweat, and Sun: An Exploratory Study of the Labor Market for Gardeners in South Texas." *Social Science Quarterly* 86, no. 1 (2005): 229–251.

———. "The Maid Trade: Cross-Border Work in South Texas." *Social Science Quarterly* 83, no. 2 (2002): 568–579.

———. "Opportunity Knocks: Entrepreneurship, Informality & Home Gardening in South Texas." *Journal of Borderlands Studies* 21, no. 2 (2006): 59–76.

———. "'*Por Necesidad*'—Transnational Labor Movements, Informality and Wage Determination: An Exploratory Study of Maids on the U.S.-Mexican Border." *Journal of Borderlands Studies* 16, no. 1 (2001): 67–82.

Portes, Alejandro. *The Economic Sociology of Immigration: Essays on Networks, Ethnicity, and Entrepreneurship.* New York: Russell Sage Foundation, 1995.

———. "Social Capital: Its Origins and Applications in Modern Sociology." *Annual Review of Sociology* 24 (1998): 1–24.

Portes, Alejandro, Manuel Castells, and Lauren A. Benton, eds. *The Informal Economy: Studies in Advanced and Less Developed Countries.* Baltimore: The Johns Hopkins University Press, 1989.

Portes, Alejandro, and William Haller. "The Informal Economy." in *The Handbook of Economic Sociology*, 2nd edition, eds. Neil J. Smesler and Richard Swedberg, 403–425. New York: Russell Sage Foundation, 2005.

Portes, Alejandro, and Kelly Hoffman. "Latin American Class Structures: Their Composition and Change During the Neoliberal Era." *Latin American Research Review* 38, no. 1 (2003): 41–82.

Portes, Alejandro, and Richard Schauffler. "Competing Perspectives on the Latin American Informal Sector." *Population and Development Review* 19 (March 1993): 33–60.

Portes, Alejandro, and Julia Sensenbrenner. "Embeddedness and Immigration: Notes on the Social Determinants of Economic Action." *American Journal of Sociology.* 98, no. 6 (1993): 1320–1350.

Rakowski, Cathy A. "The Informal Sector Debate, Part I: 1984–1993." In *Contrapunto: The Informal Sector Debate in Latin America*, ed. Cathy A. Rakowski, 31–50. Albany: State University of New York Press, 1994.

Real Estate Center at Texas A&M University. "Market Report 2010 – Laredo." http://recenter.tamu.edu/mreports/Laredo.pdf (accessed July 12, 2010).

Rector, Robert. "Amnesty and Continued Low Skill Immigration Will Substantially Raise Welfare Costs and Poverty." Backgrounder on Immigration, #1936, The Heritage Foundation. http://www.heritage.org/research/reports/2006/05/amnesty-and-continued-low-skill-immigration-will-substantially-raise-welfare-costs-and-poverty (accessed September 12, 2008).

Resendiz, Rosalva. "Taking Risks within the Constraints of Gender: Mexican-American Women as Professional Auto Thieves." *The Social Science Journal* 38, no. 3 (2001): 475–481.

Richardson, Chad. *Batos, Bolillos, Pochos, & Pelados: Class & Culture on the South Texas Border.* Austin: University of Texas Press, 1999.

Richardson, Chad, and Rosalva Resendiz. *On the Edge of the Law: Culture, Labor & Deviance on the South Texas Border.* Austin: The University of Texas Press, 2006.

Rivera, José O., Melchor Ortiz, and Victor Cardenas. "Cross-Border Purchase of Medication and Health Care in a Sample of Residents of El Paso, Texas, and Ciudad Juarez, Mexico." *Journal of the National Medical Association* 101, no. 2 (2009): 167–173.

Robertson, Robert E. "Food Stamp Program: Program Integrity and Participation Challenges." (Testimony before the Subcommittee of Department Operations, Oversight, Nutrition, and Forestry, Committee on Agriculture, U.S. House of Representatives). http://www.gao.gov/new.items/d01881t.pdf (accessed August 23, 2009).

Rocha, Jessica. "The Underground Economy Business: Informal Economy Turns Brownsville's Economic Engine." *The Brownsville Herald,* January 27, 2003. http://old.brownsvilleherald.com/comments.php?id=P47711_0_1_0_C (accessed January 27, 2003).

Roebuck, Jeremy. "Sheriff Indicted." *The Monitor,* October 15, 2008.

Rumbaut, Rubén G., and Walter A. Ewing. "The Myth of Immigrant Criminality and the Paradox of Assimilation: Incarceration Rates Among Native and Foreign-Born Men." In *Border Battles: The U.S. Immigration Debates,* Immigration Policy Center special report. http://www.immigrationpolicy.org /sites/default/files/docs/Imm%20Criminality%20%28IPC%29.pdf (accessed May 12, 2008).

Salmón, Roberto M. "Zapata, Antonio." In *The Handbook of Texas Online,* Texas State Historical Association. http://www.tshaonline.org/handbook/online /articles/ZZ/fza3.html (accessed September 27, 2010).

Sampson, Robert J. "Rethinking Immigration and Crime." *Contexts* 7, no. 1 (2008): 28–33. http://contexts.org/articles/files/2008/01/contexts_winter08 _sampson.pdf.

Sanders, Jimy, Victor Nee, and Scott Sernau. "Asian Immigrants' Reliance on Social Ties in a Multiethnic Labor Market." *Social Forces* 81, no. 1 (2002): 281–314.

Schneider, Freidrich, and Christopher Bajada. "An International Comparison of Underground Economic Activity." In *Size, Causes and Consequences of the Underground Economy: An International Perspective,* eds. Christopher Bajada and Freidrich Schneider, 73–106. Aldershot, U.K.: Ashgate, 2005.

Seid, Michael, Donna Castañeda, Ronald Mize, Mirjana Zivkovic, and James W. Varni. "Crossing the Border for Health Care: Access and Primary Care Characteristics for Young Children of Latino Farm Workers along the US-Mexico Border." *Ambulatory Pediatrics* 3, no. 3 (2003): 121–130.

Seiff, Kevin. "Midwives Struggle against New Fears and Horror Stories among Patients." *The Brownsville Herald,* August 23, 2008.

Sharif, Mohammed. *Work Behavior of the World's Poor: Theory, Evidence and Policy.* Aldershot, U.K.: Ashgate, 2003.

Sharp, John. "Bordering the Future: Challenges and Opportunities in the Texas Border Region." Office of the Comptroller of Public Accounts, State of Texas. http://www.window.state.tx.us.

Simms, Margaret C., Karina Fortuny, and Everett Henderson. "Racial and Ethnic Disparities Among Low-Income Families." The Urban Institute. http://www.urban.org/uploadedpdf/411936_racialandethnic.pdf (accessed November 18, 2009).

Slack, Tim, Joachim Singelmann, Kayla Fontenot, Dudley L. Poston, Jr., Rogelio Saenz, and Carlos Siordia. "Poverty in the Texas Borderland and Lower Mississippi Delta: A Comparative Analysis of Differences by Family Type." *Demographic Research* 20, no. 15 (2009): 353–376.

Spener, David. *Clandestine Crossings: Migrants and Coyotes on the Texas-Mexico Border.* Ithaca, N.Y.: Cornell University Press, 2009.

Staudt, Kathleen A. *Free Trade: Informal Economies at the U.S.-Mexican Border.* Philadelphia, Pa.: Temple University Press, 1998.

Steger, Manfred B. *Globalisms: The Great Ideological Struggle of the Twenty-First Century,* 3rd ed. Lanham, Md.: Rowman & Littlefield Publishers, Inc., 2009.

Stoddard, Ellwyn R. *U. S.–Mexico Borderlands Issues: The Bi-national Boundary, Immigration and Economic Policies.* El Paso, Tx.: The Promontory, 2001.

Strayhorn, Carole Keeton. "Undocumented Immigrants in Texas: A Financial Analysis of the Impact to the State Budget and Economy." Special Report from the Texas Comptroller, State of Texas. http://www.window.state.tx.us/specialrpt/undocumented/undocumented.pdf (accessed July 13, 2007).

Taylor, John M. "Imported Drugs." Testimony before the U.S. Senate Committee on Health, Education, Labor and Pensions. http://www.fda.gov/NewsEvents/Testimony/ucm113825.htm (accessed August 23, 2007).

Tellas, Edward E., and Vilma Ortiz. *Generations of Exclusion: Mexican Americans, Assimilation, and Race.* New York: Russell Sage Foundation, 2008.

Texas Comptroller of Public Accounts. "Convenience Store Owner Arrested for Tax Fraud Under New Law." Criminal Investigation Division—Case Spotlight. http://www.window.state.tx.us/about/cid/casespotlightarchive.html (accessed July 24, 2010).

Texas Department of Human Services. "Texas Food Stamp Corrective Action Plan." http://www.window.state.tx.us/tpr/tpr4/c6.fr/c601.html (accessed on March 12, 2007).

Texas Department of Public Safety—Public Information Office. "Recovery of Stolen Vehicles from Mexico Rises." http://www.txdps.state.tx.us/director_staff/public_information/pr013002.htm (accessed October 1, 2010).

Texas Department of State Health Services. "Demographic and Health Profile of Hidalgo County, 2001." Selected Fact Sheets. http://www.dshs.state.tx.us/borderhealth (accessed July 19, 2008).

Texas Higher Education Coordinating Board (THECB). "Enrollment Data." http://www.txhighereddata.org/Quick/enroll.cfm.

Thevenot, Brian. "Bureaucratic Delays Create Huge Food Stamp Backlog." *The*

Texas Tribune, December 7, 2009. http://www.texastribune.org/texas-issues /food-stamps-program/bureaucratic-delays-create-huge-food-stamp-back log/ (accessed January 14, 2010).

Thompson, Jerry. *Cortina: Defending the Mexican Name in Texas*. College Station: Texas A&M University Press, 2007.

————. *Juan Cortina and the Texas-Mexico Frontier*. El Paso: Texas Western Press, 1994.

Thorpe, Helen. "The Great Hand-Me-Down Heap." *The New York Times*, October 15, 2000.

Tienda, Marta, and Rebecca Raijman. "Immigrants' Income Packaging and Invisible Labor Force Activity." *Social Science Quarterly* 81, no. 1 (2000): 291–310.

Timoshenkov, Miguel. "Adios, 'Santa Muerte.'" *Laredo Morning Times*, March 25, 2009. http://www.lmtonline.com/articles/2009/03/25/news/doc4 9c9d8ec2945e991324659.txt (accessed October 2, 2009).

Torres, Cruz C., and Steven R. Applewhite. "Mexican American Attitudes Towards Crime: A Border Study." *Journal of Ethnicity in Criminal Justice* 2, nos. 1–2 (2004): 47–65.

Turner, A.N., C. Ellertson, S. Thomas, and S. Garcia. "Diagnosis and Treatment of Presumed STIs at Mexican Pharmacies: Survey Results from a Random Sample of Mexico City Pharmacy Attendants." *Sexually Transmitted Infections* 79, no. 3 (2003): 224–228.

U.S. Census Bureau. "American Fact Finder." http://factfinder.census.gov /servlet/ACSSAFFFacts?_event (accessed May 2, 2010).

————. "Hispanic-Owned Firms: 2002—2002 Economic Census, Survey of Business Owners." http://www2.census.gov/econ/sbo/02/sb0200cshisp.pdf (accessed March 30, 2010).

————. "Income, Poverty, and Health Insurance Coverage in the United States: 2004." http://www.census.gov/prod/2005pubs/p60-229.pdf (accessed May 12, 2009).

————. "2002/2006/2007/2008/2009 American Community Survey." http:// www.census.gov/acs/www/ (accessed June 20, 2011).

U.S. Congress. House. "Prescription Drug Pricing in the 7th Congressional District of Maryland: An International Price Comparison." Minority Staff Report, Committee on Government Reform and Oversight, Prepared for Rep. Elijah E. Cummings. http://cummings.house.gov/pdf/intl.pdf (accessed January 7, 2008).

U.S. Department of Defense. "U.S. Casualty Status." November 3, 2011. http:// www.defense.gov/news/casualty.pdf (accessed November 6, 2011).

U.S. Department of Health and Human Services. "The 2009 HHS Poverty Guidelines." http://aspe.hhs.gov/poverty/09poverty.shtml (accessed August 4, 2010).

U.S. Department of Health and Human Services, Administration for Children & Families. "Table 6—Temporary Assistance for Needy Families—Active Cases Percent Distribution of TANF Families with One Adult by Number of Recipient Children, October 2007–September 2008." http://www.acf.hhs .gov/programs/ofa/character/FY2008/tab06.htm (accessed May 28, 2010).

U.S. Department of Homeland Security. "Fact Sheet." Press Office. http://www.ice.gov/doclib/pi/news/factsheets/worksite_strategy.pdf.

———. *Yearbook of Immigration Statistics: 2005.* Washington, D.C.: U.S. Department of Homeland Security. http://www.dhs.gov/files/statistics/publications/yearbook.shtm (accessed May 13, 2006).

U.S. Department of Justice—National Drug Intelligence Center. *National Drug Threat Assessment 2010.* http://www.justice.gov/ndic/pubs38/38661/38661p.pdf (accessed August 9, 2010).

U.S. Department of Labor. "A Demographic and Employment Profile of United States Farm Workers" (Findings from the National Agricultural Workers Survey [NAWS] 2001–2002). http://www.doleta.gov/agworker/report9/toc.cfm (accessed March 21, 2010).

U.S. Department of Labor—Bureau of Labor Statistics. "May 2008 State Occupational Employment and Wage Estimates – Texas, May 2008." http://www.bls.gov/oes/2008/may/oessrcma.htm (accessed July 12, 2010).

U.S. Department of State. "Visitor Visas—Business and Pleasure." http://travel.state.gov/visa/temp/types/types_1262.html (accessed July 22, 2010).

U. S. General Accounting Office. "Illegal Aliens: Extent of Welfare Benefits Received on Behalf of U.S. Citizen Children." http://www.gao.gov/archive/1998/he98030.pdf (accessed December 10, 2008).

U.S. Immigration and Customs Enforcement. "50 Indicted as Part of National Marriage Fraud Scheme—Individuals Entered into Sham Marriages to Gain Citizenship." (News release), August 11, 2009. http://www.ice.gov/pi/nr/0908/090811cincinatti.htm (accessed August 9, 2010).

Valdez, Avelardo, and Charles Kaplan. "Conditions that Increase Drug Market Involvement: The Invitational Edge and the Case of Mexicans in South Texas." *Journal of Drug Issues* 37, no. 4 (2007): 893–918.

Valdez, Zulema. *The New Entrepreneurs: How Race, Class, and Gender Shape American Enterprise.* Stanford, Calif.: Stanford University Press, 2011.

Valenzuela, Abel Jr., Nik Theodore, Edwin Meléndez, and Ana Luz Gonzalez. "On The Corner: Day Labor in the United States." Working Paper, University of California at Los Angeles. http://www.sscnet.ucla.edu/issr/csup/uploaded_files/Natl_DayLabor-On_the_Corner1.pdf (accessed May 12, 2007).

Venkatesh, Sudhir A. *Off the Books: The Underground Economy of the Urban Poor.* Cambridge, Mass.: Harvard University Press, 2006.

Voas, Robert B., Eduardo Romano, Tara Kelley-Baker, and A. Scott Tippetts. "A Partial Ban on Sales to Reduce High-Risk Drinking South of the Border: Seven Years Later." *Journal of Studies on Alcohol* 67, no. 5 (2006): 746–753.

Vogel, Richard D. "Harder Times: Undocumented Workers and the U.S. Informal Economy." *Monthly Review* 58, no. 3 (2006): 29–39.

Wadsworth, Tim. "Is Immigration Responsible for the Crime Drop? An Assessment of the Influence of Immigration on Changes in Violent Crime Between 1990 and 2000." *Social Science Quarterly* 91, no. 2 (2010): 531–553.

Wall Street Journal. 2006. "Immigration Consensus." June 20.

Ward, Peter M. *Colonias and Public Policy in Texas and Mexico: Urbanization by Stealth.* Austin: University of Texas Press, 1999.

———. "Informality of Housing Production at the Urban-Rural Interface: The 'Not so Strange Case' of Texas *Colonias*." In *Urban Informality: Transnational Perspectives in the Middle East, Latin America, and South Asia*, eds. Ananya Roy and Nezar Alsayyad, 243–270. Lanham, MD: Lexington Books, 2004.

Weigand, Bruce. *Off the Books: A Theory and Critique of the Underground Economy*. Dix Hills, N.Y.: General Hall, Inc., 1992.

Wolf, Martin. *Why Globalization Works*. New Haven, Conn.: Yale University Press, 2004.

Zapata, Jeiny, and Raelene Shippee-Rice. "The Use of Folk Healing and Healers by Six Latinos Living in New England: A Preliminary Study." *Journal of Transcultural Nursing* 10, no. 2 (1999): 136–142.

Zedlewski, Shelia R., and Ei Yin Mon. "Many Low-Income Working Families Turn to the Supplemental Nutrition Assistance Program for Help." The Urban Institute. http://www.urban.org/UploadedPDF/411938_snapforhelp.pdf (accessed September 22, 2009).

Index

CPSIA information can be obtained at www.ICGtesting.com
Printed in the USA
BVOW01s1614070314

347015BV00001B/22/P